T...DREN

TEACHING CHILDREN MUSIC

G R A N T
N E W M A N
■
F O U R T H
E D I T I O N

Boston, Massachusetts   Burr Ridge, Illinios   Dubuque, Iowa
Madison, Wisconsin   New York, New York   San Francisco, California   St. Louis, Missouri

McGraw·Hill

A Division of The McGraw·Hill Companies

Book Team

Acquisitions Editor *Christopher Freitag*
Associate Publisher *Rosemary Bradley*
Senior Developmental Editor *Deborah David Reinbold*
Production Editor *Peggy Selle*
Designer *Lu Ann Schrandt*
Art Editor *Carla Goldhammer*
Photo Editor *Shirley M. Lanners*
Visuals/Design Freelance Specialist *Mary L. Christianson*
Marketing Manager *Kirk Moen*
Production Manager *Beth Kundert*

Executive Vice President/General Manager *Thomas E. Doran*
Vice President/Editor in Chief *Edgar J. Laube*
Vice President/Marketing and Sales Systems *Eric Ziegler*
Vice President/Production *Vickie Putman*
Director of Custom and Electronic Publishing *Chris Rogers*
National Sales Manager *Bob McLaughlin*

President and Chief Executive Officer *G. Franklin Lewis*
Senior Vice President, Operations *James H. Higby*
Corporate Senior Vice President and President of Manufacturing *Roger Meyer*
Corporate Senior Vice President and Chief Financial Officer *Robert Chesterman*

Cover photo © David Young-Wolff/PhotoEdit

Copyedited by Rosemary Wallner

Library of Congress Catalog Card Number: 93-74704

ISBN 0-697-12540-8

Printed in the United States of America

10 9 8 7 6

For Patricia, Allen, and Joe

CONTENTS

3 | *MELODY* 53

4 | *TEXTURE AND HARMONY* 105

8 SINGING 237

9 MUSIC READING AND WRITING 267

10 PLANNING AND EVALUATION 299

PREFACE

Teaching Children Music is a textbook for the prospective classroom teacher. It introduces the fundamentals of music and presents specific and practical suggestions for teaching music to children in the elementary school. Suggested songs, activities, and experiences are presented at a level appropriate for the college student, but in relation to their application in the elementary classroom. This edition of *Teaching Children Music* contains more than 180 songs that represent the diverse musical heritage of today's school children. It offers increased flexibility and choice of materials for study in the methods class and serves as a resource for future use in the elementary classroom.

A background of music lessons or experience as a participant in school bands, orchestras, or choral ensembles is advantageous for the classroom teacher who enrolls in the college methods course. An extensive background of musical training is not assumed in *Teaching Children Music,* however; students without formal musical training can succeed in developing significant musical knowledge and skills that they can apply with confidence in the elementary classroom.

The ten chapters of *Teaching Children Music* are entitled (1) Teaching Music, (2) Rhythm, (3) Melody, (4) Texture and Harmony, (5) Form, (6) Tempo, Dynamics, and Tone Color, (7) Listening to Music, (8) Singing, (9) Music Reading and Writing, and (10) Planning and Evaluation. Each chapter is filled with songs and activities to develop the teacher's awareness of materials and teaching techniques for use in the classroom. Skills and music fundamentals are integrated so that the student has opportunities to apply new information in a meaningful context. Chapter 3 (Melody), for example, introduces the piano keyboard; students combine the study of melody with an extensive section on playing the soprano recorder. Chapter 4 relates the study of texture and harmony to experiences in singing and listening, builds on keyboard knowledge, presents a brief discussion of electronic pianos, and introduces the Autoharp, Omnichord, and guitar.

Varied activities—including singing, playing instruments, movement, listening, improvising, creating music, and music reading and writing—are integrated into the presentation of music skills and knowledge throughout the book. Related listening suggestions offer a wealth of possibilities for correlating specific songs with recorded listening examples, and up-to-date information identifies specific compact discs and cassettes from current catalogs. *Teaching Children Music* provides useful information on classroom percussion instruments as well as orchestral instruments and discusses techniques and activities for teaching music listening, singing, and music reading and writing. A final chapter on planning and evaluation brings the book to its conclusion, providing information on important aspects of planning and illustrating the process with examples of long-range and daily lessons.

Appendices contain information on music for special learners, information on the approaches of Émile Jaques-Dalcroze, Zoltán Kodály, and Carl Orff, fingering charts for guitar and recorder, and a summary of music symbols. *Teaching Children Music* lists current instructional materials and resources: music books, equipment, films, videos, and includes information on computer software and electronic instruments.

ACKNOWLEDGMENTS

The author is indebted to the following reviewers for their many helpful and thoughtful suggestions.

> Michael Braz, Georgia Southern University
> Karen Carter, Oklahoma State University
> Jana Fallin, Kansas State University
> William Hawkins, Palomar College
> Kenneth Jones, Kentucky Christian College
> Edwin Schatkowski, University of Pennsylvania
> Betty Shaw, University of Texas at Houston

Appreciation is also expressed to the publishers who have granted permission for the use of copyrighted songs and materials. Conscientious attempts were made to contact all copyright holders, and appropriate permission notice appears with each song or excerpt. In the event that any copyright owners have been overlooked, it is hoped that they will kindly give notice of the omission.

TEACHING MUSIC

Music, an important part of daily life, also plays a prominent role in the ceremonies, celebrations, rites, and rituals associated with special occasions in each of our lives. Music exists in every culture, and the music of each culture offers a rich heritage for study.

THE PURPOSE OF MUSIC EDUCATION

John Dewey said that schools simplify, purify, and balance the various parts of the child's environment, "to see to it that each individual gets an opportunity to escape from the limitations of the social group in which he was born."

The first office of the social organ we call the school is to provide a simplified environment. It selects the features which are fairly fundamental and capable of being responded to by the young. Then it establishes a progressive order, using the factors first acquired as means of gaining insight into what is more complicated.[1]

In music, the teacher *simplifies* the environment by leading the child from the obvious to the subtle. The teacher *purifies* the child's musical environment by omitting the trivial and selecting the best examples of each type of music to be studied. The teacher *balances* the child's musical environment by providing a wide variety of selected music that children might not learn without schooling.

There is little need for instruction in music that is widely available and uncomplicated, especially if it is music children can learn by themselves. Education makes it possible to broaden and deepen knowledge and understanding. Instruction in music improves musical perception and increases children's ability to respond to a wide range of music of all types. The task of schooling is to give children "keys that unlock profound human understanding and accomplishment" in music and the other arts.[2]

VALUES OF MUSIC EDUCATION

Music is worthwhile for its intrinsic values and for its extramusical values as well. The primary reasons for music education deal with musical values.

INTRINSIC VALUES

Music studies offer students experiences with a unique nonverbal symbol system. Music is the most abstract of the arts and its symbols deal with subjective reality rather than the quantifiable objective reality of science and mathematics or the specific meanings conveyed by everyday language. "Music sounds as feelings feel."[3]

A whole world of human achievement exists outside the realm of verbal and mathematical symbols. Music, a truly unique symbol system, has enabled human beings to express their loftiest thoughts and feelings about all that makes life worth living—love in its myriad forms, religion, patriotism, and nature. An educational program that neglects the rich and powerful system of symbols found in music is barren and incomplete.[4]

Music studies help students discover the richness and breadth of our musical heritage. Without music studies, many students would have limited opportunities to explore the many types and styles of music that are part of our American tradition. These include Western art music, folk music, traditional songs, patriotic music, jazz, and the many varieties of popular music. Music studies in the upper grades help children discover more about the historical context of various types of music. Music studies give students a basis for making informed judgments about music.

Music studies help students explore the music of other cultures. Through experiences in performance and listening, children discover the ways world cultures use components of music and build awareness of performance styles and instruments unlike those of traditional Western music. Music studies help children discover more about the unique characteristics and functions of each culture's music.

Music studies help students discover relationships between music and other arts: literature, the performing arts (dance, drama, opera, music theater), the visual arts, and media art (film, television, radio).

Music studies help students discover the degree of musical talent they possess. Research by Howard Gardner, a leading cognitive scientist, has produced evidence that music is one of seven basic types of intelligence possessed by all humans. Music studies offer *all* students, not just those with financial resources for private lessons, opportunities to develop their musical talents.

Music appeals to the imagination and gives opportunities for self-expression and creativity. For young children, who learn by doing, experiences in singing, playing instruments, and creating or improvising music build skills that can be developed in no other way.

Music study can increase the amount of pleasure we derive from music. Music reading skills are a valuable aid to the study of music. Music listening activities improve perception of the elements and structure of music and provide opportunities to experience music from other times and places in addition to the familiar music that is widely available in daily life.

Music and the other arts balance schooling's emphasis on acquiring facts and "correct" answers with creative activities that emphasize feeling, intuition, and alternative approaches. Composers invent new music, performers create differing interpretations, and listeners find multiple meanings in the music they hear.

Music brings opportunities for success and increases children's joy and pleasure in life, both in and out of school. Research indicates that music is one of the best-liked subjects, and for some students, music is the most rewarding component of the school curriculum.

EXTRAMUSICAL VALUES

We hear music on recordings, radio, and television. We hear background music everywhere (even at the dentist's office). Music at parades, sports events, ceremonies, and rituals is part of our daily lives. It signals the arrival of dignitaries ("Hail to the Chief"), adds to graduation ceremonies ("Pomp and Circumstance"), celebrates weddings ("Here Comes the Bride"), marks the New Year ("Auld Lang Syne"), enhances worship, provides therapy, brings relaxation, inspires athletes and fans, and contributes to nearly every form of entertainment.

In the seventeenth century, the English poet John Milton recommended music as a respite from academic work. In the twentieth century, a similar idea was expressed by the Hungarian music educator Klara Kokas.

Today's children, especially those in cities, receive an overdose of cortical burdening because they have little free time and free ground for movement, and an increased school load. The school requires cortical activity during nine-tenths of the time spent there. . . . The increasing percentages of childhood hypertension and neurosis warn about the need for much more active recreation. . . . Combined singing and movement enables the child to react to his subcortical impulses in a socially desirable manner.[5]

It has been reported that playing recorded music in school reduces discipline problems by as much as 50 percent. In a different study, researchers concluded that "easy listening music," played during a fifth-grade science class, led to a significant gain in time-on-task behavior.[6] It is claimed that the study of music builds self-confidence, cooperation, responsibility, teamwork, physical coordination and dexterity, and many other desirable outcomes.

Less plausible claims are not uncommon: music teaches children to respect teachers, love nature, and be kind to dumb animals;[7] music makes good citizens ("Teach a boy to blow a horn and he'll never blow a safe."); music by Bach soothes indigestion, Mozart relieves rheumatic pain, Schubert helps insomniacs sleep, and Handel eases emotional distress.[8] These claims may make us smile, but they lack credibility.

Some research indicates that music studies contribute to gains in other subjects, especially language arts. The Music Educators National Conference (MENC) reports that students taking arts courses generally earn higher SAT scores than other students, and that there is a correlation between test scores and the ratio of music teachers and music pupils: schools with higher numbers of students per music teacher had lower scores. A summary of research on the nonmusical outcomes of music training, however, reports that there is insufficient evidence to conclude that music training transfers directly to gains in subjects such as social studies or mathematics.[9]

NO TIME FOR FRILLS?

In a recent Gallup Poll concerning the importance of various subjects for high school students, music was rated last in importance.[10] This view of the arts, while common, is disputed by experts. In his book, *Crisis in the Classroom*, Charles Silberman says, "Poetry, music, painting, dance, and the other arts are not frills to be indulged in if time is left over from the real business of education; they are the business of education."[11]

The notion that the arts are unimportant is troublesome, and so is the belief that there is not enough time to teach them. In his book, *A Place Called School*, John Goodlad notes that the usual 23.5 hours of instructional time in each week would allow an hour daily for mathematics, one and one-half hours daily for language arts, and one-half hour daily for each of the following: science, social studies, and combined health/physical education. This leaves three and one-half hours for the arts each week—sufficient time to make a balanced and comprehensive program feasible for all students in the elementary grades.[12]

MUSIC SPECIALISTS AND CLASSROOM TEACHERS

MENC recommends that music should be taught by music specialists and reinforced by classroom teachers. (Classroom teachers should have completed a minimum of twelve semester hours of credit in methods and materials for teaching the arts.)[13]

According to psychologist Benjamin Bloom, the early years of school establish the child's self-image, for better or worse. Research indicates that children see themselves as successes or failures in certain subjects, or even in the total school experience, by the end of the third grade.[14] Music education research indicates that the child's musical aptitude is fully established by the age of nine.[15] The early years appear to be crucial for the child's music education; children in the primary grades, however, are less apt to have the services of a music specialist than children in the upper grades.

The music specialist provides music classes as part of a comprehensive and sequential music program for grades K–6.[16] (Although MENC recommends that the teacher-pupil ratio for the specialist should be no greater than 1:400, some music specialists are expected to teach 400 to 1,000 children each week.) The music specialist has the advantage of extensive musical preparation, but must teach a large number of students within a fixed schedule that limits opportunities to correlate music instruction with the work of the classroom.

As a classroom teacher, you may lack the extensive musical training of the specialist, but you will have the advantage of being well acquainted with every student. You can introduce music activities at any time during the school day and correlate music with other subjects throughout the seasons of the year. Consult the music specialist for suggestions or needed resources and share information about your goals and concerns. Working in cooperation, you and the music specialist can produce more satisfactory results than either could obtain independently. By demonstrating enthusiasm for music, through your attitude or by direct involvement, you can make a valuable contribution to the child's musical development.[17]

Daily experiences involving singing, listening, playing instruments, and other musical activities will give students in your classroom opportunities to discover the expressiveness of rhythm, melody, harmony, form, tempo, tone color, dynamics, and all of the other components of music. You can stimulate children's creative abilities by giving them opportunities to experiment with sounds of every kind. You can encourage the development of musical thought processes by introducing the study of notation and assisting children in finding ways to symbolize what they hear, what they imagine, and what they find interesting in their musical world. You can expand children's musical horizons by introducing the music of many cultures, eras, and styles. As you study music and this book, you should increase your musical skills, knowledge, and understanding and acquire information that will assist you in teaching music in your classroom.

Lack of extensive musical training or concern about their personal level of achievement discourages some teachers from presenting music in the classroom. Nevertheless, there is evidence that students taught by classroom teachers "perform as well or better on [music] tests than those taught by music specialists, markedly so in the lower elementary grades."[18] Although one college course cannot supply all the skills and confidence that you would like to have, remember that helping children learn to sing and play instruments will give you opportunities to improve your own skills. Seek assistance from the music specialist and from musically proficient teacher aides, parents, or local musicians. Continue to develop your abilities through participating in music workshops, private lessons, summer music courses, and informal reading and listening.

A musical background resulting from experiences in school bands, orchestras, choral groups, or private lessons is helpful as you begin this course, but students with little musical experience will find that they can make a very good beginning at the college level. In the words of the American music educator James Mursell: "Technical competence will take care of itself in its own good time."[19]

NOTES

[1]John Dewey, *Democracy and Education* (New York: Macmillan Publishing Co., 1916); *The Middle Works of John Dewey, 1899–1924,* Volume 9 (Carbondale and Edwardsville: Southern Illinois University Press, 1980), p. 24. By permission of the Center for Dewey Studies, Southern Illinois University, Carbondale.

[2]William J. Bennett, *First Lessons, A Report on Elementary Education in America* (Washington, D.C.: U.S. Government Printing Office, 1986), p. 35.

[3]Susanne K. Langer, *Problems of Art* (New York: Charles Scribner's Sons, 1957), p. 26.

[4]Charles Leonhard, *A Realistic Rationale For Teaching Music* (Reston, Virginia: Music Educators National Conference, 1985), p. 8.

[5]Klara Kokas, "Kodály's Concept of Music Education," *Bulletin of the Council for Research in Music Education,* Fall 1970, pp. 51–53.

[6]"Research," *Phi Delta Kappa,* January 1987, pp. 399–400.

[7]See Michael Mark's *Source Readings in Music Education History,* pp. 127–54.

[8]David Chagall, "How Music Soothes, Stirs and Slims You," *Family Weekly,* January 30, 1983.

[9]Karen Wolff, "The Nonmusical Outcomes of Music Education: A Review of the Literature," *Bulletin of the Council for Research in Music Education,* Summer 1978, pp. 1–27.

[10]MENC, *Soundpost,* Winter 1991, p. 3.

[11]From *Crisis in the Classroom* by Charles Silberman. Copyright © 1970. Random House. Used by permission.

[12]John Goodlad, *A Place Called School* (New York: McGraw Hill, 1984).

[13]MENC, "Issues in Music Education, An Advisory from Music Educators National Conference," Reston, Virginia: Music Educators National Conference, May 1991.

[14]Benjamin Bloom, *Human Characteristics and School Learning* (New York: McGraw-Hill, 1976), pp. 141–60.

[15]Edwin E. Gordon, *Learning Sequences in Music: Skill, Content and Patterns* (Chicago: G.I.A. Publications, 1984).

[16]"The teacher-pupil ratio in general classroom music [should be] no greater than 1:400. No music educator teaches more than 24 contact hours per week or more than 8 classes per day of 30 to 35 minutes each." (Recommended basic program, *The School Music Program: Description and Standards,* 2d ed. (Reston, Virginia: Music Educators National Conference, 1986), p. 26.

[17]*Music and Art in the Public Schools,* Research Monograph 1963-M3 (Washington, D.C.: National Education Association, 1963).

[18]Charles Leonhard and Richard J. Colwell, "Research in Music Education," *Bulletin of the Council for Research in Music Education,* Winter 1976, p. 7.

[19]James Mursell, *Music and the Classroom Teacher* (New York: Silver Burdett Co., 1951).

HYTHM

> *Every sound is music. If you drop a stone on someone's foot and they say ouch, that's a sound. Do it three times and you've got a waltz.*

Victor Borge
Concert Pianist, Entertainer, and
Author

Music has many definitions: "noise with discipline," "the shorthand of emotion," or "the art of sound in time," to list three. The sounds we hear in music result from vibrations produced by instruments, voices, or other sources. Regular patterns of vibrations produce *tones*. Irregular patterns of vibrations are called *noise*.

Musical tones have *loudness* (amplitude), *pitch*, *duration*, and *timbre* or "tone color"—the special sound quality of each voice or instrument. Loudness is measured in *decibels*. Rustling leaves produce about ten decibels. Loud rock music has been measured at more than 110 decibels, approaching the "threshold of pain"—130 decibels. Pitch (high/low) depends on the number of vibrations per second (*frequency*). We perceive low frequencies as "low" sounds and high frequencies as "high" sounds.

Duration (long/short) refers to the length of a sound or silence. Duration can be clocked in seconds and minutes, but musical time is usually measured in relation to the steady beat. Beats occur at regular intervals along a time span. Music's "heartbeat" goes faster or slower in a *tempo* that suggests physical movement and human feeling, not just the mechanical ticking of a clock.

BEAT

Music often has an underlying beat. The beat may be obvious or barely perceptible. The steady beat is obvious in music for marching and dancing. Focus on the beat through activities such as these:

- Chant rhymes and other speech rhythms with a strong beat.
- Pat, clap, or step to the beat while listening or singing.
- Play the beat on rhythm instruments.
- Combine the beat with the other components of rhythm.

Relate the steady beat to familiar experiences. Examples include the heart beat, a ticking clock, a dripping faucet, automobile windshield wipers, or automobile turn signals. Children can experience the beat in speech rhythms by chanting rhymes with one syllable to a beat.

- *One, two, sky blue, All out but you.*
- *Sky blue, sky blue, Who's it ? Not you.*
- Chant rhymes and pat the thighs with both hands, then with alternate hands ("one hand, other hand"). Other movements: clapping the beat, finger snapping, bouncing, or stepping in place.

■ Chant and play an unpitched percussion instrument (for example, hand drum, woodblock, sticks, and so forth).

■ Think the words without saying them aloud and clap their rhythm ("Inner hearing").

"Johnny Works With One Hammer" is an action song that emphasizes the steady beat.

Burnett "Johnny Works with One Hammer" *from ORFF-SCHULWERK MUSIC FOR CHILDREN, VOLUME I, American Edition. Copyright © 1982 by Schott Music Corporation. All Rights Reserved. Used by permission of European American Music Distributors Corporation, sole U.S. and Canadian agent for Schott Music Corporation.*

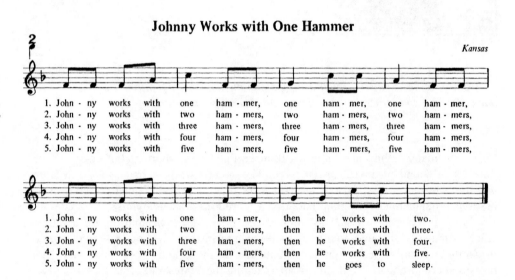

Johnny Works with One Hammer

Kansas

1. John - ny works with one ham - mer, one ham - mer, one ham - mer,
2. John - ny works with two ham - mers, two ham - mers, two ham - mers,
3. John - ny works with three ham - mers, three ham - mers, three ham - mers,
4. John - ny works with four ham - mers, four ham - mers, four ham - mers,
5. John - ny works with five ham - mers, five ham - mers, five ham - mers,

1. John - ny works with one ham - mer, then he works with two.
2. John - ny works with two ham - mers, then he works with three.
3. John - ny works with three ham - mers, then he works with four.
4. John - ny works with four ham - mers, then he works with five.
5. John - ny works with five ham - mers, then he goes to sleep.

In verse one the children, who are seated, imitate the teacher's movement—one fist playing the beat on one knee.

Second verse, both fists playing on both knees . . .
Third verse, add one foot tapping . . .
Fourth verse, add two feet tapping . . .
Fifth verse, add head nodding.

Action songs such as "Johnny Works with One Hammer" give young children practice in keeping a steady beat. They should hear the song several times to learn the words and the melody. Focus children's attention with questions. (For example, "How many times did you hear the words 'one hammer' in this song?") Repeat the first verse and ask the children to tap the beat with "one hammer." Children will learn this short song quickly, and they may be able to join in the singing after hearing the first verse a few times. If children find it difficult to concentrate on singing and movement at the same time, invite half of the class to sing while the other half does the actions; then exchange parts. On another day, add a few instruments to accompany the song: rhythm sticks, woodblocks, or repeated "C's" on bells or xylophones.

Prepare construction paper "hearts" to represent the "heartbeat" of "Love Somebody." Distribute sets of four paper hearts and have each student align them on the floor or on a desk. Instruct students to touch or tap the hearts in rhythm with the steady beat as they sing. (Teachers often find that they can integrate music with a special day, in this case Valentine's Day.)

Love Somebody

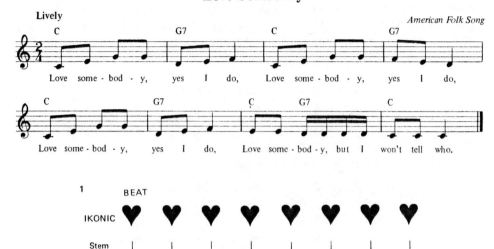

According to reported research, stepping to the beat is more difficult than patting the beat on the body. In one study only 37 percent of first-grade children had "beat competency"—the ability to walk in rhythm with the beat. After instruction, all the students had developed beat competency.[1]

VISUALIZING THE BEAT

Pictures or diagrams often convey more to young children than standard music notation. In this example, each box stands for one beat. An empty box is a silent beat.

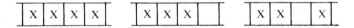

Pat the beats on your knees. Touch a different part of your body on the silent beats. Have children pat beats with *both* hands and show rests by a different motion (e.g., touching their shoulders). They could say "beat" on each audible beat and "shhh" or "rest" on the silent beat. After trying the examples shown, make and notate some new patterns. Find a variety of ways to tap the beat and to show the silent beat.

RHYTHM AND BEAT

Distinguish between the rhythm of the words or melody and the rhythm of the beat. The rhythm of the words in the melody of a song usually contain a mixture of longer and shorter sounds.

To help younger children distinguish between rhythm and beat, align several chairs to represent beats. A child seated on a chair represents one sound to one beat. An empty chair is a rest, or silent beat. Two children per chair represent two sounds on one beat.[2]

Show reading readiness "ikons" of things with one-syllable names. (For example, pictures of a bear, bee, cat, cow, dog, duck, fish, frog, horse, mouse, snake.) Blank cards represent silent beats. Chant the names and pat the beat. Make up rhyming words for additional practice.

Add new pictures to practice words with two sounds on one beat or silent beats. Sounds longer than a beat might include the hiss of a snake or the buzz of a bee. Colorful and imaginative "visuals" in K–6 music books and charts offer additional ideas to assist you in teaching lessons that focus on specific skills and concepts.[3]

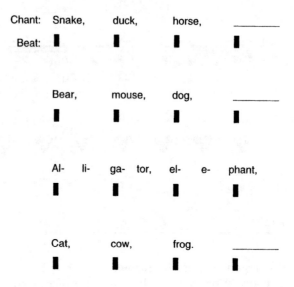

Use contrasting *tone colors* to express beat and rhythm. For instance, play the beat on a drum and the word rhythm with claves, woodblock, or rhythm sticks. Let one group step the beat as another claps the rhythm of the words. Tap the beat with plastic drinking straws or chop sticks while chanting the rhythm of the words or listening to a recording of instrumental music.

Speech rhythms—names, sayings, rhymes—help children develop greater rhythmic awareness. "Choosing rhymes," for example, are useful when it is time to decide who gets the next turn at an activity.

> *One* potato, *two* potato,
> *Three* potato, *four*,
> *Five* potato, *six* potato,
> *Seven* potato, more.

(The children hold out their clenched fists as the leader taps each one, in turn.)

DURATION

The length of a sound or silence is known as its duration. In music, the duration of a sound is *equal* to a beat, *longer* than a beat, or *shorter* than a beat. Pat the steady beat as you sing or chant "Rain, Rain, Go Away."

Rain, Rain, Go Away

Children's Song

In "Rain, Rain, Go Away" the quarter note gets one beat and there are two eighth notes to each beat. Quarter notes and eighth notes are shown below in conventional and simplified (stem) notation.

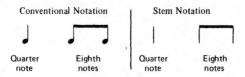

Single eighth notes may be written with a *flag* attached to the *stem*. Two or more eighth notes may be joined by a horizontal *beam*. In simplified rhythm notation, quarter and eighth notes are written without *note heads*.

QUARTER NOTE, QUARTER REST, EIGHTH NOTE

The rhythm of "Bow, Wow, Wow" includes quarter notes (♩), eighth notes (♪), and a quarter rest (𝄽), which indicates a silent beat. Sing the song and tap the steady beat. Make a silent gesture on the quarter rest (for example, touch your shoulders). Notice that the quarter note and the quarter rest each receive *one* beat. The eighth notes represent *two* sounds on *one* beat.

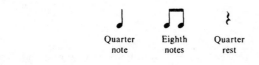

Bow, Wow, Wow

Here are the directions for "Bow, Wow, Wow" in a children's singing game. Form a circle and have partners face each other.

1. "Bow, wow, wow"—Clap hands three times.
2. "Whose dog art thou?"—Shake index finger three times, as if scolding.
3. "Little Tommy Tucker's dog"—Take partner's hands and exchange places in 4 steps.
4. "Bow, wow, wow."—Stamp feet three times. Turn about on the rest (𝄽) and face a new partner. Repeat until the original partners are facing each other again.

HALF NOTES

Sing "Hot Cross Buns" and pat the steady beat. Clap the rhythm of the melody as you tap the beat. Notice that the half note (♩) gets two beats. Introduce the half note to children by showing two quarter notes joined into one longer duration by a *tie,* which is a curved line joining notes of the same pitch into a longer duration equal to their combined value.

Traditional counting systems assign numbers to the beats. When a quarter note gets one beat, the half note gets two beats. There are two eighth notes to a beat, and they are counted "one-and" "two-and."

Quarter   Eighth   Half
note   notes   note

Hot Cross Buns

England

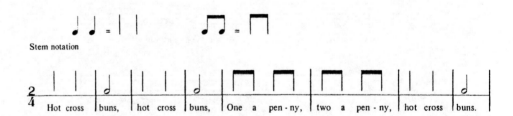

STEM NOTATION

To write "Hot Cross Buns" in stem notation, show the quarter and eighth notes without note heads. The half note is written with a note head. A child can write stem notation easily, avoiding the labor of drawing and filling in the note heads. (When writing standard notation on the chalkboard, draw note heads with a short length of chalk turned on its side.)

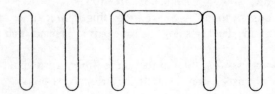

Children can show rhythm patterns in stem notation by arranging popsicle sticks, coffee stirrers, or short lengths of soda straws.

The teacher claps or chants a simple rhythm. The children echo it, and then show its notation with sticks. This activity helps to make notation more vivid for the young child, and popsicle stick notation is often easier for the teacher to observe and correct than paper and pencil activities. Children in first grade enjoy a "living notes" activity, with small groups showing rhythm patterns for the class to perform.

ta   ta   ti - ti   ta

RHYTHM AND DURATION SYLLABLES

Rhythm syllables help children label the various rhythm patterns they experience. The quarter note sounds like *ta* (tah). Two eighth notes are *ti ti* (tee tee). A half note is *too* (sustained for two beats). Say "rest" or "shh" on a quarter rest. (Children should also learn the name of each note value: quarter, eighth, etc.) Practice chanting rhythm syllables to the rhythm of "Hot Cross Buns."

ta ta too   ta ta too   ti ti ti ti   ti ti ti ti   ta ta too

♩ = ta (tah)   ♫ = ti ti (tee tee)   ♩ = too

The erasing game

The erasing game calls for concentration and memory skills. The teacher places the rhythm notation of a song ("Bow, Wow, Wow") on the chalkboard.

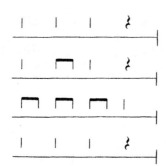

Using questions, the teacher helps students discover that the song has two lines that are the same (one and four). They say the rhythm with rhythm syllables, and then memorize it.

Next, the teacher erases lines one and four and the children say the rhythm again, chanting the erased lines from memory.

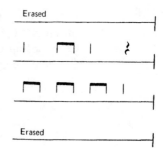

The remaining lines are then erased and the children perform the entire song from memory. After they have successfully memorized the rhythm, the teacher calls on volunteers, who come to the chalkboard one at a time and renotate a line of the song, reversing the earlier erasing process.

Echo singing and chanting

The teacher can make a game out of "echo singing" and chanting. Short sessions at each music class build habits of concentration and quick response. Select rhythm patterns from songs the children have already learned. Begin with rote learning, then help children associate the patterns with rhythm syllables.

1. The teacher sings each rhythm on a "neutral" syllable (that is, a syllable that does not duplicate any of the rhythm syllables), then the students echo.

2. Later, the teacher presents the pattern using rhythm syllables which are echoed by the students.

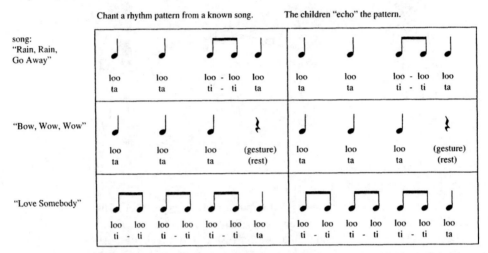

Echo responses lead to *identification* of patterns by sound. The teacher claps or sings on a neutral syllable such as "bom." The children translate the sounds into rhythm syllables.

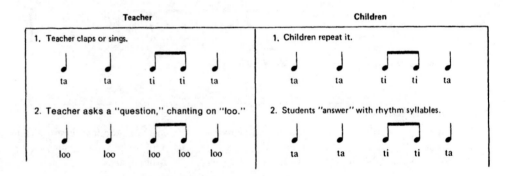

The song "Good News!" contains a whole note, which is equal to two half notes, or four quarter notes. The rhythm syllable for a whole note is "toe" or *too-oo-oo-oo,* sustained for four counts. (The sound ends just before the fifth count begins.) Sing the song with words, clap its rhythm, and chant the rhythm syllables.

Good News!

Beat Compared to Rhythm

Use rhythm syllables to contrast sounds equal in length to the beat, or sounds that are longer or shorter than a beat. Pat the steady beat as you sing, omitting a letter of B-I-N-G-O with each repetition. Clap the recurring rhythm pattern of "Bingo" and chant its pattern with rhythm syllables (*ta ta ti ti ta*) while stepping to the steady beat. Write the pattern in stem notation.

The Ostinato

An *ostinato* is a recurring tonal or rhythmic pattern that accompanies a melody or a song. An ostinato to accompany "Bingo" is shown in picture notation for primary grades singers, who "bark" on the beats showing the dog but not on the silent beat indicated by the empty dog house.[4]

Note Values and Learning Sequence

Many music teachers follow a "prepare-present-practice" structure in planning and teaching music reading skills. Each new learning is **prepared** through speech, song, movement, and many other activities that do not use notation or rhythm syllables. When children are familiar with the new element, it is **presented** (named and identified), then **practiced** in other songs and activities in the lessons that follow.

Quarter notes, quarter rests, and eighth notes are the note values presented to children during grade one music reading activities. Half notes and whole notes are usually presented during grade two.

As the sequence of learning continues, children become increasingly aware of notation relationships: each note or rest is equal to two of the next smaller units. Graphics help in clarifying note value relationships. In the following diagram, the notes of "Hot Cross Buns" are shown in relation to eight notes, the shortest note value. The child can see that each quarter note is equal to two eighth notes, while each half note is equal to two quarter notes or four eighth notes. A similar technique is the use of Cuisenaire rods in arithmetic. (Cuisenaire rods are graduated by length from one to ten, with each length in a different color. Their advantage is that a child can learn relationships through a concrete rather than a verbal operation.)

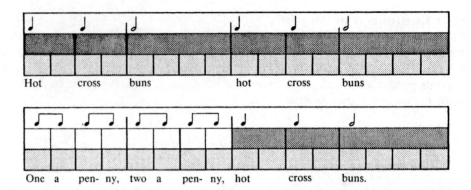

In music the most common note values are whole notes, half notes, quarter notes, eighth notes, and sixteenth notes along with their corresponding rests. Children begin with quarter notes, quarter rests, and eighth notes, before learning longer and shorter note and rest values.

The relationships of these notes and rests are shown graphically in the following chart. The longest value, the whole note, is equivalent in duration to two half notes, four quarter notes, eight eighth notes, or sixteen sixteenth notes. These same relationships can be shown by comparing a whole note to an inch on a ruler.

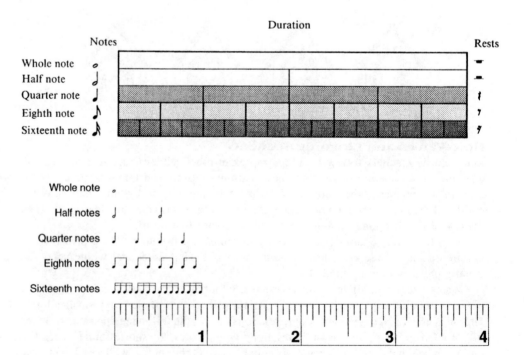

The durations of "Bounce High, Bounce Low" are easy to picture with "rhythm bars," which are lengths of poster board cut to represent durations of quarter notes, eighth notes, and so forth.

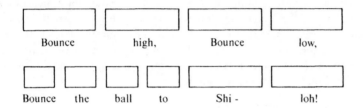

ACCENT AND METER

Recurring groups of strong and weak beats create meter. Activities to show meter include speech, body rhythms (stamping, patting, clapping, snapping the fingers), bouncing a ball on the accented beat, playing percussion instruments, strumming the Autoharp or guitar, and conducting.

ACCENTS

Beats may be accented or unaccented. Express accents through chanting, singing, playing instruments, and movement. Children in the early grades enjoy the strong rhythms of nursery rhymes. Rhythms derived from names, proverbs, tongue twisters, palindromes, knock-knock jokes, limericks, and song lyrics are appropriate for different ages and levels of development. [5]

■ Suggest categories, such as names, cities, states, foods, and invite students to choose words with various accent patterns.

mus-ic   com-**po**-ser   clar-i-**net**

■ Chant words that express the strong-weak accents of duple meter:

Base-	ball,	**Base-**	ball,	**Foot-**	ball.
pat	clap	pat	clap	pat	clap

■ Compare words that express the strong-weak-weak pattern of triple meter:

Bas-	ket-	ball,	**Bas-**	ket-	ball,	**Vol-**	ley-	ball.
pat	clap	clap	pat	clap	clap	pat	clap	clap

Accent Marks

An accent mark (>) placed over a note indicates that it is to be emphasized, usually by making it louder. Regular patterns of strong and weak beats form measures that are separated by vertical bar lines.[6] The first beat of each measure is understood to be an accented beat, even though it has no accent mark (>).

Scotland's Burning

Meter Signature (Time Signature)

The beats in "Scotland's Burning" are grouped in sets of two.[7] The upper number of the meter signature usually, but not always, indicates the number of beats to a measure. The lower number of the meter signature refers to a note value—in this case, a quarter note. The upper number specifies the number of these quarter notes that are needed to make a complete measure. A measure of 2/4 might contain two quarter notes, four eighth notes, one half note, etc. Any combination of note values may be used, provided that the total is equal to two quarter notes.

Duple meter (groups of two)

1	2	1	2
strong	weak	strong	weak

Triple meter (groups of three)

1	2	3
strong	weak	weak

DUPLE METER

Music for marching offers a clear example of duple meter, with two beats per measure (**one,** two, **one,** two). In marching, the meter matches the left-right pace of the marcher. Alternating strong and weak beats (accented and unaccented beats) are emphasized by heavy and light beats on the drums.

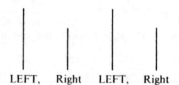

LEFT, Right LEFT, Right

Related Listening: "March of the Siamese Children" from *The King and I*, Classics for Kids, RCA Victor CD 090266–61489–2.

Jessel-MacDonald: "Parade of the Wooden Soldiers" *Classics for Kids*, RCA Victor CD 09026–61489–2.

Listening to Music in Duple Meter

Listen to recorded selections in duple meter. Instruct the children to swing both arms from side to side, with emphasis on the strong beat. Invite young children to create a "parade" as they march to recorded music. Suggest other ways for children to show duple meter through movement: patting two parts of the body (knees, shoulders), double motions such as stamp-clap, and conducting gestures in duple meter.

Conducting Duple Meter

The orchestral conductor holds a baton in the right hand and shows the **strong**-weak accents of duple meter with a downbeat on **one** and an upbeat on two. The left hand indicates dynamics, gives cues to performers, and reinforces the right hand when extra emphasis is needed. In the classroom, children usually show the basic conducting patterns with both hands. Children perform movements similar to the conductor's downbeat-upbeat pattern when they sing "Bounce High, Bounce Low" (page 17) and simulate "**bounce**-catch" movements.

To lead singing in duple meter, sound the starting pitch and conduct the upbeat to beat **one** or sing "ready sing" on the starting pitch.

TRIPLE METER

The waltz is a dance in triple meter. The recurring accent pattern in triple meter is **strong**-weak-weak (**one**-two-three, **one**-two-three). Partners can clap rhythms in triple meter. On beat one, clap both hands with your partner; on beats two and three, clap your own hands.

In stepping to the triple meter of a waltz, students will notice that the accent falls alternately on the left or right foot. Accent beat **one** by stepping on the whole foot, and tip-toe on steps two and three.

Related Listening: Saint-Saëns: "The Elephant" from *Carnival of the Animals*, London CD 425 505 2 or RCA Victor *Classics for Kids*, CD 09026–61489–2.

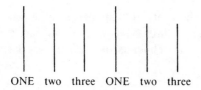

Conducting Triple Meter

The conductor shows triple meter with a downbeat on **one,** an outward beat on two, and an upbeat on three.

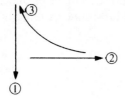

The German folk song, "The Cuckoo," is in triple meter. Its meter signature (3/4) indicates that each measure must contain three quarter notes or their equivalent. The accent pattern is **one**-two-three, **one**-two-three in each measure.

From Holt Music, *Teacher's Edition, Grade 3.* © *1988, Holt, Rinehart and Winston, Inc. Used by permission.*

The Cuckoo

German Folk Song

To lead singing in this triple meter song, sound the starting pitch and conduct the upbeat to beat one or sing "one-two-*sing*" on the starting pitch.

The rapid speed of the beats in "Chiapanecas," a traditional Mexican folk song, gives a rhythmic feeling of three beats to one foot tap. Conductors show fast triple meter with a downbeat that rebounds *immediately* to the starting point, conducting "one to a bar."

Sound Gestures

"Sound gestures"—foot tapping, *patschen* (patting the thigh or knee), clapping, or finger snapping—allow children to show meter through movement. Because sound gestures resemble the actions used in playing percussion instruments, they may also be used to practice a part before playing it on a classroom instrument. Work with a partner and devise gestures that match the triple meter of "Chiapanecas." Replace the sound gestures with percussion instruments (e.g., maracas, rhythm sticks, drums, or cowbell) to accompany the song.

Chiapanecas

Mexican Folk Song

Sing, chia - pa - ne - cas, Ay, Ay! Ay, Ay!

Dance, chia - pa - ne - cas, Ay, Ay! Ay, Ay!

Sing, chia - pa - ne - cas, Ay, Ay! Ay, Ay!

Dance, chia - pa - ne - cas, Ay, Ay! O - le!

QUADRUPLE METER

"Jinny Go Round" is notated with four beats in each measure. Beat one receives a *primary* accent; beat three has a lighter, *secondary* accent (**one,** two, *three,* four). Measures of four beats are called *quadruple meter.*

> Notice that line one of "Jinny Go Round" ends with two notes joined by a *slur,* a curved line between notes of different pitch. The *tie* joins notes of the same pitch into a single, longer duration. The slur indicates that the notes are to be performed in a smooth, connected *legato* style. (See page 30.) To lead singing, sound the starting pitch and show the upbeat before beat **one** or sing "one-two-three-*sing*" on the starting pitch.

Jinny Go Round

Missouri

Jin - ny go round and a - round and a - round, __

Jin - ny go round and a - round and a - round.

Jin - ny go round and a - round and a - round, Way

down in Rock - in - ham.

Primary Accent   Secondary Accent

From Sing It Yourself: 220 Pentatonic American Folksongs, *ed. by Louise Larkins Bradford. Copyright © 1978. Alfred Publishing Co.*

Related Listening: Victor Herbert's *March of the Toys* offers a familiar example of music in quadruple meter. RCA Victor *Classics for Kids*, CD 09026–61489–2.

Conducting in Four

The conducting pattern in four beats is **down,** left, *right,* and up. Each beat should have a slight rebound. Practice the four-beat conducting pattern as you sing the song. Be sure that the downbeat moves straight down, not to either side.

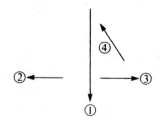

Quadruple Meter Conducting Pattern

Other activities to teach meter may include the following.

Pass a bean bag around the circle in rhythm with the accented beat. (Students should be seated in small groups.)

1. "Pass the bean bag to your left. Say 'pass' on the accented beat and 'hold' on the other beat(s)." The teacher plays "strong-weak" patterns on the drum for duple meter.

Pass, hold

2. "When the meter changes, pass the bean bag in the opposite direction." The teacher plays patterns in threes (strong-weak-weak).

Pass, hold, hold

3. Continue each duple or triple meter pattern for four to eight measures before changing. Later, when children show that they can distinguish between duple and triple meter, less predictable changes between duple and triple meter will encourage concentration and quick responses.

Toss a yarn ball from one hand to the other on beat *one* in duple meter or triple meter, bounce a ball as part of a singing game such as "Bounce High, Bounce Low," or keep a balloon in the air by tapping it on beat one.

Sound gestures (body rhythms) may be combined with speech rhythms, singing activities, or listening experiences. Use finger snaps, clapping, patting the thighs, or stamping to establish metric patterns in two, three, four, or other meters. Sound gestures are listed below in order from high to low. After deciding on a pattern, transfer the rhythms to instruments. Examples are shown here.

Finger snap	transfer to	triangle, finger cymbal, cowbell
Clap	transfer to	wood block, claves, rhythm sticks
Pat	transfer to	hand drum, bongos
Foot tap	transfer to	bass drum, conga drum

PICKUP NOTES

Some songs begin with a "pickup note" that precedes the strong downbeat. A note or group of notes preceding the first strong accent is also known as an *anacrusis*.

"Sweet Betsy from Pike" begins with a *pickup* note on count "three," preceding the first downbeat. The pickup is counted in relation to the final measure, which has beats "one" and "two." The total of the pickup notes and the final measure equals one complete measure.

The conductor signals the moment to begin by giving a silent "warning beat" known as a preparatory beat. For music that starts on count "one," the preparatory beat is the upbeat. When music does not begin on beat **one,** the conductor gives the beat just before the pickup beat. "Sweet Betsy from Pike" begins on beat three; sound the starting pitch and conduct beat *two* as the preparatory beat or sing "one-two-three-one-**sing**" on the starting pitch.

SIXTEENTH NOTES

The song "Clocks" matches clock sounds with note values: quarter notes, eighth notes and sixteenth notes. Rhythm syllables for sixteenth notes (*ti-ka-ti-ka*) can be substituted for the words "tick-a-tock-a" in the last line of the song. After learning the song with the words, substitute rhythm syllables for clock sounds throughout.

Focus attention on the new rhythm by selecting songs with clear examples of the sixteenth note pattern. (See "Love Somebody," page 9.) "Paw Paw Patch" repeats the pattern several times.

Speech rhythms and rhythm syllables are useful in learning new rhythms. Help children discover words (names, states, places, and so forth) with the sixteenth-note sound of four-on-one-beat: "Mississippi," "Huckleberry," "watermelon."

Sixteenth notes are identified ("made conscious") in music reading activities after many experiences with songs that contain sixteenth notes. Music reading lessons to present sixteenth notes are found in the basic music series as early as grade three and as late as grade five. (Review the "prepare-present-practice" pattern described on page 15.)

Listen to the Mockingbird

Related Listening: *Listen to the Mockingbird,* New York Vocal Arts Ensemble, Arabesque ABQ 6555.

The melody of "Listen to the Mockingbird" begins with a group of four sixteenth notes. Practice the rhythm syllables for the basic rhythm pattern of the song: *ti-ka-ti-ka ti-ti-ta (rest)*. Follow the notation of the song as you pat the beat and chant the sixteenth notes. Show the quarter rest with a gesture or replace it with a finger snap.

> The time signature of "Listen to the Mockingbird" is a large C, which indicates 4/4 time.[8] The song has four beats per measure and begins on beat four. (The final measure contains beats one, two, and three.) Conduct beat three as a preparatory beat or sing "One-two-sing" on the starting pitch.

Kookaburra

From The Ditte Bag *by Janet E. Tobitt.*

Another song that begins with four sixteenth notes is "Kookaburra." (The kook-aburra is an Australian bird.) Sing the song in unison or as a four-part round. Substitute rhythm syllables for the four sixteenth notes each time they occur.

BEAT, METER, AND RHYTHM

Point out the three "layers" of rhythm in songs: (1) the underlying steady beat; (2) the rhythm of the accented beat (meter); and (3) the long and short sounds that make up the rhythm of the melody. Focus on these rhythms by having one group step the beat, one group clap the accented beats, and another group pat or chant the rhythm of the melody.

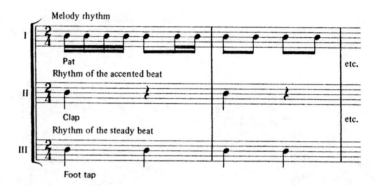

Practice the rhythms in layers, beginning with the steady beat, then adding the other parts. (Children sometimes have difficulty staying together rhythmically because of poor listening or inattention.) Once the rhythms are combined accurately, substitute simple percussion instruments and perform the three rhythms with the instruments. Perform the song in unison, then with a percussion instruments interlude, then as a round.

Clarify rhythmic relationships by using diagrams, charts, and other visual aids along with problem-solving activities. Strengthen the association between ear and eye by relating music reading experiences to songs the children know and enjoy. Written work sheets and problem-solving exercises can also be of value.

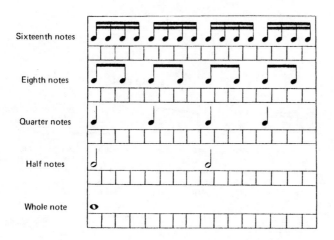

How many sixteenth notes fill up the time used by one quarter note? _____

How many quarter notes fill up the time used by one half note? _____

How many eighth notes fill up the time used by one whole note? _____

How many sixteenth notes fill up the time used by one eighth note? _____

How many half notes fill up the time used by one whole note? _____

Rhythm Patterns Combining Eighth Notes and Sixteenth Notes

Discover rhythm patterns containing mixtures of eighth notes and sixteenth notes. Three basic patterns are emphasized in the following songs.

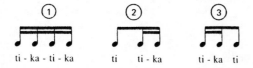

Sing "Kookaburra," then identify patterns one (*ti-ka-ti-ka*) and two (*ti ti-ka*) in the rhythm of the melody. Practice with rhythm syllables and stem notation until you know the patterns by sound and sight. (See page 25.)

Pattern number three (*ti-ka ti*) matches the sound of "Fin-ne-gan" in the song "Michael Finnegan." Circle the eighth rest after line four. (The pickup and the final measure equal one complete measure.)

ti - ka   ti

Michael Finnegan

Rhythm

> The conductor's preparatory beat to the pickup note in this song is beat number two. (Or, sing, "One-two-ready-sing" on the starting pitch.)

Locate the sixteenth-note rhythm pattern(s) in "Jingle Bells." Chant the rhythm syllables. ("Jingle Bells" also has a slur and a breath mark in its notation. Can you find these markings?)

Jingle Bells

James Pierpont

The rhythm patterns for the words "buttermilk" and "skip to my Lou" of "Skip to My Lou" are the same as patterns you have learned. Circle the eighth rests at the end of lines two and four. Rests are often used to indicate breathing points. After singing the song, chant its rhythm syllables and step the beat.

ti   ti - ka ti - ka ti

Skip to My Lou

American Folk Song

DOTS, TIES, AND PAUSES

Two notes can be joined by a *tie* to produce a longer duration equal to their combined value. A *dot* placed after a note increases its value by one half.

TIES

The tie is a curved line connecting two notes of the *same pitch.* Ties are often used to produce durations not otherwise available or to join notes separated by a bar line. For example, two quarter notes joined by a tie equal one half note. Two half notes joined by a tie equal one whole note.

Notation of Ties

Write the tie next to the note head on the side opposite the stem. (The tie should not actually touch the note head.) Keep the curve of the tie distinct from the lines of the staff.

For whole notes, write the tie above notes higher than the third line of the staff and below notes lower than the third line (the same as if they had stems).

Slurs and Ties

Tied notes have the same pitch. A *slur* is a curved line between notes of different pitch. The slur indicates a smooth, connected style known as *legato.*

Dots placed above or below notes indicate *staccato,* a detached style, in which notes are sustained for less than their full value.

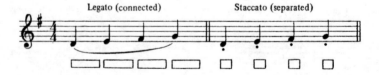

Compare these look-alike musical symbols:

DOTS

A dot placed *after* a note increases its value by one half. If a half note gets two beats, a dotted half note gets three beats. A dotted half note is equal in duration to three quarter notes. If a whole note gets four counts, a dotted whole note gets six counts. To explain a dotted half note to children, show the basic note value. Then show the half note tied to a quarter note. Because a dot is easier to write than a note *and* a tie, musicians replace the tied note with a dot.

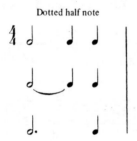

Basic note values have a 2:1 ratio. Each basic note divides into *two* notes of the next smaller value.

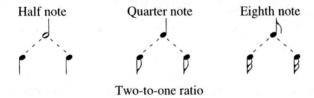

Dotted notes have a 3:1 ratio. Each dotted note divides into *three* notes of the next smaller value.

Notation of Dots
Place the dot to the right of a note. If the note is on a line, place the dot in the space above the line.

Invent a triple meter rhythm (such as pat-clap-clap) as you sing the familiar melody "Bicycle Built for Two."[9]

Related Listening: *Holt Music,* Grade 5 or *World of Music,* Grade 3.

Bicycle Built for Two

Notice that notation of "Bicycle Built for Two" includes thirteen dotted half notes and five ties. For a brief music notation review, replace the missing dots in this excerpt from the melody.

THE DOTTED QUARTER NOTE
"Chairs to Mend" is a musical setting of eighteenth century London street vendors' cries. Tap the steady beat as you sing the song in unison or as a round.

Chairs to Mend

Chairs   to   mend,   old   chairs   to   mend,   Mack - er - el,   fresh

mack - er - el;   An - y   old   rags;   An - y   old   rags?

Teach the dotted quarter note rhythm step-by-step. Show and clap a quarter note followed by two eighth notes, then tied to an eighth note, then with a dot replacing the tied note. The rhythm syllables for measure one are *tum-ti ta ta.*

Dotted quarter note

Tapping the shortest note value is another way to feel the dotted quarter note rhythm. Tap a steady series of eighth notes as you chant the rhythm of "Chairs to Mend." Notice that each dotted half quarter note equals three eighth notes.

Instrumental students who count with numbers should realize that the quarter note takes all of beat one and the dot takes half of beat two. Count "one-and-two" on the dotted quarter note. The foot tap pattern is "down-up-down."

Step the beat and chant the rhythm. The eighth note after the dotted quarter comes halfway between beats two and three. Show the rhythm in graphic form to clarify the relationship between note values.

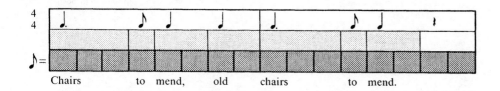

Children need practice with many examples of each new rhythm pattern. The dotted quarter rhythm is found in "America," "America the Beautiful," "The Birch Tree," "Do-Re-Mi," "My Home's in Montana," "Streets of Laredo" (all in this book), and in the next song.

The traditional New Year's song "Auld Lang Syne" (meaning "for old time's sake") begins with a pickup note on the fourth beat. Practice the rhythm of the song by chanting the dotted quarter rhythm with rhythm syllables as you tap the steady beat. How many times does the dotted quarter note rhythm occur? How many ties are shown? How many slurs?

Auld Lang Syne

foot taps

Auld Lang Syne

Robert Burns

Scottish Folk Song

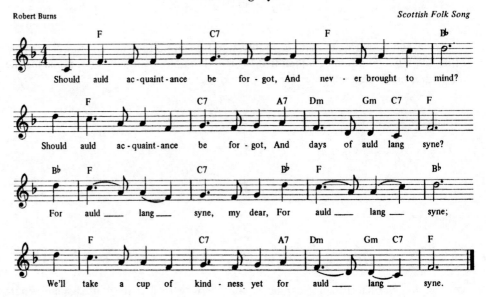

Should auld ac-quaint-ance be for-got, And nev-er brought to mind?

Should auld ac-quaint-ance be for-got, And days of auld lang syne?

For auld ___ lang ___ syne, my dear, For auld ___ lang ___ syne;

We'll take a cup of kind-ness yet for auld ___ lang ___ syne.

Three parody versions:

1. Mules
(Tune: Auld Lang Syne)

On mules we find two legs behind,
   and two we find before,
We stand behind before we find
   what the two behind be for.
When we're behind the two behind
   we find what these be for,
So stand before the two behind,
   behind the two before.

2. Advertise
(Tune: Auld Lang Syne)

The fish, it never cackles 'bout
   it's million eggs or so,
The hen is quite a different bird,
   one egg—and hear her crow.
The fish we spurn, but crown the hen,
   which leads me to surmise:
Don't hide your light, but blow your horn,
   it pays to advertise.

3. We're here because we're here, because we're here . . . (repeat throughout).

"Auld Lang Syne" and other melodies often have "parody" (humorous) words as well as the standard lyrics. Three examples are shown.

DOTTED EIGHTH NOTES

The rhythm of the dotted eighth-sixteenth note pattern is uneven because the dotted note is three times the length of the sixteenth note. This rhythm pattern is usually "presented" during fifth-grade music reading activities, but children's "preparatory" experiences should include many songs that contain the pattern.

Merrily We Roll Along

Relate the dotted eighth-sixteenth note notation to sixteenth note patterns students have learned. Move from familiar to unfamiliar, as shown.

Practice the pattern against a background of four even sixteenth notes. Help students visualize it with graphics that show the three-to-one ratio of the rhythm pattern.

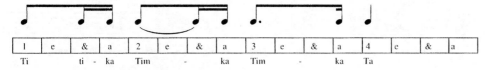

(Each rectangle equals one sixteenth note.)

"The Hokey-Pokey" begins with a dotted rhythm pickup. Conduct beat number three as the preparatory beat. The pickups and the final measure combined equal one complete measure of four counts. Rhythm syllables (*tim-ka*) and number counting for the dotted eight-sixteenth note pattern are shown.

The Hokey-Pokey

The rhythm of "I've Been Working on the Railroad" includes dotted quarter notes and dotted eighth notes.

I've Been Working on the Railroad

Notice the use of dotted notes, slurs and a *fermata* (⌢) in the notation of "Joy to the World." The fermata sign indicates that the note is to be prolonged beyond its usual duration.

Joy to the World

Isaac Watts

Lowell Mason*

Joy to the world! the Lord is come; Let earth re - ceive her King; Let

ev - 'ry__ heart__ pre - pare_ Him__ room__ And heav'n and na - ture_

sing, and_ heav'n and na - ture_ sing, And_heav'n_and heav'n_ and na - ture sing.

*This melody is frequently but questionably attributed to Handel.

SIMPLE METER AND COMPOUND METER

Meters are often classified as *simple* or *compound.* Simple meter time signatures have a two, three, or four as the upper number (e.g., 2/4, 3/4, or 4/4). Compound meters have a six, nine, or twelve as the upper number (e.g., 6/8, 9/8, or 12/8).

CONDUCTING AND COUNTING 6/8 RHYTHMS

"Silent Night," "Home on the Range," and "Greensleeves" are familiar melodies in 6/8 meter. These melodies are relatively slow in tempo and are usually conducted and counted in six, with accents on beats one and four: *one*-two-three-*four*-five-six. The conducting pattern is shown here.

Home on the Range

Peacefully

Cowboy Song

1. Oh, give me a home where the buf - fa - lo roam, Where the

deer and the an - te - lope play;___ Where sel - dom is heard a dis -

cour - ag - ing word, And the skies are not cloud - y all day.___

Chorus:

Home, home on the range, ___ Where the deer and the an - te - lope

play; ___ Where sel - dom is heard a dis -

cour - ag - ing word, And the skies are not cloud - y all day. ___

Conducting Slow $\frac{6}{8}$

We identify simple and compound meters *aurally* by the way the beats are divided. Beats regularly divide into *two* equal parts in simple meter (two sounds on one beat). Beats regularly divide into *three* equal parts ("three sounds on one beat") in compound meter.

Compare the speech rhythms of the two nursery rhymes that follow.

Simple Simon (chant)

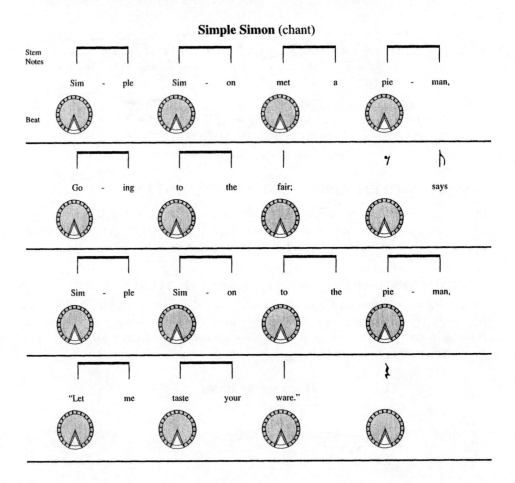

Hickory, Dickory Dock (chant)

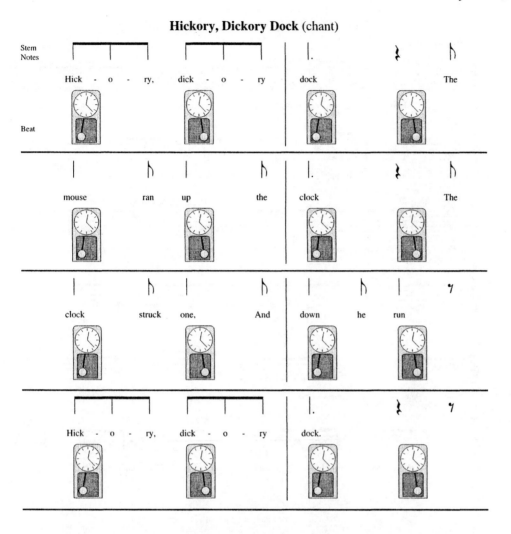

Tap the steady beat as you chant each rhyme. Notice that the beats in "Simple Simon" regularly divide into two parts (simple meter). The beats in "Hickory, Dickory Dock" regularly divide into three parts (compound meter).

The time signature of "Oh, Dear! What Can the Matter Be?" is 6/8, indicating six eighth notes per measure. The eighth notes are grouped in threes, and the dotted quarter note gets one beat. Pat the steady beat as you sing or chant the rhythm of the melody.

Oh, Dear! What Can the Matter Be?

Oh, dear! What can the mat- ter be? Oh, dear! What can the mat- ter be?

Oh, dear! What can the mat- ter be? John- ny's so long at the fair.

Verse

1. He prom- ised to buy me a trin- ket to please me, And

then for a kiss, O he vowed he would tease me, He

prom- ised to bring me a bunch of blue rib- bons to

tie up my bon- nie brown hair. So it's

2. He promised to bring me a basket of posies,
   An arm full of lilies, a bunch of red roses,
   A pretty straw hat to set off the blue ribbons
   That tie up my bonnie brown hair; so it's, etc.

Beats

The time signature 6/8 does not specify six *beats* per measure, but only indicates that each measure has six eighth notes or the equivalent. We feel *two* main beats per measure. A meter signature showing a two above a dotted quarter note gives an accurate picture of compound duple rhythm: two beats per measure, each beat divided into three parts. The conducting pattern for fast 6/8 meter songs is the same as that for duple meter songs. (See page 19.)

Meter signature

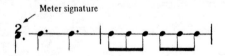

Tap the beat and clap the rhythm of "The Mulberry Bush." Notice that the dotted quarter note gets one beat, and that the eighth notes divide beats into three equal parts. Divide the class into three groups. One group performs the beat (dotted quarter). One group chants the rhythm of the melody. One group taps the divided beat in eighth notes. Select rhythm instruments that contrast in sound and and play the three rhythms.

The Mulberry Bush

2. This is the way we wash our clothes, etc.
3. This is the way we dry our clothes, etc.
4. This is the way we iron our clothes, etc.
5. This is the way we fold our clothes, etc.
6. This is the way we mend our clothes, etc.
7. This is the way we scrub the floor, etc.
8. This is the way we play on the drum, etc.
9. This is the way we play on the sticks, etc.
10. This is the way we walk all around, etc.
11. This is the way we skip all around, etc.
12. This is the way we clap our hands, etc.
13. This is the way we stamp our feet, etc.

Sing the round "Little Tom Tinker." Notice that this song is also in compound meter (three eighth notes to each dotted quarter note beat). Tom's loud cry ("Ma!") gives children a good opportunity to explore dynamics.

Little Tom Tinker

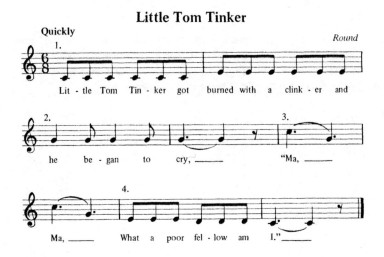

"Rig-a-Jig-Jig" begins in simple duple (2/4) meter and changes to compound duple (6/8) meter.

Rig - a Jig - Jig

In the first part of the song, the beats are regularly divided into two equal eighth notes. In the refrain, "Rig-a-Jig-Jig" changes to 6/8 meter. Dotted quarter note beats are regularly divided into three equal eighth notes.

Invite children to sing "Rig-a-Jig-Jig" as they walk to the rhythm of the first half of the song and skip to the rhythm of the second half. For another activity, form two circles, one inside the other. Each circle moves in opposite directions, stepping to the beat for the 2/4 section of the song, and then changing direction and skipping to the 6/8 rhythm. Singing games for this song are presented in *Song and Dance Activities for Elementary Children,* by Harriet R. Reeves[10] and in *120 Singing Games and Dances for Elementary Schools,* by Lois Choksy and David Brummitt.[11,12]

TRIPLETS

A *triplet* is three notes in the time usually taken by two notes of the same value. For example, three eighth notes in the time of two eighth notes. Notice the triplets in the third line of "The Frog in the Bog." In this 2/4 simple meter melody, triplets are an exception to the normal two-part division of the beat.

The Frog in the Bog

Trip - le - ti

Triplet syllables

Gertrude Mander

Harvey Worthington Loomis

1. There once was a frog who lived in a bog and played the bass
2. His mu - sic was short for soon he was caught and now in the

fid - dle in the mid - dle of a pud - dle, what a mud - dle
mid - dle of a grid - dle he is fry - ing and he's cry - ing

Bet - ter go round.
"Rath - er be drowned.

Bet - ter go round.
Rath - er be drowned."

Composers divide beats into threes with triplets or by using compound meter. The notation does not change the sound. "The Swan Sings," for example, sounds the same in 3/4 with triplets or written in 9/8 compound meter. First, in 3/4 meter with triplets:

The Swan Sings

Canon

The swan sings teer - i - li - o, teer - i - li - o, teer - i - li - o.

In compound meter (9/8), each dotted quarter note divides into three equal eighth notes. Follow the notation as you sing and conduct in three for both versions of the song.

The Swan Sings

Canon

The swan sings teer - i - li - o, teer - i - li - o, teer - i - li - o.

Both examples sound the same.

SYNCOPATION

Music often contains syncopation—the temporary displacement of the normal accent pattern. Syncopation contrasts with the regular, unsyncopated background rhythm. The composer creates syncopation by stressing a weak beat or the weak part of a beat. Syncopation also results when a rest appears in place of an expected strong beat.

In "Hop Up, My Ladies" the pattern accents the weak half of beat one and creates syncopation.

Hop Up, My Ladies

Traditional

The rhythm syllables for this rhythm pattern are syn-**co**-pa or ti-**ta**-ti.

Hop up, my la - dies

Kodály duration syllables: *syn - co - pa - ta - ta*

In the second measure of "Hop Up, My Ladies," an eighth rest replaces the expected accent on "one" and the result is also syncopation.

Mister Banjo

In "Mr. Banjo" the syncopated pattern of the refrain contrasts with the even rhythm of the verse.

Another song with syncopation is "Tinga Layo." Notice the syncopated rhythm pattern on the words "Run, little donkey, run."

1. Which melodic pattern is repeated?
2. How many times does the syncopated pattern appear in the song?

The short-long-short pattern of "Tinga Layo" is like a speeded-up version of the "syncopa" rhythm of "Hop Up, My Ladies." Show the rhythms on a chart or on the chalkboard to help students compare them.

Tinga Layo

*Calypso Song
from the West Indies*

Accompany "Tinga Layo" with bongo drums, wood block, maracas, guiro, triangle, bells, recorder, cowbell, claves, or other percussion instruments. (These instruments are described in chapter 6.) Assign a specific rhythm pattern to each instrument.

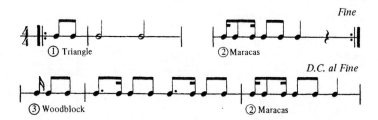

For a different accompaniment, a guiro, bongos, and claves might repeat the following patterns throughout the song:

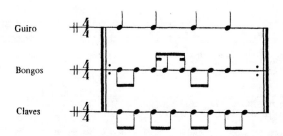

Students develop skill and learn a song more thoroughly when it is reviewed over several days. With repetition, new activities are possible and add additional interest.

1. Accompany "Tinga Layo" with the Autoharp. (The chord symbols are given in the music.)
2. Add a bells ostinato:

3. Create an instrumental *interlude* between verses. Play the melody with recorders, using the Autoharp and rhythm instruments as accompaniment.
4. Add a four-measure *introduction* based on rhythms from the song.
5. Create a brief instrumental ending section (known as a *coda*).

CHANGING METER

In syncopated music, accents are temporarily displaced. In songs with changing meters, measures vary in their patterns of strong and weak beats. "Little Bird" alternates between duple and triple meter.

Related Listening: Pete Seeger: *Birds, Beasts, Bugs, and Little Fishes,* Folkways FCS 7610.

Little Bird

Game: Children make a circle and join hands, raising their arms to form arches and "windows." One child goes in and out of the windows as they all sing. Repeat with a new child. Substitute names of other birds in each verse: robin, bluebird, sparrow, etc.

Invent a clapping pattern to show the twos and threes of "Little Bird." Practice conducting the meter changes of the song. Rehearse at a slower tempo before switching to a faster tempo.

pat   clap   pat   clap   clap

The meter of ''The Swallow'' begins in three and changes to two.

The Swallow

From 150 American Folk Songs, *selected and edited by Peter Erdei and Katalin Komlos.* © *Copyright 1974 by Boosey & Hawkes. Reprinted by permission.*

Game: This game is like "Drop the Handkerchief." "The swallow" moves around the outside of the circle during the song and drops an object behind someone. This person picks it up and tries to catch "the swallow" before he or she can run around the circle to the space left by the pursuer. The song should be repeated so that each child has a chance to be "it."

Shenandoah

Related Listening: "Shenandoah," *The Music Book* (5).

* The chord symbol F/C indicates the F chord with C as the bass note.

Described as the most beautiful of all sea songs in English, "Shenandoah" began as a rowing song on American rivers and later became a favorite of American sailors and cavalrymen. The changing meter of the melody contributes to the expressive qualities of the song, which is said to be a capstan shanty, sung while hoisting the anchor. One explanation for the changing meter is that the uneven rhythm may suggest an embedded anchor.[13]

ASYMMETRIC METERS

The Greek folk song "Ta Kalotykha Vouna" ("The Fortunate Mountains") has seven beats per measure. A clapping pattern will help you feel the metric pattern.

Ta Kalotykha Vouna

Greek Folk Song from Thessaly
Collected and transcribed by Ellen Frye
Edited and translated
by Nicholas M. England

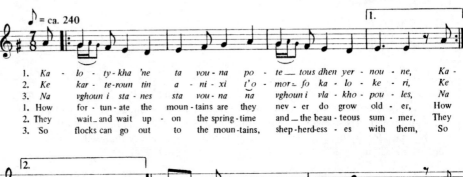

1. Ka - lo - ty - kha 'ne   ta   vou - na   po - te ___ tous dhen yer - nou - ne,   Ka -
2. Ke   kar - te - roun tin   a - ni - xi t'o - mor- fo ka - lo - ke - ri,   Ke
3. Na   vghoun i sta - nes   sta vou - na na   vghoun i vla - kho - pou - les,   Na
1. How for - tun - ate the   moun - tains are they   nev - er do grow old - er,   How
2. They wait _ and wait up - on   the spring - time   and _ the beau - teous sum - mer, They
3. So   flocks can go out   to   the moun - tains, shep - herd - ess - es with them,   So

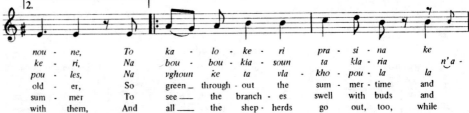

nou - ne,   To   ka - lo - ke - ri   pra - si - na   ke
ke - ri,   Na   bou - bou - kia - soun   ta kla - ria   n'a -
pou - les,   Na   vghoun ke ta   vla - kho - pou - la   la
old - er,   So   green _ through - out   the   sum - mer - time   and
sum - mer   To   see ___ the branch - es   swell with buds   and
with them,   And   all ___ the shep - herds   go   out, too,   while

to ___ ki - mo - na ___ hio - ni.   To   to ___ ki - mo - na   kio - ni.
ni - xou - ne ___ ta ___ dhen - dra.   Na   ni - xou - ne ta   dhen - dra.
lon - das tis ___ flo - ye - res.   Na   lon - das tis flo - ye - res.
snow - y in ___ the ___ win - ter.   So   snow - y in the   win - ter.
all ___ the trees _ in ___ blos - som.   To   all ___ the trees in   blos - som.
play - ing their flutes so ___ sweet - ly.   And   play - ing their flutes so   sweet - ly.

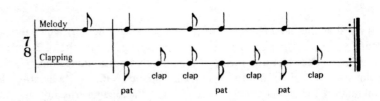

Examples of music with meters in five or seven include dance music of eastern Europe and jazz compositions such as Dave Brubeck's *Take Five.* Music in five can be grouped as two plus three or three plus two. Listen to *Take Five.* How are the beats grouped: "O*ne* two three *four* five," or "*One* two *three* four five"? Have students create speech rhythms showing meter in fives. (For example, "**Bas**-ket-ball, **Foot**-ball," repeatedly.)

Related Listening: Dave Brubeck: *Unsquare Dance* (in 7), *Time Further Out*, Columbia PCT–08490 or *SB Music* (8) p. 13; *Take Five* (in 5) *Time Out*, Columbia PC–8192; Bela Bartok, *Fifteen Hungarian Peasant Songs*, No. 6 CBS M–36712; Aaron Copland, *Jarabe, Billy the Kid*, Sony Classical SMK47543.

Offer experiences in creating asymmetric rhythms that students can notate and perform.

1. Invent a one-measure rhythm in 5/4 meter, using only quarter notes and eighth notes.

2. Rehearse the rhythm, using two different sound gestures (stamp, patschen, clap, finger snaps).

3. Notate the rhythm and decide which percussion instruments should play the accented and unaccented beats.

4. Perform your rhythm with a partner.

Leonard Bernstein's *America,* from *West Side Story,* alternates groups of three eighth notes with sets of three quarter notes.

Brubeck's *Blue Rondo ala Turk* divides nine's into three two's and one three.

Related Listening: Leonard Bernstein: *America*, from *West Side Story*, Columbia OL5230; Dave Brubeck: *Blue Rondo ala Turk*, Columbia CK–40585.

NOTES

[1]Phyllis Weikart, *Teaching Movement and Dance* (Ypsilanti, Mich. The High/Scope Press, 1982), pp. 3–11.

[2]Jim Solomon, *Monkey Business!* (Boca Raton, Fla.: Comprehensive Music Services, Inc., 1987).

[3]See for example, the ikonic examples in *World of Music,* K, p. 251.

[4]Mary Helen Richards, *Threshold to Music* (Belmont, Calif.: Fearon Publishers, 1971). Second edition by Eleanor Kidd, 1975. Mary Helen Richards' contributions to music education are discussed in the article "From Hungary to America: The Evolution of Education through Music," by Peggy Bennett (*Music Educators Journal,* September 1987), pp. 36–40.

[5]Iona and Peter Opie's famous collections, including *The Lore and Language of Schoolchildren, The Singing Game, The Oxford Dictionary of Nursery Rhymes, The Oxford Book of Children's Verse,* and the recently published *I Saw Esau,* offer an introduction to the surprising wealth and variety available, and classroom teachers will be aware of many additional sources, including the poetry of John Ciardi, Ogden Nash, or Shel Silverstein, or even some of the "subversive children's literature" described in Alison Lurie's *Don't Tell the Grown-ups.*

[6]Measures are sometimes called "bars." *A Dictionary of Musical Quotations* says, "Bar: Where to find orchestral musicians whenever they are not actually playing. . . . In America the term *measure* is used instead, probably because during Prohibition conductors didn't wish to make the players break down at the mention of the word 'bar.' " (Antony Hopkins, *Downbeat Music Guide*)

[7]The words refer to the appearance of the heather in bloom, a wee jest, according to information given in *An Integrated Music Program for Elementary School* by William Young (Prentice-Hall, 1990).

[8]Because 4/4 meter is very common in music, the C is often thought to be an abbreviation for "common time." Its origin, however, is in the Middle Ages, when "perfect" time had three beats per measure, corresponding with the Trinity. The symbol for perfect time was a circle. Music in four beats was considered "imperfect," and its symbol was an incomplete circle, our present day C.

[9]Though dating back to 1893, the melody has remained popular, passing the "test of time," which is one consideration in selecting music for the classroom. The music and background for "Daisy Bell" and 99 other American favorites are given in Theodore Raph's *The American Song Treasury* (New York: Dover Publications Inc., 1986).

[10]Harriet R. Reeves, *Song and Dance Activities for Elementary Children* (West Nyack, N.J.: Parker Publishing Co., 1987).

[11]Lois Choksy and David Brummitt, *120 Singing Games and Dances for Elementary Schools* (Englewood Cliffs, N.J.: Prentice-Hall, Inc., 1987).

[12]A collection of fifty musical fingerplays, *Eye Winker, Little Tom Tinker, Chin Chopper* by Tom Glazer (New York: Doubleday and Company, Inc., 1973), has directions for "Eensie Weensie Spider" and includes other 6/8 meter songs, such as "The Bear Went Over the Mountain," "Charlie Over the Water," "Jack and Jill," and "The Mulberry Bush."

[13]Charles Leonhard, Beatrice Krone, et. al., *Discovering Music Together* (Chicago: Follett Publishing Company, 1967.)

$\mathcal{M}$ELODY

For many listeners, melody is the most expressive element of music—the part they notice first and remember longest. A melody is an organized succession of single tones that move in rhythm. Harmony results when multiple tones are sounded together. Shown in music notation, melody and harmony are like "across and down" in a crossword puzzle: the interacting horizontal and vertical dimensions of music.

We learn about melody through direct experiences with melodies of many types and styles. Musical experiences lead to concepts and concepts help us improve our perception of what makes each melody expressive. An overview of some melodic concepts will introduce the topics discussed in this chapter.

Each melody contains pitches that are relatively high or low. The distance between the highest and lowest tone in a melody is known as its range. Melodies may have a wide, moderate, or narrow range. Some melodies are written in a high register or a low register.

Tones in melodies progress in various ways. They may repeat or move higher or lower. Melodies progress by steps, leaps, or in patterns using steps and leaps. Awareness of the distinctive shapes or contours formed by the rise and fall of the melodic line is an aid in learning and recalling different melodies. Scales of various types describe the underlying tonal relationships of melodies.

Tonal and rhythmic patterns combine to form melodic units that may be brief or lengthy. Melodies contain repeated patterns, patterns that are similar, and patterns that contrast. A melody's rhythm and shape make it recognizable despite changes in its tempo, dynamics, tone color, accompaniment, or style of performance.

Jazz musicians improvise on tunes, composers write variations on themes, singers embellish songs and arias, and arrangers present old melodies with new sounds. Melodies from different eras or different parts of the world often have distinctive qualities and styles that are similar to or unlike the melodies we know best. We can deepen and broaden our musical understanding and appreciation by learning more about music from every time and place. Experiences in singing, playing instruments, listening, moving to music, creating melodies, and reading and writing music notation lead to improved perception and musical understanding.

PITCH RELATIONSHIPS

HIGH/LOW

Pitches in a melody may be relatively high or low. During early childhood, children's physical movement is a better indicator of their perception of pitch than words. (Studies indicate that many children confuse "high" with loud and "low" with soft.) Listen to the melody of "Saint Paul's Steeple" and move your hand to trace the melody's path between high and low.

Related Listening: "Saint Paul's Steeple" is one of the melodies in *A Children's Overture* by Roger Quilter. Angel CDM 64131.

Saint Paul's Steeple

Traditional

On St. Paul's stee - ple stands a tree,

As full of ap - ples as can be.

The lit - tle boys of Lon - don town,

They run with hooks to pull them down.

Step bells, which resemble a staircase, help the child visualize the high/low dimension of pitch. Held with the smaller tone bars at the top and the longer tone bars at the bottom, melody bells also show high and low. Number the bells from C to C to match the numbers above the notes of "Saint Paul's Steeple." (Low C is one; high C is eight.) Play the melody on bells and sing it with numbers in place of words.

Glockenspiel - chalkboard

Step bells are a visual representation of the scale pattern.

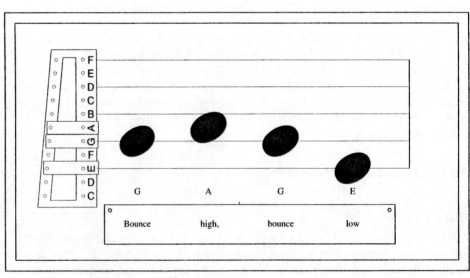

Showing and playing higher and lower pitch.

Step/Skip/Repeated Tones

Tones may repeat or move higher or lower by step or by skip. The melody of "St. Paul's Steeple" moves mostly by step. Can you find a skip? A repeated note? Conjunct melodies have smooth, mostly stepwise patterns. Disjunct melodies are more angular and contain leaps between high and low.

The melody of "Old Abram Brown" (p. 80) begins with many repeated notes, followed by an upward leap. "Hop Up, My Ladies" (p. 44) begins with a leap from low to high. "Bounce High, Bounce Low;" shown below in number notation, moves higher and lower by a combination of steps, skips, and repeated notes.

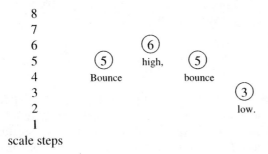

PITCH NOTATION

Pitch is shown by writing notes on a five line staff. Higher and lower *notes* represent higher and lower *tones*. The invention of staff notation is credited to Guido of Arezzo (c. 991–1033), who introduced the use of staff lines to indicate pitch relationships.

The Staff

The notes of "Saint Paul's Steeple" are written *on* the lines and *in* the spaces of the staff. The five lines are numbered from low to high, as are the four spaces between the lines.

Treble Clef

In early notation, red and green lines indicated specific pitches. Colors were replaced by letters written on a line to name its pitch. These letters evolved into modern clef signs, which are written at the left of each staff. The G clef ("treble clef")—used when writing music for high voices and instruments—encircles the second line of the staff and marks the location of G. The other pitches are named in relation to second-line G.

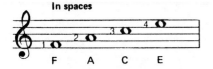

Lines and Spaces

The treble staff lines, from low to high, are E-G-B-D-F. The spaces are F-A-C-E. Among many memory aids for the lines are the following:

■ Every Good Bird Does Fly.

■ Empty Garbage Before Dad Flips.

■ Elephants Got Big Dirty Feet.

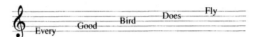

Octaves

The distance from one pitch to the next pitch with the same letter name is an *octave.* Pitches with the same name sound "alike," though they may be in different octaves. The melody of "Saint Paul's Steeple" descends eight steps from third space C to *middle C* written on a *ledger line* below the treble staff. (The space just below the staff is "D.")

Ledger Lines

Ledger lines written above or below the staff add extra range to the staff by providing additional lines and spaces. Ledger lines are just a little wider than the oval portion of a note and their spacing matches that between the regular staff lines. Identify pitch names by counting forward through the musical alphabet for notes above the top line and the reverse for notes below the bottom line.

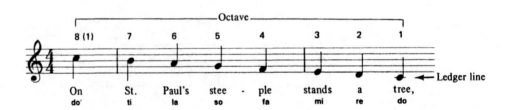

The fictional "P.D.Q. Bach," invented by humorist and composer Peter Schickele, notated his seldom-played *Trance and Dental Etudes* with quantities of ledger lines that exceed the range of the piano.

Related Listening: Franz Liszt: *Transcendental Etudes for Piano,* Claudio Arrau pianist, C.D. Phillips 416458–2 PH.

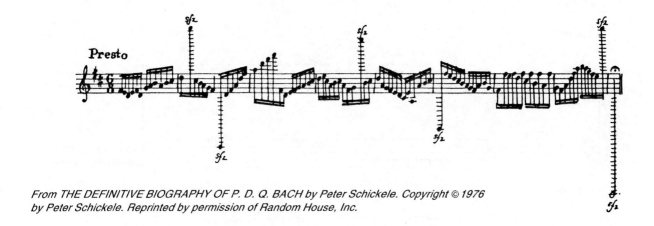

Ottava (8va)

To avoid unnecessary writing of ledger lines, the abbreviation *8va* is placed above a note or a group of notes to indicate transposition one octave higher than written. The indication *8 bassa* or *8va,* placed beneath the notes, means that they are played an octave *lower.*

Bass Clef

Music for low voices or instruments is written on the bass staff, which has a *bass clef.* This sign, derived from a Gothic F, designates the fourth line as F below the middle C of the piano. The bass staff lines are G-B-D-F-A. The spaces are A-C-E-G.

- ■ Good Birds Do Fly Always. (lines)
- ■ Get Busy, Don't Fall Asleep.[1] (lines)
- ■ All Cows Eat Grass. (spaces)

The Grand Staff

The grand staff combines the treble and bass staves to present a wider pitch range than a single staff. Music written for piano usually shows the right-hand part in the treble staff and the left-hand part in the bass staff.

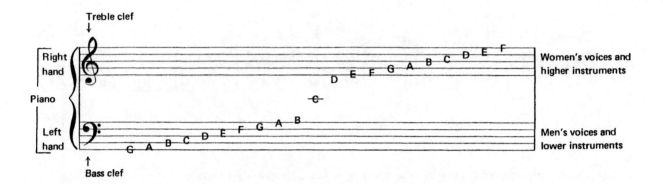

THE PIANO KEYBOARD

You will find it helpful to study the following material while seated at a piano. Refer to the fold-out, four-octave keyboard in the back of your textbook as needed.

The standard keyboard has a total of eighty-eight keys. The white keys begin with low A at the far left of the keyboard and proceed by repeating the letters A-B-C-D-E-F-G from low to high, ending with a final A-B-C at the right of the keyboard.

"C" is a white key to the left of two black keys. "Middle C" is near the center of the keyboard, just below the manufacturer's label. "F" is a white key to the left of three black keys. Use C and F as reference points to locate and identify the other white keys. (For example, play each different letter name from low to high several times. Learn to name any white key quickly and accurately.)

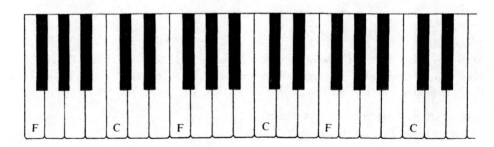

Practice naming the white keys by completing the following exercise. Cover the answers in the right-hand margin, then use them to check your responses to the questions below.

For items 1–12, name the key marked by an arrow. (Cover the answers with a piece of paper.)

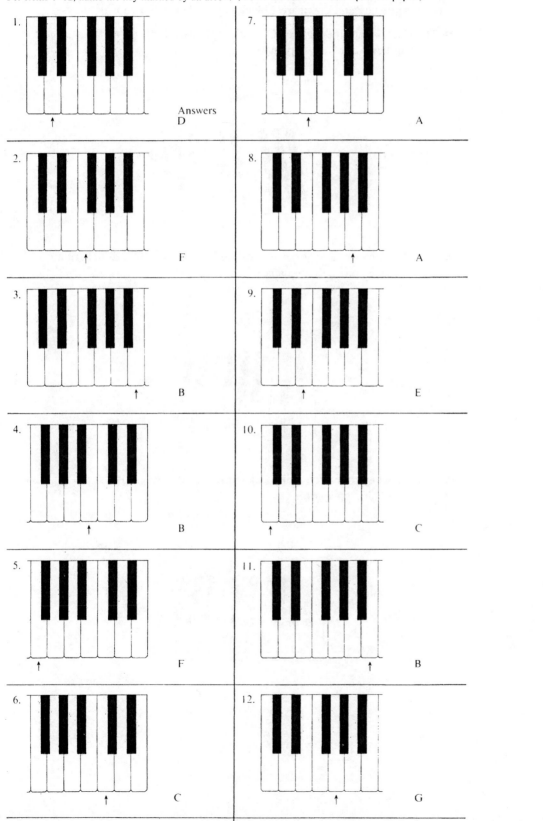

1. Answers
   D

2. F

3. B

4. B

5. F

6. C

7. A

8. A

9. E

10. C

11. B

12. G

HALF STEPS

Half steps and whole steps are the basic intervals you must know in order to understand the scales and chords used in traditional music. A half step, the smallest keyboard interval, is the distance from any piano key to the adjacent (nearest) black or white key on either side. (Adjacent keys are always a half step apart.) Half steps may occur between a white key and the nearest black key, or between two *white* keys.

■ The black key to the *right* of C is called C-sharp (C$^\sharp$). C and C-sharp are adjacent keys, one half step apart.

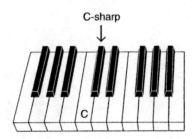

■ The black key to the *right* of F is called F-sharp (F$^\sharp$). F and F-sharp are adjacent keys, one half step apart.

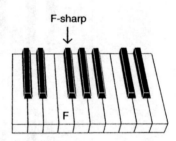

■ The black key to the *left* of B is called B-flat (B$^\flat$). B and B-flat are adjacent keys, one half step apart.

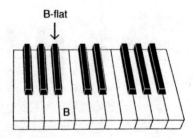

■ The black key to the *left* of A is called A-flat (A♭). A and A-flat are adjacent keys, one half step apart.

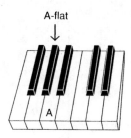

■ The white key to the *right* of E is F. The *white* keys ⏢E and F⏢ are adjacent keys, one half step apart.

■ The white key to the *right* of B is C. The *white* keys ⏢B and C⏢ are adjacent keys, one half step apart.

Practice identifying half steps by completing the following exercise. Cover the answers, then use them to check your responses.

For items 13–18, name the key one half step *higher* than the key marked by an arrow.

For items 19–24, name the key one half step *lower* than the key marked by an arrow.

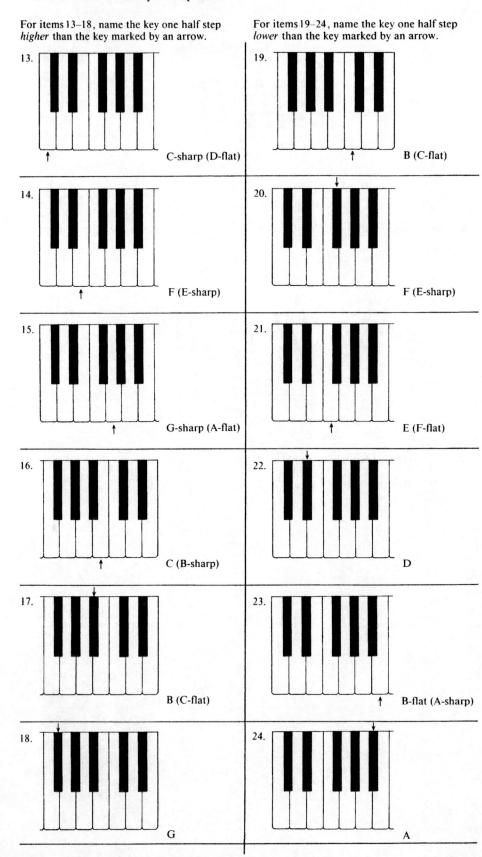

13. C-sharp (D-flat)

14. F (E-sharp)

15. G-sharp (A-flat)

16. C (B-sharp)

17. B (C-flat)

18. G

19. B (C-flat)

20. F (E-sharp)

21. E (F-flat)

22. D

23. B-flat (A-sharp)

24. A

WHOLE STEPS

Two half steps make a whole step. Spell whole steps with *consecutive letters* of the musical alphabet: C-D, D-E, and so forth.

■ From C to D is a whole step. There is a black key between C and D.

■ From D to E is a whole step. There is a black key between D and E.

■ From E to F-sharp is a whole step. There is a white key between E and F-sharp.

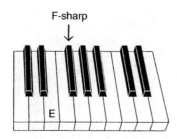

■ From B-flat to A-flat is a whole step. There is a white key between B-flat and A-flat.

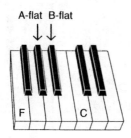

Practice identifying whole steps by completing the following exercise. Cover the answers, then use them to check your responses.

For items 25–30, name the key one whole step *higher* than the key marked by an arrow.

For items 31–36, name the key one whole step *lower* than the key marked by an arrow.

25. D

31. B-flat (A-sharp)

26. F-sharp (G-flat)

32. E (F-flat)

27. F (E-sharp)

33. C-sharp (D-flat)

28. C-sharp (D-flat)

34. E-flat (D-sharp)

29. C (B-sharp)

35. G-sharp (A-flat)

30. G-sharp (A-flat)

36. F-sharp (G-flat)

ENHARMONIC NAMES

Each black key has two names: C-sharp and D-flat are *enharmonic* spellings for the black key between C and D. Enharmonic pitches have one sound but two names.

Examine the enharmonic names for black keys on the keyboard diagram below, then complete the exercise that follows on page 66.

Enharmonic: alike in sound; different in notation.

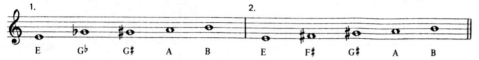

Which measure shows stepwise movement more clearly?

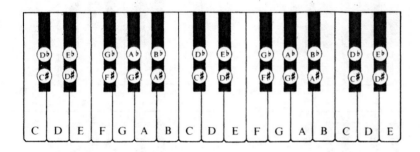

Cover the answers before you practice naming the black keys.

For items 37–42, give the "sharp name" for each black key marked by an arrow.

For items 43–48, give the "flat name" for each black key marked by an arrow.

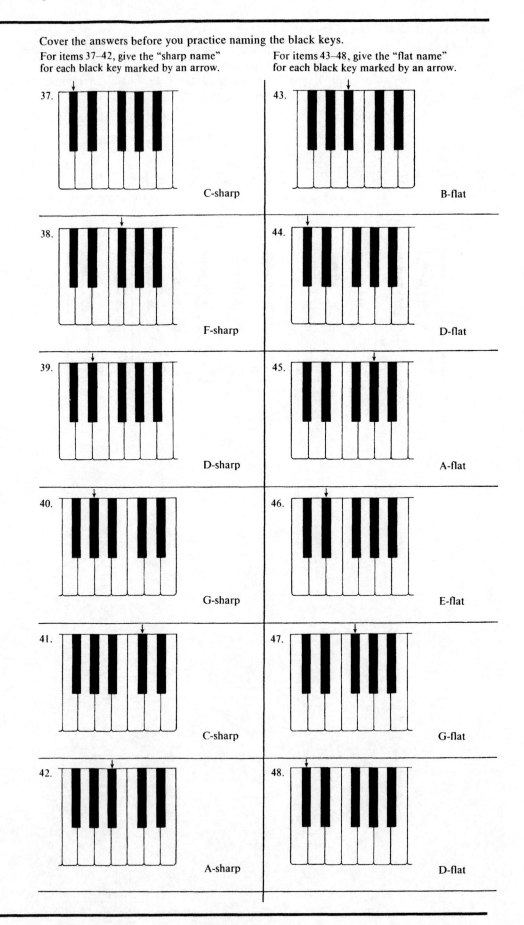

37. C-sharp

38. F-sharp

39. D-sharp

40. G-sharp

41. C-sharp

42. A-sharp

43. B-flat

44. D-flat

45. A-flat

46. E-flat

47. G-flat

48. D-flat

White keys also have enharmonic names. The white key a half step higher than E is called F or E-sharp. The white key a half step lower than F is called E or F-flat. What is the enharmonic name for "B"? For "C"?

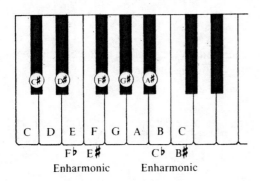

Enharmonic notes sound the same but have different spellings and musical implications. Enharmonic pitches are comparable to homophones in language: for example, *to, two,* and *too.* Write a "musical" homophone for each of the following words.

Allowed	_____	Hi	_____
Banned	_____	Him	_____
Base	_____	Liar	_____
Beet	_____	Loot	_____
Cannon	_____	Miner	_____
Coral	_____	Peddle	_____
Cord	_____	Ray	_____
Doe	_____	Sweet	_____
Frays	_____	Symbol	_____
Herd	_____	Tutor	_____

ACCIDENTALS

Sharps, flats, and naturals are called *accidentals.* The sharp sign (♯) raises a note one half step. The flat sign (♭) lowers a note one half step. The natural sign (♮) cancels a sharp or flat.

Double flats (♭♭) and double sharps (𝄪) raise or lower a note by a *whole* step. (Examples: *C-double sharp* is the same as D; *A-double-flat* is the same as G.) Double sharps and flats are infrequent in elementary music. Examine the notation of "Dry Bones" (page 83) for one example.

An accidental affects every note on the *same* line or in the *same* space within the measure, but does not apply to a note of the same letter name in a different octave.

Write the accidental to the left of a note. (We say, "G-sharp"; we write the sharp sign, then the note.)

(G♮)   (B♭)   (A♭)

An accidental is canceled by the bar line at the end of the measure, except when it is tied to a note in the following measure.

The following excerpt from "I've Been Working on the Railroad" shows a "courtesy accidental" (G natural) to remind the performer that the previous accidental (G-sharp) no longer applies.

Don't   you   hear   the whis-tle blow   -   ing?

Carolyn Wells

PLAYING THE RECORDER

A tutor who tooted a flute
Tried to teach two young tooters to toot.
Said the two to the tutor,
"Is it harder to toot, or
To tutor two tooters to toot?"[2]

Related Listening: *The Virtuoso Recorder*, Michala Petri. RCA 7749-4-RC.

Reports from the elementary classroom indicate that experiences with instruments are preferred musical activities at all age levels.[3] Students develop music reading and performance skills as they apply their musical knowledge, putting theory into practice. The soprano recorder is introduced here in order to provide "hands-on learning" early in your study of music fundamentals. The suggested materials may be studied during the remainder of the course to help you develop recorder and music reading skills simultaneously.

Varying in size from small "sopranino" to larger alto, tenor, and bass instruments, recorders are part of a family of instruments with a long history. Today, as in the past, the recorder offers rewarding challenges and an extensive repertoire of solo and ensemble music to students and advanced musicians at all levels of skill. The soprano recorder, which is more versatile than flutophones, tonettes, and similar instruments, is widely used in elementary music classes.

SELECTING A RECORDER

"Baroque"("English") and "German" models of soprano recorders are available. The baroque fingering system is generally preferred and is used in this book. Wooden recorders costing hundreds of dollars are available, but high quality and inexpensive instruments made from plastic are well-suited to use in the classroom and may be obtained from local music stores or by ordering from the sources listed in Appendix 6.

PLAYING POSITION

Hold your recorder with the left hand at the top. Cover the single hole on the back of the instrument with the left-hand thumb and cover the first (top) tone hole with the left-hand index finger. Put your right-hand thumb underneath the recorder, between holes four and five to support the recorder. (If you have a two-piece or three-piece recorder, line up the holes when you assemble it. If you have a three-piece recorder, set the holes of the bottom joint slightly to the right.)

STARTING THE TONE

Place the tip of the recorder mouthpiece on the lower lip and close your lips around the mouthpiece. (The teeth should not touch the mouthpiece.) The angle of the recorder to the head is about 45 degrees. Blow lightly, because blowing *too hard* causes an out-of-tune, unpleasant sound.

Pronounce a silent "du," and blow gently to start the tone. As the tip of the tongue drops away from its starting position just behind the upper teeth, it releases the air stream. The action of the tongue is called "tonguing."

FINGERINGS

Cover the tone holes with the fingerprint portion of your fingertips. Avoid holding the fingers too straight or too sharply angled to cover the tone holes completely. Fingers not covering tone holes should be raised only slightly, remaining about a half-inch from the recorder. Small, quick, and precise movements are the goal.

The recorder fingering chart on page 81 shows fingerings with circles and numbers. Cover the holes indicated by filled-in circles; the others are left uncovered. The left-hand fingers cover the upper tone holes: 1-2-3; the right-hand fingers cover the lower tone holes: 4-5-6-7. (The bottom two have double openings to allow for playing C-sharp and D-sharp above middle C.) The circle to the left of the diagram indicates the left-hand thumb hole ("T") on the back of the recorder.

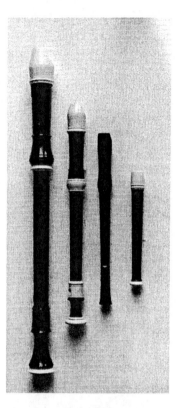

Recorders (left *to* right): Alto, soprano, sopranino, kleine sopranino.

PLAYING MELODIES

Learn each song by singing it with words and also with the letter names of the notes. When you know the song, it is easier to concentrate on the physical actions needed in playing the recorder.

Melodies with B A G

After singing "Hot Cross Buns," play the pitch "B" in the rhythm of the melody. Do the same with "A," then with "G."

- Play B with the thumb and first finger of the left hand.
- Play A with the thumb and the first two fingers.
- Play G with the thumb and three fingers.

Now play the melody as shown below.

Hot Cross Buns

Thumb →

Hot   cross   buns,   hot   cross   buns,   One a pen - ny,   two a   pen - ny,   hot   cross   buns.

● = Cover tone hole.   ○ = Leave tone hole uncovered.

Support the recorder with your right hand and finger the notes B, A, and G as shown.

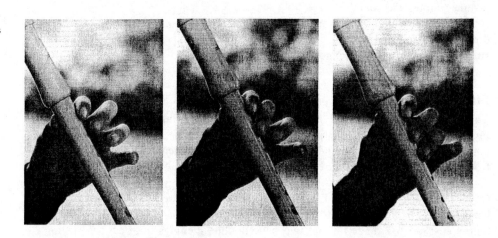

The next songs also use the notes B-A-G. Sing them with letter names, then play them on your recorder.

Good News!

Spiritual

Good news!   Char - i - ot's com - ing!   Good news!   Char - i - ot's com - ing!

Good news!   Char - i - ot's com - ing!   Don't leave   me   be - hind.

From On the Trail of Negro Folk Songs *by Dorothy Scarborough, © 1925 Harvard University Press; renewed 1953 by Mary McDaniel Parker. Reprinted by permission of the publishers.*

Hop, Old Squirrel

American Folk Song

Hop, old squir-rel,   ei - dle-dum, ei - dle-dum   Hop, old squir-rel,   ei - dle-dum, dee!

Hop, old squir-rel,   ei - dle-dum, ei - dle-dum   Hop, old squir-rel,   ei - dle-dum, dee!

Shoheen Sho

Welsh Folk Song

Sho - heen sho, Ba - by boy, Fa - ther's pride, Mo - ther's joy.

Old MacDonald Had a Farm

United States

1. Old Mac - Don - ald had a farm, E - I - E - I - O!
2.

And on this farm he had some chicks, E - I - E - I - O! With a
And on this farm he had some ducks, E - I - E - I - O! With a

Chick, chick here, and a chick, chick there,
Quack, quack here, and a quack, quack there,

Here a chick, there a chick, Eve - ry where a chick, chick.
Here a quack, there a quack, Eve - ry where a quack, quack.

Old Mac - Don - ald had a farm, E - I - E - I - O!

The notes B-A-G match the pitches of the "E-I-E-I-O" pattern in "Old MacDonald Had a Farm." After singing the entire song, divide the class into two groups. The singers begin and the recorders enter each time on the B-A-G pitches. Exchange parts, and repeat the song. Dividing a melody into small, easy-to-learn patterns is often a helpful procedure in teaching the recorder to groups of children. The complete melody of "Old MacDonald" adds two new notes—low E and low D.

Try a listen-sing-and-play approach with children. After introducing the fingerings for B, A, and G, have the class echo the rhythm patterns you play on each pitch.

Play tonal patterns in even quarter note rhythm using different tonal patterns: B-A-B, A-B-A, B-A-G, G-A-B, etc. Instruct the class to sing or hum the patterns on a neutral syllable ("loo"), then with the letter names. (Do not use scale step numbers, which get confused with numbers for fingerings.) If the children close their eyes and listen, they will learn more quickly and avoid the habit of watching your fingers.

After learning each song on your recorder, play it on other instruments that may be available: the piano or tone-bar instruments such as glockenspiels, xylophones, metallophones, or song bells. Chord symbols above the notes indicate the letter names of chords that may be used to accompany the songs on the piano, Autoharp, ukulele, or guitar.

The songs and fingerings that follow may be introduced and learned on the recorder as you continue your studies. The sequence shown here is merely suggested and may be adapted to meet the particular objectives that you or your instructor may have. The discussion of melody continues on page 82 ("Scales.")

Adding Low E and D

The fingerings for low E and low D are shown together with several songs that introduce these pitches. See "Skin and Bones" page 249 and "The Swallow page 49".

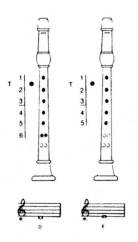

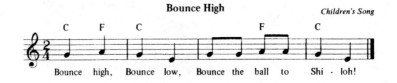

Also, see "Who's That, Tapping At the Window?" page 74.

Playing C and D

The fingering for third-space C and high D are shown. Notice that high D is played without the thumb (LH no. 2 only.) The following songs use B-A-G plus the new notes C and high D.

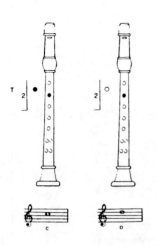

Who's That Tapping at the Window?

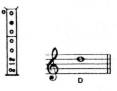

Virginia Folk Song

Who's that tap-ping at the win - dow? Who's that knocking at the door?

From On the Trail of Negro Folk Songs *by Dorothy Scarborough,* © 1925 Harvard University Press; renewed 1953 by Mary McDaniel Parker. Reprinted by permission of the publishers.

When the Saints Go Marching In

New Orleans

Oh, when the saints _____ go march - ing in, _____ Oh, when the saints go march - ing in, Lord, I want to be in that num - ber, _____ when the saints go march - ing in. _____

Go Tell Aunt Rhody

American Folk Song

Go tell Aunt Rho - dy, Go tell Aunt Rho - dy, Go tell Aunt Rho - dy, The old grey goose is dead. _____

Lightly Row

German Folk Tune

Light - ly row, light - ly row, o'er the shin - ing waves we go, Smooth - ly glide, smooth - ly glide, on the si - lent tide.

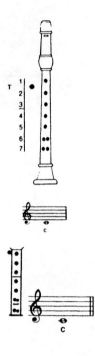

Playing Low C

All the tone holes must be covered for low C. Lead in by starting on E or D to make it easier. Problems in sounding low C are usually caused by blowing too hard, or forgetting to cover all of the tone holes. Tell children to check the fingering low C by pressing the tone holes more firmly than usual, then looking for a circular imprint in the middle of the fingerprint area of each hand. (Incorrect finger placement will show only a partial circle, or a circle not centered on the fleshy part of the fingertip.) In normal playing, use only a light amount of finger pressure.

Hot Cross Buns

England

Hot cross buns, hot cross buns. One a pen-ny, two a pen-ny, hot cross buns.

Who's That Yonder ?

Spiritual*

Who's that yon-der dressed in red? Must be the child-ren that Mo - ses led.

2. Who's that yonder dressed in white?
   Must be the children of the Israelite.

3. Who's that yonder dressed in green?
   Must be Ezekiel in his flying machine.

4. Who's that yonder dressed in blue?
   Must be the children that are coming through.

*The verses of *Who's That Yonder?* are part of the spiritual *Oh, Won't You Sit Down?*

From 150 American Folk Songs, selected and edited by Peter Erdei and Katalin Komlos. Copyright © 1974. Boosey and Hawkes. Used by permission.

Let Us Chase the Squirrel

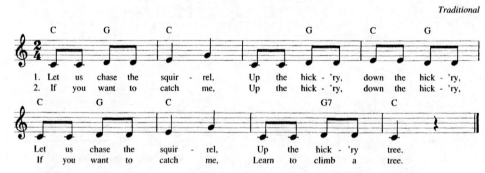

Traditional

1. Let us chase the squir - rel, Up the hick - 'ry, down the hick - 'ry,
2. If you want to catch me, Up the hick - 'ry, down the hick - 'ry,

Let us chase the squir - rel, Up the hick - 'ry tree.
If you want to catch me, Learn to climb a tree.

> Practicing fingering without blowing is often helpful. Have the children hold the recorders in a position that will allow them to observe their finger placement over the tone holes. Use a quick, light motion with only a little finger pressure—like "moving your fingers on top of a bubble."[4]

Playing F

Cover all the tone holes for low C. To play F after playing low C, lift the right-hand middle finger. (F uses all the tone holes except for the right-hand middle finger.)

Scotland's Burning

Traditional Round

1. Scot - land's burn - ing, Scot - land's burn - ing,
2. Fetch the en - gines, Fetch the en - gines,
3. Fire! Fire! Fire! Fire!
4. Pour on wa - ter, Pour on wa - ter.

Old MacDonald Had a Farm

United States

Old Mac - Don - ald had a farm. E - I - E - I - O!
Old Mac - Don - ald had a farm. E - I - E - I - O!

And on this farm he had some chicks, E - I - E - I - O! With a
And on this farm he had some ducks, E - I - E - I - O! With a

Chick, chick here, and a chick, chick there,
Quack, quack here, and a quack, quack there,

Here a chick, there a chick, Eve - ry where a chick, chick.
Here a quack, there a quack, Eve - ry where a quack, quack.

Old Mac - Don - ald had a farm. E - I - E - I - O!

Hot Cross Buns

England

Hot cross buns, hot cross buns, one a pen - ny, two a pen - ny, hot cross buns.

Who's That Yonder?

Spiritual

Who's that yon - der, dressed in red? Must be the child - ren that Mo - ses led.

Taffy

Also, see "Saint Paul's Steeple," page 54.

Playing F# - G♭

The fingering for F# (or G♭) is T 123 || 56. (Finger "G," skip one tone hole and cover the next two.)

The Birch Tree

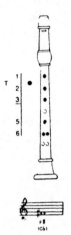

(Also, see "Bicycle Built for Two," "Bingo," "Michael Finnegan," "Mr. Banjo," and "Teddy Bear.")

Here is a way to remember the fingerings for B♭, A♭, and G♭.

- ■ To play B♭ use the fingering for "B," *skip one hole and cover the next two.*
- ■ To play A♭ use the fingering for "A," *skip one hole and cover the next two.*
- ■ To play G♭ use the fingering for "G," *skip one hole and cover the next two.*
- ■ Apply the rule with enharmonic notes: F# = G♭ A♭ = G# B♭ = A#.
- ■ *Check your fingering chart when you are in doubt.*

Playing B♭ - A♯

J'ai perdu le do (I Have Lost the Do)

French Folk Song

From Making Music Your Own,
*Grade 4, Copyright © 1968.
Silver Burdett and Ginn, Inc.
Used by permission.*

J'ai per-du le do de ma cla-ri-net-te,
I have lost the do on my clar-i-net, oh,

J'ai per-du le mi de ma cla-ri-net-te.
I have lost the mi on my clar-i-net, oh.

Sol sol la sol fa mi fa fa fa fa,

Fa fa sol fa mi re mi mi mi mi, Sol

mi mi mi mi sol mi mi mi mi sol la sol fa mi fa, Fa

re re re re fa re re re re fa sol fa mi re do.

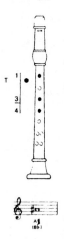

These songs also include B♭ in their melody: "America" (in F), "Bow Belinda," "The Cuckoo," "My Darling Clementine," and "See the Little Ducklings."

Playing A♭ - G♯
To play G♯ use the fingering for A, skip one hole and cover the next two. Songs with G♯ in their melody include "Do Re Mi," "Hava Nagila," and "Ta Kalotykha Vouna."

Hava Nagila

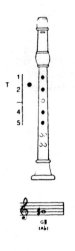

Israeli Folk Song

	Pronunciation	Meaning
	hah - vah nah - ghee - lah (three times)	Let us be happy and rejoice
	veh - nees mĕ - khah	
	hah - vah nĕ - rah - nĕ nah (three times)	Let us be singing
	veh - nees mĕ - khah	
	oo - roo oo - roo - ah - kheem	Wake up, brothers, with glad hearts
	bĕ - lehv sah - meh - akh	

Playing C♯ (Third Space)

The following have third space C♯ in their melody. (No thumb, cover holes 1 and 2.)

See also, "Rig-a-a-Jig-Jig."

D Major Scale

Do Re Mi Fa So La Ti Do Ti La So Fa Mi Re Do

D Minor Scale: Three Forms

Natural (pure) minor　　　　　　　　　　　　　Harmonic minor

Melodic minor (ascending form)　　　　　　Melodic minor (descending form)

Do, Re, Mi, Fa (Four - Part)

English (1852)

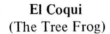

Do, re, mi, fa, I'm quite tired of this sol-fa-ing

I've for-got all you've been say-ing Do, re, mi, fa, sol, la, ti, do!

From Old and New Rounds and Canons, *compiled and edited by Harry R. Wilson. Copyright* © *1967. Harold Flammer, Inc. Shawnee Press, Inc., Music Sales Corporation. Used by permission.*

El Coqui
(The Tree Frog)

Puerto Rican Folk Song

El Co-qui sings his songs oh so sweet-ly,
El co-qui, el co-qui a mi me en-can-ta,

I can hear El co-qui all night long;
Es tan lin-do el can-tar del co-qui,

As I lie fast a-sleep in the moon-light,
Por las no-ches al ir a a-cos-tar-me,

In my dreams comes his sweet lit-tle song. Co-
Me a-dor-me-ce can-tan-do a si:

qui! Co-qui! Co-qui-qui-qui-qui! Co-

qui! Co-qui! Co-qui-qui-qui-qui!

Playing High E

Finger fourth space E like low E, but uncover a small portion of the thumb hole. This thumb position, called "cracking," "pinching," or half-hole, raises the pitch one octave. Experiment to get the thumb position just right. Do *not* blow harder to produce high E, since blowing hard will cause a harsh, out-of-tune pitch.

Text by Walter de la Mare from "Tom Tiddler's Ground." Music by Benjamin Britten from Friday Afternoons, *Copyright © 1936 by Boosey and Co., Ltd. Copyright renewed. Reprinted by permission of Boosey and Hawkes, Inc.*

See also "America" (in G major), "Come, Follow Me," "Saturday Night" (in F).

Old Abram Brown

Words by
Walter de la Mare

Music by Benjamin Britten

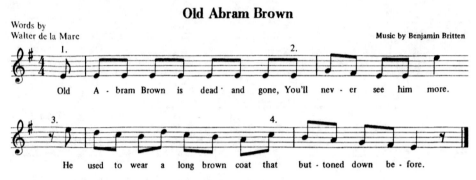

Old A - bram Brown is dead · and gone, You'll nev - er see him more.

He used to wear a long brown coat that but - toned down be - fore.

Sounds of the Singing School

American Round

I will sing you a song of the sing - ing - school, And the

sounds you there may____ hear of the *do re mi,* and the

A B C and the voi - ces ring - ing clear.

Beat the time with ac - cent strong,

Full and strong the tones pro - long.

La la la la la la la la la la la.

La la la la la la la la la la la.

Name the mea - sure, sound the key, All must sing the E.

Do re mi fa so la ti do are in ev - er - y song you know;

Two-beat, four-beat, three-beat mea-sures too, are a - mong the man - y things we do.

Playing High F

To play high F, cover holes 1-2-3-4-6, cracking the left-hand thumbhole. Consult the recorder chart, then practice the following scales.

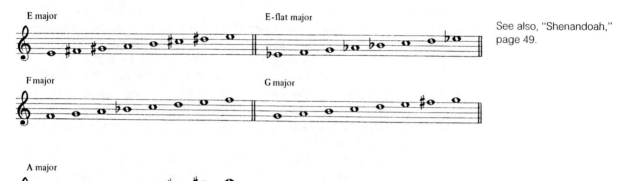

See also, "Shenandoah," page 49.

RECORDER FINGERING CHART

Fingerings are indicated visually and with numbers for the single or double holes on the front of the recorder.

Figure 3.68   Soprano Recorder Fingerings (Baroque System)

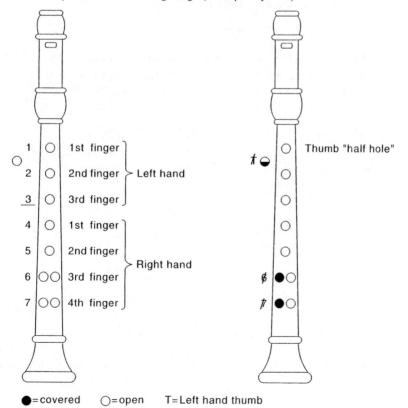

●=covered   ○=open   T=Left hand thumb

GENERAL GUIDELINES FOR RECORDER

- Schools usually begin recorder instruction in grade four or later. You will find information on playing the recorder in basic music series books, together with helpful photographs and many enjoyable melodies for children to play.
- Tune the soprano recorder to written G above middle C, since this is usually a stable and accurate recorder pitch. (Other notes may be unduly affected by adjusting the head joint.) The basic pitch can be adjusted by pulling out the head joint (if the pitch is too high) or pushing it in (if the pitch is too low).
- Breathe in relation to the phrase. A breath mark (') may be written in the music as a reminder. Try not to break a phrase in the middle. Breathe after the cadence, or take a quick breath after a long note (borrowing a fraction of the note's duration for the breath).
- Introduce songbooks and recorder method books after the children have learned to listen and imitate. The ability to read music is not essential for the beginning recorder player, but music reading skills often improve as a result of recorder instruction. Give advanced players more to do, but reinforce less advanced players with music easy enough to offer them success. Children may also gather materials distributed in class into individual recorder notebooks.
- Teach students how to use a fingering chart so that they can refer to it to review any fingering.
- Supplement group instruction with individual help and attention. Achievement—which is related to ability, attitude, and effort—will vary, but many children can experience the pleasure of making music through recorder playing.
- If instruments are available, explore basic music series books containing songs arranged for singers, recorder players, and accompanying instruments (Autoharps, bells, or percussion).

SCALES

A scale is an inventory of the most important notes used in a piece of music. Five types of scales are discussed in this chapter.

> Chromatic: a scale built of consecutive half steps
> Whole tone: a scale built of consecutive whole steps
> Major: the pattern represented by the white keys from C to C
> Minor: the pattern represented by the white keys from A to A
> Pentatonic: the pattern represented by the five black keys

CHROMATIC AND WHOLE TONE SCALES

Related Listening: Debussy: Piano Preludes, Book 1, No. 2—*Voiles* (1910).

Chromatic scales are made entirely of half steps. Whole tone scales are made entirely of whole steps. The chromatic scale has twelve half steps per octave; the whole tone scale has six whole steps per octave.

Chromatic scale: Play all twelve half steps.

Whole tone scale: Play the six white *notes* or the six black *notes*.

Chromatic or whole tone passages occur in many works, though few compositions use only half steps or whole steps. The song "Dry Bones" moves by chromatic half steps while explaining basic anatomy. Notice the use of E-sharp and F-double sharp in its notation.

Dry Bones

From Silver Burdett Music, *Grade 4, Copyright © 1985 Silver Burdett and Ginn, Inc. Used by permission.*

Black Spiritual

Sports enthusiasts are familiar with amplified keyboard fanfares that climb the chromatic scale one step with each repetition.

Fanfare on the chromatic scale

MAJOR SCALES

Major and minor scales are *diatonic scales*—mixtures of whole steps and half steps. The white keys of the C-major scale illustrate the pattern found in every major scale: half steps between tones 3–4 and 7–8, and whole steps between the other tones. "Saint Paul's Steeple," "Taffy," and "Joy to the World" are songs that trace the major scale in their melodies.

To write the G-major scale, list the letters from G to the next G and number them. Scale steps one and eight have the same letter name. The other steps have different letter names. Mark the points where half steps *should* occur.

```
G   A   B - C   D   E   F - G
1   2   3 - 4   5   6   7 - 8
```

In G major, B and C are white keys a half step apart. Change F to F♯ to make a half step between 7–8.

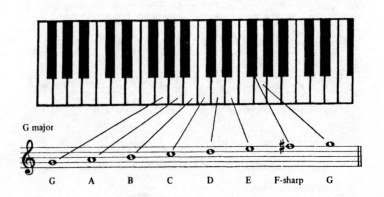

G major

To write the F-major scale, list the letters from F to the next F and number them. Mark the points where half steps should occur.

```
F   G   A - B   C   D   E - F
1   2   3 - 4   5   6   7 - 8
```

Change B to B♭ to make a half step between 3–4. There is a half step between the white keys E and F. Notice that seven different letter names are used for the notes of each major scale, and no letter within the octave is repeated.

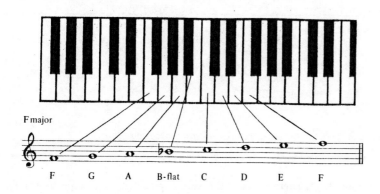

MOVABLE *DO* SYLLABLES

The "do-re-mi" syllables name scale tones and express tonal relationships. Music reading syllables were developed long ago by the Italian music theorist and teacher Guido of Arezzo. The song "Do-Re-Mi" from *The Sound of Music* is a well-known modern version of these syllables.

Do - Re - Mi

Related Listening: *"Ut queant laxis."* Gregorian Chant. Sony Classical CD SK 53899.

The original syllables came from *Ut queant laxis* (Hymn to St. John the Baptist), a Latin hymn with an unusual feature: each of its first six lines begins one step higher than the preceding line. The first syllable of each line was used to label each scale step and, with small changes, the syllables have been used ever since as an aid to music reading.[5] The syllables, their pronunciation, and their abbreviation are shown in the following table.

		Syllable	Pronounced	Abbreviation
High	½ step	Do (Ut)	doh	d'
		Ti	tee	t
		La	lah	l
		Sol*	soh	s
	½ step	Fa	fah	f
		Mi	mee	m
		Re	ray	r
Low		Do (Ut)	doh	d

*The syllable *sol* is usually spelled *so* in American and British music books.

The "movable *do* system" uses the same syllables for a scale in any key. When you sing the same song in different keys, the letter names change but the syllables stay the same. "Hot Cross Buns" is shown below with fourteen different sets of letter names. Every pattern sounds like *mi-re-do.* Syllables make music reading easier.

Children learn syllables through a carefully prepared learning sequence that begins with rote songs. Songs prepare them for lessons that present appropriate tonal or rhythm patterns derived from known songs. After sufficient practice in singing, hearing, and reading tonal patterns with syllables, they progress to staff notation.

PENTATONIC SCALES

Pentatonic scales (Greek: pente—five) have five different tones. Pentatonic scales based on *do, re, mi, so,* and *la* have no half steps. Examples of songs in this book that contain only notes from the pentatonic scale are "Auld Lang Syne," "Bounce High, Bounce Low," "Bow, Wow, Wow," "Bluebird," "Down in the Meadow," "Get On

Board," "Hop up, My Ladies," "Jinny Go Round," "Johnny Works with One Hammer," "Rain, Rain, Go Away," "Scotland's Burning," "Skin and Bones," "Starlight," "Teddy Bear," and "Who's That Tapping at the Window?"

Pentatonic songs help develop in-tune singing and are often used in playing xylophones, metallophones, and glockenspiels, which are instruments with removable tone bars. Children prepare these instruments for pentatonic by removing the *fa* and *ti* tone bars (major scale steps four and seven). Pentatonic scales starting on C, F, and G require no sharps or flats.

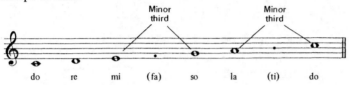

Xylophone

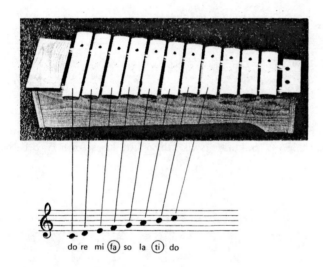

To play the G pentatonic scale, remove the tone bars corresponding to steps four and seven (*fa* and *ti*) in the G *major* scale. The scale that results has no half steps.

To play the G pentatonic scale, remove the tone bars corresponding to steps four and seven (*fa* and *ti*) in the G *major* scale. The scale that results has no half steps.

The Korean folk song "Ahrirang" is shown here in "G pentatonic." This melody contains no half steps. (Notice that *fa* and *ti*—C and F sharp—do not occur in the melody.)

Related Listening: "Ahrirang" in
*Korea: Vocal and Instrumental
Music,* sung by Kim Ok-Sim
Folkways FE 4325.

Ahrirang

M. T. K.

Korean Folk Song

Ah - ri - rang,   Ah - ri - rang,   ah - ra - ri   yo, _____

Walk - ing o'er the   moun - tain peak ___ of ___   Ah - ri - rang.

Fine

1. You,   who   left   me   be - hind,   sweet - heart, ___   Ah - ri rang,
2. As man - y   stars   as   there   are   in ___ the ___ sky, _____

D.C. al Fine

You ___ will ___ hear ___ in your heart the   song   that I   sang.
So ___ are my   sor - rows ___ since you   said ___   good - bye.

Related Listening: *Japanese
Melodies,* Yo-Yo Ma, cello CBS
FM 39703.

"Sakura," a famous Japanese melody, is based on a pentatonic scale that *does* contain half steps. The scale of "Sakura" is like the white keys from E to E, but omitting G and D.

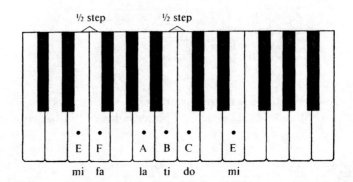

Sakura
(Cherry Blossoms)

English version by
Katherine S. Bolt

Japanese Folk Song

From The Magic of Music. *Graded Four. Copyright © 1971, 1967 by Ginn and Company. Used by permission of Silver Burdett and Ginn, Inc.*

Sa - ku - ra, Sa - ku - ra, Love - ly blos - soms
Sa - ku - ra, Sa - ku - ra, Ya - yo - i no

fill - ing the trees, Love - ly blos - soms scent - ing the breeze,
so - ra___ wa, Mi - wa - ta - su ka - ghi - ri;

Pink and white the pet - als will fall, Spread - ing sweet en -
Ka - su - mi ka? ku - mo___ ka? Ni - o - i zo

chant - ment on all. Sa - ku - ra, Sa - ku - ra,
i - zu - ru; I - za - ya! I - za - ya!

Gong

Be - hold, cher - ry trees bloom. *pp*
Mi - ni yu - ka - n.

KEY SIGNATURES: MAJOR KEYS

Sharps or flats that occur regularly in a composition are gathered at the beginning of each staff as a key signature. (The scale of C major, which has no sharps or flats, has a "key signature" of no sharps or flats.) Music based on the C scale is in the "key of C." Melodies in C major usually end on C, the keynote or "tonic."

When F-sharp is written on the fifth line of the staff, just after the clef sign, it signifies that *all* the F's in the music are raised to F-sharp. The music has a key signature of one sharp. Melodies usually end on the keynote (tonic), which in this case is G. Circle every pitch affected by the F-sharp in the key signature of "America." What is the final pitch of the melody? Name the keynote.

Key signature of one sharp

F- sharp

America (one sharp)

Samuel Francis Smith

Tune: God Save the King

Verse 1. My coun - try, 'tis of thee, Sweet land of lib - er - ty,

Of thee I sing. Land where my fath - ers died, Land of the

Pil - grims' pride, From ev - 'ry___ moun - tain - side Let___ free - dom ring.

When B-flat is written on the third line immediately after the treble clef sign, it signifies that every B shown in the music is lowered to B-flat. The music has a key signature of one flat. Circle every note affected by B-flat in the key signature of the second verse of "America." What is the final pitch of "America" in this key? Name the keynote.

Key signature of one flat

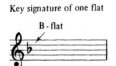

Circle the notes affected by the key signature for the third verse of "America." What is the final pitch of "America" in this key? Name the keynote.

Circle the notes affected by the key signature for the fourth verse of "America." What is the final pitch of "America" in the key of four sharps? Name the keynote.

FINDING THE KEYNOTE

Each scale or key, such as F major or G major, is represented by a key signature. Scale step number one is the same as the letter name of the scale and serves as the "home base," "keynote," or ⎡tonic⎤ of each key. The tonic functions as a tone of repose, and most melodies end by coming to rest on the keynote. The key signature indicates the location of "do," the first syllable of the major scale.

LOCATING *DO* IN KEYS WITH SHARPS

The sharp farthest to the right in the key signature is always step seven of the major scale (*ti*). Count up one half step to find *do,* which is step eight or one of the major scale.

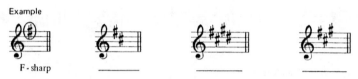

Circle the last sharp to the right. Write its letter name beneath the staff.

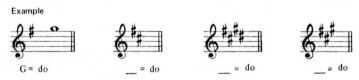

Name the note that is one half step higher than the last sharp.

KEYS WITH FLATS IN THEIR KEY SIGNATURE

The flat that is farthest to the right in the key signature is step four (*fa*) in the major scale. Count up or down to find *do* (step one). For example, if B-flat is step four, count down from B-flat to F (4 3 2 1, or *fa mi re do*). ⎡Shortcut⎤ When the key signature has two or more flats, *do* has the same letter name as the next-to-last flat.

Circle the last flat. Write its letter name beneath the staff.

Call the last flat *fa* and count down to *do.*

Shortcut: *Do* has the same name as the next-to-last flat.

The regular order of the sharps in the key signature is F-C-G-D-A-E-B. The first sharp is always F-sharp. The second sharp is always C-sharp, and so forth. The flats occur in the reverse order (B-E-A-D-G-C-F). The memory aid "Father Charles Goes Down And Ends Battle" names the sharps, and in reverse, gives the order of the flats: "Battle Ends And Down Goes Charles Father."

The following example shows key signatures using sharps or flats as they appear on the treble and bass staff. The letter name of *do* in each key is shown above the staff.

C major and key signatures with sharps

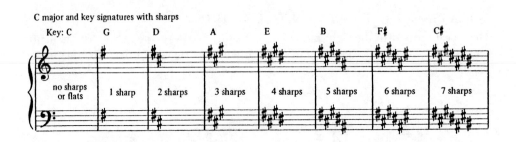

C major and key signatures with flats

> Review:
>
> The major scale is like a staircase: an eight-note pattern with half steps between steps 3–4 and 7–8. At the piano, the major scale corresponds to the pattern of the white keys from C to C. There are half steps between scale steps 3–4 (E-F) and 7–8 (B-C).

W = whole step
H = half step

MINOR SCALES AND KEYS

The minor scale corresponds to the pattern of the white keys from A to A. There are half steps between scales steps 2–3 (B-C) and 5–6 (E-F).

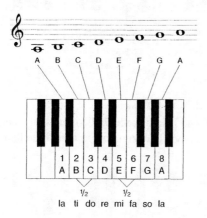

RELATIVE MAJOR AND MINOR KEYS

C major and A minor share the same key signature (no sharps or flats) and are called *related* or *relative* major and minor keys. Every key signature represents a major key and its related minor key. Both C major and A minor use the seven white keys but they differ in their patterns of half steps and whole steps.

To find the starting pitch of the relative minor scale, count up or down to step six in major. The sixth note of C major is the first note of A minor. Major scales start on *do*. Minor scales start on *la*. To find the relative minor, sing up or down to *la*.

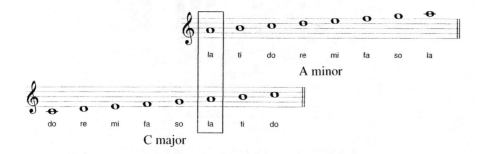

FINDING THE KEYNOTE

You have learned how to find *do*, which is the keynote in major. The keynote of the minor scale is *la*. The syllable *la* is the sixth degree of the major scale and the first degree of the related minor scale. Shortcut Notice that *la* is always three half steps lower than *do*. If *do* is on a line, *la* will be on the line beneath it. If *do* is in a space, *la* will be in the space beneath it. To discover whether a notated melody is in major or minor, examine its key signature and the last note of the melody. Melodies in major end on *do;* melodies in minor end on *la*.

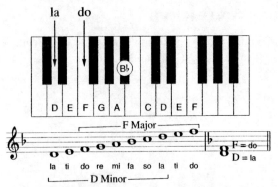

When *do* is in a space, *la* is in the space beneath.
The distance between *do* and *la* is three half steps.

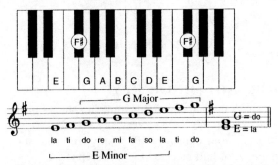

When *do* is on a line, *la* is on the line beneath.
The distance between *do* and *la* is three half steps.

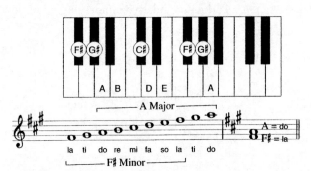

When *do* is in a space, *la* is in the space beneath.
La is F♯. The distance between F♯ and A *(do)* is
three half steps.

The following diagram shows keys with one to seven sharps in clockwise order and keys with one to seven flats in counterclockwise order. Major keys are at the outer edge of the circle. Related minor key signatures are within the circle. (For example, F major and D minor share the key signature of one flat; G major and E minor share the key signature of one sharp.) Each new key with sharps is five letter names higher than the preceding key. Count up four letters to find the next keynote in flats.

C	D	E	F	G	A	B	C	D
1	2	3	4	5				
				1	2	3	4	5

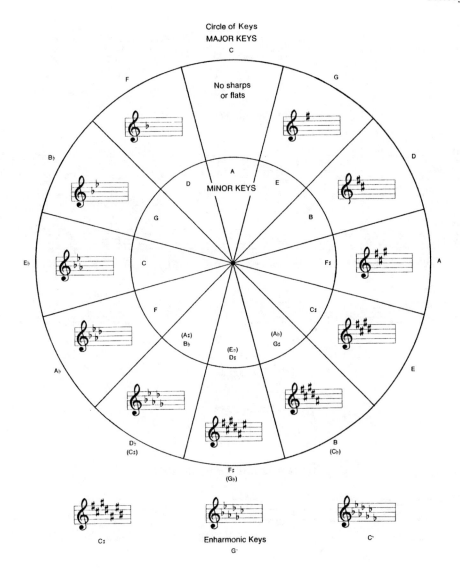

PARALLEL MAJOR AND MINOR

"Go Tell Aunt Rhody," "Lightly Row," "Love Somebody," "When the Saints Go Marching In," and "Winter, Goodbye" are major key melodies that use only the first five steps of the scale. Lower scale step three of a song in major to make it sound like a song in minor. Play "Winter, Goodbye" on the piano or with bells, then change its melody from major to minor by substituting E-flat for E natural. Compare the sounds of C major and C minor. Try the same experiment with the melodies listed above by changing them from major to minor.

C Major

Winter, Goodbye (C major)

Slowly

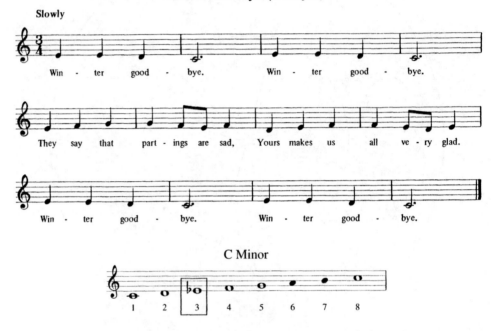

Win - ter good - bye. Win - ter good - bye.

They say that part - ings are sad, Yours makes us all ve - ry glad.

Win - ter good - bye. Win - ter good - bye.

C Minor

Winter, Goodbye (C minor)

Win - ter good - bye. Win - ter good - bye.

They say that part - ings are sad, Yours makes us all ve - ry glad.

Win - ter good - bye. Win - ter good - bye.

> Major key melodies can be changed to the parallel minor key by lowering scale steps three, six, and seven a half step.

The melody of "The Swan Sings" has a descending scale pattern in C major. To change it to C minor (the parallel minor) lower steps 3 (E), 6 (A), and 7 (B) a half step.

The Swan Sings (C minor)

Canon

The swan sings teer - i - li - o, teer - i - li - o, teer - i - li - o.

Compare the C major and C minor scales, shown below in staff notation. Notice that syllables for major scales begin and end on *do;* minor scales begin and end with *la.*

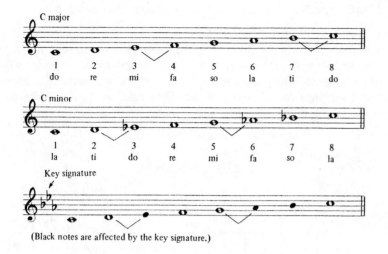

(Black notes are affected by the key signature.)

Mark the statements that are true.

_____ C major and C minor have the same keynote.

_____ C major and C minor have different keynotes.

_____ C major and C minor have the same key signature.

_____ C major and C minor have different key signatures.

_____ C major and C minor are *relative* major and minor scales.

_____ C major and C minor are *parallel* major and minor scales.

_____ To change a major scale to its parallel minor, lower steps three, six, and seven by a half step.

Invite students to play scales on resonator bells, recorders, keyboards, or melody bells. Experiences with instruments help to make scale structure vivid and concrete. If students with resonator bells stand in scale step order, a student "conductor" can point to individuals to play simple melodies, scales, or tonal patterns. Aligned like the black-and-white keys of the piano, students can play the pitches of major or minor scales on signal. (Distribute bell mallets and resonator bells to thirteen students to play the complete chromatic scale.)

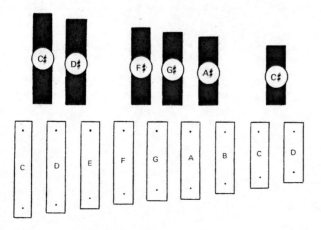

In the classroom, clarify scale structure with diagrams or charts. Combine sound and sight: sing or play the scales in the classroom while following diagrams that show their structure.

| Major | : half steps 3–4, 7–8. | Minor | : half steps 2–3 and 5–6.

Prepare activity sheets to show scale structure. Let boxes represent half steps and construct major or minor scales by writing the letter names in the appropriate squares. In the example below, the letter names of the black-and-white keys are shown in the top line of the diagram. The pitches of the C scale are shown on the middle line. Write the scale step numbers in the boxes on the lower line, as shown. Write the pitches needed to form the F major, D minor, and G minor scales in the diagrams that follow the example.

Scale Activity Sheet

C major (example)

C	C#/Db	D	D#/Eb	E	F	F#/Gb	G	G#/Ab	A	A#/Bb	B	C
C		D		E	F		G		A		B	C
1		2		3	4		5		6		7	8

F major: half steps between 3–4 and 7–8.

F	F#/Gb	G	G#/Ab	A	A#/Bb	B	C	C#/Db	D	D#/Eb	E	F

D minor: half steps between 2–3 and 5–6.

D	D#/Eb	E	F	F#/Gb	G	G#/Ab	A	A#/Bb	B	C	C#/Db	D

G minor: half steps between 2–3 and 5–6.

G	G#/Ab	A	A#/Bb	B	C	C#/Db	D	D#/Eb	E	F	F#/Gb	G

THREE FORMS OF MINOR SCALES

Minor scales have three slightly different forms, resulting from changes that affect steps six and seven. The first five notes of all forms of the minor scale are alike. The "natural minor" has no alterations, and uses the notes indicated in its key signature. The seventh step of the scale is raised a half step in the "harmonic minor" scale, and steps six and seven are raised in the ascending "melodic" form of the scale. Practice the three forms of the D minor scale on your recorder. Notice the syllable names for harmonic and melodic minor. The syllable *so* is raised to *si* (see). The syllable *fa* is raised to *fi* (fee).

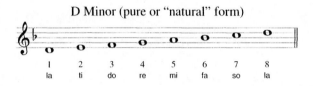

D Minor (pure or "natural" form)

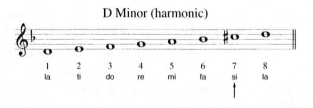

D Minor (harmonic)

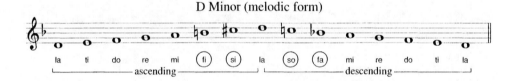

D Minor (melodic form)

Compare the following melodies. Which one is based on the natural minor scale? Which contains a raised seventh step (harmonic minor)? Which has raised six and seven (melodic minor)?

Old Abram Brown

Words by Walter de la Mare

Music by Benjamin Britten

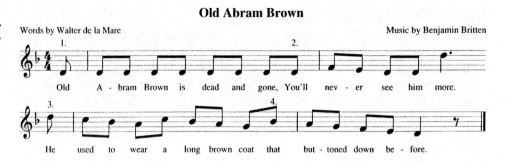

Old A - bram Brown is dead and gone, You'll nev - er see him more.

He used to wear a long brown coat that but - toned down be - fore.

Joshua Fought the Battle of Jericho

Spiritual

Josh - ua fought the bat - tle of Je - ri - cho, _ Je - ri - cho, _ Je - ri - cho, _

Josh - ua fought the bat - tle of Je - ri - cho, _ And the walls came tum - bl - in' down.

1. You may talk a - bout your kings of Gi - de - on, You may talk a - bout your men of

Saul, but there's none like good old Josh - ua, At the bat - tle of Je - ri - cho. Oh!

2. Now the Lord commanded Joshua:
   "I command you and obey you must;
   You just march straight to those city walls
   And the walls will turn to dust."

3. Straight up to the walls of Jericho
   He marched with spear in hand,
   "Go blow that ram's horn," Joshua cried,
   "For the battle is in my hand."

4. Then the lamb ram sheep horns began to blow,
   And the trumpets began to sound,
   And Joshua commanded, "Now, children, shout!"
   And the walls came tumbling down.

Greensleeves

England (c. 1580)

A - las my love _ you do me wrong _ to cast me off _ dis - court - eous - ly; And

I have loved _ you for so long, _ De - light - ing in _ your com - pa - ny.

Chorus

Green - sleeves _ was all my joy. _ Green - sleeves _ was my de - light.

Green - sleeves was my heart of gold _ And who but my la - dy Green - sleeves.

2. I long have waited at your hand
   To grant whatever you would crave,
   And waged, have I, both life and land
   Your love and goodwill for to have.
   (CHORUS)

3. Alas, my love, that yours should be
   A heart of faithless vanity,
   So here I meditate all alone
   Upon your insincerity.
   (CHORUS)

TRANSPOSITION

When a melody is changed from one key to a higher or lower key it is *transposed.* Transposition is used when—

1. A higher or lower vocal range is more suitable than the notated range of the song.

2. A new or different key is better suited to an instrument. Here are some examples:

   (a) Orff instruments have supplementary tone bars for F-sharp and B-flat only.

   (b) Autoharps usually are 12-chord or 15-chord models and play in a limited number of keys.

   (c) Keys with sharps are usually easier than keys with flats for the beginning guitar player.

   (d) Keys with numerous sharps or flats require more complicated recorder fingerings.

3. Transposition adds interest to repetitions of a melody. Recordings of popular music often use the device of raising the key of each new verse in order to heighten the feeling of excitement. (The process of changing to a new key is known as *modulation.*)

To transpose a melody, substitute the notes of a new scale for those of the old scale.

1. Write the scale of the original key and number its notes from one to eight.

C	D	E	F	G	A	B	C
1	2	3	4	5	6	7	8

2. Give each note in the melody its corresponding scale step number: C is one, D is two, E is three, and so forth.

Little Chickens

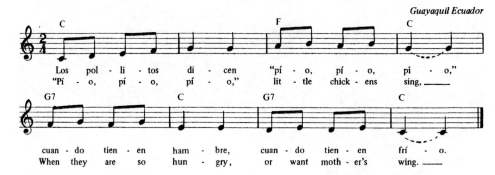

Guayaquil Ecuador

Los pol - li - tos di - cen "pí - o, pí - o, pí - o,"
"Pí - o, pí - o, pí - o," lit - tle chick - ens sing, _____

cuan - do tien - en ham - bre, cuan - do tien - en frí - o.
When they are so hun - gry, or want moth - er's wing. _____

3. Write the scale of the new key and number its notes from one to eight.

D	E	F#	G	A	B	C#	D
1	2	3	4	5	6	7	8

4. Replace each note of the original key with the note that has the same number in the new key.

Little Chickens

Guayaquil Ecuador

Los pol - li - tos di - cen "pí - o, pí - o, pí - o,"
"Pí - o, pí - o, pí - o," lit - tle chick - ens sing, _____

Cuan - do tien - en ham - bre, cuan - do tien - en frí - o.
When they are so hun - gry, or want moth - er's wing. _____

Pentatonic scale melody improvisation. Use the rhythm of a known rhyme as the basis for a melodic improvisation with instruments. Limit the difficulty of the task by using only two to five notes of the pentatonic scale. Divide the class into four groups. Each group invents a melodic pattern for one of the four phrases. Listen to the ideas in each group and select one of them for each phrase. Have the entire class learn the new song and play it on bells, xylophones, recorders, or other instruments available in your room.

Improvising a new melody to the rhythm of
"Go Tell Aunt Rhody"

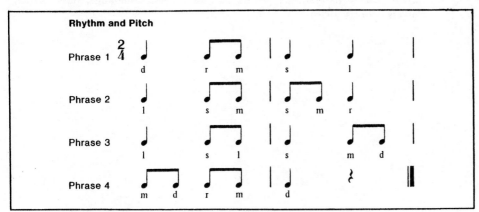

Rhythm

Phrase 1 $\frac{2}{4}$

Phrase 2

Phrase 3

Phrase 4

Rhythm and Pitch

Phrase 1 $\frac{2}{4}$

d   r   m   s   l

Phrase 2

l   s   m   s   m   r

Phrase 3

l   s   l   s   m   d

Phrase 4

m   d   r   m   d

Scale numbers	1	2	3	5	6
Letters	C	D	E	G	A
Syllables	d	r	m	s	l

Create a melody using the whole tone scale.

1. Notate the rhythm of a song you have selected.

2. Choose notes from the pentatonic scale to go with your rhythm.

3. Practice your melody and make any changes you think necessary.

4. Play your melody.

5. Listen to the following example of a melody using the whole tone scale.

Debussy, *Piano Preludes,* Book 1, No. 2, *Voiles* (1910).

NOTES

[1]William S. Newman, *Understanding Music,* 2d ed. (New York: Harper and Row, 1961).

[2]Bennett Cerf, comp., *Out on a Limerick* (New York: Pocket Books, 1962), 121.

[3]Wallace Nolin, "Patterns of Attitudinal Development in General Music Classes," *Update, The Application of Research in Music Education,* 7 no. 1 (Fall 1988), 33. "Playing classroom instruments and playing band and orchestra instruments were highly regarded by most students. The attitudes toward these activities actually increased as students grew older—one of the few categories in which this occurred."

[4]The phrase "moving your fingers on top of a bubble" is quoted from *Jump Right In, Teacher's Guide, Soprano Recorder, Book One* by Richard Grunow and Edwin E. Gordon (Chicago: G.I.A. Publications, Inc. 1987), 73.

[5]"Ut" was changed to *do* in the seventeenth century, and *ti,* the seventh syllable, was added to complete the scale. (The melody of *Ut queant laxis* is shown in modern notation in the *Juilliard Repertory Library,* published by Canyon Press, Inc.) A concise summary of the history of syllables is found under "Solmization" in the *New Harvard Dictionary of Music,* Don Michael Randel, ed. (Cambridge, Mass.: Harvard University Press, 1986).

*T*EXTURE AND HARMONY

4

Harmony developed much later than rhythm and melody in Western music. For centuries church music consisted of a single line of melody sung by a soloist or a choir. Experiments with the possibilities of simultaneous tonal combinations during the Middle Ages led to music with parallel melodic lines four or five notes apart. Contrary motion—with parts moving up or down in opposite directions—emerged during the eleventh century. The gradual development of music notation made more complex music possible, including polyphonic music combining two or more independent melodies. During the fifteenth century, advances in music printing made polyphonic music available to be sung at home in secular rounds and madrigals. Later, chords of three tones became the norm and the possibilities of melody against a background of chords led to the development of modern harmony and varied types of music using combinations of rhythm, melody, and harmony.

TEXTURE

Words such as "megaphone," "microphone," "phonograph," "saxophone," "telephone," and "xylophone" share the Greek word *phone,* meaning "sound." *Phonics* are vocal sounds and the words "monophonic," "polyphonic," "homophonic," and "heterophonic" label musical textures: the horizontal and vertical lines of melody and harmony, which can be interwoven like threads in fabric.

MONOPHONIC TEXTURE

Melody alone makes one line of sounds, or *monophonic* texture (Greek, *monos,* "single"). Monophonic music preceded harmony by many centuries. An example of monophonic music is Gregorian Chant, the unison melody of the Catholic liturgy. You could picture monophonic texture on the felt board with a single horizontal strand of yarn shaped in a contour like a melody's line of notes. Monophonic texture occurs in music of every time and place. Compositions for unaccompanied instruments or solo voice are also examples of monophonic music.

Related Listening (monophony): Debussy: "Syrinx" for Flute Unaccompanied. "Music of Debussy," James Galway, flute. CD: RCA RCDI-7173.

POLYPHONIC TEXTURE

Polyphonic music (Greek, *polys,* "many") has a texture made from interweaving two or more independent melodic lines. Polyphonic music, also known as contrapuntal music, originated in the Middle Ages, when musicians added a new melody to an existing one.

Related Listening (polyphony): Handel: "For Unto Us a Child Is Born" from *Messiah,* Leonard Bernstein, New York Philharmonic, Westminster Choir, CD: CBS MYK 38481.

HOMOPHONIC TEXTURE

Homophonic music (Greek, *homos,* "same") has a texture made from prominent horizontal lines of melody against a vertical background of chords. Homophonic texture predominates in much of the art music, folk music, and popular music of today.

HETEROPHONIC TEXTURE

Related Listening (heterophony): Igor Stravinsky: "The Shrove-Tide Fair," *Petrushka,* CD: London 417619–2.

In *heterophonic* music (Greek, *heteros,* "other") performers combine simultaneous, but differing, versions of the same melody. Heterophonic texture occurs in orchestral music as well as in the music of Africa, Asia, Eastern Europe, and the Near East. Unintentional heterophonic music is not uncommon when singers in a group differ in their recollection of the tune.

You can illustrate contrasting textures in the classroom by performing a familiar round such as "Row, Row, Row Your Boat" or "Three Blind Mice."[1]

- ■ Sing it unaccompanied in unison to illustrate   monophonic texture.
- ■ Add chords to the tune to make   homophonic texture.
- ■ Sing it as a round to demonstrate   polyphonic texture.

Related Listening: *Old Abram Brown,* The Tapiola Children's Choir, Deutsche Grammophon 2530812, or *Holt Music,* Grade 6, or Silver Burdett and Ginn *World of Music,* Grade 5.

Listen to a recorded performance of "Old Abram Brown" (the melody is shown on page 100) and notice the interplay of melody, harmony, and textures in the performance of a round. Notice that mixtures of polyphonic and homophonic texture result when a polyphonic round is accompanied by chords.

Developing a musical vocabulary

Musical terms such as *homophonic* and *polyphonic* are useful because they help us to focus and conceptualize. Children usually describe what they hear with gestures or other types of movement, or picture it with drawings, or use words that they find meaningful. One of the teacher's tasks is to help children develop a musical vocabulary. Introduce new terms when they are needed, just as in other subjects. Ask questions that focus on the music: "Was it accompanied or unaccompanied?" "Did you hear melody alone or two different melodies?" "Did the second melody sound like the first melody?" "Was this music polyphonic or homophonic?" "How could we make a different texture?"

HARMONY

The term "harmony" refers to the structure and functions of chords in music. Tones in succession make melody. Tones sounded together make harmony.

Some melodies outline the tones of a chord. The chord tones C-E-G sound like "The Marines' Hymn." Played in reverse order (G-E-C), the tones become "The Star-Spangled Banner." Buglers toot a whole repertoire of different melodies by changing the rhythm and sequence of the pitches C-E-G. In harmony, however, a C chord is a C chord, no matter how its notes are stacked.

G	E	C	G	E	C
E	G	G	C	C	E
C	C	E	E	G	G

Composers and arrangers create new and different sounds with chords by writing them higher or lower or by changing the spacing between chord tones.[2]

The Marines' Hymn (excerpt)

From the halls of Mon - te - zu - ma to the shores of

The Star-Spangled Banner (excerpt)

Oh! — say can you see by the dawn's ear - ly light,

CHORDS

Triads are chords with three different tones. The C chord (C-E-G) is a triad, built on the first step of the C scale. Repeating a chord tone in different octaves is known as *doubling*. A chord remains a triad, however, even when one of its notes is doubled. Doubling adds emphasis to a tone and is necessary when writing triads in four-part harmony.

Related Listening: J. Strauss II: *The Blue Danube,* Op. 314, EMI CDZ 762503 2.

Root, Third, and Fifth

The C triad is built from steps one, three, and five of the C scale. The notes of a triad are the root, third, and fifth. Chords may be constructed on any note. The C triad (C-E-G) on the first degree of the C scale has the same letter name as its root. A chord is in root position when the chord root is the lowest note.

In C major, the C chord is called the I chord because its root is the same as the first step of the C scale. The D chord is a II chord because its root is the same as the second step of the C scale. Each chord is numbered according to the scale step number of its root.

Triads in C major

Triads and Larger Chords

The C triad uses steps 1-3-5 of the C scale. Steps 1-3-5-7 would result in a seventh chord. Steps 1-3-5-7-9 produce a ninth chord, and so forth. The size of the chord refers to the distance between its root and its upper note. Contemporary music may include chords based on scale steps four notes apart, such as 1-4-7. Chords built from clusters of adjacent tones are also used.

Spacing

Notes in chords are written on consecutive lines or spaces or distributed more widely in "open" spacing. A chord is in root position when its root is the lowest tone.

R = Root   3 = Third   5 = Fifth

Chord Inversion

E   C   E
G   G   C
C   E   G

A chord is "inverted" when a tone other than the root is the lowest pitch. A *triad* is inverted when its third or fifth is the lowest chord tone. In root position the C chord is C-E-G. When E or G is the lowest note of the C chord, the chord is inverted. Chords in root position sound more stable and conclusive than inverted chords, but chord inversion allows for smoother movement between chord tones.

KEYBOARD EXPERIENCES WITH HARMONY

PLAYING TRIADS

Keyboard experience offers one of the best ways to approach the study of chords. Begin keyboard practice with triads by playing the chord tones one at a time—as "broken" chords—then play the notes together as "solid" chords (Numbers above or below the notes indicate fingerings for the right or left hand.)[3]

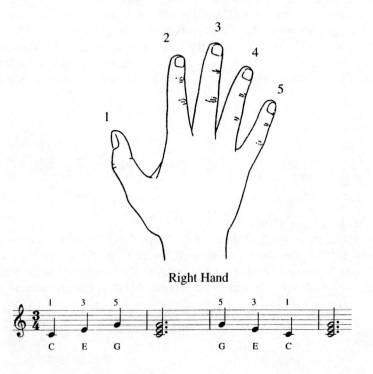

Right Hand

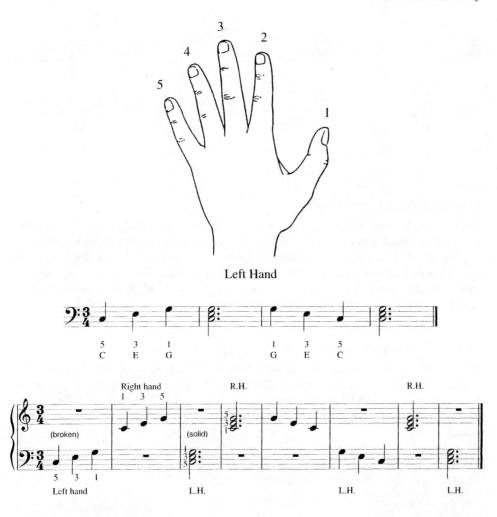

Left Hand

Practice chord *arpeggios* to increase your facility and your skill in reading bass and treble staff notation.

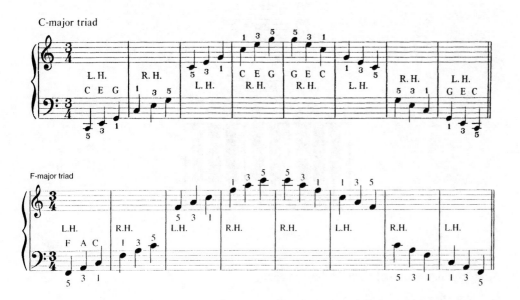

THE TONIC (I) CHORD

The *tonic* or **I** chord in the key of C uses scale steps 1-3-5 (C-E-G). Chords can be indicated by chord symbols written above the staff. **C** indicates the chord C-E-G.

Play the C-E-G chord in the middle register of the piano, with its chord root no lower than one octave below middle C. You can accompany some songs with only the tonic chord (for example, "Little Tom Tinker" or "Row, Row, Row Your Boat") but most accompaniments use two or more different chords.

THE DOMINANT SEVENTH (V7) CHORD

The G chord (G-B-D), which is built on step five of the C scale, forms the *dominant* triad (V). In C major the tonic chord (C-E-G) is the musical "home base," whereas the dominant is a chord of tension that resolves to the tonic. The notes G-B-D-F form the dominant seventh chord (V7). Dominant seventh chords often replace dominant triads.

A smoother chord change between tonic and dominant results from a simplified G7 chord, played **B-F-G.** Compare the change from C to G7 as shown below, first with G7 in root position, then with the simplified G7 chord.

Study the pattern for the I to V7 chord change:

> The *top* note stays the same.
> The *middle* note moves up a half step.
> The *bottom* note moves down a half step.

Use a consistent fingering pattern when you play the B-F-G chord: left hand: **5-2-1;** right hand: **1-4-5.** Practice the chord pattern C—G7—C with each hand and then with hands together. Notice that "G" occurs in both chords as a "common tone." The common tone remains in place during the chord change.

Key of C major

Accompanying Melodies with I-V7-I

Begin the melody of "Go Tell Aunt Rhody" with the right hand playing the E above middle C. Place the little finger of your *left* hand on the C below middle C. Practice melody and chords separately until you can play each part smoothly and with a steady beat. Then practice with hands together.

Go Tell Aunt Rhody

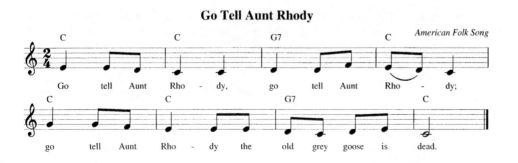

"Winter, Goodbye" is shown on page 96 in C major. Keep a steady beat as you count in three. Play the melody and chords in the same keyboard positions used for the preceding melody.

Practice the melody and chords of *"Lightly Row"* separately, then with hands together. Set a comfortable tempo and keep a steady beat. Try to keep your eyes on the music rather than looking at your hands.

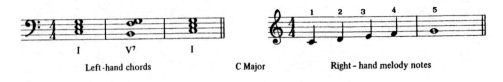

Left-hand chords   C Major   Right-hand melody notes

Lightly Row

In "Merrily We Roll Along" the melody passes from the right hand to the left hand. Practice the right- and left-hand parts separately, then play the song with hands together. Play the chords as background to the melody. Sing the melody with letter names to develop your reading skills in bass and treble clef.

Merrily We Roll Along

Traditional

Mer - ri - ly we roll a - long, roll a - long, roll a - long.

Mer - ri - ly we roll a - long, o'er the deep, blue sea.

Playing the I-IV Chord Pattern

The F chord (F-A-C) is the **IV** chord ("subdominant" chord) in the key of C major. The notes of the F chord are arranged as C-F-A to make smooth movement between the C and the F chords.

(broken)   (solid)

Right hand

Left hand

F chord (IV chord)

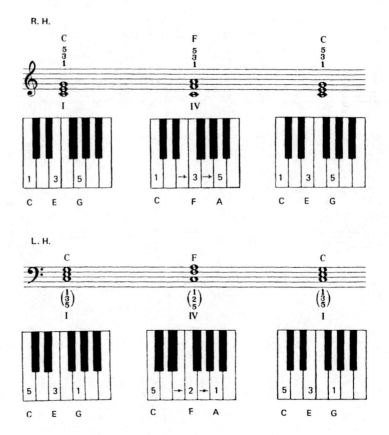

Study the pattern for the chord change between I and IV:

> The *top note* moves up a whole step.
> The *middle note* moves up a half step.
> The *bottom note* remains the same.

Play the F chord with the fingerings shown here: left hand: **5-2-1;** right hand: **1-3-5.** Practice the chord pattern C—F—C with each hand and then with hands together.

"C" occurs in both chords as a "common tone." The common tone remains in place during the chord change. After practicing the F chord in broken and solid chord styles, practice making the chord change between C and F, hands separately, then with both hands.

Accompany the melody of "Oh, How Lovely Is the Evening" with the C and F chords.

Oh, How Lovely Is The Evening

THE PRIMARY CHORDS

Chords built on the tonic, subdominant, and dominant (scale steps one, four, and five) are the principal chords or *primary* chords in each key. In C major the tonic, subdominant, and dominant seventh chords are C, F, and G7.

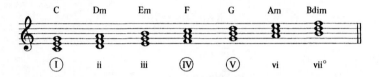

Many children's songs and folk songs require only three chords for a satisfactory accompaniment. The I-IV-I-V7-I pattern combines the patterns you have learned. Practice the pattern in C, as shown here.

Accompanying Melodies with Three Chords

Practice the melody and chord changes for "See the Little Ducklings," then play it with hands together. Practice at a comfortable tempo, keeping a steady beat. Can you play the song without errors? Can you play it three times in a row without error?

See the Little Ducklings

The melody of "Kum-ba-yah" begins with pickup notes (no chord) on beat three. The song's phrases are shown on separate lines to make it easy to compare them. The rhythms of the first three phrases are identical. Notice that the missing third beat at the end of each line is found in the "pickup notes" of the next line. Use consistent fingerings, practice with each hand separately, then play the song with hands together.

Kum-ba-yah

African–American

The melody of "El Coqui" begins with the notes of the C triad (C-E-G); its accompaniment skips from one chord tone to the next. For a simpler accompaniment, use the chord patterns you have practiced in the preceding songs. (Notice the chord symbols above the melody.)

El Coqui
(The Tree Frog)

Puerto Rican Folk Song
arr. by G.N.

PLAYING SONGS IN OTHER KEYS

The preceding songs have emphasized the primary chords (I-IV-V7-I) in the key of C major. The chord patterns and fingerings can be used in any key, however.

Playing Major Triads in Twelve Keys

The structure of chords can be determined by calculating the number of whole steps or half steps between chord tones. The visual patterns of black keys and white keys offer a different way to learn them. Notice that three of the chords use only the white keys. Their pattern is white-white-white. Chords in group two are white-**black**-white. The chord patterns are shown below.

Group one: the triads of C, F, and G major have three *white* keys: C-E-G; F-A-C; G-B-D.

Group two: the A, D, and E major triads have the pattern white-**black**-white.

❏ ❏ ❏ (C-major triad)
❏ ❏ ❏ (F-major triad)
❏ ❏ ❏ (G-major triad)

❏ ■ ❏ A C♯ E (A-major triad)
❏ ■ ❏ D F♯ A (D-major triad)
❏ ■ ❏ E G♯ B (E-major triad)

Group one

White and Black Key Pattern

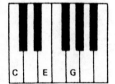

C major

white — white — white

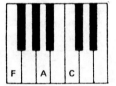

F major

white — white — white

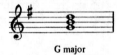
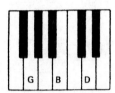

G major

white — white — white

Group two

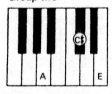

A major

white — black — white

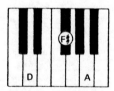

D major

white — black — white

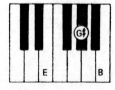

E major

white — black — white

Group three: the A♭, D♭, and E♭ major triads have the pattern **black**-white-**black**.

Group four has three major triads with unlike patterns of black-and-white keys.

■ ❑ ■ A♭ C E♭ (A♭-major triad)
■ ❑ ■ D♭ F A♭ (D♭-major triad)
■ ❑ ■ E♭ G B♭ (E♭-major triad)

■ ❑ ❑ B♭ D F (B♭-major triad)
❑ ■ ■ B D♯ F♯ (B-major triad)
■ ■ ■ G♭ B♭ D♭ (G♭-major triad)

Group three

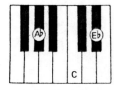
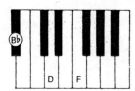

A - flat major

black — white — black

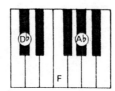
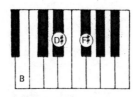

D - flat major

black — white — black

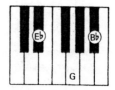
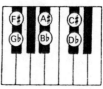

E - flat major

black — white — black

Group four

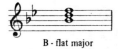

B - flat major

black — white — white

B major

white — black — black

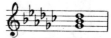

(Enharmonic spellings)

G - flat major

F - sharp major

Take one group at a time and play its three triads in different octaves and different sequences until you can locate, play, and spell each chord from memory. Then practice the I-IV-V7 chord pattern in the three keys represented by the chords in each group. (Group one, for example, represents the keys of C, F, and G major.)

It is not essential to practice all twelve of these chords during your beginning sessions at the keyboard. Instead, focus on a single group of three chords. Play each chord in different registers at the keyboard—high, middle, low—and play the chords in different orders. Learn to find each chord quickly and to play it accurately. Add new chords at the next practice session.

Short amounts of daily practice are usually more productive than the same amount of practice time in long, infrequent practice sessions.

Songs with I and V7 in F Major

The following songs are written in F major, which has one flat in its key signature. Notice that the fourth finger of the right hand is placed on B-flat.

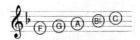

Right-hand melody pattern

Key of F major

Left-hand chord patterns

Tonic
I
F major

Dominant
V7
C7

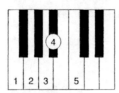 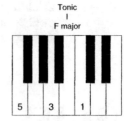 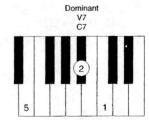

Left-hand chord patterns

Key of F Major

F

C7

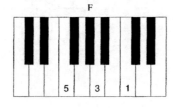 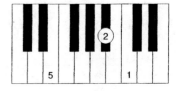

I (Tonic)   V7 (Dominant)

Winter, Goodbye

Win - ter, good - bye.   Win - ter, good - bye.   They say that   part - ings are sad,

Yours   makes us   all   ver - y glad!   Win - ter, good - bye.   Win - ter, good - bye.

"Love Somebody" also uses the tonic and dominant seventh chords. Notice that the left hand has the melody and the right hand the chords in lines three and four.

Love Somebody

American Folk Song

Love some-bod-y, yes, I do! Love some-bod-y, won-der who;

Love some-bod-y, 'deed I do! Love some-bod-y but I won't tell who;

Love some-bod-y, yes, I do! Love some-bod-y won-der who;

Love some-bod-y, 'deed I do! Love some-bod-y but I won't tell who.

Songs that share the same chord pattern are called "partner songs." Partner songs combine two independent melodies, and thus illustrate a simple type of "non-imitative polyphony" in their texture. The songs "Mistress Moore," "Sandy Land," "The Mulberry Bush," "This Old Man," "Paw Paw Patch," and "Skip to My Lou" can be accompanied with the same chord pattern, shown below. (Later you may wish to use a more varied accompaniment style.)

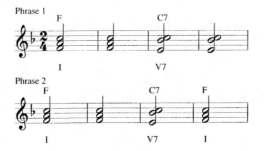

Playing the Primary Chords in F Major

In F major the primary chords are F, B♭, and C7. The chords in "See the Little Ducklings" follow the sequence I-IV-I-V7-I. Notice the B♭ in the melody and in the IV chord.

See the Little Ducklings

Traditional

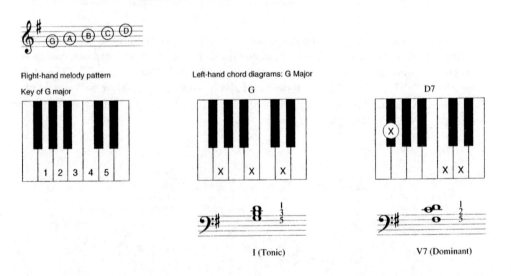

F major I   IV   I   V7   I

Playing Songs in the Key of G

In G major the primary chords are G, C, and D7. The following "five finger" melodies use the tones G A B C D. The pitch F♯ occurs in the V7 chord, which is played F♯ C D to allow for smooth movement between the I-V7 chords.

Right-hand melody pattern
Key of G major

Left-hand chord diagrams: G Major

G

D7

1 2 3 4 5

X   X   X

X

X   X

I (Tonic)

V7 (Dominant)

Also see "Lightly Row," page 73.

Winter, Goodbye

Playing the Primary Chords in G Major

"Listen to the Mockingbird" (page 25) includes the primary chords G, C, and D7. Notice that the melody begins with pickup notes on beat four. Practice at a comfortable tempo and keep a steady beat.

Key of G Major

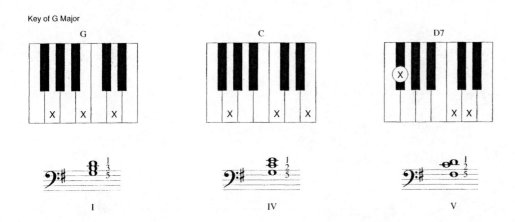

A consistent fingering pattern for I-IV-V7-I facilitates learning songs in different keys and is helpful when playing "by ear." Review the right- and left-hand fingerings in the key of C major. Use the same fingerings in every key.

Syllables or *scale step numbers* describe the chord changes without reference to right- or left-hand fingers.

To change from I to IV
The top note moves up from **so** to **la** (5 to 6).
The middle note moves up from **mi** to **fa** (3 to 4).
The bottom note remains on **do** (1).

To change from I to V7
The top note stays on **so** (5).

The middle note moves up from **mi** to **fa** (3 to 4).
The bottom note moves down from **do** to **ti** (1 to low 7).

Start from the tonic chord in any key to find the IV and V7 chords in this keyboard pattern.

CHORDING STYLES

The pianist uses varied styles to play the primary chords. One style is to alternate between left-hand bass notes on the chord roots and chords in the right hand. The illustration shows left-hand bass notes on F and C, the chord roots of the F and C7 chords in the right hand. Practice the chords, then apply the style to an accompaniment for "Love Somebody."

Basic Chords

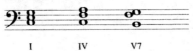

Accompaniment styles in two, three, four, or six.

Saint Paul's Steeple

Chord Symbols

A lead sheet is a shorthand musical score with melody, chord symbols, and lyrics. You can translate the chord symbols (written above the melody) into accompaniments for piano, guitar, or other classroom instruments.

Four Types of Triads

Here are chord symbols designating four different types of C triads: C major (C), C minor (Cm), C diminished (C dim), and C augmented (C aug). The following example shows the chord symbol for each triad of the major scale. In major keys, I, IV, and V are major, and ii, iii, and vi are minor. (Major chords use upper case Roman numerals; minor triads use lower case.)

Triads in major keys

Major triads	I	IV	V
Minor triads	ii	iii	vi
Diminished triad	vii°		

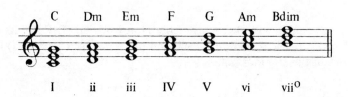

Minor chords are based on the harmonic minor scale, which has a raised seventh step. The triads for each step of the *harmonic* minor scale are shown next, together with their chord symbols. Notice that $\boxed{\text{i}}$ and $\boxed{\text{iv}}$ are **minor** chords but $\boxed{\text{V}}$ is major. In the example (A-minor) G$\sharp$, the raised seventh step of the scale, results in a **major** triad (E-G$\sharp$-B) for the V chord.

Triads in minor keys

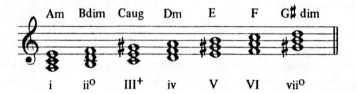

Major triads	V	VI
Minor triads	i	iv
Diminished triads	ii^{O}	vii^{O}
Augmented triad	III^{+}	

The Birch Tree

Russian Folk Song

"Don Gato" begins with the notes of the D minor triad (D-F-A). Its chords are Dm, Gm, C, and A7. The C chord (C-E-G) and the A7 chord (A-C$\sharp$-E-G) result from different forms of the D minor scale:

D E F G A B$^{\flat}$ $\boxed{\text{C}}$ D   D E F G A B$^{\flat}$ $\boxed{\text{C}\sharp}$ D
1 2 3 4 5 6 7 8   1 2 3 4 5 6 7 8
D minor (natural form)   *D minor (harmonic form)*

Don Gato

English by Margaret Marks

Mexican Folk Song
Arr. by B. Beagle

From Sing Together Children.
Copyright © World Around
Songs. *Used by permission.*

Use the major triad as a guide to the structure of minor, diminished, and augmented triads.

Minor Triads

The chord symbol for a minor triad is a capital letter followed by a small "m" or the letters *min*. The chord symbol Cm or C min indicates the C minor triad: C-E♭-G. Major triads use steps 1-3-5 of the *major* scale; minor triads use steps 1-3-5 of the *minor* scale. The A minor triad (A-C-E) are pitches 1-3-5 in A minor. The D minor triad (D-F-A) are pitches 1-3-5 of D minor, and so forth.

Minor Triads

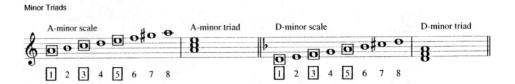

Playing Minor Triads

Change a major triad to minor by lowering its third a half step (C-E-G becomes C-E♭-G). "White key" major triads (C, F, and G) change from ☐ ☐ ☐ to ☐ ■ ☐. Replace each of the following major triads with a *minor* triad. Write the new triad in the empty measure. Play each of the triads at the piano and compare the sound of major and minor triads.

Example

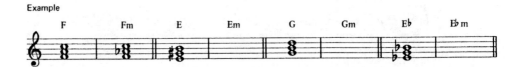

Diminished Triads

The chord symbol for a C diminished triad is C dim. Change the minor triad to diminished by lowering its fifth a half step. Replace each of the following minor triads with a *diminished* triad. Write the new triad in the empty measure. Play each of the triads at the piano and compare the sound of minor and diminished triads.

Example

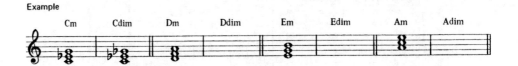

Augmented Triads

The chord symbol for the C augmented triad is C aug. Change the major triad to augmented by raising its fifth a half step, as in the example below. Play the four types of triads at the piano and compare their sounds.

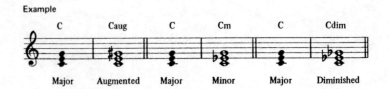

Augmented and diminished chords are not uncommon in music, though they are used less often in children's songs than in classical music or jazz. Notice the diminished chords used in "America the Beautiful" on page 159.

ELECTRONIC INSTRUMENTS

Electronic instruments and computer-assisted instruction offer exciting new avenues for music-making, creativity, music reading, and aural skills training.

ELECTRONIC KEYBOARDS

Students in many schools use inexpensive electronic keyboards to gain knowledge of melodic patterns, chord formation, transposition, and other basic music skills.

Electronic keyboards with automatic chord functions simplify the playing of three- or four-note chords and offer added rhythmic effects plus a variety of tone colors. The Casio and Yamaha systems are representative. With a Casio keyboard, press the chord root to sound the major triad (e.g., C major). For minor chords (e.g., C minor), press the root and the key above it. For the dominant seventh chord (e.g., C7), press the chord root and the two keys above it. For a minor seventh chord, press the chord root and the three keys above it (e.g., C m7). With Yamaha keyboards, make the change from major to minor by pressing the chord root and the *black* key to the left of it. Change from major to seventh chord (e.g., C to C7) by playing the *white* key to the left of the chord root. Each type of keyboard comes with an instruction manual that supplies the details needed to produce results. You may also wish to inquire about the "Miracle Piano Teaching System," which combines a velocity sensitive electronic keyboard, instructional software, and the computer or Nintendo Entertainment System into a keyboard learning program. (The Software Toolworks, 60 Leveroni Court, Novato, CA 94949.)[4]

THE OMNICHORD

The Omnichord is a portable, battery-operated electronic chording instrument that can be strummed like a guitar or an Autoharp. You can program background chords and rhythms and then add the melodic line during playback. The instrument's MIDI capability (musical instrument digital interface) allows you to connect it to a computer for additional applications. Using one finger, you can play four types of triads and three types of seventh chords in any key. It never needs tuning and has adjustable tempo and volume controls plus a choice of ten tone color "voices." Optional accessories include power amplifiers, headphones, and A/C adapters.

Suzuki Omnichord

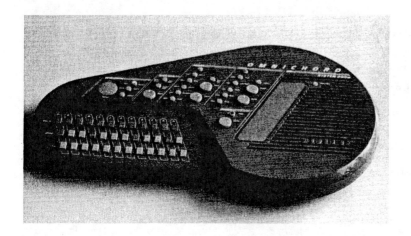

THE AUTOHARP

Patented in 1881 by Charles F. Zimmerman, the Autoharp[5] has had a lengthy career as a folk instrument and classroom instrument. Twelve-chord, fifteen-chord, and twenty-one-chord instruments in various models are available. Information on current models and prices of Autoharps and similar instruments is available in the catalogs listed in appendix 6.

BASIC PLAYING TECHNIQUE

The Autoharp player creates an accompaniment by pressing chord bars and strumming. Players also may use melodic strums and create various other special effects.

Introducing the Autoharp

Choose a familiar song that can be harmonized with only one or two chords and introduce the Autoharp by demonstrating its sound and the basic playing position. After letting the children listen to "melody with chords," demonstrate the basic playing technique.

Strumming

- Place the Autoharp on a level surface. The longer, thicker (low) strings should be next to you. Strum with a pick held in your right hand and press the chord bar marked "C Maj." with your left-hand index finger.

  Felt picks give a softer tone; plastic picks give a louder, more brilliant tone. Reach over your left hand and strum across the full range of strings from low to high in the area to the left of the Autoharp bridge.

  Adapt the strum to the music. For example, strum from left to right (low strings to high strings) on beat **one,** and in the opposite direction for unaccented beats. Short, quick strums fit a rapid tempo; longer, slower strums match a slower tempo.

- Change to the G7 chord by pressing its chord bar with your middle finger.
- Alternate between the C and G7 chords until you can change from one to the other with ease.
- To accompany singing, you may decide to strum on every beat or only on accented beats, depending on the tempo and style of the music. In fast moving songs, for example, strumming only the accented beats may give a more musical result.
- Younger children may divide the task: one child strums, the other presses the chord bars.

ACCOMPANYING MELODIES WITH I AND V7

Begin with one-chord or two-chord songs or a song with an ostinato chord pattern. The following words, sung to the tune of "Frère Jacques," combine the two-chord pattern with the ostinato concept.

Ostinato

The accompaniment of "The Bus" also uses two chords—F and C7—the tonic and dominant seventh chords in F major.

The Bus

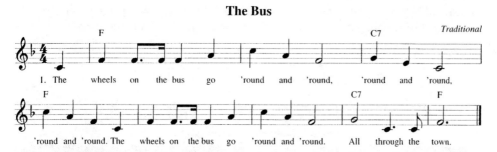

2. The money on the bus goes "clink, clink, clink" . . .

3. The driver on the bus says, "Move on back" . . .

4. The horn on the bus goes "beep, beep, beep," . . .

5. The wipers on the bus go "swish, swish, swish." . . .

6. The windows on the bus go up and down. . . .

7. The baby on the bus goes "wah, wah, wah" . . .

*8. The parents on the bus go "read, read, read" . . .

(*suggested by a child in our music labs.)

Scale letter	F	G	A	B♭	C	D	E	F
Scale step number	1	2	3	4	5	6	7	(1)
Chord symbol	F				C7			
Roman number	I				V7			

Explain to the students that Roman numerals label chords, while figures (1–8) indicate scale steps. In the key of F major the tonic chord (F) is "home base," and the dominant seventh chord (C7) is "away from home."

Recognizing I and V7 (Tension and Repose)
Correlate tension-repose (V7-I) with physical movement.

> *Listen to the Autoharp. Move when you hear this chord.* (Play V7)
> *"Freeze" when you hear this chord.* (Play I)

Play eight strums on the first chord, then change to the new chord for eight strums. When children begin to anticipate a change after the eighth beat, make less predictable changes, but allow enough time for perception and response to occur. Some children will confuse changes in volume or tempo with changes in harmony, but listening and practice will bring rapid improvement.

Three Types of Chords
The 15-chord Autoharp plays major ("Maj."), minor ("Min."), and dominant seventh chords (C7, G7, etc.).

G Maj.	Gm	G7
(major)	(minor)	(seventh chord)

ACCOMPANYING MELODIES WITH I-IV-V7
For practice, touch the chord bars on the chord bar diagram in your book: place your left-hand index finger on the C chord, your middle finger on the G7 chord, and your ring finger on the F chord bar. These are the I, V7, and IV chords in C major. The chord bars are arranged for ease of playing: if your left-hand index finger is on I, the

middle finger will land on V7, and the ring finger on IV. Try the I-IV-V7 pattern in the keys of B♭, F, C, and G major and in D or A minor. Remember: point with your *left*-hand index finger to the major or minor chord that is the tonic chord (I) of the key. The dominant (V7) chord will be under your middle finger and the subdominant (IV) chord will be under your ring finger. The simplicity of this arrangement is one of the advantages of teaching children about chords with the aid of an Autoharp.

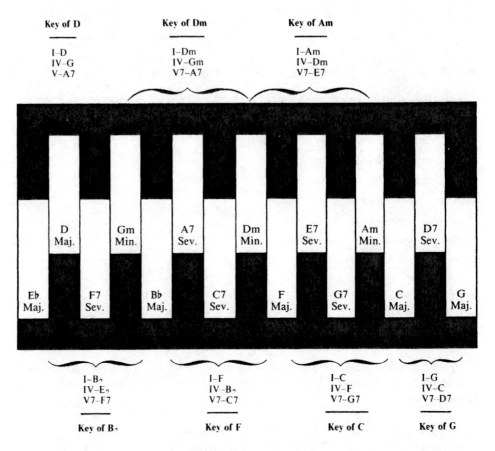

The accompaniment of "My Home's in Montana" uses three chords—C, F, and G7—built on steps one, four, and five of the C major scale.

My Home's in Montana

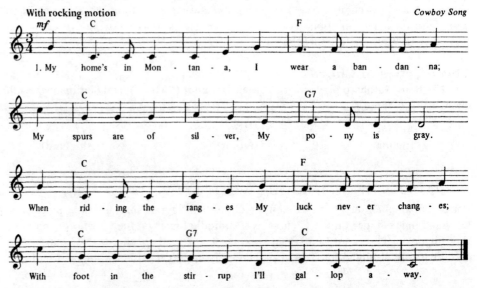

Scale letter		F	G	A	B♭	C		D	E	F
Scale step number		1	2	3	4	5		6	7	(1)
Chord symbol		F			B♭	C7				
Roman number		I			IV	V7				

Have students listen for the number of *different* chords in a song. Begin by singing and accompanying a song with one, two, or three chords. Ask the children to signal you when they perceive a chord change. A variation on this idea is playing the song without making the necessary chord changes: Where does it sound wrong? How could it be made to sound right? Ask the children to signal—raise one thumb, in front of and close to the body—when they hear the need for a chord change. (Let half of the class sing while the other half listens.)

The number of Autoharps available in the classroom may limit individual playing opportunities during a single lesson. Students may take turns, however, while classmates work with full-size Autoharp chord bar diagrams. Practice singing, touching the chord bars, and rhythmic "strumming." Some students may wish to make arrangements for individual practice outside of class or after school.

BLUES HARMONY

The twelve-bar blues pattern consists of three four-measure phrases. Children can explore blues harmony with Autoharps, keyboards, resonator chords, or guitars.

Music Series Correlation: See the lessons on the "Joe Turner Blues" in *Holt Music,* Grade 6, or *Music and You* (Macmillan), Grade 6.

BLUES CHORDS

Measure	1	2	3	4	5	6	7	8	9	10	11	12
Chord	I	I	I	I	IV	IV	I	I	V7	V7	I	I
Strums	////	////	////	////	////	////	////	////	////	////	////	////
		Phrase one				*Phrase two*				*Phrase three*		

The blues scale, with steps three, five, and seven lowered a half step, adds "blue notes" against the I-IV-V7 chord background. Many variations on the basic chords are used by blues musicians. As shown here, the "Joe Turner Blues" follows the basic chord pattern. The C7 chord is spelled C-E-G-B♭ and the F7 chord is F-A-C-E♭.

Joe Turner Blues

American Blues

1. They tell me ___ Joe Turn-er's ___ come and gone, ___
2. He came here ___ with for-ty ___ links of chain, ___
3. Joe Turn-er, ___ he took my ___ man a - way, ___

They tell me ___ Joe Turn-er's ___ come and gone. ___
He came here ___ with for-ty ___ links of chain. ___
Joe Turn-er, ___ he took my ___ man a - way. ___

He left me ___ here to sing ___ this ___ song.

SONGS IN MINOR

The melody of "The Birch Tree" uses scale steps one through five. Its chords are based on the harmonic minor scale, with raised step seven (A7 chord: A-C♯-E-G).

The Birch Tree

Russian Folk Song

Recognizing Major and Minor Chords by Ear

Strum several major chords on the Autoharp, then strum several minor chords. Ask the class to listen and decide whether the chords were the same or different. Introduce the terms major and minor and practice again, playing contrasting sets of major or minor chords. Students may use a signal or write answers on a worksheet to show what they hear.

	Teacher strums chords.	*Students respond.*
Set 1	A A A A	Student's answer: M M M M
Set 2	Am Am Am Am	Student's answer: m m m m

For a movement activity, suggest, "Walk when you hear major chords, 'freeze' when they change to minor." (Select other appropriate movements as desired.) Students also should construct and play major and minor chords on bells, piano, or barred instruments.

Charting Chords

Taking "inventory" of the chords used in songs gives students another way to become familiar with chords and chord patterns.

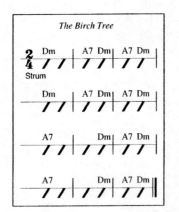

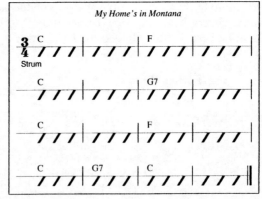

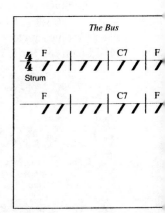

Charts or chalkboard diagrams are sometimes easier to follow than the notation in songbooks. The charts on page 134 show two strums per measure for the duple meter of "The Bus" and three per measure for the triple meter of "My Home's in Montana." The chord changes are less regular for "The Birch Tree." Notice that the player repeats the previous chord in measures without a chord symbol until a change is marked by a new chord symbol.

■ Make chord charts or flash cards with a marker and poster board. Like charts, transparencies can be saved and filed for later use.
■ Color coded charts with matching colored tape or labels on the chord bars help younger students and special learners. (e.g., C = yellow, G7 = blue, F = red.)
■ After children have learned to follow chord diagrams, guide them to playing directly from chord symbols shown above the five-line staff in their music books.

SPECIAL EFFECTS

The unique sounds of folk instruments from other cultures are heard on many recordings. The Autoharp can imitate some of these instruments when the sound fits a particular song you have chosen.

Oriental (imitation koto): Pluck individual strings.
Scottish: Press two chord bars at once (G and Gm or D and Dm) to get a drone sound on strings a fifth apart.
Slavic: One player pushes chord bars while another plays the strings with light wooden mallets. This makes the Autoharp sound like a dulcimer (a folk zither played by striking rather than plucking).
Harp: Strum from high to low and vary the length of the strums.

TUNING THE AUTOHARP

Ask a music specialist or band director to assist you if you need help in tuning an Autoharp for your classroom. Here is a general procedure.

Tune the Autoharp to match the pitch of a well-tuned piano or use an electronic tuner. Begin with the notes of the F chord (F-A-C). Listen to F on the piano, pluck it on the Autoharp and compare. Turn the tuning wrench clockwise to raise pitch, counterclockwise to lower it. (Normally the tuning wrench need not turn more than an eighth of an inch, except when stretching a new string into place. Strings will break if tuned too tightly or if you "tune" the one next to the one you meant to—for example, playing F on the piano and mistakenly turning the tuning peg for E on the Autoharp.

After tuning all the F's, continue with the A's and C's to complete the F chord. Then tune the notes of the C chord (C-E-G) and the G chord (G-B-D). Strum each chord and adjust any pitch that sounds too high or too low in relation to the other chord tones. The five "black key" strings come next, in the order shown below. Notes tuned in the preceding chord are shown in [brackets].

F A C	[C] E G	[G] B D	[D] F$^\sharp$ [A]	[A] C$^\sharp$ [E]	[E] G$^\sharp$ [B]	E$^\flat$ [G] B$^\flat$
F chord	C chord	G chord	D chord	A chord	E chord	E$^\flat$ chord

THE GUITAR

Basic guitar chords offer another possibility for the study of harmony. Starting with a tuned guitar, try these simplified chords and continue by adding new chords. (See pages 144–145 for a method of tuning the guitar yourself.)

CHORD ROOTS AND SIMPLIFIED CHORDS

From high to low, the open strings of the guitar are E B G D A E, with high E numbered as string "one." The beginner can pluck open strings with the right hand to create a chord root type of accompaniment. Try "She'll Be Coming 'Round the Mountain," using strings three (G), four (D), and five (A), to play chord roots beneath the melody.

She'll Be Coming 'Round the Mountain

U. S.

open
string
④   ④   ④   ④
D   D   D   D

2/2 1. She'll be | com - ing 'round the | moun - tain when she | comes, ———|— She'll be

④   ④   open string ⑤   ⑤
D   D   A   A

com - ing 'round the | moun - tain when she | comes, ———|— She'll be

④   ④   open string ③   ③
D   D   G   G

com - ing 'round the | moun - tain, She'll be | com - ing 'round the | moun - tain, She'll be

⑤   ⑤   ④   ④
A   A   D   D

com - ing 'round the | moun - tain when she | comes. ———|—   ‖

2. She'll be driving six white horses when she comes, etc.

3. Oh, we'll all go out to meet her when she comes, etc.

4. Oh, we'll kill the old red rooster when she comes, etc.

5. And we'll all have chicken dumplings when she comes, etc.

Appropriate sound and actions can be performed during the long notes in the melody, for example:

Coming 'round the mountain—toot-toot.
Driving six white horses—whoa; back.
All go out to meet her—hi, y'all.
Kill the old red rooster—hack hack.
All have chicken dumplings—yum, yum.

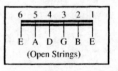

Try the song again, this time in E major, using strings one or six (E), five (A), and four (D) as chord roots.

Easy-to-play C and G7 chords allow you to accompany many I-V7 songs like those you learned earlier at the keyboard.

Simplified Chords

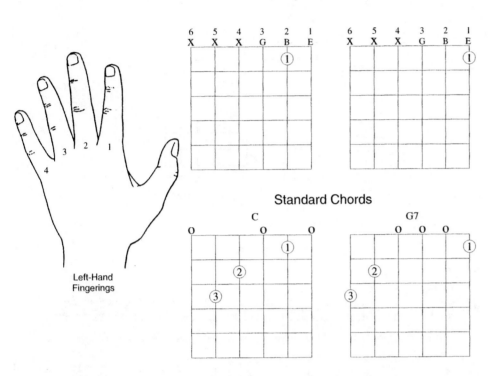

Standard Chords

"X" indicates **omit**: do not strum the string.

Another player can pluck single strings on a second guitar to add a bass part made from chord tones in C and G.

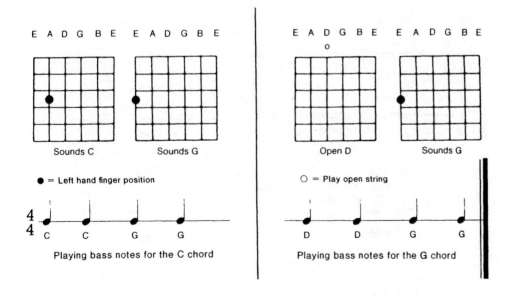

ONE-CHORD SONGS

The E-minor chord harmonizes several one-chord songs. Rest the guitar on your lap and place your left-hand fingers on the strings as shown in the E-minor chord diagram. With your right-hand thumb, strum across all of the strings on the accented beats.

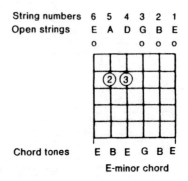

Hey, Ho! Nobody Home

Key: E minor   *English Round*

Zum Gali Gali

Key: E minor   *Israeli Round*

Translation: The Pioneer's purpose is labor.

Change the chord to E *major* to accompany "Make New Friends," "Clocks," "Frère Jacques," "Little Tom Tinker," or "Row, Row, Row Your Boat" as you strum on the accented beat.

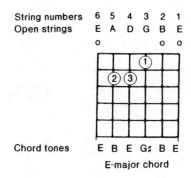

Make New Friends

PLAYING POSITION

Rest the guitar against your body rather than supporting it with your hands. The left-hand fingers should press hard enough to put the strings into contact with the frets, but not so hard as to produce tired, stiff fingers. Arch the fingers and press the fingertips straight down, *directly behind the frets.* (If the fingers are not close enough to the frets a buzzing sound may result.) Place the thumb on the underside of the guitar neck and keep the palm of the hand away from the back of the guitar.

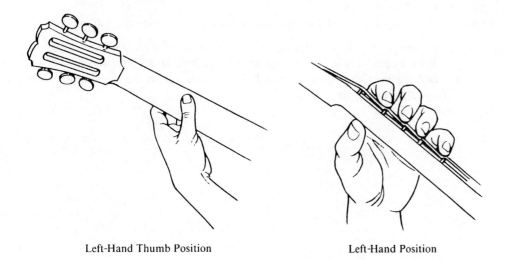

Left-Hand Thumb Position   Left-Hand Position

The right hand should be relaxed with the fingers slightly curved. Finger the E chord with your left hand and try various strums until you get a clear sound on each string. Be patient and listen carefully.

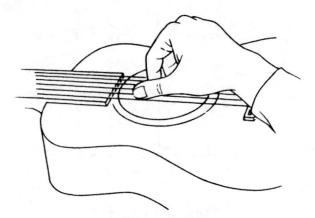

Right-Hand Position

Right-Hand Position

GUITAR STRUMS

Examples of strums that may be used in accompaniments include the following.

1. The *sweep strum* is a downward motion of the thumb across all the strings. In a slow tempo, play on every beat; in quicker tempos, play on accented beats.
2. Pluck the bass note with the thumb, then sweep across the remaining strings for a different strum.

3. The *brush strum* is done with the backs (fingernails) of the first three fingers across the strings.
4. The *thumb-brush strum* combines the thumb bass note (as in number 2) and the brush strum.
5. Another version is the thumb-index finger strum. The first finger does either a *downstroke* (away from the guitar player) or an *upstroke* (toward the player).

6. Plucked strings add still more variety. The thumb plays a bass note, and the fingers pluck upwards on the three top strings. For example, the thumb sounds string 6, and the first three fingers (placed on strings 3, 2, 1) pluck upwards toward the thumb (toward the player).

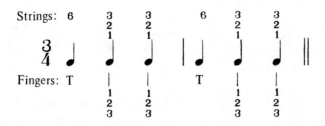

7. Arpeggio (broken chord) accompaniments are not difficult in slow tempos. To accompany in slow 6/8 meter, for example, sound the bass string with the thumb, then pluck the upper three strings separately with the right-hand fingers (1, 2, 3) on strings 3, 2, 1.

Two-Chord Songs

The E-minor and A-minor chords make an easy accompaniment for "Joshua Fought the Battle of Jericho."

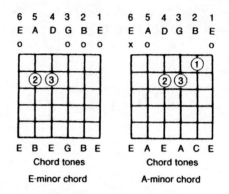

Joshua Fought the Battle of Jericho

Spiritual

2. Now the Lord commanded Joshua:
   "I command you and obey you must;
   You just march straight to those city walls
   And the walls will turn to dust."

3. Straight up to the walls of Jericho
   He marched with spear in hand,
   "Go blow that ram's horn," Joshua cried,
   "For the battle is in my hand."

4. Then the lamb ram sheep horns began to blow,
   And the trumpets began to sound,
   And Joshua commanded, "Now, children, shout!"
   And the walls came tumbling down.

The Primary Chords

The primary chords in D major and A major are relatively easy to learn. Their chord diagrams are shown below.

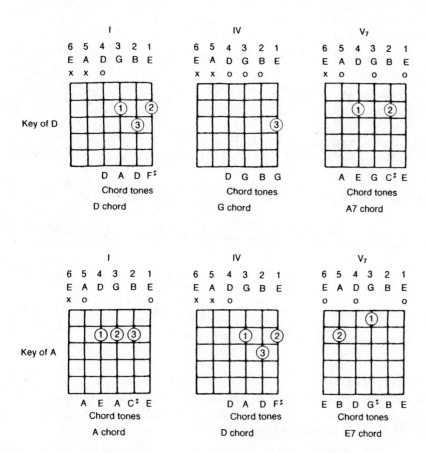

Frets on the guitar fingerboard are a half step apart. When you press behind a fret, you shorten the vibrating portion of the string. Ascending pitches on the same string move from the tuning pegs toward the body of the guitar. You can practice the chromatic scale (consecutive half steps) by fingering behind successive frets on each string. Find major scale tones by using the pattern you have learned: half steps between steps 3–4 and 7–8; whole steps between the other tones. The guitar, used in this way, is an excellent aural/visual teaching tool to help children understand scales as well as chords. The following chart shows the pitches produced on each string up to the twelfth fret.

Selecting a Guitar

There are many different types of guitars. Two main categories are electric and acoustic. Acoustic guitars are preferred for use in the elementary classroom. Nylon strings are easier on the fingers than steel strings.

TUNING THE GUITAR

Tune the guitar with the help of guitar pitch pipes, an electronic guitar tuner, a tuning fork, or another instrument. Twisting the tuning pegs raises or lowers pitch. Tighten a string to raise its pitch; loosen it to lower the pitch. Turn the pegs only a little at a time. Overtightening can break the string or harm the guitar. Notice that the guitar sounds one octave lower than written. Match the pitch of the open strings to E A D G B and E on the piano, as shown in the illustration that follows.

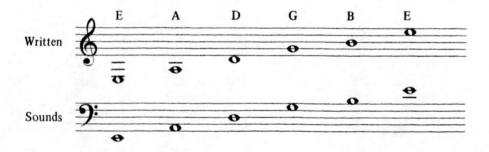

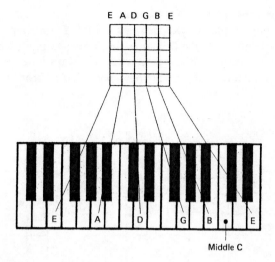

The following method of tuning the guitar is also used.

- Tune string six to low E, and then proceed as follows:
- Place your finger just behind the fifth fret of string six to get the correct pitch for string five. Tune string five to match this pitch.
- Tune string four to match the pitch of string five, fifth fret.
- Tune string three to match the pitch of string four, fifth fret.
- Tune string two to match the pitch of string three, *fourth* fret.
- Tune string one to match the pitch of string two, fifth fret.

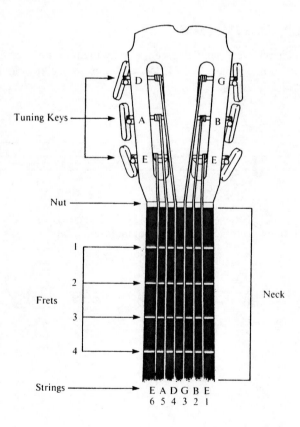

Simplified Chords: Open Tunings

Guitars can be adapted to play chords on open strings. For example, two guitars, one tuned to the G chord and one to the D chord, can furnish harmony for two-chord songs in the key of G. When using non-standard tunings, always tune strings to lower than standard pitch, since tuning to higher pitches may result in broken strings or damage to the guitar.

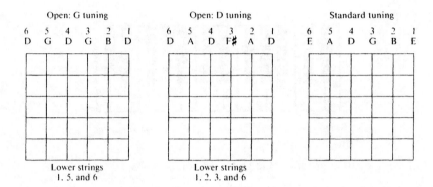

SUMMARY

Texture and harmony enrich the musical experience. By developing skills with piano and keyboards, as well as the Omnichord, Autoharp, and guitar, you can enhance the musical activities in your classroom and increase children's opportunities to discover the ways that rhythm, melody, and harmony combine to make music expressive.

SUGGESTED ACTIVITIES

1. Build triads on every scale degree and play them on bells or piano. Listen to the sound of major chords on I, IV, and V in major keys and minor chords occur on ii, iii, and vi.

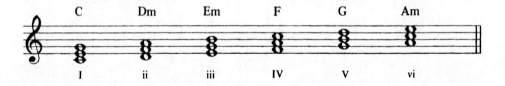

2. Invent an ostinato to accompany a pentatonic melody on bells or xylophone.

3. Listen to non-traditional harmonies: chords built on adjacent scale degrees, intervals four steps apart, or clusters of tones played by the fist. Encourage children to experiment with consonant sounding major and minor triads compared to the more dissonant sounds of melodies harmonized with chords built in half steps, fourths, tone clusters, and so forth.

4. Investigate the piano accompaniments found in the basic music series. Use these materials to increase your piano skills.

5. Instruction books for individual piano studies offer a wealth of music at all levels of difficulty. Local music dealers will be happy to show you books written for the adult learner.

Related Listening: Béla Bartók: *Mikrokosmos* No. 107, SVBX 5425; Henry Cowell, Piano Music No. 8 (*Tiger*), *Doris Hays Plays the Piano Music of Henry Cowell,* Finnadar SR 9016.

NOTES

[1] Rounds produce "imitative polyphony"; partner songs (contrasting tunes with the same harmony) have "non-imitative polyphony."

[2] It is said that Haydn accepted Mozart's bet that he could not perform a piece Mozart had written for the piano. When Haydn began to play, he came to a point where the music specified a note at each end of the keyboard as well as one in the middle. Unable to play it, Haydn asked Mozart to do so. Mozart leaned forward at the keyboard and played the middle note with his nose. Both composers could also play by ear.

[3] At the keyboard the thumb is number one. In playing the recorder the index finger is number one. Anthony Smith points out that every state except California has adopted a standard system for naming the fingers, but that the effort has led to ten different systems. Anthony Smith, *The Body,* (New York: Viking-Penguin, 1985), 507.

[4] See "Is the Miracle a Miracle?" by George F. Litterst, *Piano Quarterly,* 29, no. 156, Winter 1991–92, 49–54.

[5] Autoharp is the registered trademark of Oscar Schmidt-International, Inc.

*F*ORM

Every art expresses our human need for meaning and order. The plan of organization in music is called *form*. In musical form the composer seeks a design in which the parts are related to the whole in such a way as to produce both unity and variety.

FORM IN MUSIC

Form has a *general* meaning that refers to the way the parts are related to the whole, and a *specific* meaning that refers to a particular form. Nursery rhymes, limericks, and sonnets are poetic forms that differ in their use of words, rhythms, meters, and rhyme schemes. For example, all limericks have a similar pattern, but each has its own unique content.

A professor stopped off in Hong Kong	*There was an old man with a flute,*
And composed an original song.	*A sarpint ran into his boot;*
It was all on one note,	*But he played day and night,*
This song that he wrote,	*Till the sarpint took flight,*
But it sounded just great on a gong.	*And avoided that man with a flute.*
(author unknown)	*(Edward Lear)*

REPETITION AND CONTRAST

Repetition and contrast are basic principles of musical form. Repetition gives unity; contrast brings variety. Because music occurs in time, repetition is important for the listener, who can't go back and re-examine a section as in reading a book. The composer balances repetition and contrast to achieve unity with variety—a balance of same, similar, and different patterns of sound and silence. (The French composer Eric Satie tested the limits in his composition entitled *Vexations for Piano,* which he indicated should be repeated 840 times. A performance of the piece lasts more than eighteen hours.)[1]

Songs with repeated music but different words are called "strophic" songs. "America," "The Star-Spangled Banner," and many hymns and folk songs are strophic songs.

Mini quiz. Select the better example.
(a) "1-2, button my shoe."
(b) "1-2-3, button my shoe."

STRUCTURE IN MUSIC

In language individual letters form words and words form clauses, sentences, paragraphs, and longer sections. Music, too, is organized into shorter and longer sections. A melody's form is based on the organization of all its individual parts.

Phrases

The phrase is the basic building block of music. A musical phrase is a coherent unit, comparable to a phrase or clause in language. Music moves in phrases like a ball in a game of catch. There is a constant pattern of *tension* (throw the ball) and *repose* (catch the ball). A cadence is a temporary point of repose at the end of a phrase. The last note of the phrase is often a longer note, or a note followed by a rest, which gives the performer a place to take a breath. Phrases differ in length, though four measure phrases are very common. In songs, the phrase usually matches a line of text. Lower case letters are used to describe phrases.

Four identical phrases:	a a a a
Four similar phrases, each slightly varied:	a a′ a″ a‴
Four unlike phrases:	a b c d

(Children also represent same-different patterns with pictures of objects and animals or with colors.)

Motive

Phrases are often built by linking smaller melodic patterns. Each of the four phrases in "Are You Sleeping? (Frère Jacques)" contains repeated measures. Repeated measures are also found in "Scotland's Burning" (page 18).

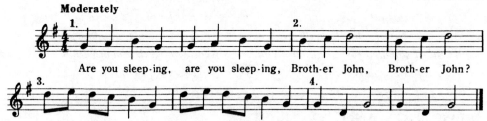

Are You Sleeping? (Frère Jacques)

Frère Jacques
Brother John

ROUND/FRANCE

Frère Jacques, Frère Jacques, dormez-vous, dormez-vous?
Sonnez les matines, Sonnez les matines, ding, din, don, ding, din, don.

"Motives" are distinctive patterns of two or more tones that serve as unifying elements in a melody. "The Cuckoo" melody has four phrases, represented by the letters a a′ b a′ or with shapes: ◯ ◯ ▢ ◯. The phrases marked "a" contain a two-note "cuckoo" motive representing a bird call. How many times does the "cuckoo" motive occur in this song?

The Cuckoo

German Folk Song

A repeated rhythmic motive unifies the melody of "My Darling Clementine." How many times does the rhythm pattern occur in each chorus of this song? Repetition is a prominent feature in this familiar song. Notice that all of the verses repeat the same music, and so does the chorus.

My Darling Clementine

United States

2. Light she was, and like a fairy,
   And her shoes were number nine,
   Herring boxes without topses,
   Sandals were for Clementine.

3. Drove she ducklings to the water
   Every morning just at nine,
   Hit her foot against a splinter,
   Fell into the foaming brine.

4. Ruby lips above the water
   Blowing bubbles soft and fine;
   As for me, I was no swimmer
   And I lost my Clementine.

5. How I missed her, how I missed her,
   How I missed my Clementine,
   Then I kissed her little sister,
   And forgot dear Clementine.

The musical content of two phrases may be the same (repetition), similar, or different (contrasting). Phrases are represented by lower case letters in the following diagrams.

Repeated Phrases
Each three-measure phrase in "The Birch Tree" (page 76) is repeated: a a b b.

Similar Phrases
"Hop Old Squirrel" (page 70) has four phrases that are similar, but not identical (a a' a" a''').

Contrasting Phrases
The phrases of "See the Little Ducklings" (page 115) are contrasting (a b). Phrase "a" has an upward contour; phrase "b" moves downward. Compare the phrases of "Love Somebody." Phrases one and three are identical, phrases one and two are similar, and phrase four contrasts.

Love Somebody

Examine the patterns found in the following songs, all found in this book. Create several other possible arrangements of four phrases.

Hickory, Dickory Dock	a a b c
Hop, Old Squirrel	a a' a a"
Hop Up, My Ladies	a a' a b
Jingle Bells (chorus)	a b a b

Children's music books use pictures of familiar objects or animals, geometric shapes, and colors to represent phrases that are the "same" or "different."

- ■ Four identical phrases: a a a a.   □ □ □ □
- ■ Four different phrases: a b c d.   □ △ ○ ◇
- ■ Similar phrases: a a' or aᵛ.   □ ■

Melodic Contour
Awareness of contour is an aid in learning a melody and in analyzing its form. A line tracing the notes in a melody shows contour (melodic shape), like a connect-the-dots drawing. The melodic line may rise or fall within a narrow or wide range and its contour may be smooth or angular. Each melodic shape is expressive in its own way. (For example, a rising line suggests energy; a descending line suggests repose.)

The four phrases of the song "Pussy Cat" have distinctive shapes. Write the number of the phrase beside the statement that describes it.

_____ This phrase moves upward in stepwise patterns to reach the melody's highest note.

_____ The contour of this phrase is similar to the phrase just before it, but at a lower pitch level.

_____ This phrase moves downward by steps, then leaps and lands on the keynote.

_____ This phrase moves by downward melodic skips followed by repeated notes.

Related Listening. Rossini: "Cats Duet," Felicity Lott (soprano), Ann Murray (mezzo soprano), EMI CDC754412.

Songs of the Cat, Garrison Keillor (baritone) and Frederica von Stade (mezzo soprano), High Bridge Co. HBP 17399.

Melodic Contours

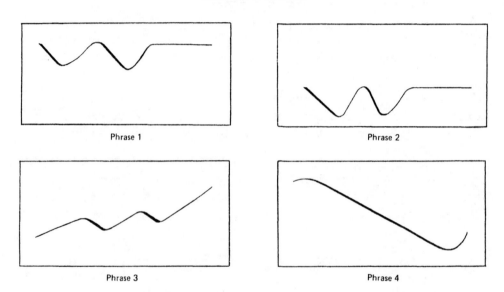

Phrase 1   Phrase 2

Phrase 3   Phrase 4

Pussy Cat

Mother Goose Rhyme
J. W. Elliott

Sequence

A tonal pattern that repeats at a higher or lower pitch level is called a "sequence." A sequence is a type of varied repetition that plays an important part in melodies and in harmony as well.

Line three of "The Cuckoo" (page 151) has a tonal pattern that repeats at a higher pitch level. The motive of "Skip to My Lou" repeats at a lower pitch level. Can you identify a melodic sequence in the melody of "Pussy Cat" (page 153)?

Skip to My Lou

American Folk Song

Sequential repetition is found in music at every level, from the simplest tune to music for orchestra. The melody of Beethoven's *Fifth Symphony* opens with a four-note motive that is restated at a lower pitch level, then repeated eleven times in changing forms as it moves throughout the orchestra to a melodic high point.

Related Listening: Beethoven: *Symphony No 5 in C Minor,* 1st Movement, CD: London 430 218–2.

Beethoven: Symphony no. 5, first movement (excerpt)

Repetition and contrast occur in many different ways in the melody of "America" ("My country, 'tis of thee . . ."). The melody moves in two-measure units and is divided into two phrases, each one ending on a longer note. (Phrase one is six measures in length; phrase two contains eight measures.) Study the song carefully and answer the following questions.

_____ 1. Which measures have a rhythm using even quarter notes?

_____ 2. Which measures contain a rhythm pattern using a dotted quarter note followed by an eighth note?

_____ 3. Does the melody move mainly by step or by skip?

_____ 4. Can you find a sequence in the melody?

_____ 5. Where is the melodic high point?

Copy the melody on music paper, then try to write it from memory. (Notice that music writing reinforces learning and makes us focus on musical details.)

Related Listening: *America Sings,* The Eric Rogers Chorale and Orchestra, London 433 686–2.

Answers: (1) Measures 1, 3, 5, 7, 9. (2) Measures 2, 4, 8, 10, 12. (3) By step.
(4) Measures 9 and 10 repeat the pattern of measures 7 and 8. (5) Measure 13 has the highest pitch.

America

Samuel Francis Smith

Tune: God Save the King

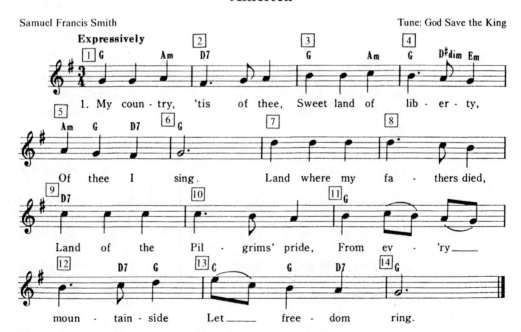

Introductions and Codas

Added sections called introductions, interludes, and codas are found in songs and instrumental music. When children sing with recorded songs in the classroom, the recording usually begins with an instrumental introduction, and may include an interlude between verses, followed by a short instrumental coda to mark the conclusion of the song. Students can discover the length of the introduction or interlude by listening and by counting the beats. Invite children to create verbal or instrumental introductions, interludes, or codas for chants and rhymes, then identify these features in songs and recordings.

Introduction	*Splish, splash, splish, splash.*
Rhyme	*Dr. Foster went to Gloucester,*
	In a shower of rain.
	He stepped in a puddle, up to his middle,
	And never went there again.
Coda	*Splish, splash, splish splash.*

PHRASES AND CADENCES

What is the difference between a cat and a comma? A cat has claws at the end of his paws; a comma is a pause at the end of a clause.

The chord pattern IV-V sounds incomplete.
The chord pattern IV-I is played on the words "Amen" at the conclusion of hymns.
The chord pattern V-I sounds complete because it ends on the tonic.

A phrase sounds unfinished if its last note is *not* the tonic. Arrival at the tonic, however, completes the musical thought. Review the relationship of tones to the home tone with children. Stop on the next-to-last note of a song and discover the tendency or expectation that the music will move to the home tone. A cadence is a momentary point of repose at the end of a phrase.

In harmony, chord patterns establish different types of cadences. Listen and compare the following chord patterns. Does the pattern IV-V sound complete or incomplete? Does the pattern V-I sound complete or incomplete? Which pattern ends on the tonic? Listen to the chord pattern IV-I. Why is it called an "Amen cadence"?

Cadences are like vocal inflections that tell the listener whether the speaker is asking a question or making a statement. Compare the following two excerpts from an old English comedy. Punctuation and phrasing give the same words different meanings.[2]

1.

Do and say what you wish, you shall never please me;
But when you are merry, I will be all sad;
When you are sorry, I will be very glad;
When you seek your heart's ease, I will be unkind;
At no time in me shall you much gentleness find.

(Act III, Scene 4)

2.

Do and say what you wish. You shall never please me
But when you are merry. I will be all sad
When you are sorry; I will be very glad
When you seek your heart's ease. I will be unkind
At no time. In me shall you much gentleness find.

(Act III, Scene 5)

ONE-PART FORM

Incomplete or *complete* cadences are found in song forms. Forms with a single complete cadence are classified as "one-part forms." "See the Little Ducklings" has two phrases. Compare the cadences that end each phrase.

The first phrase moves upward. The second, contrasting phrase, moves downward with repeated notes.

See the Little Ducklings

The melody of phrase one ends on "G," an active tone; phrase two ends on the tonic ("C").

"The Muffin Man" has two four-measure phrases. Are the phrases identical or similar? Phrase one ends with a "half cadence" (I-V7); phrase two ends with a "full cadence" (V7-I). This two-phrase "question and answer" structure is called a *period* or a *sentence*.

The Muffin Man

"America the Beautiful" has four phrases, the last ending with a complete cadence. (Phrases one, two, and three end with incomplete cadences.) Some of the other examples of one-part songs (only one complete cadence) in this book are "Bicycle Built for Two," "Pussy Cat," and "When the Saints Go Marching In."

Related Listening: "America the Beautiful," *Americana*, Robert Merrill (baritone), London 430 132–2 (compact disc).

America the Beautiful

Katharine Lee Bates
Samuel A. Ward

1. O beau - ti - ful for spa - cious skies, For am - ber waves of grain, For
pur - ple moun - tain maj - es - ties A - bove the fruit - ed plain! A-
mer - i - ca! A - mer - i - ca! God shed His grace on thee, And
crown thy good with broth - er - hood From sea to shin - ing sea!

2. O beautiful for Pilgrim feet,
Whose stern impassioned stress
A thoroughfare for freedom beat
Across the wilderness.
America! America! God mend thine every flaw,
Confirm thy soul in self-control,
Thy liberty in law.

3. O beautiful for heroes proved
In liberating strife,
Who more than self their country loved.
And mercy more than life.
America! America! May God thy gold refine
Till all success be nobleness
And every gain divine.

4. O beautiful for patriot dream
That sees beyond the years.
Thine alabaster cities gleam
Undimmed by human tears.
America! America! God shed His grace on thee,
And crown thy good with brotherhood
From sea to shining sea.

TWO-PART (BINARY) FORM

In binary (two-part) forms, each *section* ends in a complete cadence. Capital letters designate sections (AB) and lower case letters designate subsections.

"The Birch Tree" has two sections that contain repeated three-measure phrases (aabb). Each section ends with a V7-I cadence on the tonic. Which of the following diagrams—AA or AB—describe its form?

The Birch Tree

Russian Folk Song

Sil - ver birch a - lone in the mead - ow, Stand - ing all a - lone in the mead - ow,
Lone - ly birch tree in the mead - ow, Love - ly birch tree in the mead - ow.

Repeat signs save space and effort in writing music. The repeated phrases of "The Birch Tree" could be notated as follows:

"Jingle Bells" has two sections: verse and refrain. How many phrases are in the first section? Which phrases end on the tonic? Is the melody of the refrain the same as or different from the melody of the verse?

Section one has four phrases. Only phrase four ends on the tonic (F). The two sections are different (AB).

Jingle Bells

Words and Music by James Pierpont

First and second endings save unnecessary recopying of music notation. Take the first ending (⌐1.____⌐) the first time and substitute the second ending (⌐2.____⌐) after making the repeat. Analyze the form of "El Coqui" on page 117. Is it an example of two-part form? Why or why not?

See "Greensleeves," "Home on the Range," and "Rig-a-Jig-Jig" for some additional examples of songs in binary (AB) form.

THREE-PART (TERNARY) FORM

In ternary form the pattern is restatement after contrast: ABA. "Get on Board" has three sections, each one ending in a complete cadence. (The marking *"D.C. al Fine"* above the last measure of section B means to repeat the first section from the beginning and end at *fine*.) Robert Schumann's composition "Dreaming" (*Scenes from Childhood*) is also in ABA form.

Related Listening: Schumann: "Dreaming" (*Scenes from Childhood*), *Bowmar Orchestral Library*, BOL 63.

Get on Board

See "Oh, Dear, What Can the Matter Be?" "Tinga Layo," and "The Cuckoo" for some additional examples of repetition after contrast (ABA).

Listen to Aaron Copland's "Circus Music" from *The Red Pony*. The melody in section "A" (in triple meter) features trumpets and trombones and begins with skips through chord tones (*do-mi-so-ti*). It ends with a sudden loud chord. Section "B" features high woodwinds and has faster, circling, or "whirling"' music. After discovering that the music is in three sections (ABA), use costumes, masks, puppets, pictures, or other materials to represent circus acrobats, clowns, or animals to match the sounds of the three sections.

Related Listening: Aaron Copland: *The Red Pony* (symphonic suite from the film score), New Philharmonia Orchestra, Aaron Copland, conductor, CD: CBS MK-42429.

LONGER MUSICAL FORMS

Theme and variations and rondo forms are discussed in chapter 7. Musical forms are sometimes classified as sectional forms (binary, ternary, rondo, and sonata allegro form), polyphonic forms (rounds, canons, and fugues), variation forms (theme and variations, ground bass [basso ostinato, passacaglia, and chaconne]), and forms with extramusical elements (songs, program music, music drama, and so forth). Symphonies, concertos, sonatas, and string quartets are examples of multi-movement forms, with separate movements in contrasting keys and tempos. Operas, like plays, are divided into acts and scenes.

A particular form may have different names. For example, a sonata is a multi-movement instrumental work, often for a soloist. A sonata for two violins, viola, and cello is a *string quartet.* A sonata for orchestra is called a *symphony,* though it is called a *concerto* when written for soloist and orchestra. The term *genre* (*zhahn*-ruh) rather than form is sometimes used when referring to symphonies and other large works that are composed in different forms. Concise articles in music dictionaries are convenient sources for additional information about traditional musical forms.

Aria	Blues	Canon	Cantata
Chorale	Concerto	Fugue	Madrigal
March	Mass	Motet	Musical
Opera	Oratorio	Sonata	Song Forms
Suite	Symphony	Theme and Variations	Tone Poems

The following diagram outlines the basic forms described in this book.

DIAGRAMS OF BASIC FORMS

I. One-Part Forms

Phrase

	cadence

Period

incomplete	complete
cadence	cadence

Phrase Group

incomplete	incomplete	complete

Double Period

Period I		Period II	
incomplete	semi-final	incomplete	complete

II. Sectional Forms

Binary Form

Part I (A) Phrase, period, phrase group, etc.	Part II (B)
Home key	New Key New Key

Home key
complete

Ternary Form

Part I (A)	complete cadence	Part II (B)	complete cadence	Part III (A)	complete cadence

Rondo

A	B	A	C	A
	contrasting		contrasting	

Theme and Variations

A	A^1	A^2	A^3	A^4

TEACHING SUGGESTIONS

Children discover form through movement, by singing, by playing instruments, by composing their own music, and by representing "same-different" with geometric shapes, pictures, or letters (aaba).

The more children perceive, the more they gain from the musical experience. The musical vocabulary that labels concepts about form facilitates musical thinking and allows children to use language meaningfully in describing music relationships. One task of music education is to assist children in building a musical vocabulary.

MOVEMENT

Young children who lack the musical vocabulary to explain what they perceive, often demonstrate their awareness of form through movement responses and activities. The information that follows includes some general suggestions and information concerning movement activities and then lists some specific movement activities to show form.

Guidelines

To avoid bumping and collisions, invite students to "find an empty space" in which to stand. Help students find positions equally far apart in a defined area, but arranged so as to use all the space available. After they position themselves throughout the room, emphasize moving without touching others and keeping equally far apart.

Use verbal instructions to help children develop a movement repertoire. "Walk all around the room without touching anyone." "Now find a different way to walk." "Walk as if you were (excited—tired—happy—sad, etc)."

Nonlocomotor Movements

The availability of space for movement activities affects planning and the choice of various types of locomotor and nonlocomotor movements. Typical nonlocomotor movements are bending-stretching, pushing-pulling, twisting-turning, swinging, bouncing, and shaking. Nonlocomotor movements, which are done in place, are often a better starting point than locomotor movements, especially for students who may be hesitant about participation. Introduce new movements by comparing them to familiar activities: an accordion *bends* and *stretches,* a rower *pushes* and *pulls* on the oars; a door knob *twists,* a wheel *turns.* A pendulum or a windshield wiper *swings,* a coiled spring has a *bouncing* action, and *shaking* is like shivering on a cold day. A characteristic of all of these movements is that they do not involve a shift in weight, as in moving from one foot to the other foot.

- Begin by moving a single part of the body: "Move one arm." "Now find a different way."
- Help children become aware of contrasting movements: out/in, high/low, over/under, fast/slow, etc.
- Establish problems for children to solve: move one body part, two parts, three parts, the entire body.
- Use questions to stimulate creative movement responses. ("Can you . . .)

   "Move one arm slowly?"
   "Draw a letter in the air with one finger?"
   "Move a part of your body that begins with the letter *e*?"
   "Make fast, jerky movements with your arms? Slow, smooth movements?"

- Pantomime also suggests movements.[3] "Move like a robot, an egg beater, a windshield wiper," etc.

Locomotor Movements

Locomotor movements, which include walking, running, leaping, jumping, galloping, sliding, and skipping, require a transfer of weight. Movements such as sliding, galloping, and skipping are easy for some children and rather difficult for others. Galloping is a run-leap combination, with either foot leading. A gallop to the side is called a *slide*.

Explore these movement possibilities: direction (forward, backward, to the side, straight lines, zig-zag, circles), tempo (fast/slow), levels (high/low), force (strong/weak, heavy/light), locomotor movements (walk, run, hop, jump, leap), and combinations of these.

Props

Scarves, streamers, masks, hats, balloons, or hoops may enhance movement responses as you introduce patterns, pathways, and shapes. *Hoops* can make *patterns* on the floor, or mark off a child's personal space. *Balloons,* floating in the air, suggest a smooth, graceful movement. Tie a string to the balloon and let the child pull the balloon along varied movement pathways. *Streamers* swing, twirl, or float in the air.

Movement and Musical Form

Illustrate repetition and contrast with movements that are the same or different. For example, (1) pat the beat in the A section, clap the beat in the B section; (2) move clockwise in the circle for the A section, turn and step to the center and back during the B section, move clockwise when the A section returns.

- Show phrases with arm movements. Move both arms in arcs that begin and end with the phrases.
- Show contour by tracing the shape of the phrase or the melody in the air while singing or listening.
- Tell the children to move when you move and stop when you stop. Sing, or play a recorded selection. Move during the first section, stop during the next. Ask questions about the rhythm, melody, tone color, or some other feature. Repeat the first part as needed. For the next section use a different type of movement, the children moving when you move, stopping when you stop. Continue until the students have heard the entire song. "How many sections did we discover?" "Was section two the same or different from section one?" (Use questions and discussions to focus attention and call attention to significant details in the song or recording.) With longer recorded works, match the duration of the experience to the amount the children can assimilate without loosing interest during a single class session. Repeated listening over several days is usually necessary to help fix important details in memory.
- Move, then stop at a designated point in the music. ("Step the beat and stop when the contrasting section begins.")
- Stand or sit to show the beginning of a new section in a song or listening example.
- Hold up cards with letters that represent section A or B when you hear each section.

SINGING

- Highlight exact repetition in songs like "Scotland's Burning" and "Frère Jacques." Sing the songs with one group taking the first measure and a second group singing its repetition throughout the song.
- One group sings pattern "a." One group sings pattern "b."
- One group sings the verse; one group sings the chorus.
- A soloist or different soloists sing(s) the verses; the class sings the chorus.

PLAYING INSTRUMENTS

- Accompany different sections with instruments of different timbre. For example, play the rhythm of the beat and the accented beat on drums during the A section; accompany the B section with rhythm patterns using maracas and rhythm sticks.
- Improvise eight-beat question and answer patterns with percussion instruments. End each section with a rest on beat number eight.
- Improvise tonal patterns in major. End the question on a tone other than *do*. End the answer on *do*.
- Improvise tonal patterns in minor. End the question on a tone other than *la*. End the answer on *la*.

CREATING, COMPOSING

Creative activities using uncomplicated tasks invite children to demonstrate their awareness of form through meaningful activities that allow for open-ended responses.

- Create, perform, and notate short rhythm patterns to illustrate repetition and contrast.

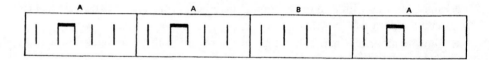

- Invent a piece in two parts (AB) that are different in sound.
  1. In part **A** get louder, little by little (crescendo). In part **B** get softer little by little (diminuendo). Use percussion instruments that can make loud sounds, medium loud sounds, and soft sounds or, focus on tempo.
  2. In part **A** start slowly and get faster (accelerando). In Part **B** start fast and get slower (ritardando). Use percussion instruments that can make short, quick sounds and instruments that can make long, sustained sounds or, focus on meter.
  3. In part **A** use body percussion (snap, clap, pat, stamp); let the sounds move in twos. In part **B** use body percussion and let the sounds move in threes.
- Invent a piece in three sections (ABA) form. Both "A" sections will be the same.
  1. Make one part loud and the contrasting part soft. Use one or more percussion instruments in each part or, focus on timbre, or pitch.
  2. Make one part with scraping sounds and the other with sounds that ring.
  3. Use the bells C D E and end on C in one part. Use the bells A B C and end on A in the other part. Make your rhythm from quarter notes and eighth notes, with each part lasting for eight counts.

VISUALIZING, DRAWING, WRITING

- Show contour with strands of yarn on a felt board. Invite students to place colored shapes to show different patterns in music.
- Invite children to create sequential patterns with numbers. Write a pattern and leave a blank: "What should be the next number?" Examples: 1-3-5-7-_?_; 1-4-7-10-_?_ Follow by creating melodic sequences. What is the next note? C-E-D-F-E-_?_

■ Use geometric shapes to illustrate repetition and contrast.

	Sing and move.	**Play instruments.**
△	*Hot Cross Buns.* Step, step, stop.	wood block
△	*Hot Cross Buns.* Step, step, stop.	wood block
☐	*One a pen-ny, two a pen-ny* (Clap the rhythm.)	rhythm sticks
△	*Hot Cross Buns.* Step, step, stop.	wood block

■ Illustrate repetition and contrast with colors and objects.

■ Illustrate repetition and contrast with pictures and photographs.

■ Arrange visuals (theme charts, colored sheets of construction paper, contour cards, examples of rhythm patterns, titles of familiar tunes, pictures, and so forth) to show the order of events in a listening selection. For example, the melodies in Edwin Franko Goldman's "Children's March" quote well-known children's songs, sometimes more than once. The songs appear in the following order:

> "London Bridge Is Falling Down"
> "Mary Had a Little Lamb"
> "Jingle Bells"
> "The Farmer in the Dell" combined with "Jingle Bells"
> "Sing a Song of Sixpence"
> "The Farmer in the Dell"
> "Lazy Mary Will You Get Up?"
> "Hickory, Dickory Dock"
> "Three Blind Mice"
> "Rockabye Baby"
> "Pop! Goes the Weasel"
> "London Bridge . . ." and "Pop! Goes the Weasel"
> "London Bridge Is Falling Down"
> "Pop! Goes the Weasel"
> "London Bridge"

Related Listening: Edwin Franko Goldman: "Children's March," Eastman Wind Ensemble, conducted by Frederick Fennell, CD Mercury Living Presence 432019–2 or *Music and You*, Grade K.

■ Encourage students to use notation to guide them in discovering form. Analyze familiar tunes and indicate repeated, similar, and contrasting phrases with lower case letters. For example, "Match these songs with their diagrams":

1. "Jingle Bells" (chorus)	_____ a a b b′
2. "The Birch Tree"	_____ a b c d
3. "Twinkle, Twinkle, Little Star"	_____ a b a b
4. "Taffy"	_____ a a b a

■ Write contrasting rhythms on the chalkboard. Assign two groups to clap them, play them with body rhythms, or perform them with percussion instruments. Decide which rhythm to call "A" and which to call "B." Perform a rhythm piece in AB form. Perform a rhythm piece in ABA form.

Binary

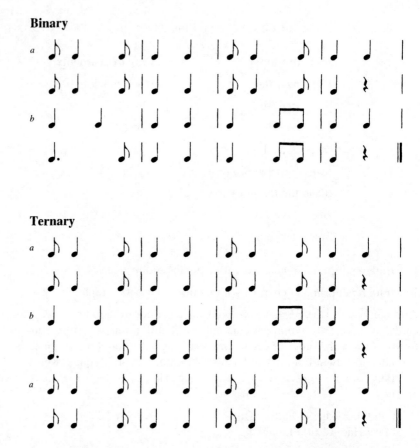

Ternary

- ■ Examine the illustrations in basic music series books, charts, and transparencies for examples of repetition, contrast, same, different, similar, and other ideas in musical form. Collect examples from other sources: Repetition: the slats in a picket fence or in venetian blinds, railroad ties; Contrast: pictures showing different seasons, day or night, wet weather, dry weather, colors, fabrics, shapes, and so forth.

VERBALIZING

- ■ **Illustrate** repetition and contrast in language and poetry or with synonyms ("words with the same meaning") and antonyms ("words with opposite meanings") or punning contrasts such as the following.

    overcome-undergo; ant hill-Uncle Sam; cargo-bus stop; common sense-rare coins

- ■ **Find** language examples of repetition:

    Walla, Walla; Mau Mau, beri-beri, "To the swinging and the ringing/Of the bells, bells, bells . . . (Edgar Allen Poe); "Break, break, break,/On thy cold gray stones, O Sea! . . ." (Alfred, Lord Tennyson).

- ■ **Discuss** the structure and content of a song or listening selection. "What produced [repetition, similarity, contrast]? Was it the words? rhythm? melody? tone color? harmony?" Guide the students in their discoveries. Examples of the ways repetition and change are intermixed are found in songs like "My Darling Clementine" with its repeated rhythmic pattern and changing words. The *verses* are different, the *chorus* is the same. The *tune* is the same in the verse and in the chorus.

■ **Tell.** "Tell how many times you heard the following [word, rhythm, motive, pattern]." "Was this section of the music [louder, softer, faster, slower, higher, lower]? (More difficult questions combine two or more elements: "Which part was louder and lower? Higher and softer? Lower and faster?")

■ **Compare** and **Contrast.** For example, compare AB or ABA patterns in music to similar patterns in nature, clothing, building, and so forth. Compare music to language: In what ways do both have form? Examine two songs: How are they alike? How do they differ? Relate the comments to actual experiences with music.

■ **Learn.** Teach and learn the musical terms and vocabulary that match the children's perceptions of music after they have had a variety of musical experiences to build conceptual awareness. Children often communicate through movement or other responses, but learning music terms will give them tools that facilitate more learning, just as vocabulary contributes to development in other subjects. When teaching about form, introduce and use terms such as cadence, phrase, motive, contour, sequence, repetition, contrast, variety, unity, section, binary, ternary, verse-refrain, introduction, interlude, and coda.

NOTES

[1] In 1963 ten pianists, taking turns, played it in 18 hours and 40 minutes. A member of the audience who had remained for the entire performance shouted "encore."

[2] From *Ralph Roister Doister* by Nicholas Udall (1505–1556). *The Dramatic Writings of Nicholas Udal* (New York: Barnes and Noble, Inc., 1966).

[3] Whether or not to emphasize imagery in teaching movement is controversial. Some say that indefinite approaches ("Move to the music . . . anyway you wish.") are too vague and too difficult for beginners, who may lack a vocabulary of movements. Telling children to "be" an elephant or a butterfly also ignores their need to know how their movements can be like something else. It is also argued that referential meanings ("Gallop like wild horses.") tend to distract learning from actual dance concepts of movement, space, force, and time. See, for example, Mary Joyce's *First Steps in Teaching Creative Dance to Children,* 2d. ed. (Palo Alto, CA: Mayfield Publishing Company, 1980). This book, written for the classroom teacher, contains thirty-four dance lessons, with much other useful information.

TEMPO, DYNAMICS, AND TONE COLOR   **6**

Rhythm, melody, harmony, form, tempo, dynamics, and tone color all contribute to the expressiveness of music. The elements that are most direct and easy to perceive—tempo, dynamics, and tone color—attract children very early in life, often in the kitchen, where numerous cooking utensils supply a variety of resources for the young musician.

TEMPO

TEMPO AND THE BEAT

The pace of music is called "tempo," and it is based on the speed of the beats rather than the long and short durations that make up the rhythm of the words or melody.[1] Shakespeare's schoolboy, "creeping like snail / Unwilling to school," adapted tempo and movement to express mood, no doubt returning from school at a faster pace.

Movement

Learning to walk in rhythm with the beat is easier when the tempo matches the moderately fast pace of the child. Movement with the beat is more difficult in slow tempo. Nevertheless, children should experience music in varied tempos as well as music with tempo changes.[2] Children who have learned to move in rhythm with a steady drum beat are ready to explore activities such as the following.

- "Listen to the drum. When it is fast, pat your knees fast. When it goes slowly, pat your knees slowly." "How else could we show fast and slow?"
- Use movement to demonstrate tempo associations. "How would a [turtle, cheetah, etc.) move?"
- "Show fast or slow by the way you run [or walk]." Call on others to clap in rhythm with these movements, then invite a new student to demonstrate tempo by movement.
- Starting from a circle formation, invite the children to walk around the room, telling them to stop on your signal and walk back to the circle. (Remind them not to touch or bump anyone.) After noting the average tempo of the group, ask them to repeat their movement away from and back to the circle. This time, play the drum at the group's "average tempo." (Use some other unpitched rhythm instruments—claves, woodblocks, etc.—or improvise pentatonic patterns on the black keys of the piano, if you prefer). Repeat the sequence, this time in a running movement, once again matching the children's tempo on the drum.
- Later, move in tempo with the teacher's rhythm. "Follow the rhythm of the drum." Play sets of steady beats. Stop and repeat the activity in a different tempo.

■ Children can do the improvising, too. Let one group move as others play pentatonic tones on instruments with removable tone bars. Exchange parts to give everyone opportunities to explore tempo through movement and by creating music with percussion instruments.

■ Experiment with contrasting versions of a known song by having children sing in a slower tempo, or a faster tempo, as they pat or step the underlying steady beat. After singing in the new tempo, ask them if it was faster or slower.

Moving to Recorded Music

Related Listening: Hap Palmer: *Learning Basic Skills Through Music,* Education Activities, Inc., AR 514.

Recorded music gives additional possibilities. For example, in Hap Palmer's "The Elephant" the elephant moves very slowly until he encounters tigers and hunters. Then he runs, making the jungle shake. *The Carnival of the Animals* by Saint-Saëns includes "Tortoises," "Kangaroos," and the birds in "The Aviary."

Chant the rhyme "Engine Number Nine." For an introduction, the children may imitate the sounds of a train gathering speed—a whispered chug-chug sound—followed by the spoken rhyme once the train has gained speed. (The musical term for a gradual increase in tempo is *accelerando*.) At the end of the chant, improvise sounds like those of a train slowing down and coming to a stop. (The musical term for a gradual decrease in tempo is *ritardando*.)

Game: Follow the leader (the "engine") around the room. Have the children bend their arms at the elbow and "pump" back and forth to the beat.

Engine Number Nine

Eng - ine, Eng - ine, Num - ber Nine,

Go - ing down Chi - ca - go Line,

If the train goes off the track,

Do you want your mon - ey back?

Related Listening: Villa-Lobos: "The Little Train of the Caipira", *Bowmar Orchestral Library,* No. 64. **Film:** *The Little Train of the Caipira,* 13 minutes, Instructional Media Services, Inc.

"The Little Train of the Caipira" from *Bachianas Brasileiras* No. 2 by Heitor Villa-Lobos is an orchestral work depicting a steam-powered train that gathers speed, stops to take on passengers, and slows down at journey's end. (Detailed listening guides for this selection and many others are found in booklets accompanying RCA's *Adventures in Music,* a set of twelve LP records that is now out of print but still available in many schools.) Refer to the description of "The Little Train of the Caipira" (Grade 3, vol. 1). Examine the listening lessons on this work in current music series: *Holt Music,* Book 4, *World of Music,* Grade 2, *Music and You,* Grade 2. Another listening resource, currently available on cassette tapes, is the *Bowmar Orchestral Library.*

Play the singing game "Obwisana" at a slow and then a fast tempo.

Obwisana

Ghana

Ob-wi-sa-na   sa-na-na   Ob-wi-sa-na   sa.

Ob-wi-sa-na   sa-na-na   Ob-wi-sa-na   sa.

Related Listening: "Obwisana" Silver Burdett and Ginn *World of Music,* Grade 1, CD 2.

> **Obwisana**
>
> *Game:* Kneel or sit in a circle. Place an object (a stick, a shoe, a ball of paper, etc.) in front of each child. On beat *one,* lift the object. On beat *two,* put it down in front of the person to the right of each player. After learning the song and playing the game in a slow tempo, try it at a fast tempo.

Italian Tempo Terms

Italian tempo terms, which serve as an international vocabulary for musicians, usually label the separate movements of symphonies and other instrumental works.

Term	Metronome	Approximate Tempo
largo	42–44	broad
lento	52–108	slow
adagio	50–76	slow
andante	56–88	walking
moderato	66–126	moderate
allegro	84–144	fast
vivace	80–160	lively
presto	100–152	very fast

Tempo markings also indicate tempo changes.

accelerando	increase speed gradually
piu mosso	more motion
ritardando	decrease speed gradually
meno mosso	less motion
a tempo	return to the previous tempo
tempo rubato	free, a flexible tempo
tempo giusto	a strict tempo

Related Listening (accelerando): Edvard Grieg: "In the Hall of the Mountain King," *Peer Gynt Suite No. 1. World of Music,* Book 2, or *Bowmar Orchestral Library,* No. 59.

The Metronome

Like a clock, the metronome measures time with precision. Metronomes indicate the speed of the beats with a ticking sound and are adjustable to a rate of 40 to 208 beats per minute. (MM = 60 indicates one beat per second.)[3]

As part of a lesson on tempo you might show children a metronome from your school's music department. After demonstrating the metronome, help children discover more about its uses.[4] Ask them to listen for eight beats and then tap eight beats in the same tempo, but without the metronome. Turn the metronome on again to test the results. Did they keep the same tempo, or change to a slower or faster tempo? Explore

Related Listening: Beethoven: "An Maelzel" (To Maelzel), *The Comic Beethoven,* Seraphim S-60180. Beethoven: *Symphony No. 8,* Second Movement, RCA *Adventures in Music,* Grade 6, vol. 1, New York, RCA Victor Record Division.

several different tempos. (At present, electronic metronomes, ranging from the size of a credit card to the traditional size, are widely used. Some metronomes also have a flashing light to show the speed of the beat.)

Modern metronomes

Tempo markings are guidelines rather than indicators of a single "correct" tempo. Other tempo considerations include the mood and text of the song, the musical content, and the ability of the performers. Recordings of songs in classroom music books are another guide, although the recorded tempos may be somewhat fast for children who are first learning a song.

DYNAMICS

Related Listening: Ibert: "Parade," *Music and You*, Grade 2, *World of Music*, Grade 1. Also, Morton Gould: "Parade (for percussion), *Brass & Percussion*, CD: RCA 09026–61255–2 or *Holt Music*, Grade 2.

Sounds vary in loudness—from the barely audible to those that are painfully loud. We speak of silence, but children will notice that the classroom is alive with sounds even when they are as quiet as possible. "Listen and name the sounds you hear."

Some games and activities develop the child's awareness of musical sound and silence. "Musical chairs" is an example—move to the music, run to the chairs when the music stops—but the game can become so boisterous that little learning occurs.[5] Try a modified version—move to the music and drop to the floor when the music stops. (The last one down is "out.") Better still, if children move to the music and stop in place when it stops, everyone can participate throughout the game.

Dynamic markings indicate the relative loudness of music. A sudden dynamic change from soft to loud, such as the loud chord in Haydn's "Surprise" Symphony, is intended to awaken the listening ear, while a gradual change from soft to loud can make a repetitive melody grow increasingly exciting, as in Ravel's *Boléro* or Grieg's "In the Hall of the Mountain King." In Ibert's "Parade," the distant parade's approach is suggested by an increase in volume, and its departure by a decrease in volume. A similar dynamic contrast occurs in Morton Gould's "Parade" (for percussion). "John Jacob Jingelheimer Schmidt" begins with a full tone and gets softer with each repetition. (Sometimes it is performed in the opposite way, as additional singers join in each time the words announce "That's my name, too."[6])

John Jacob Jingleheimer Schmidt

Camp Song

John Ja - cob Jin - gle - heim - er Schmidt. That's my name, too;

When - ev - er I go out, the peo - ple al - ways shout:

John Ja - cob Jin - gle - heim - er Schmidt! Dah dah dah dah dah dah dah - da!

DYNAMIC MARKINGS

Traditional Italian terms (or their abbreviations) indicate points on a scale of dynamics from the barely audible to extremely loud[7]:

pp	*(pianissimo)*	very soft
p	*(piano)*	soft
mp	*(mezzo piano)*	medium soft
mf	*(mezzo forte)*	medium loud
f	*(forte)*	loud
ff	*(fortissimo)*	very loud

Sudden changes between loud to soft in music are obvious, but awareness of the need for dynamic contrasts is not always evident in children's singing or instrument playing. Changes in dynamics are an important means of making music expressive. Gradual dynamic changes are indicated by the terms *crescendo* (getting louder) and *diminuendo* (getting softer), or by signs that indicate these changes:

Related Listening (crescendo) "Meadowlands," *Soviet Army Chorus and Band,* Monitor MCD 61500 (compact disc). Listen to the long crescendo. For a seventeen-minute crescendo, listen to Ravel's *Boléro.*

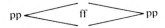

pp ◁ ff ▷ pp

Emphasize dynamics through movement activities and by singing or playing instruments. "Listen to the piano. Are the sounds loud or soft? Show me by the way you move." (A song such as "Hey, Betty Martin" may suggest loud or soft movements such as walking on tiptoe or stamping the feet.)

"Little Tom Tinker" (page 41) has obvious dynamic contrasts. Sing it at a moderate volume, then emphasize the loud cry on the word "Ma." Children's voices may become harsh or strident, however, if very loud singing is emphasized on a regular basis. Avoid overly loud instrumental accompaniments, too. Strive for a musical balance between voices and accompaniment.

To help children gain increased awareness of their vocal potential, compare whispering, the speaking voice, the singing voice, and the playground voice. Avoid "loud" singing, but do ask for a bigger sound when children are not using sufficient breath support and energy. Build variety in dynamics by occasionally singing a loud passage softly (or the reverse) so that children learn to sing or play with a wider, more expressive dynamic range.

TONE COLOR (TIMBRE)

EXPERIMENTING WITH TONE COLOR

Children's fascination with sounds of all types becomes evident very early in life. Play activities, environmental sounds, and the sounds made by musical instruments provide an inexhaustible variety of listening experiences. Focus on tone color through activities such as the ones that follow.

Preschool and Primary Grade Children

- Partially fill containers (sealed plastic cups, empty tape cassette boxes, etc.) with rice, corn, beans, paper clips, and other materials that will produce interesting sounds. Let children shake them and decide which ones sound the same and which sound different.

- "Listen to the drum. Circle this way (clockwise) when I play on the rim. Circle the other way when I play on the drum head."

- Play "Simon Says." ("Simon Says, 'Take three steps.'") Use an instrument with the words, "Simon Says." Tell children to move only when they hear the sound of the specified instrument along with the command. (If the triangle is "Simon," the children should not respond to a different sound such as a woodblock.)

- Match pictures or words to possible sounds. Explore the variety of sounds that young children know and enjoy. For example:
  "Draw a line connecting each sound and its likely source."[8]

meow	firecracker
arf	thunder
peep	dog
tweet	mouse
sniff	sports car
chirp	cat
boom	baby chick
vroom	cricket
bang	canary
squeak	nose

- Label the sounds of classroom instruments (clicking, ringing, scraping, jingling, rattling), and group the instruments according to tone color.

- Have students identify other members of the class by the sound of their voices.

- Sing songs that imitate animal sounds ("Bought Me A Cat," "Old MacDonald," etc.). Extend the activity by substituting classroom instrument sounds to represent various animals.

- Sound effects, another aspect of tone color, can be added to songs like "Bill Grogan's Goat." Designate a narrator, conductor, and instrumentalists. The narrator recites the words and the conductor cues the performers, who create instrumental or vocal sounds to represent the goat, the train, and the events of the song. Additional examples: "Twinkle, Twinkle Little Star": Have children explore instruments that make "star sounds"— e.g., a triangle. "Hickory, Dickory Dock": Add sounds to suggest the ticking clock, the clock striking "one," and the mouse running up or down.

- Use tape recordings of different environmental sounds and have children identify the sources. Children can "collect" sounds on tape as individual projects.

■ Identify "mystery sounds" (thunder, fog horns, bells, animal sounds, etc.) from sound effects records, which are available in many libraries.

■ Devise games based on timbre. For example, "Name the instrument." Place several instruments (e.g., triangle, woodblock, sleighbells, tambourine) in the center of the circle. Have a child play sounds from one instrument while the class listens with eyes closed. Invite a different child to move to the center of the circle and find the instrument that made the sound the class just heard. (If possible, have two identical sets of the instruments, and play the "mystery sounds" on a set concealed from the children's vision.) For a more challenging game have students identify a *sequence* of sounds by listening. "I heard a woodblock, then bells, then a tambourine. The triangle was last."

Primary and Middle Grade Children

■ Correlate music and science. Pour some water into a shallow, transparent container placed atop an overhead projector. Strike a tuning fork and dip it into the water, setting up little waves.

■ Use an *oscilloscope* to picture the wave forms produced by different sound sources.

■ Make a collection of sounds. Invite students to demonstrate various sounds made by objects in the room, or by clapping, snapping, or some other type of body percussion. (Use a tape recorder to gather sounds for children to identify.) List the sounds on the chalkboard and classify them as loud/soft, high/low, long/short, or according to their timbre. Invite students to explore all kinds of sound-makers: paper, plastic, glass, rubber, wood, metal, etc.

■ Invite band and orchestra students or community musicians to the class to demonstrate their instruments.

■ The following categories (shown with examples) classify all types of instruments.[9]

Idiophones	*Chordophones*	*Membranophones*	*Aerophones*	*Electrophones*
castanets	banjo	bass drum	bassoon	electric guitar
chimes	cello	bongos	clarinet	electric organ
cowbells	guitar	hand drum	harmonica	synthesizer
maracas	harp	timpani	recorder	tape recorder
xylophone	violin		whistle	

■ Refer to the information on timbre in the basic music series books. (See, for example, "The Sound Bank" in Silver Burdett & Ginn's *World of Music*.)

■ Combine the study of timbre with movement to music. (See pages 162–167.)

■ View films or videotapes about musical instruments. (See appendix 6.)

■ Arrange a visit to a children's concert. (University and community orchestras often provide concerts of music especially for young listeners.)

THE ORCHESTRA

The orchestra of the eighteenth century, with approximately forty-five players, was much smaller than the orchestras of today, which may have more than a hundred performers. The instruments of the orchestra cover a wide pitch range and are highly developed technically, though modern instruments are not always preferred over historical instruments created by skilled instrument makers in the past.

RANGES OF INSTRUMENTS AND VOICES

The following chart shows the ranges of voices and instruments in relation to the eighty-eight black and white keys of the modern piano. As you will notice, each written pitch has a definite frequency of vibrations. Doubling the frequency raises the pitch an octave. (The frequency of the pitch A, for example, is 27.5, 55, 110, 220, 440 . . .) The chart will give you a general map of the higher and lower voices and instruments used in music. By looking at it you can find answers to questions such as the following. Which *instrument* has middle C as its lowest note? Which instrument has the widest range? How many *ledger lines* does the highest C have?

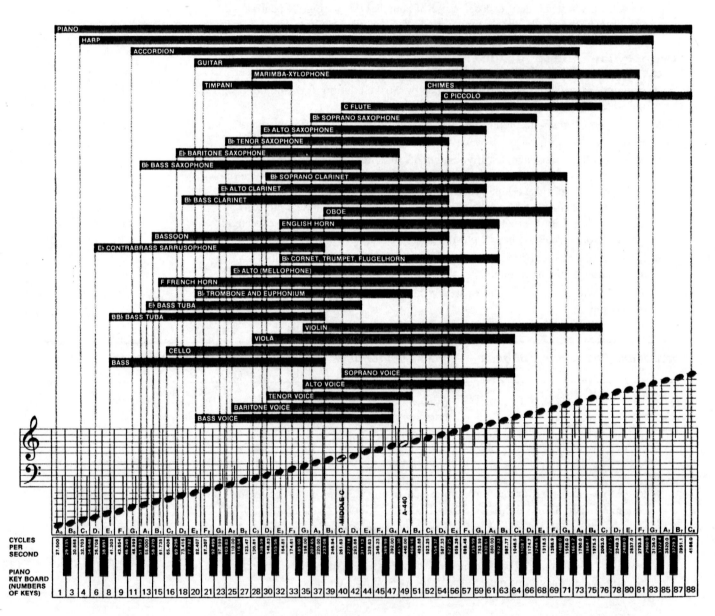

Used by permission of C. G. Conn, A Member Company of United Musical Instruments, Inc. Copyright © 1936, C. G. Conn, Inc.

The orchestra has a variety of tone colors that may be used singly or in combinations. Tone color is often used to highlight a melody or to emphasize structure and form through the use of contrasting the tone colors in different phrases and sections in a composition. The orchestra's four "families" of instruments are strings, woodwind, brass, and percussion.

STRINGED INSTRUMENTS

String instruments include violins, violas, cellos, and string basses. The violin has a wide range that covers the soprano and the alto register. Its open strings are tuned to G D A and E. Sound is produced by bowing across the strings or by plucking them ("pizzicato"). A violin made in 1698 by Stradivarius sold for more than one million dollars in 1988.

Violin
All orchestral instrument illustrations, unless noted otherwise, are reprinted from Ready-to-Use Classical Music Illustrations by Bob Guiliani. Copyright © 1990, and used by permission of Dover Publications, Inc.

Like the violin, the viola is held between the chin and shoulder and may be played while standing or seated. Its lowest tone is the C below middle C and its open strings are tuned to C G D and A. The viola has a darker sound than the violin and plays a supporting harmonic role in the tenor register.

Viola

The cello, twice the size of a violin, rests on a peg and is played while seated. Its full name is violoncello (not "violincello"). The cello sounds in the bass register, with open strings tuned to C G D and A, an octave lower than those of the viola. The cello's rich tone is featured in "The Swan" from *The Carnival of the Animals* by Saint Saëns.

Cello

The string bass, or double bass, is over 6 feet in length. The player usually perches on a stool and supports the neck of the instrument, which rests on an end pin that touches the floor. Its strings are tuned in fourths from low E (E A D G). Famous passages for the double bass include the trio from the third movement of Beethoven's *Symphony No. 5* and "The Elephant" from *The Carnival of the Animals.*

Double bass

The harp (6 feet in height) has forty-seven strings and seven pedals connected to discs. When the pedals are pressed, the discs rotate and raise the pitch of the strings. All of the C strings are red; all of the F strings are blue. The performer plucks the strings and can produce arpeggios and glissandos—showers of tones in rapid succession.

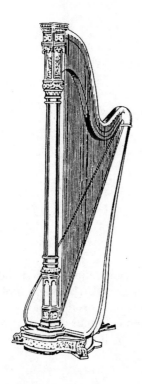

Harp

WOODWIND INSTRUMENTS

The woodwind family—piccolo, flute, clarinet, oboe, English horn, bassoon, and saxophone—covers a wide pitch range. The tiny piccolo can play very high. The tubing of the 16-foot contrabassoon, folded into a more convenient height of about 4 feet, produces low tones at the bottom of the woodwind range.

Flute and piccolo tones are produced by blowing against the edge of a hole in the mouthpiece (like blowing across the top of a pop bottle). The oboe, English horn, and bassoon have a double reed. The clarinet and saxophone have a single reed. Blowing into the flattened end of a soda straw (trim the ends into an inverted "V" shape first) or against a blade of grass held taut between the thumbs illustrates the action of the reed in tone production.

The flute (26.5 inches) has thirteen sound holes and sixteen keys. The piccolo is only 12.5 inches in length. The sounds of these instruments are familiar in music for band as well as for orchestra.

Flute

The oboe (25 inches) has a penetrating, nasal quality. The alto oboe is called an English horn. It has a bulb-shaped bell. The bassoon plays in the tenor and bass registers and may be assigned music that is serious or comical in sound. It would be more than 8 feet long if its four wooden joints were assembled in a straight line, but a U-shaped connection at the bottom allows the assembly to form two parallel tubes and a more convenient size.

Oboe

English horn

Bassoon

Contrabassoon

The clarinet family includes soprano, alto, bass, and contrabass instruments. The clarinet has a wide range and is capable of rapid trills, scales, and arpeggios as well as beautiful legato melodies. The clarinet was a favorite of Mozart and it has a wealth of solo literature along with many solo passages in orchestral music.

Clarinet

The saxophone is made of metal but belongs to the woodwind family, even so. It was invented by Adolphe Sax around 1840 and has several sizes—soprano, alto, tenor, and baritone being the most common.

Saxophone

BRASS INSTRUMENTS

The trumpet, horn, trombone, and tuba make up the orchestral brass section. Bands include baritone horns, euphoniums, and sousaphones in addition to the orchestral brass instruments. The brass player's lips vibrate when air is blown through them into the brass mouthpiece, and these vibrations are amplified by the instrument. Unlike military bugles, orchestral brass instruments can play the complete chromatic scale: the trombonist varies the length of the instrument by moving the trombone slide; the trumpet, horn, and tuba have valves that add additional tubing when used singly or in various combinations.

The trumpet plays brilliant fanfares as well as lyrical melodies and is equally at home in the band or jazz ensemble. The cornet, which has a more mellow sound, is often used in band music.

Trumpet

The horn has 12 to 16 feet of tubing which is coiled into a circular design. The horn (also called the French horn, but not by horn players) has a deeper tone than the trumpet. Its wide range and varied tone qualities allow it to blend equally well with the brass or the woodwind family.

Horn

The tenor trombone has a deeper and darker tone than that of the horn. Composers have written music to take advantage of the trombone's power, as well as special effects such as the glissando, or its solemn-sounding tones in music for a processional.

Trombone

The tuba, the lowest sounding brass instrument, has a dark, sonorous tone. It is also surprisingly agile when played by a skilled performer, who may play music intended for the tuba or transcriptions of music written for other instruments. Some tuba players even manage a bass register version of the famous piccolo part from Sousa's "Stars and Stripes Forever."

Tuba

PERCUSSION INSTRUMENTS

Orchestral bells, marimbas, xylophones, and kettledrums are percussion instruments with definite pitch. Triangles, woodblocks, tambourines, and cowbells are percussion instruments with indefinite pitch. The family of percussion instruments includes snaredrums, bass drums, and even automobile brake drums—nearly anything that produces a sound when struck, shaken, or rattled. Classroom percussion instruments are discussed later in this chapter.

Snare drum

Cymbals

Xylophone

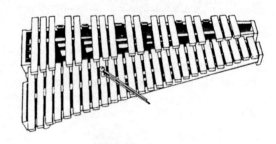

Bass drum

Kettledrum

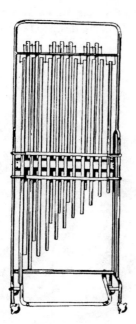

Tubular bells

EXPERIENCES WITH ORCHESTRAL INSTRUMENTS

Whenever possible children should have opportunities to hear orchestral instruments and other instruments in live performance.

- ■ Invite local musicians or members of school ensembles to demonstrate the sounds and capabilities of orchestral instruments.
- ■ Attend children's concerts by orchestras, bands, or smaller ensembles, which are often scheduled by community arts associations or available through school field trips.

Supplement concerts and other live performance experiences with recordings and other audiovisual resources. Recorded examples of tone color are abundant in the various basic music series cassettes and compact discs. *World of Music*'s "Sound Bank," for example, includes classroom, electronic, folk, and orchestral instruments, as well as sounds from nature and the environment: fog horns, sirens, animals, and so forth.

Related Listening: *Peter and the Wolf, Holt Music,* Grade 1, *Music and You,* Grade 1; *Carnival of the Animals, Bowmar Orchestral Library, No. 51.*

Prokofiev's *Peter and the Wolf,* Kleinsinger's *Tubby the Tuba,* and Saint-Saëns' *Carnival of the Animals* continue to be favorite listening experiences and there are numerous recordings, filmstrips, and videotapes from which to choose. (See the catalogs listed in appendix 6.) *Meet the Instruments,* an audiovisual resource with color pictures, a filmstrip set, and video and "*André Previn's Guide to Music,* an audiovisual set containing wall charts, cassettes, activity books, topic books, a quiz book, and a teacher's manual are available from Bowmar, c/o Columbia Pictures Publications, 15800 N.W. 48th Avenue, Miami, FL 33014.

CLASSROOM INSTRUMENTS WITH DEFINITE PITCH

Direct experiences with classroom percussion instruments offer children many avenues to musical growth.

BELLS

Bells of many kinds are available for classroom music. Some are similar to the bells used in orchestras and bands. Others are designed especially for children's use.

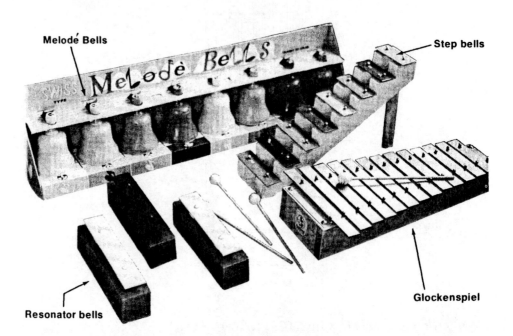

The bars of resonator bells are individually mounted so that each bell can be used separately or arranged in small groups to form tonal patterns, scales, or chords. "Hot Cross Buns," for example, requires just three different tones. Select the resonator bells indicated by letter names in each of the following examples and play the melody of "Hot Cross Buns" in the rhythm you have learned.

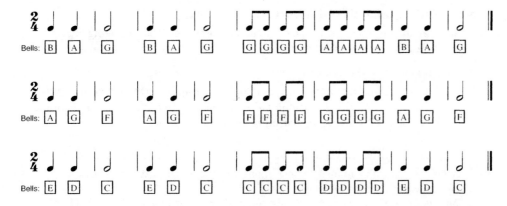

Playing bells often makes the study of chords or scales more concrete and more interesting, and you can distribute resonator bells to involve a number of students at one time. With practice and concentration, students can even play melodies in "hand-bell style"—each player responsible for a single tone. Scale pattern melodies (such as "Do Re Mi") or melodies with a small number of different pitches are easier than melodies with many skips.

Metal bars mounted on a rack are called song bells or melody bells. Glockenspiels with metal bars that can be removed give added flexibility. Aligned with a staff drawn on the chalkboard, melody bells help students connect sight and sound.

Three-line Staff: do = G

Melody bells and chalkboard with staff

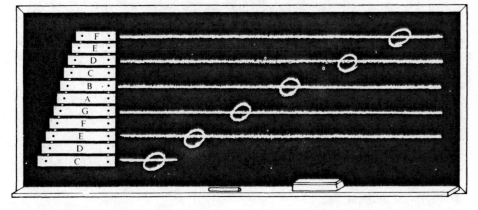

Swiss Melodé bells are color coded for each pitch. Played like miniature hand bells, they can be used by very young children for simple melodies or chords.

Step bells, which are arranged like a staircase, help children comprehend the meaning of higher and lower pitch in music.

USES FOR BELLS IN CLASSROOM MUSIC

Bells have many possible uses in the elementary classroom. The following suggestions illustrate a few of these possibilities.

■ Teach melody and accompaniment.

Teach tunes or accompaniments on bells by rote or through a combination of rote and simplified music notation. Some children may sing the melodies, while others play bells or barred instruments.

Pentatonic songs with a limited number of different tones make excellent choices. Useful collections are the following:

Sing It Yourself, 220 Pentatonic American Folk Songs by Louise Larkins Bradford (Sherman Oaks, CA: Alfred Publishing Company, Inc., 1978).

Pentatonic Song Book by Brian Brocklehurst (New York: Schott Music Corporation, 1968).

Second Pentatonic Songbook (1976).

■ Reinforce music reading skills.

Number bells with a crayon or use color coding to help children match bells with notation.

■ Play short tonal patterns in songs.

Intervals, recurring motives, or any simple pattern may be used. For instance, in "Good News!" play the notes for "Chariot's coming" on bells each time it appears in the melody.

■ Play the starting pitch of a song.
■ Play an ostinato.
■ Use ear-training and tone-matching games such as the following:

Sing and play common tonal patterns: 1 3 5, 5 3 1, 5 3 6 5 3, etc.

"Play what you hear me sing." (For example, *so–mi* = 5–3.)

■ Combine bells with wind, percussion, and chording instruments.
■ Play major, minor, pentatonic, chromatic, and whole-tone scales by ear and from notation.
■ Play chords, chord roots, and cadences.

Bells help children discover how chords are made and used. For example, play the chords for "Joe Turner Blues" (see page 133).

■ Improvise short melodies.

For example, invent an eight-beat phrase that ends on scale step five (*so*) followed by an eight-beat phrase that ends on scale step one (*do*).

■ Highlight musical details.

Play bells on a tonal pattern, on the first note of each measure, on the highest or lowest note of a phrase, on the first or last note of a phrase, or on the final cadence of a song.

■ Create sound effects for stories, songs, and poems.

■ Use resonator bells to compare pentatonic, major, minor, or chromatic scales through sight and sound. Arrange bell players in consecutive half steps from low to high for the chromatic scale. Have the "black keys" step back, so that a pattern like that of the keyboard results. Let student conductors signal to each player so as to sound successive notes of various scales or tunes the group has studied.

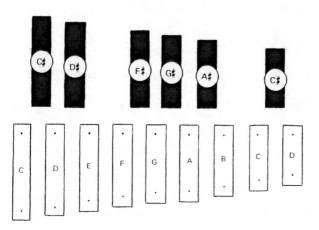

■ With only one bell, a child can play a repeated note in a singing round, then a chord root in a one-chord song or the common tone in a two-chord song. (For instance, G is a common tone between the C and G chords.)

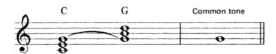

■ Play a bell ostinato.

Related Listening: Carillon: *L'Arlésienne Suite No. 1* by Georges Bizet, *Bowmar Orchestral Library*, no. 78 or *World of Music*, Grade 4.

Carillon

■ Play simple melodies or simple tonal patterns from difficult melodies.
■ Play simple patterns from notation.
■ Play bell parts given in basic music series books.
■ Play chords.
■ Play chords or chord roots with a recording. You can accompany many songs by using notes indicated in the chord symbols above the songs.

TONE BAR INSTRUMENTS

The German composer and music educator Carl Orff (1895–1982) advocated high quality instruments especially designed for children. In today's classrooms "Orff instruments" include a variety of percussion instruments of all types. Xylophones, glockenspiels, and metallophones have removable or interchangeable tone bars. The use of these instruments facilitates learning and helps children visualize and experience tonal relationships in scales, chords, and melodies.

- Xylophones have wooden tone bars.

- Glockenspiels have thin metal tone bars and produce a brilliant tone color.

- Metallophones have thicker metal bars and produce a mellow, long-lasting tone.

RANGE

Abbreviations for the instruments indicate names and range. For the sake of simplicity, the notated range of the instruments is the same, though their actual ranges differ as shown here.

	Glockenspiel	*Xylophone*	*Metallophone*
Soprano	SG	SX	SM
Alto	AG	AX	AM
Bass	—	BX	BM

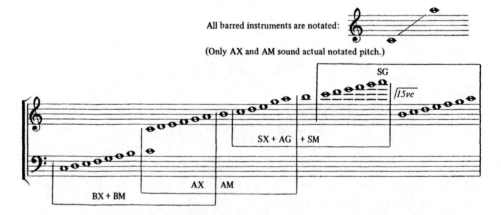

All barred instruments are notated:

(Only AX and AM sound actual notated pitch.)

Glockenspiels	Actual sound	Metallophones	Actual sound	Xylophones	Actual sound
Soprano (S G)	two octaves higher	Soprano (S M)	one octave higher	Soprano (S X)	one octave higher
Alto (A G)	one octave higher	Alto (A M)	as written	Alto (A X)	as written
		Bass (B M)	one octave lower	Bass (B X)	one octave lower

Diatonic instruments have interchangeable tone bars for F and F-sharp and for B and B-flat. *Chromatic* instruments also are available.

Orff instruments
Photo courtesy of MMB Music, Inc. Used by permission.

PLAYING TECHNIQUE

Position the instruments at a comfortable height for the player—waist-level if standing, knee-level if seated. Children waiting a turn should sit by the instrument, facing the teacher, so that they learn the part, too. Often children can teach each other, as they take turns. The longest (lowest) tone bars should be at the player's left. (See the comments about "mirroring" in the box below.)

When the teacher faces the class the teacher's right is the child's left, and vice-versa. To minimize the need for lengthy verbal explanations, movement patterns can be taught visually as the children make a "mirror image" of the teacher's gestures. For example, when facing the class, a movement of the teacher's right hand is mirrored by a movement of a student's left hand. After learning the needed movements through imitation, the patterns are then sung with note names, played with fingers on the tone bars and then with mallets. The teacher may demonstrate from an instrument turned so that low C is at the teacher's right (but at the children's left) so that they can imitate patterns by observing the teacher's mallet direction from low pitches to higher pitches.

Mallets with plastic or wooden heads are used for glockenspiels and xylophones. Mallets with felt or yarn-wrapped heads generally produce a more pleasing tone on bass xylophones and metallophones. Children can experiment with different mallets and sounds to discover ways to produce contrasts in tone quality.

Grip a mallet lightly between the thumb and the first two fingers of each hand: palms down; fingers curled around the stick. (Do not place the index finger along the top of the stick because muscular tightness may result.) Hold the elbows away from the body as in riding a bicycle or motorcycle.

Basic mallet techniques include (1) striking two tone bars with both mallets simultaneously; (2) striking with alternating mallets (like walking up or down the scale); (3) tremolo (quick, repeated strokes on one tone bar with alternating mallets); and (4) glissando (sweep up or down across the tone bars and strike the last note of the glissando with the other mallet).

Borduns are a basic type of accompaniment played on xylophones and metallophones. Played on strong beats, a bordun uses scale notes one and five *within the same octave*. Four types of simple borduns are: chord borduns, broken borduns, level borduns, and arpeggiated borduns.[10]

From St. Helena Island Spirituals *by N. G. J. Ballanta. Copyright © 1925. G. Schirmer, Inc. Used by permission.*

I Got a Letter This Morning

*Sounds one octave lower than written

Removable tone bars make Orff instruments adaptable to various tonal patterns and scales. When removing a tone bar, lift it straight up with both hands to avoid bending the retaining pin. Replace all tone bars at the conclusion of the activity or the lesson.

The young child can begin with only a few tone bars and add other notes when they are needed. Pentatonic music, which has no half steps, precedes the study of major and minor scale songs. Set up the pentatonic scale by removing the tone bars corresponding to steps 4 and 7 of the major scale.

C pentatonic: CDEGA without F(4) or B(7) of the C major scale.
F pentatonic: FGACD without B♭(4) or E(7) of the F major scale.
G pentatonic: GABDE without C(4) or F♯(7) of the G major scale.

Simplify playing techniques when possible. Here are two examples.

■ For repeated low-middle-high patterns, let one hand play the middle note while the other alternates between low and high.

■ In the next illustration, the second stick pattern is easier than the first.

Alternating mallets (hands must cross over)

Right hand stays in position on repeated note.

PERCUSSION INSTRUMENTS WITH INDEFINITE PITCH

Bells and xylophones are examples of percussion instruments with *definite* pitch. The classroom percussion instruments described next differ in tone color and produce contrasts in duration (long-short), dynamics (loud-soft), and pitch register (higher-lower), though their sounds have *indefinite* pitch.

Agogo Bells

Agogo bells produce a ringing sound when struck with a small metal beater. Each bell has a different, but indefinite pitch.

Agogo bells

Bongo Drums

Bongos are pairs of small drums of different size and sound. They are usually played while seated, with the drums held between the knees. Strike the drums with the tips of the first and second fingers of each hand. Different sounds can be obtained by striking various areas of the heads.

Cabasa (Afuche)

The cabasa, a corrugated aluminum cylinder covered with metal beads, is played by rotating the cylinder. Hold the rounded section in one hand and turn the handle to obtain the scraping produced as the metallic "beads" rub against the cylinder.

Casaba

Castanets

Castanets are made from hollowed hardwood or plastic "shells" mounted on a stick. Hold the stick in one hand and shake or snap it for moderate volume. Tap the handle just back of the castanet with the fingers of the other hand for soft passages.

Castanets

Claves (CLAH-*vehs*)

Claves are round, hardwood sticks. Medium size orchestral claves are about 1 inch thick and 9 inches in length. Hold one hand in a cupped position with the palm facing up. Rest one clave on the thumb and fingers of the cupped hand and strike it with the other clave. (The cupped hand serves as a resonator.)

Claves

Coconut Shells

Tap two coconut halves against the floor or a board to produce an imitation of galloping horses.

Conga Drum

The conga drum has a single head mounted on a cylindrical shell about 28 inches deep, and produces a deep sound. It is played with cupped hands or with flat fingers.

Cowbell

Hold the cowbell in the left hand with the open end facing right. Strike with a stick. Different areas of the cowbell give different tones.

Cymbals

Grasp the cymbal straps firmly, one in each hand. To play a crash, hold one cymbal stationary and pass the face of the other against it with a glancing blow. Do not hit them directly together as if clapping your hands.

Finger Cymbals

These small cymbals produce high sounds of indefinite pitch. When playing two together, strike the upper surface of the edge of one with the under surface of the edge of the other.

Gong

Gongs are large discs of heavy, hammered metal. Strike the gong with a felt beater. The softer the beater, the softer the tone. Strike *near* the center, not dead center.

Gong

Guiro (GWEE-*rob*)

This is a gourd with ridges cut in its surface that is played by scraping it with a stick.

Guiro

Hand Drum

The hand drum has a round frame and a single drum head. Hold the frame at waist level with one hand and strike it with the fingertips of the other. To avoid monotony, vary the section of the head that is struck. Also, strike with the base of the thumb or alternate the fingertips and thumb.

Hand drum and triangle

Jingle Clogs

Jingle clogs—metal disks mounted on a stick—are held in one hand and shaken, or struck against the other hand to make a jingling sound.

Maracas (mah-RAH-*kabs*)

These Latin American instruments are gourds with pebbles or dried seeds inside. Shake the maracas with a sharp wrist motion to make the pebbles or seeds strike against the shell wall.

Maracas

Rattles (Chocallo)

This tube, filled with seeds or shot, is played by shaking it in a circular motion.

Rhythm Sticks

Rhythm sticks, often made from dowels, are smooth or narrow sticks that can be struck together. Like the guiro, the ridged sticks can produce a scraping sound.

Rhythm sticks

Sand Blocks

Rough-textured sandpaper attached to wooden blocks produces a louder sound than finer grades of sandpaper. Play by rubbing two sand blocks together.

Sleigh Bells

These bells are attached to a strap and produce a jingling sound when shaken.

Tambourine

Hold the tambourine with one hand and strike it with the fingertips, palm, or knuckles of the other. Move the free hand to the tambourine, not vice-versa. For very soft or rapid playing, place the instrument (rim up) on a soft pad and strike the rim lightly with the fingers of both hands. Shake the instrument to get a tremolo.

Temple Blocks

Temple blocks, carved from wood, are mounted on a stand. Each block is a different size and has a slit in the center. When struck, the smaller temple blocks produce a higher sound than the larger, lower ones.

Triangle

Suspend the triangle from a cord that is clamped to a music rack held in one hand. Strike the triangle on the side opposite the open end with a metal beater. Control the dynamic level by using heavier or lighter beaters and by striking with different amounts of force.

Triangle

Woodblock

Place the woodblock on a table with a pad underneath to stop extra noise. The long tone-slot should be toward the top of the block, facing the player. Strike the center of the top surface with a medium hard rubber tip xylophone mallet.

Two-tone woodblock

Other unpitched percussion instruments, including chime trees, log drums, ratchets, sirens, and slapsticks, to name but a few, may be found in the music classroom. Use the classified index found in any of the classroom music series to locate additional information and teaching suggestions for instrumental activities at each grade level.

Icons may be substituted for names of percussion instruments on the music score.

Classroom instruments		Orff notation	Classroom instruments		Orff notation
	triangle	△		maracas	
	cow bell			rattles	∅
	wood block	⊟		sand block	
	claves	✕		bongo drums	⊡—⊡
	hand drum	○		tambourine	

Teachers will find many Orff instrument pieces for the classroom in Shirley McRae's *Playtime* (Memphis Musicraft Publications, 3149 Southern Ave, Memphis, TN 38111) and in the many publications listed in appendix 6.

LEARNING TO PLAY INSTRUMENTS

To play an instrument, children need to acquire a concept of the desired sound and develop the physical responses needed to produce the sound.

Build concepts of sound and physical movement by providing a model to imitate. Explain how to produce the desired result, help children as they make provisional tries, and guide them in their subsequent practice.

The beginner's first attempts may be far from the desired result, but reinforcement of correct responses over a period of time should help the child fill in the details of good performance. Here are some suggestions:

1. Let the musical menu consist primarily of genuine, expressive music. Provide relevant exercises and study materials as needed to build skills necessary for expressive music making.
2. Start with music that is easy enough to be learned quickly. Success is reinforcing and contributes to motivation that produces further learning. Stress fundamentals before advancing to subtle aspects of performance. Be sure your instruction is consistent with what you know about the physical, mental, and emotional characteristics of the age group.
3. Provide for ample practice before introducing new chords, new fingerings, or more complicated skills. Small amounts of daily practice are more effective than large amounts of practice at irregular intervals. Don't try to teach everything there is to know about a particular song in one lesson, but do use a concept or a song in varying contexts. When you come back to a song another day, add something new to what has been learned in earlier lessons.
4. Keep the children involved. Ask children what they think they need to practice. Make them responsible for their own learning. For example, use sound gestures to prepare for playing instrument accompaniment parts.

highest sound	finger snap
high sound	clap
low sound	patschen
lowest sound	stamp

At first, compare only two different pitches. Later, match pitch registers to instruments (e.g., snap = triangle), practice "sound gestures," then transfer each gesture to the corresponding instrument. Everyone can practice the sound gestures, then take turns playing the instruments.

5. Include individual, small-group, and large-group experiences so as to increase opportunities for musical growth and provide a high level of motivation. Opportunities for individual responses make instruction more effective, and allow children to show others what they can do. Encourage capable students to demonstrate skills and assist students who need additional help.

6. Combine and coordinate experiences in singing, playing, listening, reading, writing, experimenting, and moving to music. Even the simplest song may offer a large number of interesting learning experiences.

7. Some students prefer visual, aural, or tactile learning modes. Lessons involving sight, sound, and touch are likely to have broader appeal and greater impact than lessons based on only one learning mode. Singing, chanting rhythms, playing instruments, reading music, movement activities, and guided discussion are all useful possibilities. Learning aids such as charts, filmstrips, films, flannel boards, posters, pictures, recordings, and tape recorders can build interest and increase learning.

8. Introduce notation *after* students have acquired basic playing techniques. Even adult learners find it difficult to concentrate on details of notation at the same time they are attempting to master a new chord or fingering on an instrument.

9. Focus on one thing at a time, but help students find relationships between old and new learnings.

LISTENING AND TONE COLOR

Benjamin Britten's *The Young Person's Guide to the Orchestra* offers a rewarding and worthwhile listening experience for children in the upper elementary grades as well as for adults.

BENJAMIN BRITTEN: *The Young Person's Guide to the Orchestra*

Benjamin Britten's *The Young Person's Guide to the Orchestra* (written in 1946) begins with a theme composed much earlier by Henry Purcell (1659–1695). Originally written for the film, *The Instruments of the Orchestra,* the work may be presented to children in several ways. The 1947 film has the London Symphony Orchestra with conductor Sir Malcolm Sargent as commentator. More recent recordings include one with Antal Dorati as conductor and Sean Connery as narrator as well as recordings without narrator. For computer-assisted learning, "The Orchestra," a CD-ROM version of Britten's composition, is available from Warner Audio. It has 500 extra CD audio examples and on-screen commentary. Your school's instructional materials center may have it.

The following is a brief guide to the work:

> **Theme** (heard six times): (1) full orchestra, (2) woodwinds, (3) brasses, (4) strings, (5) percussion, (6) full orchestra. Presentation of the instruments of each family (13 variations):
> *woodwinds:* (1) flutes and piccolo, (2) oboes, (3) clarinets, (4) bassoons
> *strings:* (5) first and second violins, (6) violas, (7) cellos, (8) double basses, (9) harp
> *brass:* (10) French horns, (11) trumpets, (12) trombones, tuba
> *percussion:* (13) timpani, bass drum, cymbals, tambourine, triangle, snare drum, woodblock, xylophone, castanets, gong, whip

Related Listening: *The Young Person's Guide to the Orchestra*, New York Philharmonic, Leonard Bernstein, conductor. Narrated by Master Henry Chapin, Columbia M 31808. See also *Holt Music*, Grade 6, *Music and You*, Grade 6, or *World of Music*, Grade 6. Without narration: The Philadelphia Orchestra, Eugene Ormandy, conductor, RCA ARL1–2743.

Fugue: a new melody by Benjamin Britten is presented and imitated by each instrumental family, then it is heard in combination with the original theme by Purcell.

Distribution of Instruments in a Modern Orchestra

Woodwinds:

2 to 4 flutes and piccolo
2 to 4 oboes and English
  horn
2 to 4 clarinets
2 to 4 bassoons

Piano: 1

**(occasionally used as an
  orchestral instrument)**

Brass:

2 to 8 French horns
2 to 4 trumpets
2 to 3 trombones
1 to 2 tubas

Strings:

12 to 16 first violins
12 to 16 second
  violins
8 to 12 violas
6 to 10 cellos
4 to 9 double
  basses

Percussion:

2 to 5 timpani (played by
  one player),cymbals,
  triangle, snare drum,
  bass drum, gongs,
  xylophone (played by 2
  to 3 players)

Harp: 1 to 2

Twentieth-century composers have expanded the range of sounds heard in music by calling for special playing techniques with traditional instruments, by using instruments from non-Western cultures, and by introducing new electronic instruments and computer technology.

Related Listening: "The Banshee," *Holt Music,* Grade 3, *World of Music,* Grade 2, *Music and You,* Grade 3; cassette tape: Cowell, *Piano Music,* Finnadar CS-9016. A filmstrip and cassette are available from Educational Audio Visual.

HENRY COWELL: "THE BANSHEE"

Unconventional performance techniques help make "The Banshee" by American composer Henry Cowell (1897–1965) a captivating work for listeners of all ages. It is played by two performers: one stands at the curve of a grand piano, reaching inside to play on the open strings; a seated performer holds down the damper pedal of the piano so that the strings continue to vibrate when activated. The title of the work refers to an Irish ghost, or "banshee." The musical score for "The Banshee" is printed in *The Schirmer Scores, A Repertory of Western Music* by Joscelyn Godwin (New York: Macmillan, 1975). Henry Cowell's composition illustrates unusual sounds and "program music"—music that refers to something extramusical.

GUNTHER SCHULLER "THE TWITTERING MACHINE"

Lasting only two minutes, "The Twittering Machine" is music without a definite tonal center and it features unusual instrumental sounds: flutter-tonguing on trumpet, glissando on trombone, woodwind "twittering," and short sounds from woodblocks, gourd, and other instruments, all combined to portray the twittering machine (*Die Zwitschermaschine*) that is the subject of Paul Klee's painting. (The painting, part of the collection at the Museum of Modern Art, is reproduced in a color illustration in *Music And You,* Grade 3.)

Related Listening: Gunther Schuller: "The Twittering Machine" from *Seven Studies on Themes of Paul Klee, Music and You,* Grade 3, or Mercury CD 434 329–2.

SOUNDS AND PROGRAM MUSIC

Program music is music that tells a story or refers to an extramusical event. A lesson related to the sounds of rain and thunder combines tone color and program music. Any of a number of rhymes or songs about rain might be used as an introduction. ("Doctor Foster went to Gloucester," "Eency Weency Spider," "It's Raining, It's Pouring," "Rain, Rain, Go Away," and so forth.

> *It's raining, it's pouring.*
> *The old man is snoring,*
> *He went to bed*
> *With a cold in his head,*
> *And he won't get up 'till morning.*

Invite children to create non-vocal sounds that imitate the sounds of a rain storm. Focus on its beginning, climax, and gradual ending. Begin with soft sounds and a few scattered raindrops; let the storm become more intense and then fade away. Help the children discover how sounds such as hands rubbing together, soft clapping and patting, or foot stamps can imitate the storm. Next, let them transfer their ideas to percussion instruments representing the rain, wind, and thunder. Group the children according to their sound and let student conductors take turns directing the rise and fall of the storm sequence. Listen to orchestral works that depict storms (three are listed here) and discuss the orchestral sounds that were used to represent the storm.

Related Listening: Ludwig van Beethoven: *Symphony No. 6,* Fourth Movement, CBS MY 36720. Ferde Grofé: *Grand Canyon Suite,* Fifth Movement ("Cloudburst") or *Music and You,* Grade 4, or Grofé, *Grand Canyon Suite:* CD, RCA Victor 09026–61667–2. Hector Berlioz: *Fantastic Symphony,* Second Movement, *Bowmar Orchestral Library,* no. 61, or DG 410895–1GH.

SUGGESTED ACTIVITIES

1. Working with a partner, sing or play the melody of a song on the recorder or bells. Add an accompaniment, using Autoharp, guitar, piano, or percussion instruments.
2. Learn to recognize the barred instruments (glockenspiels, xylophones, metallophones) by sight and range (soprano, alto, and bass).
3. Prepare tone bar instruments to play in C, F, or G pentatonic. Create ostinato or bordun patterns as accompaniment to a pentatonic song.
4. Teach a student to play major, minor, and pentatonic scales on the recorder or bells "by ear" and from notation.
5. Play familiar melodies by ear on recorder, piano, or barred instruments.

NOTES

[1]Duke, Robert A., "Beat and Tempo in Music: Differences in Teachers' and Students' Perceptions." *Update,* 9 (Fall-Winter 1990): 8–12.

[2]Patricia E. Sink, "Research on Beat Performance and Perception Skills: Music Teaching Strategies for Developing Rhythmic Competency," *Southeastern Journal of Music Education,* 1 (1989), 1–18.

[3]The initials "MM" refer not to candy but to "Maelzel's Metronome," named after Johannes Maelzel, who patented the device. Composers including Beethoven and Ligetti have written compositions related to the metronome. Beethoven wrote a humorous metronome song, which he later used as a theme in his *Symphony No. Eight* (1812). The contemporary composer Gyorgy Ligetti has written a piece (*Poeme symphonique*) for 100 metronomes beating different tempos.

[4]Uses for the metronome include establishing the tempo indicated, using the metronome to develop a more accurate sense of divided beats (counting two, three, or four sounds to a beat), or learning complicated rhythms by taking the shortest note value as the beat and adding up the durations of longer notes in relation to the shortest value.

[5]Consult *The Guinness Book of World Records* (New York: Sterling Publishing Co.) to determine the latest record for the largest game of musical chairs. There were 1,789 participants in a 1977 game held in Utah.

[6]One TV entertainer uses the song in a routine involving airport paging systems, imagining that everyone at the terminal eventually responds with "That's my name, too."

[7]Approximate figures for levels of sound intensity in decibels are: 0-the threshold of hearing, 10-normal breathing, 20-a quiet whisper from 5 feet, 60-background music, 100-a subway train, 105-a peak level for an orchestral concert, 115-amplified rock music.

[8]*Harper's* magazine reports that a major automobile maker helps its service departments identify noises in order to diagnose mechanical problems. A *click* is a light sound, like the click of a ballpoint pen. A squeal is like the sound of "fingernails across a chalkboard." (Teachers will be pleased to learn that their occupation may offer preparation for careers in automobile service departments.) *Harper's* magazine, August 1993, p. 14.

[9]See *Musical Instruments of the World, An Illustrated Encyclopedia,* for a publication with more than 4,000 drawings of instruments of all types from all around the world. (Paddington Press, Ltd, Two Continents Publishing Group, The Diagram Group, 1976).

[10]Orff theory and curriculum are described with exceptional clarity in the following publications: *Discovering Orff* by Jane Frazee with Kent Kreuter (New York: Schott Music Corp., 1987) and *Exploring Orff, A Teacher's Guide* by Arvida Steen (New York: Schott Music Corp., 1992).

*L*ISTENING TO MUSIC 7

Listening is the basis for every musical activity. Singing, playing instruments, moving to music, composing, and music reading all depend on listening to sounds which may be audible or heard inwardly.[2]

Recordings and videotapes are essential components of the K-8 music series for each grade, and they include a wide range of music of many times, places, styles, and cultures along with guides to assist the teacher. The richness of choice made possible by modern technology is accompanied by the danger that children saturated by background music have learned to ignore it . . . and other music as well.

"Repetition is the key to making a succession of tones magically become a melody in the mind."[1]

LEARNING TO LISTEN

The skilled listener perceives and responds to the significant details that make music expressive. Research indicates that children and teenage listeners prefer popular music with an obvious beat, especially fast, loud instrumental music.[3] (Some teenagers listen to music at such high levels that loudness is its chief attribute—loudness that destroys hearing by damaging the ear's cochlear hair cells, causing deafness in young people.)[4]

Improved listening skills help children perceive what makes music expressive and expand their knowledge of the many different types of music available to them. The following suggestions offer guidelines for instruction in music listening.

- Include music of all styles, periods, and cultures in your classroom. Choose music of lasting value that is suited to the children's age level.
- Match the length of the listening experience to the child's attention span. Begin with short examples. Divide longer works into shorter sections. Come back another day, like a continued program on television.
- Be prepared. Get acquainted with the listening selection before introducing it in the classroom. Structure your lessons to progress from the obvious to the subtle, from familiar to unfamiliar, from simple to complex. Avoid too much that is new in one lesson or during one week. Depth and breadth are needed.
- Guide children's listening. Give them something specific to listen for. (For example, before playing a recording, use questions to focus attention.) Familiar melodies have a special attraction, and melody is often the center of attention, but instruction in listening should call attention to all the expressive components of music.
- The perceptive listener concentrates on music for its own sake, rather than as a mere background to nonmusical activities.
- The principles of musical form—unity, variety, and balance—are valid in planning lessons. Unify lessons by selecting some pieces for repeated listening. Vary the listening activities to maintain a high level of interest. Strike a balance among activities (listening, moving, performing, etc.) in order to promote comprehensive musical experiences.

- Integrate listening into the total musical experience, and relate it to other activities in the child's life in school and out of school.

- Accept children's verbal or nonverbal responses. It may be easier for them to show what they hear or to use their own terms—but guide them to standard musical terminology.

- Familiarity breeds enjoyment. Listeners say they "know what they like and like what they know," but meaningful experiences with unfamiliar types of music lead to an expanded range of musical tastes. As the saying goes, "That's why they make ice cream in different flavors."

SIGNIFICANT MUSICAL DETAILS

Guided listening helps to direct the child's attention to significant musical details. The following chart outlines some of these details.

Tone color	Instruments, voices, solo, small group, large group
Rhythm	Beat: strong, weak, none
	Meter: groups of twos, threes, or combinations of twos and threes
	Rhythm patterns: even, uneven, syncopated
Melody	Contour: smooth, jagged
	Direction: higher, lower, repeated tones
	Movement: steps, skips, combination of steps and skips
	Register: low, middle, high
	Pitch range: wide, narrow
	Scale type: major, minor, pentatonic, non-tonal, etc.
Harmony	Relation of melody and chords (accompaniment)
	Number of chord changes, types of chords
	Consonance—dissonance
Texture	Melody alone (monophonic)
	Combined melodic lines—rounds, canons (polyphonic)
	Melody with accompaniment (homophonic)
Form	Structure: motive, phrase, AB, ABA, ABACA, etc.
	Repetition (exact, varied, sequences, contrast)
	Introduction, interlude, coda
Expression	Tempo: slow, medium, fast, getting faster or slower
	Dynamics: soft, medium, loud, getting louder or softer
	Articulation: separated sounds, connected sounds
	Text: subject matter, relation to the music
Style	Music of different times and places
	Type: folk, popular, classical, etc.

EQUIPMENT AND CONDITIONS FOR MUSIC LISTENING

Experiences in listening to recorded music are enhanced by high quality listening materials and equipment. Your school may provide a phonograph and LP records, a tape player and cassette tapes, or compact discs and equipment. In any event, learn how to operate the playback equipment efficiently.

Before presenting the lesson note the location of the desired selection (for example: "*World of Music,* Grade 2, disc one track 17" or "record 5, side 2, band 7"). Playing the desired listening selection is relatively simple with compact discs and less so with tapes and LP records. Find the desired starting point on cassette tapes before class begins, in order to avoid time-consuming and distracting winding and rewinding during class.

Select a volume level that is audible throughout the room but not so loud as to be uncomfortable for the listeners. Test the level from the children's location as well as the way it sounds from your location.

THE TEACHER'S ROLE

Your involvement, enthusiasm, excitement, and interest set the example for the students. Observations of teachers in classrooms indicate that, like most people, we talk too much. Don't talk during the music, and don't yell out informative tidbits about the music while it is playing. ("Here comes the part I told you to listen for!") Listen with the students, without strolling around the room. Terence Dwyer puts it this way in *Teaching Music Appreciation:* "[The teacher] must learn the art of apparently listening with downcast gaze and rapt attention to the music whilst he keeps a surreptitious eye on his class to be sure that all is well. If someone does misbehave, he will get a direct stare and be dealt with afterwards."[5] Don't read a book, or use the time to grade papers.

Emphasize perception rather than liking or disliking the music. Liking a piece of music often comes with getting to know it. Later on will be soon enough for passing judgment.

Don't try to teach everything in one lesson. Limit information to what is relevant in terms of your objectives. The composer's name and date of birth are not unimportant, for example, but the information may not be needed during this particular lesson.

Extramusical information has its place, as in explaining the origins of a patriotic song, or the story that goes with a piece of program music, but lessons about music should be . . . about music.

PROGRAM MUSIC

Music for children includes program music and "absolute music"—music that has no specific associations. Grofé's *Grand Canyon Suite,* Saint-Saëns' *Carnival of the Animals,* Prokofiev's *Peter and the Wolf,* and Gershwin's *An American in Paris* are examples of program music. The extramusical elements of program music usually don't require much explanation. Therefore, in teaching program music help children discover how the composer creates the musical effect: what is it in the music that suggests thunder, kangaroos, a wolf and duck, or taxi horns in Paris? Don't attempt to turn all music into program music by making up stories where no story was intended by the composer. Bennett Reimer, the author of *A Philosophy of Music Education,* comments as follows on the detrimental effects of emphasis on the extramusical:

> *Some people have the idea that nonmusical experiences are appropriate for younger children and can be phased out as the children grow older. What this says, in effect, is, "Let us make sure that we start children out on the wrong foot. Let us teach them, at the most impressionable time of their lives, that music is not an art, that they should experience music nonmusically, that the more nonmusical they become now the more likely it is they will become musical later."[6]*

APPROACHES TO MUSIC LISTENING

Research on methods of teaching music listening to children in grades K-6 indicates that repeated listening to a work increases students' understanding and enjoyment of the music, but programmed learning materials and techniques such as projecting themes onto a screen do *not* seem to produce better results than "traditional" methods of teaching.[7] In *Lessons From the World, A Cross-Cultural Guide to Music Teaching and Learning,* Patricia Shehan Campbell says, "Music instruction might be conceived of as a balance of receptive-passive and participatory-active experiences."[8] Listening to recordings, on the receptive side of the equation, can be joined to related musical activities (singing, moving, playing instruments, and so forth) to balance the receptive and participatory modes of learning.

Combining listening with singing and playing offers a multi-sensory approach that is active, not passive. In the classroom you can use works that invite children to participate by singing or by playing tonal or rhythm patterns found in listening selections. Not every listening selection can be sung or played, of course, but the technique can be used a great deal. Composer Zoltán Kodály was convinced that this type of active learning is beneficial:

> *The singing of a Vivaldi theme, or the simple singing of the principal themes, brings the individual closer to the entire work than the best formal analysis.*[9]

Students can perform melodies and then listen to compositions that incorporate the melodies as themes. The following list of familiar melodies quoted by well-known composers will help you identify some of the many compositions that are available for participatory listening activities.

Themes and Melodies Quoted by Composers of Longer Works

Song Title	Composer/Title	Recording
Adeste Fidelis ("O Come All Ye Faithful")	Charles Ives: "*Adeste Fidelis* in an Organ Prelude" (1897)	BIS CD 510
"Alexander's Ragtime Band"	John Alden Carpenter: *Adventures in a Perambulator*—"Hurdy Gurdy"	Mercury Living Presence 434–219–2 MM or *Holt Music*, Grade 2 (Holt, Rinehart and Winston)
"All the Pretty Little Horses"	Aaron Copland: *Old American Songs*	CBS MK-42430
"America" ("God Save the King")	Ludwig van Beethoven: *Wellington's Victory*	Mercury 416–448–2
"America" ("God Save the King")	Ludwig van Beethoven: *Variations on "God Save the King,"* Opus 34	Vox CD 3X 3017
"America" ("God Save the King")	Claude Debussy: *Preludes for Piano*, Book 2, No. 9 ("Pickwick")	Philips 420 394 2 PH
"America" ("God Save the King")	Charles Ives: *Variations on "America"*	Argo 421 731–2 ZH
"America" ("God Save the King")	Muzio Clementi: *Symphony No. 3*	ASV DCA 803
"Arkansas Traveler"	David Guion: "Arkansas Traveler"	*Bowmar Orchestral Library* No. 56 (*Dances, Part II*)
"The Ash Grove"	Benjamin Britten: "The Ash Grove"	Marquis ERAD 127 or Etcetera KTC 1046
"Auld Lang Syne"	Ludwig van Beethoven: "Auld Lang Syne"	Channel Classics CCS 1491
"Austrian Hymn"	Franz Joseph Haydn: String Quartet, Opus 76, No. 3 ("Emperor")	Teldec 44081 AS
"Austrian Hymn"	Franz Joseph Haydn: *Lieder*, Elly Ameling, Soprano, Jorg Demus, Piano	Philips 420217–2 PH
"Battle Hymn of the Republic"	Morton Gould: *Battle Hymn*	*Brass and Percussion*, RCA Victor 09026–61255–2
"The Bear Went Over the Mountain" (For He's a Jolly Good Fellow")	Ludwig van Beethoven: *Wellington's Victory*	Mercury 416–448–2
"The Bear Went Over the Mountain" (For He's a Jolly Good Fellow")	Virgil Thomson: *Symphony on a Hymn Tune*	Mercury 434–310–2MM

Song Title	Composer/Title	Recording
"The Bear Went Over the Mountain" (For He's a Jolly Good Fellow")	Virgil Thomson: *Suite* from *The River* (Fourth Movement)	Vanguard Classics OVC 8013
"The Birch Tree"	Peter Tchaikovsky: *Symphony No. 4* (Fourth Movement)	CBS MK-44911 or *Holt Music,* Grade 4, (Holt, Rinehart and Winston)
"Black Is the Color of My True Love's Hair"	Roy Harris: *American Ballads for Piano*	Etcetera KTC 1036
"Black Is the Color of My True Love's Hair"	Luciano Berio: *Folk Songs*	London CD 425832–2LH
"The Boatman"	Aaron Copland: *Old American Songs*	CBS MK-42430
"Bought Me a Cat"	Aaron Copland: *Old American Songs*	CBS MK-42430
"Camptown Races"	Aaron Copland: *A Lincoln Portrait*	*Bowmar Orchestral Library,* No. 75 (*U.S. History in Music*) or Telarc CD-80117
"Camptown Races"	Charles Ives: *Symphony No. 2* (Fifth Movement)	*Bowmar Orchestral Library,* No. 65 (*Music, U.S.A.*) or Sony Classical, SMK 47568
"Camptown Races"	Louis M. Gottschalk: "The Banjo"	Nimbus CD NI5014
"Charlie Is My Darling"	Ludwig van Beethoven: Folk Song Arrangements	Channel Classics CD CCS 1491
"Chester" (Revolutionary War melody)	William Schuman: *New England Triptych* (Third Movement)	*Bowmar Orchestral Library* No. 75 (*U.S. History in Music*) or Mercury Living Presence CD 432755–2
"Cindy"	Lyndal Mitchell: *Kentucky Mountain Portraits*	Mercury Living Presence 434–324–2MM
"Columbia the Gem of the Ocean"	Charles Ives: *Symphony No. 2* (Fifth Movement)	*Bowmar Orchestral Library,* No. 65 (Music, U.S.A.) or Sony Classical, SMK 47568
"Columbia the Gem of the Ocean"	Charles Ives: "The Fourth of July" (from *Symphony: Holidays*)	CRI C-180
"Come Follow Me"	William Schuman: *Concerto on Old English Rounds*	Columbia M 35101 (LP record)
"Dixie"	Ernst Bloch: *America*	Vanguard Classics OVC 8014
"Dixie"	Virgil Thomson: *Suite* from *The River*	Vanguard OVC 8013
"East Side, West Side"	Aaron Copland: *Music for the Theater*	DG CD431672–2GH
"The Farmer in the Dell"	Edwin Franko Goldman: *Children's March*	Mercury Living Presence 432–019–2MM or *Holt Music,* Grade 1, (Holt, Rinehart and Winston)
"The Farmer in the Dell"	Harl McDonald: *Children's Symphony* (Third Movement)	*Holt Music,* Grade 1, Holt, Rinehart and Winston
Frère Jacques ("Are You Sleeping?")	*Brother John and the Village Orchestra*	Bowmar Records
Frère Jacques ("Are You Sleeping?")	Gustav Mahler: *Symphony No. 1* (Third Movement)	*Bowmar Orchestral Library* No. 62 (*Masters in Music*) or London 411731–2LH
"Funiculi, Funicula"	Richard Strauss: *Aus Italien*	London CD 425941–2LH

Continued

Song Title	Composer/Title	Recording
"Gaudeamus igitur" (German student song)	Johannes Brahms: *Academic Festival Overture*	Sony Classical CD SMK47538 or *Bowmar Orchestral Library*, No. 76 (*Overtures*)
"The Girl I Left Behind Me"	LeRoy Anderson: *Irish Suite*	Mercury 432013–2FM
"The Girl I Left Behind Me"	Roy Harris: *Folksong Symphony*, 1940 (First Movement)	Vanguard Classics OVC 4076
"Git Along Little Dogies"	Aaron Copland: *Billy the Kid*	Sony Classical CD SMK 47543
"Git Along Little Dogies"	Virgil Thomson: "Cattle" from *The Plow That Broke the Plains*	*Bowmar Orchestral Library* No. 65 (*Music U.S.A.*) or Vanguard Classics OVC 8013
"Goodbye Old Paint"	Aaron Copland: *Billy the Kid*	Sony Classical CD SMK 47543
"Good Night, Ladies"	Charles Ives: "Washington's Birthday" from *Symphony: Holidays*	CD Vox CDX 5035
"Go Tell Aunt Rhody"	Virgil Thomson: Suite from *The River*	Vanguard Classics OVC 8013
"Great Grandad"	Aaron Copland: *Billy the Kid*	Sony Classical CD SMK 47543
"Greensleeves"	Feruccio Busoni: *Turandot's Boudoir*	Arcadia CD MAD 015
"Greensleeves"	Ralph Vaughan Williams: *Fantasia on Greensleeves*	CBS MYK 38484 or *Holt Music*, Grade 6, (Holt, Rinehart and Winston)
"Greensleeves"	Gustav Holst: *Second Suite in F Opus 28, No. 2* (Fourth Movement: Fantasia on the "Dargason")	Telarc CD 80038
"Hail Columbia"	Ernest Bloch: *America*	Vanguard Classics OVC 8014
"Hail Columbia"	Charles Ives: "Putnams' Camp" from *Three Places in New England*	*Bowmar Orchestral Library* No. 75 (*U.S. History in Music*) or DG423243–2 GC
"Hail Columbia"	Louis M. Gottschalk: *The Union*	Vanguard Classics CD OVC 4051
"Hail, Hail, the Gang's All Here"	Sir Arthur Sullivan: "Come Friends" (*The Pirates of Penzance*)	EMI Classics 2 CDMB 64409
"Happy Birthday to You"	Igor Stravinsky: *Greeting Prelude*	*Holt Music*, Grade 3 (Holt, Rinehart and Winston or MusicMasters Classics) 01612–67113–2
"Hatikvah" (Varmeland)	Bedrich Smetana: *The Moldau*	*Bowmar Orchestral Library*, No. 60 (*Under Many Flags*)
"Hickory, Dickory Dock"	Edwin Franko Goldman: *Children's March*	Mercury Living Presence 432–019–2MM or *Holt Music*, Grade I (Holt, Rinehart and Winston)
"Hop Up, My Ladies"	Roy Harris: *Folk Song Symphony*, 1940 (Fifth Movement)	Vanguard Classics OVC 4076
"Hop Up, My Ladies"	Roy Harris: *American Ballads for Piano*	Etcetera KTC 1036
"Hot Cross Buns"	F. W. Scott: "Variations on Hot Cross Buns"	*Holt Music*, Grade 4 (Holt, Rinehart and Winston)

Song Title	Composer/Title	Recording
"Hot Time in the Old Town Tonight"	Virgil Thomson: Suite from *The River*	Vanguard Classics OVC 8013
"How Dry I Am"	Charles Ives: *Trio for Violin Cello and Piano* (Second Movement)	CRI CD 583
"How Firm a Foundation"	Virgil Thomson: *Symphony on a Hymn Tune*	Mercury 434–310–2MM
"If You're Happy and You Know It"	Virgil Thomson: Suite from *The River*	Vanguard Classics OVC 8013
"I'll Love My Love"	Gustav Holst: *Second Suite in F,* Opus 28, No. 2 (Second Movement:"Song Without Words")	Telarc CD 80038
"I'm Going to Leave Old Texas Now" ("Bury Me Not on the Lone Prairie")	Roy Harris: *Folksong Symphony,* 1940 (Second Movement)	Vanguard Classics OVC 4076
"I'm Just a Poor Wayfaring Stranger"	Roy Harris: *American Ballads for Piano*	Etcetera KTC 1036
"I Ride an Old Paint"	Elie Siegmeister: *Western Suite*	Vox Allegretto ACD 8155
"I Ride an Old Paint"	Virgil Thomson: "Cattle" (*The Plow That Broke the Plains*)	*Bowmar Orchestral Library* No. 65 (*Music, U.S.A.*) or Vanguard Classics OVC 4076
"I Wonder As I Wander"	Luciano Berio: *Folk Songs*	London CD 425832–2LH
"Jesu, Joy of Man's Desiring"	Johann Sebastian Bach: Cantata 147, *Herz und Mund und Tat und Leben*	Teldec CD 356542L
"Jesu, Joy of Man's Desiring"	Wendy Carlos: *Switched on Bach* (electronic synthesizer)	Telarc CD-80323
"Jingle Bells"	Edwin Franko Goldman: *Children's March*	Mercury Living Presence 432–019–2MM or *Holt Music,* Grade 1, (Holt, Rinehart and Winston)
"Jingle Bells"	Harl McDonald: *Children's Symphony* (Third Movement)	*Holt Music,* Grade 1 (Holt, Rinehart and Winston)
"Jingle Bells"	Charles Ives: *Trio for Violin, Cello and Piano*	CRI CD 583
"Joy to the World"	Charles Ives: *Symphony No. 2* (Fifth Movement)	*Bowmar Orchestral Library,* No. 65 (*Music, U.S.A.*) or Sony Classical, SMK 47568
"La Cucaracha"	Robert McBride: *Mexican Rhapsody*	Mercury Living Presence 434–324–2MM
"Land of Hope and Glory" (graduation march melody)	Edward Elgar: *Pomp and Circumstance* No. 1	*Bowmar Orchestral Library* No. 54 (*Marches*)
"Listen to the Mockingbird"	The Chestnut Brass Company	Newport NPD 85516
"London Bridge"	Edwin Franko Goldman: *Children's March*	Mercury Living Presence 432–019–2MM or *Holt Music,* Grade 1, (Holt, Rinehart and Winston)
"London Bridge"	Harl McDonald: *Children's Symphony* (First Movement)	*Holt Music,* Grade I (Holt, Rinehart and Winston)
"London Bridge"	John Alden Carpenter: "The HurdyGurdy" (*Adventures in a Perambulator*)	Mercury Living Presence CD 434–319–2 MM
"Londonderry Air" ("Danny Boy")	Percy Grainger: *Irish Tune from County Derry*	*Bowmar Orchestral Library* No. 65 (*Under Many Flags*) or Telarc CD-80059 (St. Louis Symphony Orchestra, Leonard Slatkin, Conductor)

Continued

Song Title	Composer/Title	Recording
"Long, Long Ago"	Charles Ives: *Symphony No. 2* (Fifth Movement)	*Bowmar Orchestral Library*, No. 65 (*Music, U.S.A.*) or Sony Classical, SMK 47568
"Long, Long Ago"	Charles Ives: *Trio for Violin, Cello, and Piano*	CRI-CD 583
"Mack the Knife"	Kurt Weill: *The Threepenny Opera*	London CD 430075–2LH
"March of the Three Kings"	George Bizet: "Farandole" (*L'Arlesienne Suite No. 2*)	Sony Classical CD SMK-47531
"Marseillaise, La"	Peter Tchaikovsky: *Overture, 1812*	CBS CD MLK 39433
"Marseillaise, La"	Edward Elgar: *The Music Makers*	EMI Classics CDCC-54560
"Mary Had a Little Lamb"	Edwin Franko Goldman: *Children's March*	Mercury Living Presence 432–019–2MM or *Holt Music*, Grade 1, (Holt, Rinehart and Winston)
"The Metronome" (To Maelzel)	Ludwig van Beethoven: Symphony No. 8 (Third Movement)	London CD 425525–2LH
"The Metronome" (To Maelzel)	*The Comic Beethoven*	Seraphim S 60180 (LP)
"Mexican Hat Dance"	Robert McBride: *Mexican Rhapsody*	Mercury Living Presence 434–324–2MM
"A Mighty Fortress Is Our God" (*Ein' feste Burg*)	Johann Sebastian Bach: *Cantata 80* (*Ein' feste Burg ist unser Gott*)	DG CD 427130–2AGA
"A Mighty Fortress Is Our God" (*Ein' feste Burg*)	Claude Debussy: *En blanc et noir* (II)	Music and Arts CD 709–1
"A Mighty Fortress Is Our God" (*Ein' feste Burg*)	Felix Mendelssohn: *Symphony No 5 in D Minor* (Finale)	DG CD 419870–2GGA
"Mr. Banjo"	Ernest Bloch: *America*	Vanguard Classics OVC-8014
"My Home's in Montana"	Virgil Thomson: "Cattle" (*The Plow That Broke the Plains*)	*Bowmar Orchestral Library* No. 65 (*Music, U.S.A.*) or Vanguard Classics OVC 8013
"My Old Kentucky Home"	Louis Moreau Gottschalk	Vanguard Classics CD OVC 4050
"My Old Kentucky Home"	Charles Ives: *Trio for Violin, Cello, and Piano*	CRI CD 583
"Old Chisholm Trail, The"	Aaron Copland: *Billy the Kid*	Mercury CD 434–301–2 PM
"Old Chisholm Trail, The"	Roy Harris: *Folksong Symphony* (Second Movement)	*Bowmar Orchestral Library*, No. 15 (*U.S. History in Music*) or Vanguard Classics OVC 4076
"Old Chisholm Trail, The"	Elie Siegmeister: *Western Suite*	Vox Allegretto ACD 8155
"Old Folks at Home, The"	Ernest Bloch: *America*	Vanguard Classics OVC 8014
"Old 100th" (The Doxology)	Johann Sebastian Bach: Cantata 130, *Herr Gott, dich loben alle wir*	London CD 4333175
"Old 100th" (The Doxology)	Ernest Bloch: *America*	Vanguard Classics, OVC 8014

Song Title	Composer/Title	Recording
"Old 100th" (The Doxology)	Paul Hindemith: *Trauermusik* (*Für deinen Thron Tret ich Hiermit*)	RCA Red Seal DC 60464–2-RC
"Old 100th" (The Doxology)	Henry Purcell: *Voluntary on the Doxology "Old 100th"*	Telarc CD 80218 Empire Brass
"Old 100th" (The Doxology)	Virgil Thomson: "Prelude" (*The Plow That Broke the Plains*)	Vanguard Classics, OVC 8013
"Old Joe Clark"	Charles Vardell: "Joe Clark Steps Out"	Mercury Living Presence 434–324–2MM
"On Springfield Mountain"	Aaron Copland: *A Lincoln Portrait*	*Bowmar Orchestral Library*, No. 75 (*U.S. History in Music*) or Telarc CD-80117
"Pawpaw Patch"	Lyndon Mitchell: *Kentucky Mountain Portraits*	Mercury Living Presence 434–324–2MM
"Peter, Peter, Pumpkin Eater"	Robert McBride: "Pumpkin Eater's Little Fugue"	*Bowmar Orchestral Library* No. 65 (*Music, U.S.A.*)
"Pop! Goes the Weasel"	Ernest Bloch: *America*	Vanguard Classics OVC 8014
"Pop! Goes the Weasel"	Edwin Franko Goldman: *Children's March*	Mercury Living Presence 432–019–2MM or *Holt Music*, Grade 1, (Holt, Rinehart and Winston)
"Rock-a-bye Baby"	Edwin Franko Goldman: *Children's March*	Mercury Living Presence 432–019–2MM or *Holt Music*, Grade 1, (Holt, Rinehart and Winston)
"Rule Brittania"	Ludwig van Beethoven: *Variations on Rule Brittania*	Philips 432093–2PH
"Rule Brittania"	Sir Edward Elgar: *The Music Makers*	EMI Classics CDCC 544560
"Saint Paul's Steeple"	Roger Quilter: *A Children's Overture*	Angel Studio CD CDM 64131
"*Sakura*" ("Cherry Blossoms")	*Japanese Melodies for Flute and Harp*	CBS MK34568
"Shortnin' Bread"	Morton Gould: *Spirituals for Orchestra*	Mercury Living Presence CD 432016–2MM
"Simple Gifts" (Shaker Melody)	Aaron Copland: *Appalachian Spring*	*Bowmar Orchestral Library* No. 65 (*Music, U.S.A.*) or Mercury Living Presence 434301–2MM
"Sing a Song of Sixpence"	Edwin Franko Goldman: *Children's March*	Mercury Living Presence 432–019–2MM or *Holt Music*, Grade 1, (Holt, Rinehart and Winston)
"Skip to My Lou"	Lyndon Mitchell: *Kentucky Mountain Portraits*	Mercury Living Presence 434324–2MM
"Song of the Volga Boatman"	Stravinsky: *Song of the Volga Boatman* (arr. for wind instruments)	Claves CD 50–8918
"The Star Spangled Banner"	Edwin Bagley: *National Emblem March*	RCA Victor 09026–61255–2
"The Star Spangled Banner"	Charles Ives: "Putnams' Camp" (*Three Places in New England*)	*Bowmar Orchestral Library* No. 75 (*U.S. History in Music*)
"The Star Spangled Banner"	Igor Stravinsky: "The Star Spangled Banner," (choral arrangement)	MusicMasters Classics 01612–67113–2
"The Star Spangled Banner"	Giacomo Puccini: *Madame Butterfly*	London CD 417577–2LH3

Continued

Song Title	Composer/Title	Recording
"The Star Spangled Banner"	Louis Gottschalk: *The Union*	Nimbus CD NI 5014
"The Street" (*Juilliard Repertory Library* collection)	Igor Stravinsky: "Coachman's Dance" from *Petrushka*	CBS CD MK-42433
"Streets of Laredo, The"	Roy Harris: *Folksong Symphony*, 1940	Vanguard Classics OVC 4076
"Streets of Laredo, The"	Roy Harris: *American Ballads for Piano*	Etcetera KTC 1036
"Streets of Laredo, The"	Virgil Thomson: "Cattle" (*The Plow That Broke the Plains*)	*Bowmar Orchestral Library* No. 65 (*Music, U.S.A.*) or Vanguard Classics OVC 8013
"Ta-Ra-Ra-Boom-de-ay"	Charles Ives: *Trio for Violin, Cello, and Piano*	CRI CD 583
"Tallis's Canon"	Benjamin Britten: *Noye's Fludde*	Argo ZK-1 PSI (LP)
"There's No Place Like Home"	Aaron Copland: *Our Town*	CBS MK-42429
"Three Blind Mice"	Edwin Franko Goldman: *Children's March*	Mercury Living Presence 432-019-2MM or *Holt Music*, Grade 1, (Holt, Rinehart and Winston)
"Three Blind Mice"	Aaron Copland: *Music for the Theater*	Sony Classical CD SMZK 47232
"Turkey in the Straw"	Roy Harris: *Folksong Symphony*, 1940	Vanguard Classics OVC 4076
"Turkey in the Straw"	Charles Ives: *Symphony No. 2* (Fifth Movement)	*Bowmar Orchestral Library*, No. 65 (*Music, U.S.A.*) or Sony Classical, SMK 47568
"Twinkle, Twinkle, Little Star"	Ernö Dohnányi: *Variations on a Nursery Song*	CBS SMCD-5052
"Twinkle, Twinkle, Little Star"	Harl McDonald: *Children's Symphony* (First Movement)	*Holt Music*, Grade 1 (Holt, Rinehart and Winston)
"Twinkle, Twinkle, Little Star"	Wolfgang Amadeus Mozart: Variations on *Ah, vous dirai-je, Maman*	CBS CD MLK 39436
"Twinkle, Twinkle, Little Star"	Camille Saint-Saëns: "Fossils" (*Carnival of the Animals*)	*Bowmar Orchestral Library* No. 51 (*Animals and Circus*) or London 425-505-2
"Twinkle, Twinkle, Little Star"	Roger Quilter: *A Children's Overture*	Angel Studio CDM 64131
"When Jesus Wept"	William Schuman: *New England Triptych* (Second Movement)	Mercury Living Presence 432092-2PH
"When Johnny Comes Marching Home Again"	Morton Gould: *American Salute*	RCA Gold Seal 6806-2RG or *World of Music*, *Grade* 5, Silver Burdett and Ginn

Related Listening: Bagley: "National Emblem," CD: *Brass and Percussion* (Morton Gould, conductor), RCA Victor 09026-61255.

BAGLEY: "National Emblem" and "The Star-Spangled Banner"

The following examples will help you discover more about listening materials and guided listening techniques as you add to your own repertoire of listening experiences.

The march "National Emblem" was composed in 1906 and became a hit, in part because it quotes the melody of "The Star-Spangled Banner." The composer of "National Emblem" was the American bandmaster Edwin E. Bagley (1857–1922).

Song Title	Composer/Title	Recording
"Yankee Doodle"	Ernest Bloch: *America*	Vanguard Classics OVC-8014
"Yankee Doodle"	Charles Ives: "Fourth of July" (*Symphony: Holidays*)	CRI C-180
"Yankee Doodle"	Charles Ives: "Putnams' Camp" (*Three Places in New England*)	*Bowmar Orchestral Library* No. 75 (*U.S. History in Music*)
"Yankee Doodle"	Virgil Thomson: *Chorale and Fugue on "Yankee Doodle"*	*Bowmar Orchestral Library* No. 65 (*Music, U.S.A.*)
"Yankee Doodle"	Louis M. Gottschalk: *The Union*	Nimbus NI 5014
"Yes, Jesus Loves Me"	Virgil Thomson: *Symphony on a Hymn Tune*	Mercury 434310-2

"The Star-Spangled Banner" uses a melody once known as "To Anacreon in Heaven." Its words are by Francis Scott Key, who composed them after watching the British bombardment of Fort McHenry in Baltimore during the War of 1812. In 1931 President Herbert Hoover signed the bill making "The Star-Spangled Banner" the official national anthem of the United States.

After listening to recordings of (A) "National Emblem" and (B) "The Star Spangled Banner," match the two compositions with their musical characteristics by writing the correct letter in each blank.

_____ The meter is 2/4

_____ The meter is 3/4

_____ The tempo is fast

_____ The tempo is stately

_____ The dynamics have a wide range of contrasts

_____ The dynamics have a moderate range of contrasts

_____ The form is AAB

_____ The form is Introduction AA BB: CC (Trio)

_____ The music is for band

_____ The music is for voices or voices with instrumental accompaniment

"The Star-Spangled Banner," CD: *America Sings*, The Eric Rogers Chorale and Orchestra, London 433 686–2. Related Reading: *The Star-Spangled Banner*, Illustrated by Peter Spier (New York: Bantam Doubleday Dell Publishing Group, Inc., 1973). This paperback book presents the story of "The Star-Spangled Banner" in pictures and includes a historical account as well as a facsimile of Francis Scott Key's handwritten manuscript of the poem.

GRIEG: "In the Hall of the Mountain King"

Henrik Ibsen's drama *Peer Gynt* tells the story of a legendary rascal from Norwegian folklore. Composer Edvard Grieg (1843–1907) wrote incidental music for the drama, and later selected eight of the original twenty-two pieces to make the two *Peer Gynt* Suites.

"In the Hall of the Mountain King" is Grieg's musical setting of a part of the story in which *Peer Gynt* is pursued and tormented by ugly "trolls," creatures with tails and slit eyes who lurk in dark places, avoiding sunlight.

Children can listen to the music without knowing the title or the story, however. They may prefer to imagine their own titles and stories, perhaps in connection with creative writing projects or as music for Halloween.

Related Listening: Grieg: "In the Hall of the Mountain King" from *Peer Gynt Suite No. 1*. Holt Music, Grade 2, *Music and You*, Grade 7, *World of Music*, Grade 2 and Grade 7.

Related Listening: "In the Hall of the Mountain King," *Classics from the Crypt*, BMG Classics 09026–61238–2.

Related Reading: *Trouble with Trolls* by Jan Brett (New York: G. P. Putnam's Sons, 1992).

At first children may focus on the obvious features of the music: tempo, dynamics, pitch register, and the use of instruments. They will notice that the music gets increasingly faster, louder, higher and that it uses more instruments as it moves along. The entire piece repeats a basic melodic rhythm pattern eighteen times.

The rhythm is easy to tap, step, or clap. Its basic pattern is shown here:

The melody and its rhythm is grouped into three similar sections, each consisting of six repetitions of the rhythm pattern and its slight modifications.

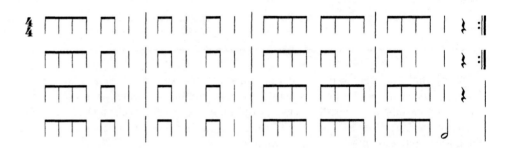

Notice that the melody is in minor. During repetitions one and two it moves up the first five steps of the minor scale then twists down in a chromatic pattern. In repetitions three and four the melody traces five steps from the major scale in a pattern similar to the minor version. Repetitions five and six are like one and two, but faster and louder. Then the entire six repetitions are heard twice more, always moving quicker, getting louder and adding more instruments.

Initial listening experiences might focus on tempo, dynamics, pitch, or tone color. Later, children can study the basic rhythm: write the pattern on the chalkboard in stem notation, then chant it with rhythm syllables or numbers.

Using plastic straws as "drumsticks," tap the rhythm of the melody. After rehearsing it without the recording, tap the rhythm while listening to the first two repetitions of the piece.

Add movement. After the group has learned to step to the basic rhythm of the melody, assign numbers to the children. Number "one" begins when the pattern first occurs, and each new number joins in at the beginning of repetitions two through eighteen to form a single line of "trolls" that follows the leader around the room. (The increase in the number of trolls, of course, parallels the music's increases in speed, loudness, and instruments.) Devise new movements to express the sounds of the brief closing section of the music.

Review the contrast between major and minor by playing the first part of the melody on resonator bells. Use bells from the C minor scale (the music on the recording is in B minor) to play the opening minor scale pattern without the recording:

C   D   E♭   F   G   E♭   G

Repetitions three and four outline pitches 1–5 of the major scale:

G   A   B   C   D   B   D

As a music notation activity, follow a copy of the melody (shown below) while listening to the recording.

In the Hall of the Mountain King

Related Listening: "Carillon" from
L'Arlésienne Suite No. 1 by
Georges Bizet, *Bowmar
Orchestral Library,* no. 78, or
World of Music, Grade 4.

BIZET: "Carillon" (*L'arlésienne* Suite No. 1)

"Carillon" from the *L'Arlésienne* (The Girl from Arles) *Suite No. 1* by Georges Bizet (1838–1875) is in ABA form. It begins with a prominent ostinato played by the horns as they imitate the ringing of the carillon with a repeated G♯ E F♯ pattern. Following a contrasting middle section in 6/8 meter, the first section and its ostinato returns. Students can play or sing the pattern (*mi do re*) as they discover that repetition may involve a short passage or an entire section.

"Carillon" from L'arlésienne Suite No. 1
(excerpt, simplified score)

Related Listening: Lucien
Cailliet's Variations on the Theme
"Pop! Goes the Weasel," *Holt
Music,* Grade 4, or *Music and
You* (Macmillan), Level 4, or RCA
Adventures in Music, Grade 4,
vol. 1.

CAILLIET: Variations on the Theme "Pop! Goes the Weasel"

The variations form, a favorite of many composers, has led to many compositions based on well-known tunes: "America," "Farmer in the Dell," "Goin' Home On a Cloud," "Pop! Goes the Weasel," "Sakura," "Twinkle, Twinkle Little Star," and "Yankee Doodle" to name a few. In a theme and variations, one element remains constant, while others are varied. Usually the theme is the constant element with variations occurring in its rhythm, meter, mode (major or minor), harmony, tone color, and other elements. Sometimes only one element is altered; sometimes everything is altered—to the extent that the original tune is completely disguised.

The seventeenth-century English song "Pop! Goes the Weasel" is heard as the theme in Lucien Cailliet's Variations on the theme "Pop! Goes the Weasel." Here the composer illustrates variants of the tune in styles ranging from an eighteenth-century fugue to twentieth-century jazz. Many teachers have found that children enjoy hearing the variations on the tune, and especially the sound effects coinciding with "Pop! Goes the weasel."[10] These include a popgun, a woodblock, a slide whistle, and a silent "pop" (in remembrance of a drummer who forgot to prepare the popgun in time).

Introduction
Theme
Variation 1—fugue
Variation 2—minuet, triple meter
Variation 3—minor, duple meter
Variation 4—major, triple meter
Variation 5—jazzy
Coda

Pop, Goes the Weasel

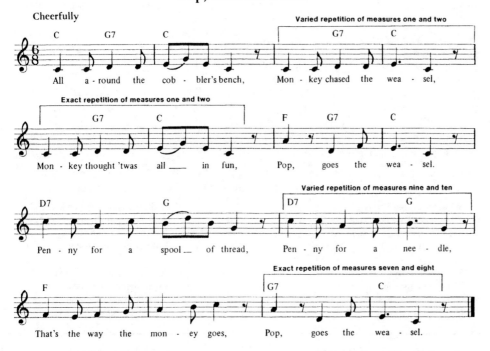

Use movement to call attention to structure in songs. For instance, form a circle with the children and sing "Pop! Goes the Weasel." Move to the right for the first two phrases and to the left for the second two phrases. (Change direction after the words "Pop! Goes the Weasel" each time.)

A tone-deaf old person from Tring
When somebody asked him to sing,
Replied, "It is odd
But I cannot tell 'God
Save the Weasel' from 'Pop Goes the King.' "

MOZART: Variations on *"Ah, Vous Dirai-je, Maman"*

The melody of "Twinkle, Twinkle Little Star" comes from the French nursery tune "Ah, vous dirai-je Maman"("Ah, I will speak of you, Mother,") and it has been used as a theme in longer works by several composers, including Mozart. The English words were written by Jane Taylor (1783–1824), who, with her sister Ann, wrote *Poems for the Nursery,* a famous nineteenth-century children's book. Among many versions of words for the melody are the following:

"Baa, Baa, Black Sheep,"
"The Alphabet Song,"
"Little Arabella Miller."
"Twinkle . . . Little Bat" (Edward Lear)
"Scintillate" *The Firestone Book of Children's Songs*

Each four-measure phrase of "Twinkle, Twinkle Little Star" has the same duple meter rhythm. The notes in phrase one outline a contour that moves upward then descends with repeated notes and steps. Phrase two has a contrasting, descending pattern that is stated twice. Phrase three is like phrase one. The melody is in major and can be harmonized with the I, IV, and V chords. Its form is diagrammed as ABA.

Related Listening: Mozart: Variations on "Ah, vous dirai-je, Maman," *Holt Music,* Grade 2, *Music and You,* Grade 4, or *World of Music,* Grade 5.

Twinkle, Twinkle, Little Star

Jane Taylor (English, 1783–1824)   *French Folk Melody*

Twin - kle, twin - kle, lit - tle star, How I won - der what you are.

Up a - bove the world so high, like a dia - mond in the sky,

Twin - kle, twin - kle, lit - tle star, How I won - der what you are.

(2) When the blazing sun is gone,
     When he nothing shines upon,
     Then you show your little light,
     Twinkle, twinkle, all the night.

(3) Then the traveler in the dark,
     Thanks you for your tiny spark,
     He could not see which way to go,
     If you did not twinkle so.

(4) In the dark blue sky you keep,
     And often through my curtains peep,
     For you never shut your eye,
     Till the sun is in the sky.

(5) As your bright and tiny spark,
     Lights the traveler in the dark—
     Though I know not what you are
     Twinkle, twinkle, little star.

Ah, vous dirai-je, Maman

1. Ah, vous dirai-je, maman,
    Ce qui cause mon tourment?
    Papa veut que je raisonne
    Comme une grande personne;
    Moi, je dis que les bonbons
    Valent mieux que la raison.

2. Ah, vous dirai-je, maman,
    Ce qui cause mon tourment?
    Papa veut que je demande
    De la soupe et de la viande;
    Moi, je dis que les bonbons
    Valent mieux que les mignons.

3. Ah, vous dirai-je, maman,
    Ce qui cause mon tourment?
    Papa veut que je retienne
    Des verbes la langue antienne;
    Moi, je dis que les bonbons
    Valent mieux que les leçons.

The Alphabet Song

A	B	C	D	E	F	G,
H	I	J	K	L	M •N	O	P
Q	R	S_____		T	U	V,
W_____		X_____	Y		and	Z,

Now I've sung my A B Cs,
Next time sing them with me, please.

Arabella Miller

Little Arabella Miller
Found a fuzzy caterpillar.
First it crawled upon her mother,
Then upon her baby brother,
They said, "Arabella Miller,
Put away that caterpillar."

Mozart's Variations on "Ah, vous dirai-je, Maman" were composed in 1781–1782 and published in 1785.

Wolfgang Amadeus Mozart:
Twelve Variations on "Ah, vous dirai-je, Maman"

K. 300e (265)

The piano states the theme to the tune we know as "Twinkle, Twinkle Little Star," and then presents twelve variations.

Variation 1	Theme (duple meter) elaborated in even sixteenth notes.
Variation 2	Theme in the treble. The left-hand part moves in sixteenth notes, in an elaborate version of the basic accompaniment.
Variation 3	The theme moves in triplet rhythm with the left-hand accompaniment in steady quarter notes.
Variation 4	The right hand plays the theme in steady quarter notes to a triplet accompaniment in the left-hand part.
Variation 5	The melody and accompaniment alternate in presenting patterns from the theme and its accompaniment.
Variation 6	The melody is presented in chordal style with a rapid sixteenth note accompaniment.
Variation 7	Scalewise patterns move above longer durations in the accompaniment.
Variation 8	Melody and accompaniment change to minor, with the melody imitated in follow-the-leader style by the left hand.
Variation 9	The melody, now in major, is imitated once again by the left hand's part.
Variation 10	The melody moves against broken chord patterns in the left hand. Chromatic scale steps vary the melodic line.
Variation 11	The tempo changes to an adagio (slow) tempo in a lyrical style.
Variation 12	The final variation moves in a fast allegro in triple meter. Both hands play rapid sixteenth note patterns with melodic ornamentation.

Related Listening: Benjamin Luxon and Bill Crofut: "Simple Gifts"/ "Lord of the Dance" (Lord of the Dance by Sidney Carter) CD: Omega OCD 3003, *Music and You*, Grade 5, *Holt Music*, Grade 5, *World of Music*, Grade 8.

Related Listening: Aaron Copland: *Appalachian Spring*. Copland Conducts Copland, CBS MK 42430.

COPLAND: Variations on a Shaker Tune from *Appalachian Spring*

The religious group known as the Shakers arrived in New York State from England in 1774 and eventually established a number of Shaker communities. (The name refers to their custom of shaking and moving during worship.) The Shaker tune "Simple Gifts" was used by Aaron Copland (1900–1990) in his ballet *Appalachian Spring*, which was awarded the 1945 Pulitzer Prize for music.

"Simple Gifts" (page 344) has a two-part (AB) form. In Copland's variations the entire melody is stated as the theme and again in the first and third variations; variations two and five use only the A section of the tune; variation four uses only the B section. Children might focus on instrument tone color, tempo, or dynamics while listening to the composition. Help them discover that the theme is repeated, but varied each time by changing its tempo, dynamics, chords, register, instruments, or by transforming the tune into a canon, which, like a round, is a form of musical "follow the leader." The following chart shows some features of the music.

Theme: 16 measures 2/4 meter *p*   Part **A** of the melody is presented by a solo clarinet with harp and flute accompaniment. Two clarinets begin part **B** of the theme with flutes in the accompaniment.

Interlude: three measures   Flute, oboe, bassoon, muted trumpet.

Variation 1	*mp*	A little faster. Oboe and bassoon duet accompanied by muted trumpet in part **A** of the theme. In part **B** flutes and horns are added, playing longer sounds in contrast to the more rapid rhythm of the melody.
Interlude: two measures		Harp, glockenspiel, piano, violins. Repeated pattern begins.
Variation 2	*mf*	Part **A** of the theme in augmented rhythm (longer note values). Violas and trombones begin the theme, which is imitated in canon by the violins. An ostinato-like rhythm is heard in the accompaniment, played by harp, piano, and violins.
Interlude: six measures		Flutes, oboes, bassoons, strings; horns, trumpets, trombones—crescendo.
Variation 3	*f*	The entire theme is played by trumpets and trombones in an emphatic style. The violins add rapid runs up and down the scale.
Variation 4	*mf*	Slower. This quiet variation uses the **B** section of the theme, played by woodwinds with cello and double bass in the background.
Variation 5	*fff*	The full orchestra plays the final variation, using part **A** of the theme. Tympani (kettle drums), harp, and double basses play a descending bass line that contrasts with the augmented rhythm of the theme.

JOHANN PACHELBEL: "Canon in D Major"

Johann Pachelbel (1653–1706) was a famous German organist and composer. His best known work, the "Canon in D Major," has been recorded in versions for strings, brass, and even as a popular song entitled "How, Where, When?"

The music begins with an eight-beat bass pattern, which occurs twenty-eight times during the composition. The bass pattern is combined with a repeated chord pattern and a series of contrasting melodies played by violins. The violins enter one at a time, each imitating the other's melody, to produce a three-part polyphonic texture in follow-the-leader style. A balance of repetition and contrast results as the listener hears the repeated bass and the rhythmically contrasting melodies of the violins.

Students can play or sing the bass line, listen for varied repetition, or even add a partner melody ("Jolly Old Saint Nicholas") to the music. After learning conducting gestures for music in fours, invite students in the middle- or upper-elementary grades to devise movements that reflect the repetition and change of the music. For example, form a circle and step the beat while conducting in four. Create patterns such as the following:

> While conducting, step on beats one, two, three, four.
> While conducting, step on beats one, two, and four.
> While conducting, step on beats one and two, hold on beats three and four.

Related Listening: "Pachelbel's Greatest Hit," (nine diverse arrangements of Pachelbel's Kanon), CD: RCA 607 12–2-RG or *Holt Music*, Grade 8 (122-123), or *Silver Burdett and Ginn World of Music* Grade 5.

Related Listening: Stravinsky: *Greeting Prelude, Holt Music,* Grade 3, *The Spectrum of Music,* Grade 5.

STRAVINSKY: "Greeting Prelude"

Our most often-played melody is Mildred and Patty Hill's "Happy Birthday to You," published in 1935 and originally sung to the words "Good Morning to All." One of the twentieth-century's most famous composers, Igor Stravinsky quoted the melody in his *Greeting Prelude,* which was composed in 1955 to honor the eightieth birthday of French conductor Pierre Monteux.

Stravinsky's composition is full of surprises, and it illustrates a number of techniques found in twentieth-century music. These techniques include canon, diminution, and inversion (turning the melody upside down) and octave displacement—the "right" note in the "wrong" octave. Stravinsky changes the sixth note of the melody ("you") so that it goes to a note an octave higher than the one expected. "Octave displacement" is a characteristic of a large number of twentieth-century melodies. Children can explore the technique with any familiar tune.

Yankee Doodle

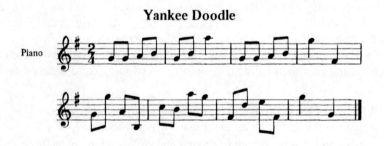

Activities related to music listening can make frequent use of the principle of teaching from the familiar to the unknown.

Children created their versions of "Happy Birthday" in work described as part of the Contemporary Music Project.[11] One version was accompanied with original instruments, including a coffee can, tin can, hollow bar, rocks in a milk carton, etc., each instrument playing one beat of the rhythm accompaniment.

THOMPSON: "Cattle" from *The Plow that Broke the Plains*

Many American composers have used familiar western melodies in their music. An extended lesson on Copland's *Billy the Kid* is presented in *Music and You,* Grade 5. *The Streets of Laredo* (*The Dying Cowboy*) is the basis for a movement of Samuel Barber's *Excursions for Piano* and for one of Roy Harris' *American Ballads for Piano.* (The latter is presented in *World of Music,* Grade 5.) These melodies are found in other works, as well. Aaron Copland quotes "I Ride An Old Paint" in the *Saturday Night Waltz* section of his ballet *Rodeo,* and Elie Siegmeister quotes the tune in his *Western Symphony.*

Three cowboy tunes ("I Ride an Old Paint," "My Home's in Montana," and "Git Along, Little Dogies") are used as themes in Virgil Thomson's "Cattle" from the 1936 film score *The Plow That Broke the Plains.*

Related Listening: Virgil Thomson: "Cattle" from *The Plow That Broke the Plains, Bowmar Orchestral Library,* no. 65, *Holt Music,* Grade 4, or CD: Vanguard Classics OVC 8013 (Symphony of the Air, Leopold Stokowski, Conductor).

Old Paint

My Home's in Montana

Git Along, Little Dogies

The melody moves in 6/8 meter, but the accompaniment sounds like *triple* meter.[12] (The accents are shown in boldface type in the diagram.) Divide into two groups and play the rhythms with instruments that contrast in tone color. Count in a steady rhythm, in a slow tempo and play the pattern several times. Repeat the rhythm pattern at a faster tempo.

Group One:	**1**	2	3	**4**	5	6
Group Two:	**1**	&	<u>2</u>	&	<u>3</u>	&

Have students learn all three songs, then listen to a recording of Virgil Thomson's composition.[13] Explain that a rondo is a musical form with a recurring "A section" sandwiched between contrasting B and C sections. There are several different rondo patterns: ABACA, ABACABA, ABACADA. Children can create a rondo by alternating a recurring rhythm pattern (A) with improvised rhythms for the B and C sections.

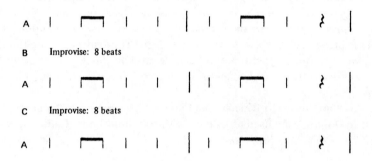

Label "I Ride an Old Paint" as "A," "My Home's in Montana" as "B" and "Streets of Laredo" as "C." Distribute A, B, or C flash cards representing each melody and listen again. Instruct the students to show the A, B, or C card when they hear its melody. Finally, have students arrange the cards to show the sequence of the themes in the order of their appearance on the recording (ABACABAC). *Holt Music,* Grade 4, and Silver Burdett & Ginn *World of Music,* Grades 4 and 6, include additional suggestions for teaching this music to children.

Related Listening: Beethoven: *Symphony No. 7, Allegretto* DG2531313 or *Holt Music,* Grade 5.

BEETHOVEN: *Symphony No. 7,* 2nd Movement

The second movement of Beethoven's *Symphony No. 7* opens with a one-chord introduction. Its sixteen-measure first theme begins on the pitch "E," which is sounded twelve times in a persistent rhythm that continues throughout the movement. In phrase one the melody moves away from the home key (A minor) to a cadence in C major. In phrase two (which is heard twice) the melody modulates back to A minor and ends in a complete cadence.

Teach the rhythm to the children and have them listen for it as you play the first few measures of the theme. As soon as they can tap the rhythm, teach them the theme. Simplified notation should help them remember it as they learn to play it on bells.

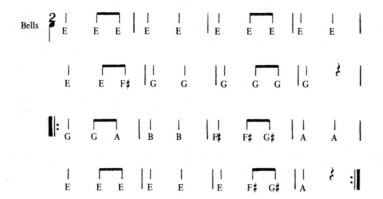

Students may also sing the theme on "loo" or with syllables. Notice that the syllables for F-sharp and G-sharp are those for steps six and seven in melodic minor: *fi* and *si*.

Following the initial statement of the melody, it is repeated, this time with an added countermelody. Follow the notation as you listen.

Symphony No. 7, **Second Movement (Theme)**

Beethoven

After learning to sing or play the melody, return to it on another day and listen to the entire *allegretto* movement. The following outline shows seven varied repetitions of the theme and two contrasting sections.

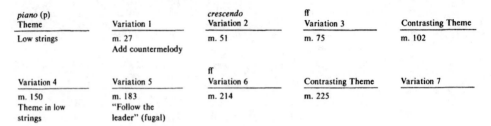

Beethoven: *Symphony No. 7*, Second Movement

Related Listening: Tchaikovsky: *Symphony No. 4*, Fourth Movement, RCA *Adventures in Music*, Grade 6, vol. 2. The *Adventures in Music* Teacher's Guide is a helpful reference for study of this composition. (See appendix 6.)

TCHAIKOVSKY: *Symphony No. 4*, Finale

The following activities suggest ways that music reading skills could be integrated in a lesson on the Russian folk song "The Birch Tree."

The Birch Tree

■ After singing the song, make an "inventory" of the notes it contains by circling the scale steps used in the melody.

■ Name the notes you circled. Which scale do they come from—F major or D minor? How many different pitch names are used?

■ Distribute resonator bells using these notes and play the first line of the melody. Does it move down or up? Does it move by step or by skip? Does it repeat?

- Is line two the same as or different from line one?
- Pat the steady beat and sing or chant the rhythm syllables for the rhythm of the melody.
- Distribute resonator bells to five players and perform the melody at a slow tempo while the rest of the class sings.[14]
- Sing the melody with syllables and show hand signs.
- Add several recorders to the vocal and bell melody. Autoharp chords are indicated by capital letters above the notes.
- Review the conducting pattern for duple meter. Have volunteers take turns conducting as the group performs the melody with voices and instruments.
- Write the melody on the chalkboard, then play the erasing game (see page 13). After completing the erasing game, by renotating the melody on the chalkboard, distribute music paper and have students copy the melody. Collect these papers and evaluate the students' success. Make use of some work in copying music as one of the best ways to improve notation skills. (You may find that students will enjoy copying music and take pride in doing neat and accurate work.)
- Listen to the melody "The Birch Tree" as it occurs in the finale of Tchaikovsky's *Symphony Number Four*. Twenty or more recorded versions of the symphony are available. Consult your local library or the current Schwann record catalog.[15] This listening selection lasts nearly eight minutes. Listening to it in shorter segments may give better results. The outline on page 228 shows that "The Birch Tree" theme is presented as a set of variations. Students could sing the melody, tap its rhythm, or listen to determine which orchestral instruments are used in each variation.

(A)

Theme 1	Theme __	Theme __	Theme __	Theme __	Variations on Theme 2 a a' a'' a''' a''''
ww st per			full orchestra		

Short transition

(A')

Theme __	Theme __	Variations on Theme 2 a a' a'' a''' a''''
	full orchestra	

Coda
 (closing section)

Theme__ tympani roll Theme__(Fragments of Themes 2 and 3)

Individualized learning, using earphones in the media center, offers other opportunities. A listening guide, to be completed by the student, might be an appropriate technique in your fifth or sixth grade classroom.

■ Show the film *The Peter Tchaikovsky Story,* which portrays an idealized version of the composer as a child and as a young man. The Bolshoi Ballet is shown in performance during the film (University of Illinois Film Center 81068).

■ For the elementary school chorus, perform "The Little Birch Tree," arranged by Mary Goetze for unison voices, piano, and recorder or flute. (Published by Boosey & Hawkes, 6130, 1984). An arrangement by Arvida Steen, for Orff instruments, is included in the Orff Activities Teachers Resource Binder for *Holt Music,* Grade 4.

Related Listening: Kabalevsky: "March" from *The Comedians, Holt Music,* Grade 2, or RCA *Adventures in Music,* Grade 3, vol. 1.

KABALEVSKY: "March" from *The Comedians*

Charts, diagrams, and activity sheets offer visual reinforcement to the listening experience and help students focus their attention on significant details in the music. The "listening grid" has empty boxes that children fill in as they listen.[16] In the following example, the children hear a march and place a dot in each square to represent each measure they hear as they silently count "1–2" in duple meter. This task may take several repetitions. When it is completed, they listen in future lessons for other details, adding information to the listening grid. The example that follows emphasizes rhythm patterns found in "March" from *The Comedians* by Dmitri Kabalevsky. (The lesson is preceded by experiences in chanting rhythm syllables and reading rhythm patterns from flash cards.)

1. "Listen and pat the steady beat with the music."
2. "Listen again. This time make a dot for each measure. There are two beats in each measure, so put one dot in each box of your listening grid for each measure that you hear."
3. "Listen for this rhythm (ti-ti ta, ti-ti ta, ta ta too) and mark the boxes where you hear the rhythm." (Play measures one to eight for the students.)

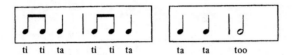

4. "Echo this rhythm after I say it. (too ta ta, too ta ta)."

5. "Now echo this rhythm. (tim-ri, tim-ri, tim-ri, tim-ri, ta ta too)."

tim – ka tim – ka tim – ka tim – ka

6. "Listen to the march again and write the rhythm patterns in the boxes of your listening grid."

Continue in a similar fashion and notate the basic rhythm of the entire melody.

1	2	3	4	5	6	7	8
clarinets	and bassoons						
9	10	11	12	13	14	15	16
strings							
17	18	19	20	21	22	23	24
25	26	27	28	29	30	31	32
33	34	35	36	37	38	39	40
oboe and clarinet							
41	42	43	44	45	46	47	48
49	50	51	52	53	54	55	56
strings							
57	58	59	60	61	62	63	64
woodwinds				orchestra		snare drum	

Related Listening: James Galway: *The Magic Flute of James Galway, Carnival of Venice,* arranged by Briccialdi. RCA LRL1–5131. Wynton Marsalis: *Carnaval, Fantaisie and Variation on The Carnival of Venice,* by Jean Baptiste Arban. Nonesuch H—71298. Philip Jones Brass Ensemble: *In Switzerland; The Carnival of Venice* (Niccolo Paganini); *Music and You,* Grade 3, HNH 4037.

"The Carnival of Venice"

Famous performers are often better known than composers in today's world of music. Comparing performances of a single composition can help children become more perceptive, as they notice how performers translate a musical blueprint into actual sounds. The following example uses the tune "My Hat, It Has Three Corners," which is nearly the same as the well-known melody called *The Carnival of Venice.*

My Hat

Recordings of *The Carnival of Venice* by James Galway, flute, Wynton Marsalis, trumpet, or by The Philip Jones Brass Ensemble highlight differences in the sound of trumpet and flute. The brass ensemble's parody of the melody has "wrong notes," vocal sounds, distortions, and a variation for tuba requiring the musical agility of a piccolo.

Students might look up information about the performers. James Galway, the Irish flute virtuoso, has written an autobiography that describes his education and career. Wynton Marsalis is, of course, famous as a musician who plays jazz or classical music with equal skill. The Philip Jones Brass Ensemble demonstrate in this recording that "serious music" can be funny.[17]

CARL ORFF: *Gassenhauer* "Street Song"

Related Listening: Carl Orff: *Gassenhauer: Street Song* (Carl Orff Conducting), Quintessence PMC7127 or *World of Music*, Grade 3.

Carl Orff. "Street Song"

Chord Sequence

C I	C I	F IV	F IV
1	2	3	4

C I	C I	G V	G V
5	6	7	8

C I	C I	F IV	F IV
9	10	11	12

C I	G V	C I	C I
13	14	15	16

F IV	G V	C I	C I
17	18	19	20

F IV	G V	C I	C I
21	22	23	24

1. Play chord root tones on bells.

2. Circle the rhythm patterns you hear.

3. Improvise new combinations of rhythms in the same chord sequence.

Carl Orff's *Street Song* shows how varied repetition provides unity and variety for the listener. A 24-measure chord pattern in triple meter is presented first by alto xylophones and then repeated seven more times as new layers of sound and rhythm are added. The dynamic level increases as soprano xylophones, timpani, sopranino recorder, and additional percussion instruments join in to increase the level of activity and intensity. Students can identify prominent rhythms and follow the patterns throughout the recording, perhaps using the example as a model for their own improvisations in a simpler context.

Related Listening: Ravel: *Rapsodie espagnole,* CD: (1) The Reiner Sound, Chicago Symphony Orchestra, Fritz Reiner, conductor, RCA 09026–61250–2 or (2) Detroit Symphony Orchestra, Paul Paray, conductor, Mercury 432 003–2.

RAVEL: "Prelude to the Night" from *Rapsodie Espagnole*

A four-note ostinato continues throughout most of Ravel's "Prelude to the Night" from *Rapsodie espagnole.* Use questions. Does the pattern move up or down? Is the beat emphasized in this music? Is the music generally loud or soft? Play the ostinato softly on bells. Discover that the rhythm is in triple meter, with a subdued feeling of pulse appropriate to the mood and title, "Prelude to the Night."

Related Listening: Poulenc: *Mouvements Perpétuels,* First Movement Angel S–37303.

POULENC: *Mouvements Perpétuals*

Composer Francis Poulenc's *Mouvements Perpétuels* lives up to its title with a repeated accompaniment that continues without change throughout the first movement. A student could play *do* (B-flat) and *so* (F) on alternating beats for a simplified version of the left-hand part.

Related Listening: Ralph Vaughan Williams: *Fantasia* on *Greensleeves; Come to the Fair, Folk Songs and Ballads,* "Greensleeves," sung by Kiri Te Kanawa Angel R 144298 "Greensleeves in Modern Dress," *Holt Music,* Grade 6.

VAUGHAN WILLIAMS: "Fantasia on Greensleeves"

Contrasting musical styles are evident in examples of *Greensleeves,* a famous melody dating back to Shakespeare's time. (See page 101.)

Related Listening: (1) Stravinsky: *Music for Two Pianos and Piano Four Hands, Five Easy Pieces.* Wergo WER 6228–2 or Chandos CHAN 6535. (2) Stravinsky: Suite No. 1 For Small Orchestra, No. 1. Sony Classical SK 45843 or London (Enterprise) 433079–2LM.

STRAVINSKY: "Five Easy Pieces"

Igor Stravinsky's *Five Easy Pieces* (1917), originally written as a piano duet, were later orchestrated by the composer. The first piece, in ABA form, has a repeated accompaniment on four notes—F E D C, a contrasting middle section, and then a repetition of the first part. Recordings of both the piano and the orchestral version are listed here.

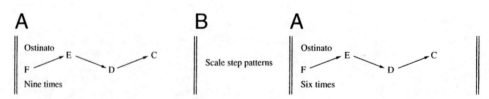

INDIVIDUALIZED LISTENING

Use computers, videodiscs, interactive CDs, and cassette recordings to reinforce or expand listening lessons. If an area of the classroom is used as a music learning center, children can work independently during free time—creating music, learning to play an electronic instrument, reading about music, listening through earphones, or exploring a project of their own choice. For example, students might practice identifying the sounds of instruments or develop listening skills: recognizing higher or lower, duple or triple meter, major or minor, movement by step or skip, intervals, scales, chords, or other tonal-rhythmic patterns.

The school or classroom music center may include visual aids, as well as work sheets to be filled in after using a filmstrip-recording set. With headphones and a CD or tape-cassette player, children can listen quietly without disturbing others. Some teachers prepare special cassettes of tonal or rhythm patterns to develop music reading skills.

Develop projects of interest to students in the upper-elementary grades with individualized listening guides based on "learning contracts." Possible topics are composers' lives and music; selected Broadway musicals; operas; or music related to other subject areas such as science, art, or social studies. Materials for special learners including the talented and gifted are available as supplements to the basic music series.

Both programmed instruction and narrative records about the lives of composers are suitable for individual listening activities. (Convenient sources for these materials are the catalogs of such firms as the Children's Book and Music Center, Gamble Musical Merchandise Catalog, Lyons, Peripole, Rhythm Band, or Silver Burdett. Addresses for these firms are listed in appendix 6.)

MUSIC LISTENING RESOURCES

(1) The *Bowmar Orchestral Library,* which is available in many classrooms, includes notated themes on posters and overhead transparencies. (2) Your school may have copies of the RCA *Adventures in Music* recordings, which are currently out of print. The companion booklets for *Adventures in Music* include themes and extensive information on recorded selections for grades one through six. (3) Most music appreciation books include notated themes along with information about the works they describe. (4) *Portraits in Music* by David Jenkins and Mark Visocchi (Oxford University Press, volume 1, 1979; volume 2, 1981) includes theme, photographs, drawings, listening guides, follow-up activities, and background information for a total of thirty-three pieces by famous composers. (Though designed for upper grades and secondary students, the materials can be adapted for use with younger listeners.) (5) *A Dictionary of Musical Themes* by Harold Barlow and Sam Morgenstern (New York: Crown Publishers, 1948) contains nearly 10,000 themes, notated and presented in alphabetical order from Adolphe Adam to Efrem Zimbalist. (For those who can hum a tune and figure out its notes, an index shows the themes in note names in the key of C major.) (6) Listening guides are included in the teacher's editions of music series books. (7) Other aids include the concise paperback *BBC Music Guides,* prepared for British Broadcasting Corporation programs. (Seattle: University of Washington Press, Gerald Abraham and Lionel Salter, general editors). A comprehensive and informative resource for the teacher is D. Kern Holoman's *Evenings with the Orchestra* (New York: W. W. Norton & Company, 1992). This book includes details about the orchestra and 73 composers and guides to 275 often-performed masterpieces. (8) Sources for multicultural materials and recordings are included in publications by the Music Educators National Conference (MENC) and the extensive catalog of multicultural books and recordings available from World Music Press, PO Box 2565 (ll Myrtle Avenue), Danbury CT 06813. The following films, originally produced during the 1970s and 1980s, are now available in video format from World Music Press: *Discovering the Music of Japan, Discovering the Music of India, Discovering the Music of the Middle Ages, Discovering the Music of Latin America, Discovering the Music of Africa, Discovering Russian Folk Music,* and *Discovering the Music of the Middle East.*

The Children's Group (561 Bloor Street W., Suite 300, Toronto, Ontario, Canada M551Y6) has created a superior series of composer stories and music that currently includes the following: *Beethoven Lives Upstairs, Mr. Bach Comes to Call, Mozart's*

Magic Fantasy, Tchaikovsky Discovers America, and *Vivaldi's Ring of Mystery.* All are available on cassette or compact disc; the Beethoven program is also available on video.

A series of publications from Gakken Co., Ltd., Tokyo, is available in English. Award-winning illustrations with texts written for young readers present stories associated with famous compositions: *Peter and the Wolf, Carnival of the Animals, Invitation to the Dance, Swan Lake, Coppelia, Hansel and Gretel, Peer Gynt, William Tell, A Night on Bare Mountain, Joey the Clown (The Comedians),* and *The Sorcerer's Apprentice.* Stories of opera can be found in anthologies and in works such as Gian-Carlo Menotti, *Amahl and the Night Visitors* (New York: McGraw-Hill, 1952), Stephen Spender, *The Magic Flute* (New York: Putnam's, 1966), John Updike, *The Ring* (New York: Knopf, 1964).

A particularly concise and informative publication for children is *An Usborne Introduction, Understanding Music* by Judy Tatchell (London: Usborne Publishing, Ltd., 1990). Norman Lloyd's *The Golden Encyclopedia of Music* (New York: Golden Press, 1968) and the latest edition of the *Oxford Junior Companion to Music* (London: Oxford University Press, 1980) are also useful reference works for young people.

Hello, I'm Music, a multimedia program (six filmstrips and records, teacher's guide, student work sheets), presents concepts of melody, harmony, rhythm, form, and tone color in nontechnical language with a humorous approach suitable for students in the intermediate grades.

Composers, Their Stories and Music (records or cassettes) provides narration and musical excerpts dealing with the lives and works of composers such as Bach, Beethoven, Berlioz, Brahms, Haydn, Mozart, Wagner, and Verdi. Composer biographies are also available with filmstrip-record sets for composers of the twentieth century.

The catalog of CLEARVUE/eav (6465 North Avondale Avenue, Chicago, IL 60631–1909) includes videos, CDs and sound filmstrips on music, including music appreciation and music fundamentals as well as music software programs for computer-assisted learning. The American Music Conference (1000 Skokie Boulevard, Willmette, IL 60091) publishes a "Film Review Service," which includes selected films, classified according to subject and age level. You could use this list as a starting point in compiling your own file of music films.

The following record-filmstrip kits (available from *Pop Hits Publishing,* 3149 Southern Avenue, Memphis, TN 38111) invite children in the upper grades to explore contemporary studio recording techniques:

- *Pop/Rock Instruments, A Demonstration Ride*
- *Studio Sounds of the '80s* (featuring the syndrum, clarinet, vocorder, synthesizers, electric piano, and recording console)

SUGGESTED ACTIVITIES

1. Prepare a listening activity based on the instruments of the band or orchestra, and explain one family of instruments: strings, woodwinds, brass, or percussion.
2. Prepare a "call chart" to guide listeners in following a brief recorded work.[18]
3. Study a listening lesson from a current music series book for a grade level of interest to you. Listen to the recording as well.
4. Attend a concert at your college or university. Identify significant details (see page 204) of one or more of the works performed.
5. Visit your campus media center and make a brief list of music listening materials of interest to you.

NOTES

[1]Allen P. Britton, "Roles of Performance and Repertory," in *Basic Concepts in Music Education II,* Richard J. Colwell, ed. (Niwot, Colo.: The University Press of Colorado, 1991), 184.

[2]Music learning theorist Edwin Gordon calls it *aural perception* when we hear sounds that are physically present, and uses the term *audiation* to describe what happens when we give meaning to this information. Aural perception requires actual sounds to be present, but audiation can take place through recall or creativity, or hearing music seen in notation whether or not actual sound is present.

[3]Steven K. Hedden, "What Have We Learned About Building Student Interest?" *Music Educators Journal,* December 1990, pp. 33–37.

[4]Diane Ackerman, *A Natural History of the Senses* (New York: Random House, 1990), p. 187.

[5]Terence Dwyer, *Teaching Music Appreciation* (London: Oxford University Press, l967), p. 97.

[6]Bennett Reimer, *A Philosophy of Music Education,* 2d ed. (Englewood Cliffs, N.J.: Prentice-Hall, 1989), pp. 124–125.

[7]Steven K. Hedden, "Development of Music Listening Skills," *Bulletin of the Council for Research in Music Education,* Fall 1980, pp. 12–22.

[8]Patricia Shehan Campbell, *Lessons From the World, A Cross-Cultural Guide to Music Teaching and Learning* (New York: Schirmer Books, 1991), p. 212.

[9]Egon Kraus, "Zoltán Kodály's Legacy to Music Education," *The Eclectic Curriculum in American Music Education* (Reston, Va.: Music Educators National Conference, 1972), p. 35.

[10]The words of the song have nothing to do with an actual weasel, but instead are Cockney slang: "pop" means pawn, and the "weasel" was whatever tool the workman had to pawn when short of money. See Theodore Raph's *The American Song Treasury* (New York: Dover Publications, Inc., l986) for information about "Pop! Goes the Weasel!" and 99 other well-known songs.

[11]*Experiments in Musical Creativity,* CMP3, A Report of Pilot Projects Sponsored by the Contemporary Music Project in Baltimore, San Diego, and Farmingdale, (Washington D.C.: Music Educators National Conference, 1966).

[12]In his autobiography, the composer writes, "Teaching a guitarist to play in three-four time against a six-eight beat cost plenty too." (Describing the rehearsals in New York City in 1936.) *Virgil Thomson* (New York: A.A. Knopf, 1966), p. 261.

[13]Record jacket notes identify one of the melodies as *Laredo,* which leads to some confusion, since there is a Mexican folk song called *Laredo* and a cowboy tune called the *Streets of Laredo* or *The Dying Cowboy.* Neither of these melodies is much like the melody used by Virgil Thomson.

[14]Arthur Schopenhauer's essay, "The Russian Horn," describes Russian bands of up to one hundred players, each player with a horn that played only one note. The single note reminded Schopenhauer of people with only one idea—only in a crowd did these people seem interesting. See Jacques Barzun, *Pleasures of Music* (New York: The Viking Press, 1951), pp. 449–50.

[15]Write to: Schwann Opus, 208 Delgado Street, Santa Fe, NM 87501, or see your local record dealer.

[16]Paul Larson, "The Listening Grid," *Music Educators Journal,* February 1971, pp. 51–52.

[17]Those who think that all classical music has to be serious may enjoy listening to Leonard Bernstein's *Humor in Music* (Columbia MS 6225). Other examples of musical humor include P.D.Q. Bach's many recordings (e.g., *The Wurst of P.D.Q. Bach* on VSD 719/20), Gerard Hoffnung's *Music Festival Concert* (Angel 35500), Allan Sherman and the Boston Pops in *Peter and the Commissar* (RCA LSC-2773), the recordings made by Spike Jones (e.g., *Spike Jones is Murdering the Classics* on RCA LSC 3235) or composer Tom Johnson's *Failing, A Very Difficult Piece for Doublebass* (Records to accompany *Music, Ways of Listening* by Elliot Schwarz, published by Holt, Rinehart and Winston, 1982).

[18]*See* "Call Charts: Tools from the Past for Today's Classroom" by Beverly Bletstein, *Music Educators Journal,* September 1987, pp. 53–56.

SINGING 8

SINGING

Singing is a central component of the elementary school music curriculum. Enjoyable experiences in singing are important in themselves, and singing is also important for what it contributes to the growth of skills in music listening or playing instruments. An old band room adage says, "You can't play it if you can't sing it."[1]

Music specialists and classroom teachers can foster singing skills that will last a lifetime if they offer singing and singing instruction daily during the primary grades. In later years, some children sing reluctantly, as a result of peer pressure or the fear of singing poorly. "Success (or adequacy) in a school subject opens it up for further consideration and use," writes Benjamin Bloom. "In contrast, failure (or inadequacy) in a school subject may effectively close this subject for further consideration."[2]

Singing is important. Some children, however, respond more positively to one activity than to another. "It would be a mistake to prevent children who do not like singing from taking part and enjoying music, for there are other ways of participating in an active way," writes a leading authority on the Orff approach to music education.[3] A British music educator says, "Singing is useful in music lessons only when the children will sing. . . . However, we must be careful to distinguish between a refusal to sing and a reluctance to *start* singing."[4]

Humorist Roy Blount, who remembers being told to move his lips without singing aloud during music programs, says, "All known melodies can be boiled down to four or five basic tunes." He proposes a "society for the singing impaired" and the slogan, "You don't sing as badly as you think you do."[5]

Research that tells us when and how children learn to sing can be useful in guiding classroom singing activities. Studies show that infants younger than six months can learn to imitate pitches and even sing them back with accuracy. According to one study, "Not only did the infants demonstrate the ability to discriminate pitches and match what they produced to what they heard, but they also appeared to enjoy the task and work hard at it."[6] Recordings of the "cooing" sounds made by infants between three and nine months of age provide data on the pitch range and contours of early "singing." These data suggest that interaction with parents and caregivers shapes singing skills very early in the child's life. The data also remind us of the singing potential of the human voice: The composite range of infants was from G below middle to C to high C above the treble staff! The infants' highest and lowest pitches were not typical, of course: most pitches in their vocalizations used a narrower range between 346 and 526 hertz—approximately F to C in the treble staff.[7]

Following a stage of "musical babble," children create their own spontaneous songs and begin to sing bits of standard tunes. By age two or two and a half, children repeat fragments of songs and at age three or four many have a fairly extensive repertoire. Preschool children usually start with the words of a song and then learn the rhythm, followed by the melodic contour. At age four the child has control of a song's lyrics, rhythm, and general contour, but tends to stray from one key to another. By age five, the child can distinguish a song's underlying beat from its rhythm, sing its intervals with some accuracy, and stay in one key.[8]

The fact that some children learn new songs at the age of one and others have difficulty with intervals and sense of key well past the age of five or six seems to suggest that singing and music are innate talents. There is evidence, however, that musical aptitude is a product of both nature and nurture. "Barring physical disability, every child can speak and every child can sing," says Edwin E. Gordon, whose research indicates that the young child's musical aptitude is developmental:

Because the level of music aptitude a child has at birth will change according to the quality of the early informal and formal music experiences he has, the music aptitude of children up to nine years of age is called developmental music aptitude. Music aptitude does not continue to develop, either positively or negatively, after a child is approximately nine years of age. The music aptitude of students nine years of age and older is called stabilized music aptitude.[9]

Gordon recommends that children should hear music as much as possible, especially during the first eighteen months of life, the period before the child's attention shifts to the development of language skills. Gordon also urges that preschool children's "informal singing" should be encouraged; that is, singing without adult attempts to correct mistakes or otherwise intervene.[10]

Because heredity and environment interact, children's home environment is reflected in their musical development. Children whose families sing, play instruments, and listen to music have a higher level of musical development when they begin school than those whose families provide fewer active musical experiences.

Even though some children enter kindergarten without the ability to carry a tune, musical skills can be developed within the limits of the child's musical aptitude. What is needed is the opportunity to learn to sing, lots of practice, and guidance in the development of singing skills and confidence.[11]

FINGERPLAYS

During early childhood, children enjoy the challenges of fingerplays, which help them build control of small muscle movement.[12] "Eency-Weency Spider," "One Finger One Thumb," "Where Is Thumbkin?" "This Old Man," and "Open, Shut Them" are typical fingerplay songs of early childhood.

Each line of "Eency-Weency Spider" has its own motions. Lines one and four use a climbing motion. The children may "walk" the fingers of one hand up the forearm of the other hand or walk the opposite thumb and forefinger of each hand. Show the "rain" by wiggling the fingers with palms turned downward. Make a circle with the hands and arms to show the "sun."

Eency-Weency Spider

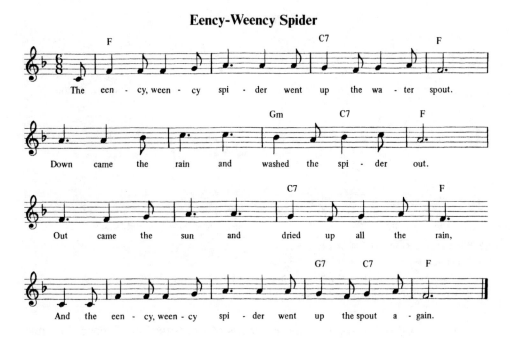

The een - cy, ween - cy spi - der went up the wa - ter spout.
Down came the rain and washed the spi - der out.
Out came the sun and dried up all the rain,
And the een - cy, ween - cy spi - der went up the spout a - gain.

The Words of "Open, Shut Them" indicate the actions.

Open, Shut Them

Lillian Wiedman

From Making Music Your Own, *Kindergarten. Copyright © 1966. Silver Burdett and Ginn, Inc. Used by permission.*

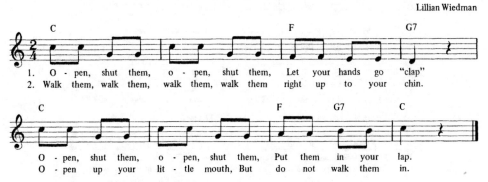

1. O - pen, shut them, o - pen, shut them, Let your hands go "clap"
2. Walk them, walk them, walk them, walk them right up to your chin.

O - pen, shut them, o - pen, shut them, Put them in your lap.
O - pen up your lit - tle mouth, But do not walk them in.

Keeping one finger and one thumb moving isn't so difficult, but wait until you get to verses two, three, and four of "One Finger, One Thumb".

One Finger, One Thumb

Traditional

1. One fin - ger, one thumb, keep mov - ing. One fin - ger, one thumb, keep mov - ing. One fin - ger, one thumb, keep mov - ing. We'll all be hap - py and bright.

2. One finger, one thumb, one foot, keep moving. . .

3. One finger, one thumb, one foot, one elbow, keep moving. . .

4. One finger, one thumb, one foot, one elbow, one head, keep moving. . .

Continue with additional movements as desired.

The tune of "Frère Jacques" has more sets of words than most songs. You may know this next version.

Where Is Thumbkin? (to the tune of Frère Jacques)

Where is Thumb-kin, where is Thumb-kin? Here I am,
PLACE BOTH FISTS BEHIND BACK.   SHOW ONE THUMB,

here I am. How are you to - day, sir?
THEN, THE OTHER.   BEND ONE THUMB.

Ver - y well, I thank you. Run a - way, run a - way.
BEND THE OTHER.   PUT ONE THUMB BEHIND BACK, THEN
                                                          THE OTHER.

2. Where is pointer?   4. Where is ringer?

3. Where is middle?   5. Where is pinky?

Remember to practice and memorize the motions and words before you try to teach children to sing "This Old Man."

This Old Man

2. This old man, he played two,
   He played nick-nack on my shoe...

3. This old man, he played three,
   He played nick-nack on my knee...

4. This old man, he played four,
   He played nick-nack on my door...

5. This old man, he played five,
   He played nick-nack on my hive...

6. This old man, he played six,
   He played nick-nack on my sticks...

7. This old man, he played sev'n,
   He played nick-nack till elev'n...

8. This old man, he played eight,
   He played nick-nack on my gate...

9. This old man, he played nine,
   He played nick-nack on my spine...

10. This old man, he played ten,
    He played nick-nack over again...

Verse 1	On *one,* hold up one finger.
	On *thumb,* touch thumbs together.
	On *nick-nack,* touch knees twice.
	On *paddywack,* clap hands twice.
	On *give a dog a bone,* extend hand toward the "dog."
	On *rolling home,* roll hands around each other.
Verse 2	On *two,* hold up two fingers.
	On *shoe,* touch shoe.
	(Repeat remainder)

ACTION SONGS

Action songs, like fingerplays, require only a limited amount of space and time. Children's responses prepare them for creative movement experiences and help to encourage participation in music activities. The child learns to imitate the teacher's actions, or creates movements that match the words of the song. Sometimes the words are fairly specific, as in "Ring Around the Rosy." Other songs invite the child to invent an individual type of movement to fit the words.

Teddy Bear

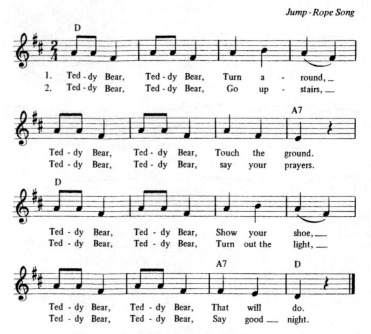

Jump - Rope Song

1. Ted - dy Bear, Ted - dy Bear, Turn a - round, ___
2. Ted - dy Bear, Ted - dy Bear, Go up - stairs, ___

Ted - dy Bear, Ted - dy Bear, Touch the ground.
Ted - dy Bear, Ted - dy Bear, say your prayers.

Ted - dy Bear, Ted - dy Bear, Show your shoe, ___
Ted - dy Bear, Ted - dy Bear, Turn out the light, ___

Ted - dy Bear, Ted - dy Bear, That will do.
Ted - dy Bear, Ted - dy Bear, Say good ___ night.

The children perform the movements indicated by the words.

From *150 American Folk Songs,* selected and edited by Peter Erdei and Katalin Komlos. Copyright © 1974. Boosey & Hawkes, Inc. Reprinted by permission.

SINGING GAMES

Bluebird

Game Song

Here comes a blue - bird through the ___ win - dow,

Hey did - dle - dum a day day day.   Take a lit - tle part - ner,

hop in the gar - den, Hey did - dle - dum a day day day.

Game: Have the children form a circle and join hands. One child (the "bluebird") skips in and out of the circle, passing under the arches formed by the arms of the other children. On "Take a little partner," the "bluebird" chooses a partner. The two join both hands and gallop out and in again through the circle opening left by the partner. If the song is sung again, the first child joins the ring, and the partner becomes the "bluebird."

The Old Grey Cat

2. The little mice are creeping . . .
3. The little mice are nibbling . . .
4. The old grey cat is waking . . .
5. The little mice are running . . .

Game: One child (the "cat") curls up on the rug. In verse two, several children (the "mice") tip-toe around the room. In verse three, they pretend to nibble. In verse four, sung more loudly, the cat awakens. Verse five is sung very quickly, as the cat chases the mice. Whoever is captured becomes the new cat. Along with the activity, be sure to emphasize mood, dynamics, and tempo during the singing.

That's a Mighty Pretty Motion

2. That's a mighty funny motion, Dee, di, dee,
That's a mighty funny motion, Dee, di, dee,
That's a mighty funny motion, Dee, di, dee,
Rise, Sugar, rise.

Game: Have the children stand, hands unjoined, in a large circle with one child in the center. As the words, "That's a mighty pretty motion, Dee, di, dee," are sung, the center child makes a motion or dance movement to the rhythm of the music. Throughout the song, the children clap loudly on the first and third beats.

At the words, "Rise, Sugar, rise," the center child leads another child into the ring and then stands in the selected child's place in the circle.

The same procedure is followed during the second verse except that the center child performs an unusual or humorous motion to the words, "That's a mighty funny motion, Dee, di, dee."

From *On the Trail of Negro Folk Songs* by Dorothy Scarborough, © 1925 Harvard University Press; renewed 1953 by Mary McDaniel Parker. Reprinted by permission of the publishers.

The Closet Key

1. I have lost the clo - set key, in my la - dy's gar - den,
2. Help me find the clo - set key, in my la - dy's gar - den,

I have lost the clo - set key, in my la - dy's gar - den.
Help me find the clo - set key, in my la - dy's gar - den.
(Solo)

3. I have found the closet key, in my lady's garden,
   I have found the closet key in my lady's garden.

Game: One child ("it") covers his or her eyes while the teacher hides "the closet key." The class observes the hiding place and sings the first verse. During verse two, "it" searches for the key, guided by the group's singing, which gets louder as the child moves closer to the "key" and softer as the child moves away. Upon finding the key, the child sings verse three as a solo, selecting a new person to be "it." While the children take their turns at singing the solo part, the teacher can assess individual progress in singing.

The Noble Duke of York

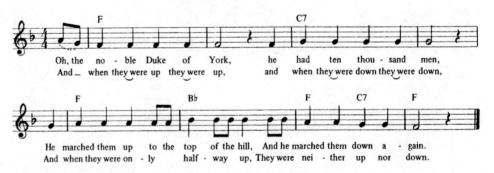

Oh, the no - ble Duke of York, he had ten thou - sand men,
And _ when they were up they were up, and when they were down they were down,

He marched them up to the top of the hill, And he marched them down a - gain.
And when they were on - ly half - way up, They were nei - ther up nor down.

Game: The song begins at a moderate tempo and is repeated at a faster tempo each time. Students rise for words indicating *up* and sit for words indicating *down.* They stand in a half up/half down position for the last line.

Singing games such as "Bow, Wow, Wow" (page 11) encourage children to participate in musical activities, and to prepare a basic vocabulary of tonal and rhythmic patterns.
Directions:
Form a circle and have partners face each other.

1. "Bow, wow, wow"—Clap hands three times.
2. "Whose dog art thou?"—Shake index finger three times, as if scolding.
3. "Little Tommy Tucker's Dog"—Take partner's hands and exchange places in 4 steps.
4. "Bow, wow, wow."—Stamp feet three times. Turn about on the rest (𝄽) and face a new partner. Repeat until the original partners are facing each other again.

Many singing games have a long history based on traditional songs, folk songs, or children's lore from various parts of the world. Their catchy tunes are easy to memorize and they lead to better participation in singing, the development of movement skills, and greater awareness of musical structure. Many of the games are closely related to folk dancing, and singing games help prepare students for more complicated types of dances.

If children find it difficult to sing as they move, you may wish to divide the class into a singing group and a group to move, and then exchange parts.

SINGING IN THE CLASSROOM
Skillful song-leading makes singing more enjoyable for children. The song leader finds worthwhile songs suited to the children's vocal range. Before starting to sing the song, the leader plays the keynote and starting pitch, sets the tempo, and signals the moment to begin singing. All of this takes some thought and practice. Read the following material carefully.

Songs in a Limited Vocal Range
On average, children entering kindergarten have a comfortable vocal range of about six notes: from D above middle C to B on the third line of the treble staff.

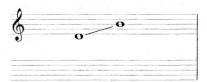

Comfortable Singing Range
Preschool to Kindergarten

Maturation and vocal experience increase the singing range, and by the end of first grade the child's six-note range expands to about one octave—middle C to third space C. (Individual ranges, of course, will vary.) The song leader chooses songs that do not greatly exceed the singing range of the children. The range of the "Star-Spangled Banner," for example, is too wide for young voices (and lots of older voices, too).

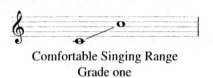

Comfortable Singing Range
Grade one

Suggested reading: Kenneth H. Phillips, *Teaching Kids to Sing,* New York: Schirmer Books, A Division of Macmillan, Inc., 1992.

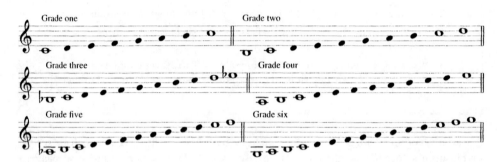

Children's singing range. (Black notes represent the comfortable range where the majority of the songs' pitches should be.)

The Starting Pitch

Singing the song in the right key for children's voices is also important. The keynote may be in the middle of the song's range, or it may be the highest or lowest pitch. Here are three examples:

- Third space C, a starting pitch in the upper part of the children's comfortable singing range, fits a song like "Saint Paul's Steeple," which begins on its *highest* note and descends one octave.
- Middle C, a starting pitch in the lower part of the children's singing range, fits a song like "Happy Birthday to You." In the key of F, C is low *so.* "Happy Birthday" begins on low *so,* reaches high *so* in phrase three, and ends on *do.* (You'll have many opportunities to sing this song with children. Start it on C or D so that they can sing the *high* note as well as the *low* note.)
- F and G, pitches in the middle of the young child's vocal range, fit a song like "Old MacDonald" which begins on its keynote, then drops four steps lower.

Before starting to sing, review the melody in your mind, and select a key that will be appropriate for children's singing.

Having chosen the desired starting pitch, use an accurate pitch reference—a piano, pitch pipe, tuning fork, or set of bells—to find it. (A study of the vocal pitch-matching skills of undergraduate education majors indicates that an electronic keyboard may produce more accurate singing than either melody bells or an Autoharp.)[13] Refer to the basic music series for guidance in selecting songs and keys that match the child's vocal range.

Establishing the Starting Pitch and Tempo

Singers go astray in pitch when they are uncertain about the relationship between the starting tone and the keytone, which is music's "home base." A procedure that clears up the problem in many cases is to have children sing the *tonic chord* and the *starting pitch* before beginning the song.

(Reminder: A melody may begin on any note, but the *last note* is usually the keynote. See pages 89–92.)

1. Sound the keynote on an instrument or with a pitch pipe.
2. Sing the keynote on "loo" and have the class sing it. Establish the basic tonality by playing or singing *do-mi-so-mi-do* in major or *la-do-mi-do-la* in minor.

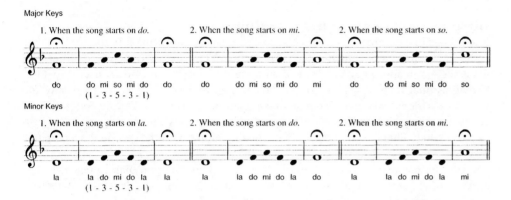

3. Have the children listen as *you* sing or play the starting tone of the melody. Then listen while the *children* sing it. (If necessary, repeat this step.)
4. Sing or play the first phrase of the song to set the tempo and the basic tonality.
5. Chant "1-2-1- *sing!*" on the starting pitch. (In triple meter, use " 1-2-sing.") Be sure to count in the same tempo that you will use for the song. A gesture on the word "sing" will remind the children to take a breath and begin with a solid vocal tone.

For review, practice giving the tempo and starting pitch for "The Cuckoo" (major mode, moderate tempo, triple meter) and for "The Birch Tree" (minor mode, faster tempo, duple meter). Select songs in other meters and keys for additional practice.

Teaching Rote Songs

Songs learned "by ear" are called *rote songs*. The teacher presents the rote song by singing it, or by playing it on an instrument or a recording. Concentration and memory skills affect the learning process, and so do the length and complexity of different songs. A child learns "Bounce High, Bounce Low" quickly; the numerous verses of "Skin and Bones" take more practice.

Knowing the song by memory will add to your confidence. When presenting the song to the children, copy the techniques used in a good speech: be expressive, maintain eye contact, and show enthusiasm. The teacher should not sing along with the children all of the time for at least two reasons: first, they become dependent; second, it is difficult to hear the children's voices while singing with them.

Whole-Part-Whole

Simplify learning tasks by dividing them into smaller parts, when necessary. Present a longer song in its entirety, so that children can sense its meaning and musical appeal, then teach it phrase by phrase.

Adapt the teaching process to fit the song, the needs of the children, and your lesson objectives.

1. Present the whole song after introducing it with some type of motivation (pictures, comments, props, etc.).
2. Use a question to direct attention to some feature of the song.
3. Sing phrase one and have the students repeat it.
4. Sing phrase two and have the students repeat it.

5. Sing phrases one and two and have the students repeat them.
6. Continue in similar fashion for the remaining phrases.
7. Sing the entire song.

Avoid singing with the children. Listen to their singing and have them listen when you sing. (Teacher sings; children listen. Children repeat the phrase; teacher listens.)

Introducing Songs with Recordings

Recordings offer a number of advantages. All of the songs printed in the basic music series books are available in compact disc format. They are performed by children and adult singers in appropriate styles and with varied accompaniments. A useful feature, known as dual track or "pick-a-track" recording, allows the teacher (1) to play the recording with melody and accompaniment combined; (2) turn off the accompaniment channel so that children can learn the song by hearing only the melody track; (3) turn off the melody channel so that children can sing along with the recorded accompaniment once the song is learned.

Use the recordings to assist you in learning songs that you plan to teach. In the classroom, you may wish to use recordings to present a song or to demonstrate another way to interpret a known song. Recordings assist students in learning a new song, and supply a vocal model. The recorded accompaniments bring instruments of all kinds— oboes, violins, synthesizers and less familiar instruments from other cultures—to classroom singing, adding variety to what children can play on classroom instruments. Recordings give the teacher's voice some rest—often much needed—and free the teacher to move around the room to listen to individual children. Recordings also contribute to other learnings, such as the study of instrumental timbre or the study of music from other times and places.

Relying on recordings has its disadvantages as well. Teachers can adapt their singing or the tempo to fit the children's needs. (Recorded tempos may be too fast for children just learning a new song.) Teachers can stop and repeat a tonal pattern or a short section more quickly than they can find and replay a small segment from a recording. The recordings you want may not be available when you want them. You may not have access to good playback equipment, either. (A report from the National Endowment for the Arts makes note that many school districts fail to supply funds to buy music textbooks and recordings.[14] One writer describes a school with "no written curricula, no recordings, no textbooks, no pianos or classroom instruments, and just one 'record player' to be shared by eighteen teachers!")[15]

When using recordings—

1. Listen to the record before you present it in class. How long is the introduction? Is there an interlude between verses? How many verses? Is there a coda (an ending section)? How does the record fit in with your teaching objectives? (For example, if your topic is the melodic contour of "America," its triple meter, or something similar, you could put off learning additional verses until another day.)
2. Introduce the song and motivate children to learn it by giving its background or story. Play the selection several times before asking the children to sing.
3. Give them something definite to listen for with each hearing.
4. Keep them actively involved as they listen.
5. Be sure they know the starting pitch.
6. Use conducting gestures as needed to help children know when to start and finish.

7. Remind them to listen to the recording as they sing.
8. Assist the children in learning the words. Write them on the chalkboard or use a transparency. Chant the words without the recording. Use questions to call attention to less common words and make sure children know what the words mean.
9. Use a mixture of whole song and phrase-by-phrase methods when appropriate. After children have heard the entire song several times, don't hesitate to stop to make corrections before continuing with the recording.

Songs with Repeated Tonal Patterns

Young children may try to sing along before they know the tune. If you select a song like "Old MacDonald," they can "chime in" on the repeated "E-I-E-I-O" tonal pattern. Look for songs with short, easy-to-learn patterns. Children with pitch-matching difficulties also benefit from practice with repeated tonal patterns. An example is the "ooo" ghost sound from "Skin and Bones."

Skin and Bones

1. There was an old wom-an all skin and bones, Oo – oo – oo – ooh!

2. She lived down by the old graveyard, Oo–oo–oo–ooh!
3. One night she thought she'd take a walk, Oo–oo–oo–ooh!
4. She walked down by the old graveyard, Oo–oo–oo–ooh!
5. She saw the bones a-layin' around, Oo–oo–oo–ooh!
6. She went to the closet to get a broom, Oo–oo–oo–ooh!
7. She opened the door and BOO!!

Here are additional examples of songs with "chime-in" patterns.

"The Cuckoo," "Down in the Meadow," "Good News," "Hey, Betty Martin," "Hop, Old Squirrel," "Hop Up, My Ladies," "Jinny Go Round," "Kum-ba-yah," "Little Tom Tinker," "Rig-a-Jig-Jig," "Teddy Bear," "Ten in a Bed," "Tinga Layo," and "Who's That Tapping at the Window?"

Songs with Repeated Phrases

The song leader and the children can take turns singing the repeated phrases of "Frère Jacques," "Old Texas," and "Scotland's Burning." Additional examples of "take turn" songs—"Oh, My! No More Pie," "Bill Grogan's Goat," "The Bear Song," "Down By the Bay," "Oh, In the Woods," "John the Rabbit," "Oh, My Aunt Came Back," and "Oh, You Can't Get to Heaven"—are included in *Music for Little People* by John Feierabend (New York: Boosey and Hawkes, 1989).

"I've Been Working on the Railroad," "Love Somebody," and "Sweet Betsy from Pike," are songs with recurring tonal patterns or phrases that children can learn quickly. (Many other examples, including "Ain't Gonna Grieve My Lord No More," "Charlie Over the Ocean," "Chichipapa," "Going On a Picnic," and "The Wheels on the Bus" can be found in the basic music series and in other collections of children's songs.) Make your own file of songs that you know and enjoy. Notice the use of repetition as you sing and listen to "Who Did?"

From Music as Experience *by Gretchen H. Beall. Wm. C. Brown Company, Publishers, 1981. Used by permission.*

Who Did?

Call and Response Song

2.
Whale did, (whale did,) whale did, (whale did,)
Both: Whale did swallow Jo - Jo - Jo - Jo.
Whale did, (whale did,) whale did, (whale did,)
Both: Whale did swallow Jo - Jo - Jo - Jo.
Whale did, (whale did,) whale did, (whale did,)
Both: Whale did swallow Jo - Jo - Jo - Jo.
Whale did swallow Jonah. (whale did swallow Jonah.)
Both: Whale did swallow Jonah down.

3.
Daniel (Daniel) Daniel (Daniel)
Both: Daniel in the Li - Li - Li - Li.
Daniel (Daniel) Daniel (Daniel)
Both: Daniel in the Li - Li - Li - Li.
Daniel (Daniel) Daniel (Daniel)
Both: Daniel in the Li - Li - Li - Li.
Daniel in the Lion's (Daniel in the Lion's)
Both: Daniel in the Lion's Den.

"Bingo," "If You're Happy and You Know It," "Paw-Paw Patch," "Rig-a-Jig-Jig," "This Old Man," and "Toodala" have repeated word patterns that are easy to learn. "Toodala" exemplifies features that appeal to young children: "a predominant rhythm pattern, repeated motifs, and lalling (nonsense syllables)."[16]

ACTIVITY SONGS

The *Wee Sing* series by Pamela Conn Beall and Susan Hagen Nipp (Los Angeles: Price/ Stern/Sloan) includes numerous songbooks, cassettes, and videos featuring fingerplay songs, campfire songs, silly songs, nursery songs, folk songs, patriotic songs, and other categories. Children who are shy or reluctant to sing may discover the joy of singing when they get caught up in activity songs. If possible, examine the songbooks and recordings by Raffi and those by Sharon, Lois and Bram for possible ideas and songs you would select for use in your classroom.

PROPS AND MOTIVATORS

Simply "practicing" a song over and over is not as enjoyable as creating something new. In songs like "Aiken Drum" props, puppets, stuffed animal toys, masks, pictures, role playing, and games make learning into fun. Primary grades children may combine art and music as they sing "Aiken Drum." Suggest that children name a new facial feature or garment for "The Man in the Moon," select an idea, and invite the child to illustrate it with crayons on a poster-sized sketch during each new verse. In the example, children named fruits and vegetables as categories in verses three and four and created a fanciful picture of the man who "lived in the moon."

Aiken Drum

Traditional Scottish Tune

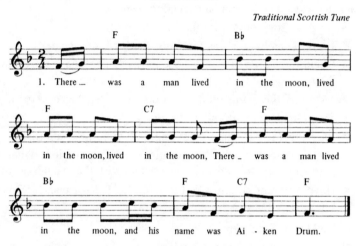

CHORUS: And he played upon a ladle, a ladle, a ladle,
And he played upon a ladle, and his name was Aiken Drum.

The chorus and the following verses use the same tune as that shown for verse one.

1. There was a man, lived in the moon, and his name was Aiken Drum.
2. And his hat was made of good *cream cheese,* and his name was Aiken Drum.
3. And his eyes were made of *strawberries,* and his name was Aiken Drum.
4. And his nose was made of *carrots,* and his name was Aiken Drum. (etc.)

Memory skills, selective attention, and active participation by the child are essentials. When you present a song, remind children to listen carefully, and give them something to listen for. The following suggestions can be applied to many different songs. Remember, children don't have to learn a song in just one day, and you don't have to use all of these activities with the same song.

1. Use questions to call attention to the words and to clarify their meaning, when necessary.
   - "Is 'Pop! Goes the Weasel!' about an animal?"
   - "Can you name some words that rhyme in this song?" "How many times was *B-i-n-g-o* repeated?"
   - "What does 'Auld Lang Syne' mean?"
   - "Who knows when Americans first started singing 'Yankee Doodle'?" "What do the words mean?"

2. Call attention to musical details.
   - "Listen to this [tonal pattern] or [rhythm pattern] and then tell me how many times you hear it in the song."
   - "Listen to this part of the melody. Does it move [higher or lower]; [by step or by skip]?"
   - "Was the music in two's or three's?"
   - "How many phrases did you hear? Was the second phrase the same or different from the first phrase? Which phrase had the highest sound(s)? Which phrase was loudest?"
   - "Should the song get [faster or slower]; [softer or louder]? Why?"
   - "What makes this song sound like the music of Japan?"

3. Vary the ways the children are asked to respond.
   - Sing the song on *loo* (without the words).
   - Hum the melody. (Lips touching, teeth slightly apart.)
   - Chant the words of each phrase in rhythm and have the children repeat them.
   - "Mouth" the words while listening to the teacher or a recording.
   - Sing aloud on every other phrase.
   - Sing specific patterns (for example, "chime-in" patterns).
   - Concentrate on improving posture, breathing, diction, dynamics, precision, pitch control, or eye contact with the teacher as you sing.
   - Have different groups take turns singing ("Row one," "Everyone on this side of the room," and so forth.)

4. Use Visual Reinforcement.
   - Use props that help create and maintain interest: puppets, stuffed animals, simulated microphones for solo singing, props that go with a particular song ("I Know an Old Woman Who Swallowed a Fly"), yarn for "Elephants Balancing Step by Step on a Piece of String," a ball for "Bounce High, Bounce Low," etc.
   - Flannel board figures or shapes have countless possibilities. For example, children arrange felt "animals" to show the word sequence in a cumulative song such as "Bought Me a Cat" (cat, hen, duck, goose, cow, dog, sheep, horse).
   - Use photographs and pictures or actual objects to add interest, clarify, or call attention to details: four similar phrases, contrasts, high-low pitch relationships; a series of pictures can serve as reminders of the words in each phrase.
   - Charts can show dynamics, form, contour, beats, meter, and other musical relationships.
   - Maps can make historical or cultural information about the song more meaningful.
   - Check your library for songbooks that illustrate "The Wheels on the Bus," the rhythmic chant of "Going on a Bear Hunt," and other well-known children's songs.
   - Write key words on the chalkboard. Relate words to class work in reading and spelling.

5. Add movement.
   - Have the children pat the beat or a simple ostinato as they listen to the song.

- Use movements in place (nonlocomotor movements): rainbow shaped arcs to show phrases length, swaying or bouncing to mark the beat, hand levels to show pitch contour, sound gestures (snap, clap, pat, stamp) to show meter or accent, hand signs to show specific tonal patterns, etc.
- Use movements from place to place (locomotor movements): step the beat, change directions for contrasting phrases, run or skip to show simple and compound meter, etc.
- "Raise your hand when you hear the [musical or song detail: keynote, interval, repeated phrase, etc.]."
- Dramatize the song. ("The Old Grey Cat," "Mary Had a Little Lamb," "A Hunting We Will Go," "Little Cabin in the Woods," and so forth.)
- Use gestures or pantomime the words.
- Play a singing game: "Bow, Wow, Wow," "Bow, Bow, Bow Belinda," etc.

THE CHILD VOICE

In order to select appropriate music and guide children's vocal development, the teacher must be aware of the child's vocal range and voice registers.

Speaking Voice and Singing Voice

The teacher should demonstrate the contrast between speech and singing ("This is my speaking voice, this is my singing voice") and call on children to imitate these two ways to use the voice. It is not necessary to single out problem singers, for all children can benefit from the practice. The child's *speaking voice* pitch is usually in the vicinity of middle C.

Developing Children's Vocal Range

A comfortable singing range for children starting school is from D above middle C to B on the third line of the treble staff. Therefore, most of the songs kindergarten children sing should be in this comfortable vocal range. With maturation and training the singing range expands, eventually extending to high F or G and to A or G below middle C. If many of the notes of a melody are in the upper part of the student's vocal range, the song may be more tiring than a song with only one or two "high notes." The "average range" of a song is known as its *tessitura*.

Individual singing ranges will differ from the group's average range, of course. One study reported individual children with vocal ranges of twenty-six or twenty-seven notes; first graders averaged slightly more than an octave, however, and most sixth graders could sing about two octaves.[17]

Male teachers may find that some children will try to match the adult male voice range, which is usually an octave lower than the unchanged child voice. A brief explanation and demonstration of the difference between the child's voice and the adult male voice is often all that is required.

Vocal Registers

The child's voice has two registers: chest voice and head voice. These terms describe the singer's vocal sensations rather than the actual resonating spaces used in tone production.[18] For children, the chest voice is in the range from the A below middle C to A one octave higher. From third line B upward is the head voice register. The two registers overlap from about D to A. Constant use of the chest voice is like driving an automobile only in low gear. Discovering the head voice register allows children to achieve their full vocal range and greater flexibility in singing.[19]

Discovering the Head Voice

The teacher's object is to encourage young singers to use the lighter head voice sound, and then bring that quality down into the range between the head voice and the chest voice. Some teachers have children sing to puppets—one with a low "speaking" voice, the other with a very high voice. Vocal sound effects added to story telling reduce children's inhibitions and increase their willingness to try vocal experiments. (For example, "The Three Bears" have high, middle, and low voices.) By imitating sirens, train whistles, Halloween ghosts, or outer space sounds children learn to move their voices into the head voice register. Musical conversations, in which the teacher or a child sings a question and another singer answers, make a game out of singing. Categories, such as pets, toys, names, rhymes, parts of speech, colors, etc., add variety and interest and can lead to related learnings in other subjects.[20] Frequent individual practice is needed in order to get results.

HELPING CHILDREN LEARN TO SING

Maturation and instruction are both factors in vocal growth. Fundamentals of singing, (including posture, breath control, tone production and diction) and concepts of sustained tone, higher and lower, tone quality, melodic contour, and vocal tone production should be included in music instruction.

1. Sustained tone. At the time they begin school, some children have not discovered how singing differs from speaking and, therefore, need to discover that singing involves *sustaining* a vocal sound, in contrast to the short, unsustained sounds of everyday speech.
2. Higher and Lower. Children in preschool and the early grades confuse the terms for pitch and volume. We say, "Turn the television down!" and mean that it is too loud. When we tell the child the music goes "up," he or she may simply sing louder on the same pitch. A tall bassoon looks "high" but makes low sounds. A short piccolo looks "low" but makes high sounds.

   The following are examples of activities to help children learn to conceptualize high and low sounds.

   - Choose a song with an octave leap in the melody and relate the sounds to movement. ("Stretch high," "bend low.")
   - Play and listen to high and low sounds on classroom instruments. (Bells held vertically show high/low.)

- Reinforce learnings with pictures or diagrams.
- Improvise games. ("Stand when you hear high sounds; sit when you hear low sounds.")
- Obtain a sound effects recording from your local library and compare high/low pitches (such as a low fog horn and high electronic "space music").

3. Tonal concept. A concept of the desired vocal tone quality is essential. Children model their own singing after the styles they know, including such diverse sources as television, family, friends, and school. Current basic music series recordings feature children's voices that serve as models of good singing.

A resonant singing tone has focus but need not be loud. Because the voice sounds different to the listener than to the singer, the beginning singer may fail to open the mouth wide enough to project a good tone. Techniques to alleviate "clenched teeth" singing include the following:

- Tell the children "raise your upper jaw," a reverse logic statement that causes the lower jaw to move downward.
- Notice a small indentation that the synovial cavity forms just in front of the middle of the ear when the lower jaw moves down. As they sing, have students touch this indentation to test for a lowered jaw position.[21]

4. Melodic contour. Illustrate contour, the rise and fall of the melodic line, and invite children to trace contour with hand movements. Sing with an "oo" vowel to match the shape of the contour lines. Draw new contours, and match them with the voice. Use contour charts to emphasize contour in melodies the children have learned.

Contours

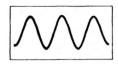  

 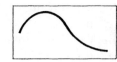 

5. Tone production. Emphasize correct posture and breath support. When standing, the singer's body should be erect, with chest raised and weight balanced forward on the feet, not back on the heels. Imagine a floppy puppet lifted into alignment by a string attached to the top of the head. When children are seated in chairs, have them sit forward, rather than recline against the back of the chair.

Breath support keeps the vocal tone alive and makes good singing possible. Inhale, and notice that the air fills the lungs as the ribs expand outward like the bellows of an accordion. As we exhale, the abdominal muscles are the "bellows" that control the release of air and enable us to sustain tones in and produce a musical phrase.

Use suggestions and exercises as posture and breath support reminders.

1. Imagine a tone as a ping-pong ball floating on a fountain of air. Without constant support, the ball will drop to the surface.

2. Inhale, then exhale with a hissing sound for a count of ten (or more).
3. Read a short poem aloud or count as far as possible in one breath. Learn to take in enough air and use it all.
4. Blow steadily on a simulated "candle" to make the flame flicker without going out.
5. Inhale while walking for six steps, then exhale completely on the following six steps. Gradually increase the count.
6. Puff at "dandelion seeds," or at a "pinwheel."
7. Imitate the buzz of a bee.[22]

Pitch Perception and Vocal Control

The cooperative efforts of the music specialist and the classroom teacher are needed to help children improve their singing skills. Daily singing in the classroom, for example, can do much to assist those children who sing out of tune primarily because of a lack of vocal experience. Like shooting free throws and other skills, singing improves with practice.

Research indicates that out-of-tune singing may be more a matter of vocal control than of inability to discriminate small pitch differences.[23] Out-of-tune singing also results from lack of concentration, poor posture, fatigue, improper room ventilation, excessively loud singing, or songs in too high or too low a singing range.

After the child has learned to distinguish between higher/lower and can show the difference between singing and speaking, there are several techniques to increase in-tune singing.

1. Sing songs on "loo" or hum part of the time so that children can concentrate on pitch and tone without the distraction of words.
2. Begin with limited range songs in the range between D and B.
3. Use musical games and movement activities combined with singing. The repetition of simple melodies is amusing for the child, who learns basic tonal and rhythmic patterns in a play situation.
4. Objectify pitch relationships by using instruments—bells, tuned water glasses, keyboard instruments—to show higher/lower pitch.
5. Melodies played on the piano have a percussive style that children unknowingly may imitate. Opinions differ as to whether or not the piano should be used to accompany young children's singing. Some teachers advocate soft chording as a support for singing; others say the piano should rarely be used with young voices.[24]
6. Once the children know a song, encourage them to sing independently. The teacher should listen to children as they sing, rather than constantly singing along with them.
7. Take advantage of the recorded materials in the basic music series to clarify pitch concepts: higher/lower, step-leap, specific tonal patterns, etc.
8. Individualize. For example, children may have trouble hearing their own voices. Have them cup their hands behind their ears as radio announcers used to do. Use a tape recorder to help in motivation and evaluation.
9. Keep progress records so that you can direct assistance to all children who need it rather than to the few most obvious voices.
10. Reinforce aural learning with visual aids: charts, pictures, diagrams, etc.
11. Use hand signs (see page 275) and movement as kinesthetic reinforcement for singing experiences.
12. Begin individual singing early in the year and try to let each lesson include activities and games with individual or small-group singing.
13. Remember that patience, persistence, and encouragement are important parts of the teaching-learning process.

14. Reinforce progress, but avoid indiscriminate praise.
15. Be sure that children share in the joy of achieving. The better they sing, the more rewarding it is. The more rewarding it is, the better they sing.

Diction

Good diction makes words easy to understand. Children's versions of well-known songs suggest that they don't always learn lyrics accurately. Writing in *Experiences in Music,* Phyllis Gelineau lists the following examples of the way they heard it: "Through the night with a light from a bulb," "Oh, beautiful for spaceship flies," "Heigh-ho the Cheerios," and "He is trampling out the vintage where the great giraffes are stored."[25]

Diction is a combination of correct pronunciation, clear enunciation, and crisp articulation. Regional pronunciations—*readin', athaletics, are* (for our), *all* (for oil), *card* (for cord)—are one diction problem, and another results when songs contain unfamiliar words, proper names, or foreign language texts. Recordings of the songs are often a helpful guide.

Focus on the five "basic" vowel sounds: *ee, eh, ah, oh,* and *oo.* Vowels, such as the *e* in *red,* have a single sound. Diphthongs join two sounds: *day* is sung *da + ee,* sustaining the first part and touching the last at the end. Without careful attention to vowel sounds, words such as *hail* and *hell* can be confused, as in "Hail, Hail, the Gang's All Here!"

Sing consonants on the same pitch as the vowel that follows, rather than gliding to the vowel sound. Do not omit final consonants or fail to articulate them clearly in words such as *little* ("liddle"). Too much "s" at the end of a word makes a group sound like a hiss or a leaky tire. Words ending in "er" have a harsh sound that is unpleasant when sustained. "Superrrrrrrrrr" sounds poor, not super.

Articulation

Practice in articulation can be enjoyable. Tongue twisters challenge the speaker or singer and can be used in vocal warmups as one way to emphasize clear articulation.

Dou - ble bub - ble, dou - ble bub - ble gum.

For additional practice, try the following tongue twisters.

Crick-et cri-tic
Yel-low yo-yo's
Six slim saplings
Truly rural
Eight apes ate eight ap-ples
Toy boat
Three tree twigs
Four fat frogs frying fritters
Double bubble gum
Some shun sunshine
Lemon liniment

Many collections of tongue twisters are available. Gyles Brandreth's *The Biggest Tongue Twister Book in the World* (New York: Sterling Publishing Co., 1980), and Alvin Schwartz's *A Twister of Twists, A Tangler of Tongues* (New York: J. B. Lippincott Co., 1977), are filled with them and with references to other sources. Tongue twisters are useful in developing pronunciation skills, as aids to creativity and writing (have children make up original tongue twisters), or as competitive games between teams: Who can score a point by repeating the tongue twister three or six times?

SINGING WITH EXPRESSION

Good tone production, correct rhythm, and accurate pitch are components of good singing. Attention to the meaning of the words and variety in dynamics and tempo help make singing more expressive.

Phrasing

Ask if there are any questions about the meaning and context of the words in a song. Have the group read aloud to improve phrasing, emphasizing the words and tones of greater importance in the musical phrase. Avoid a mechanical style of recitation. Explore contrasts in dynamics and tempo. Breathe after a longer tone or at the end of the phrase, but not in the middle of a word.

Listening to Recordings of Expressive Singing

Increase children's awareness of musical expression with questions, suggestions, class discussion, and even deliberately "wrong" interpretations. (For example, sing a slow song rapidly, a soft song loudly, or take a breath in the wrong place on purpose.) Ask students what changes they think are needed: Tempo? Dynamics? Tone quality? Make a recording of the children and ask them what they are doing well in their singing. What would they change? Listen to recordings by well-known singers and notice differences in interpretation. Here, for example, are contrasting recordings of the song "Bought Me a Cat."

Related Listening:
1. *Old American Songs by Aaron Copland,* William Warfield, Baritone. CD: CBS MK;   2. *Old American Songs* by Aaron Copland, Willard White, Bass. CD: Chandos CHAN 8960;   3. Beautiful Dreamer ("The Great American Songbook") Five Songs from Old American Songs, Marilyn Horne, Mezzo Soprano, CD: London 417242–2.

Bought Me a Cat

1. Bought me a cat, the cat pleased me,
2. Bought me a hen, the hen pleased me,

Fed my cat un-der yon-der tree.
Fed my hen un-der yon-der tree.

1. Cat went

fid-dle-i-dee,

2. 3. 4. 5. etc.

2. Hen says, "Chip-sy, chip-sy,"
3. Duck says, "Quack, Quack,"
4. Goose went sli-shy, slo-shy,
5. Cow says, "Moo, Moo,"
6. Dog says, "Bow, Wow,"
7. Sheep says, "Baa, Baa,"
8. Horse says, "Neigh, Neigh,"

> The song "Bought Me A Cat" is a simple melody with cumulative verses. With each repetition a new barnyard creature is added. The singer must list the newest animal (e.g., Horse says, "Neigh") and then the others—horse, sheep, dog, cow, goose, duck, hen—leading back to "cat went fiddle-i-dee."

Related Listening:
1. "Shenandoah," *The Music Book,* Grade 5;   2. *Music and You,* Grade 5;   3. Commercial recordings: *An Evening with Belafonte,* RCA LSP 1402;   4. Westminster Choir, *Folk Songs,* Joseph Flummerfelt, Conductor, CD: Gothic G38130.

In preschool or primary grades, individual children might imitate each animal's sound in the song. The teacher can point to soloists, or align them in sequence. A chart with pictures of the animals makes a good memory aid.

The changing meter of "Shenandoah" (page 49) has been mentioned, but the melody should also be enjoyed for its beauty and expressiveness. (In the words of one fifth grade boy, "I just can't get 'Shenandoah' out of my head.") The related listening examples provide various interpretations.

ROUNDS AND CANONS

Rounds and canons are more challenging than unison songs, but also more interesting. In a round each part follows the leader and sings exactly the same pitches. A *canon* (the word means a "rule") is also based on musical imitation, but the imitation can be at a higher or lower pitch level. Canons may involve compositional techniques such as *retrograde* (the melody moving backwards) or *inversion* (the melody turned upside down). (A *cannon* is a weapon that fires cannon balls or decorates a courthouse lawn.[26])

Some preparatory steps can lessen the beginner's difficulties in learning to sing a round. Clapping a *rhythmic ostinato* to accompany a known song introduces the challenge of two things at once. A *melodic ostinato* is only a little more difficult.

Numbers above the notes indicate parts one and two and show when to begin. Let the children sing part one and the teacher part two. Exchange parts and repeat, so that they understand how imitation works. Then have the children sing both parts. An outline of the pattern for a round follows:

> Divide the singers into as many groups as the round has parts.
> Learn the melody in unison.
> Sing it as a round. If it has two parts, each group sings the melody twice; three times for three parts, etc.
> End after each group completes the agreed-upon number of repetitions.

John Hilton's "Come, Follow Me," which is over 300 years old, is used by the contemporary American composer William Schuman in his *Concerto On Old English Rounds*. College students may wish to sing the song in a lower pitch range (see page 330).

Related Listening: William Schuman: *Concerto On Old English Rounds*, Columbia M–35101 (includes "Come, Follow Me").

PARTNER SONGS

Rounds produce imitative polyphony; partner songs illustrate non-imitative polyphony—two unlike melodies heard together. Songs with the same chord pattern can be combined as partner songs. Even though partner songs have the same underlying harmony, their contrasting rhythms and melodies call for attention to pitch and tempo, and careful listening.

"Land of the Silver Birch" and "The Canoe Song" can be accompanied by a single chord throughout. Their closely related subject matter makes them partners in text as well as in harmony.

Adapted from Honor Your Partner Songs *by Robert Perinchief. Copyright* © *1982. Perry Publications, Inc. Used by permission.*

Land of the Silver Birch and Canoe Song

"This Old Man" and "The Mulberry Bush" are partner songs that combine simple meter and compound meter. To make this rhythmic effect apparent to students, divide the class into two groups. Rehearse each song separately before singing the two melodies simultaneously. Add an instrumental interlude by playing the melody rhythms separately, then combined. Use contrasting rhythm instruments for the two songs.

The Mulberry Bush and This Old Man

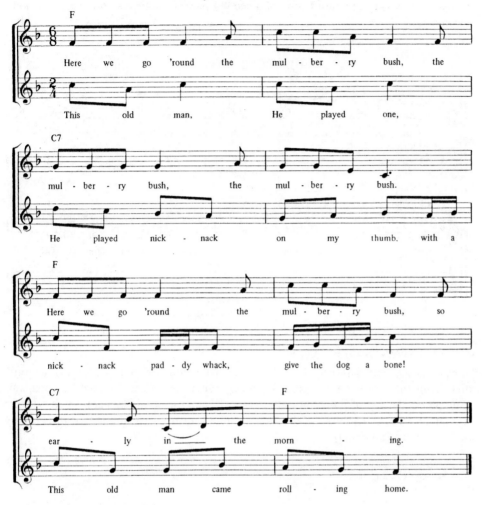

The songs in each of the following groups can be performed as partner songs.

1. "Bicycle Built for Two," "The Sidewalks of New York," and "In the Good Old Summertime"
2. "Bow Belinda," "Oh, Dear, What Can the Matter Be?," and "The Irish Washerwoman"
3. "Frère Jacques," "The Farmer in the Dell," "Row, Row, Row Your Boat," and "Three Blind Mice"
4. "Home on the Range" and "My Home's in Montana"
5. "This Old Man," "Skip to My Lou," "Sandy Land," "Here We Go 'Round the Mulberry Bush," and "Paw-Paw Patch"
6. "When the Saints Go Marching In" and "Swing Low, Sweet Chariot"
7. "Land of the Silver Birch" and "Canoe Song"
8. "Joshua Fought the Battle," "Wade in the Water," and "Hey Ho, Nobody Home"
9. "She'll Be Coming 'Round the Mountain" and "When the Saints Go Marching In"
10. "Go Tell Aunt Rhody," "He's Got the Whole World in His Hands," "London Bridge," "Merrily We Roll Along," and "Good Night, Ladies"
11. "Hop Up, My Ladies" and "Shortnin' Bread"

SINGING CHORD ROOTS

Singing or playing the chord root as a second part is another step toward harmonic awareness.

My Darling Clementine

CHANTS AND DESCANTS

A *chant* is a second part, usually added beneath a melody. Melodies based on the tonic and dominant chords have a common tone—a note that occurs in both chords. For example, in the key of F the tonic chord (F A C) and the dominant chord (C E G) have a common tone, C. A rhythmic chant on the note C results in a simple type of harmony to accompany the melody.

A more interesting chant results if a nonchord tone is added to the common tone. In this example, the nonchord tone uses scale step number six (*la*).

A *descant* is a second part, above the regular melody. A descant is added to "My Darling Clementine" in the next example.

My Darling Clementine

Descant by B. Beagle

SINGING IN HARMONY

Traditional harmony in thirds is the basis for the two-part harmony of the song "Saturday Night."

Saturday Night

Nigerian Folk Song

SUGGESTED ACTIVITIES

1. Notate your comfortable vocal range from low to high. Use a piano to help you locate your lowest and highest singing pitches.
2. Make a tape recording of a song you have memorized. After listening to the tape, record the song again as you concentrate on improving some aspect of your singing.

3. Practice the routine of starting a song (establishing the tempo and starting pitch), taking turns with several classmates. Review pickup notes and basic conducting as needed.
4. Visit music classes in a local elementary school. Observe the procedures used by the music teacher to lead the children in singing. Write a brief description of the children's singing voices, or consider the items suggested in the checklist that follows. Listen objectively to the children's singing (or make a tape recording), then assess their strengths and weaknesses. (Circle the item according to your judgment.)

Checklist

Participation	Most students involved	A few nonparticipants	Little involvement
Music	Worthwhile & expressive	Could be better words _____ music _____	Trivial & lacking in appeal
Singing			
Posture	Excellent	Fair	Unsatisfactory
Breath Control	Excellent	Fair	Unsatisfactory
Tone Quality	Satisfactory	Timid, uncertain	Strident (belting)
Volume	Satisfactory	Too soft	Too loud
Pitch	Well in tune	A few problem singers	Many students singing out of tune
Range	Well developed	Making progress	Unsatisfactory for this age level
Flexibility	Excellent	Some problems in relaxation	Too much tension, little flexibility
Diction	Very clear	Needs attention	Unintelligible
Blend	Excellent	Some voices not blending	Children not listening
Balance	Satisfactory	Accompaniment sometimes too loud	Can't hear singers
(Voices and accompaniment, if any)			
Precision	Excellent	Needs attention	Not together
Dynamic Range	Excellent	Not enough contrast	All one level
Resonance	Voices in focus	Improving	Too whispery or too forced
Vocal Independence	Students can sing without aid of teacher or recording	Improving	Students unable to get through the song unaided
Part Singing	Students can sing in parts	A few students can sing in parts	Students can sing only in unison
Style	Students match singing to style of music	Improving	Students unaware of different vocal and musical styles
Expression	Generally expressive	Improving	Needs attention

NOTES

[1] H. A. Vandercook, *Teaching the High School Band* (Chicago: Rubank, Inc., 1926), 53.

[2] Benjamin Bloom, *Human Characteristics and School Learning* (New York: McGraw-Hill, 1976), 149.

[3] Jos Wuytack, *Musica Viva: Orff Instruments* (Paris: Alphonse LeDuc, 1970), 8.

[4] William Salaman, *Living School Music* (Cambridge, Mass.: Cambridge University Press, 1983), 29–30.

[5] Roy Blount, Jr., "The Singing Impaired," *The Atlantic*, February 1982, 77–78.

[6] Ellen Winner, *Invented Worlds, The Psychology of the Arts* (Cambridge, Mass.: Harvard University Press, 1982), 232.

[7] Donna Brink Fox, "An Analysis of the Pitch Characteristics of Infant Vocalizations," *Psychomusicology*, 9, no. 1 (Spring 1990), 21–30.

[8] Lyle Davidson, Patricia McKernon, and Howard E. Gardner, "The Acquisition of Song: A Developmental Approach," in *Documentary Report of the Ann Arbor Symposium: Applications of Psychology to the Teaching and Learning of Music* (Reston, Va.: Music Educators National Conference, 1981), 301–315.

[9] Edwin E. Gordon, "The Nature and Description of Developmental and Stabilized Music Aptitudes: Implications for Music Learning," in *Music and Child Development*, eds. Frank R. Wilson and Franz L. Roehmann (St. Louis: MMB Music, Inc., 1990), 331.

[10] Edwin E. Gordon, *Learning Sequences in Music, Skill, Content, and Patterns*, Chicago: G.I.A., 1989), 274.

[11] Kenneth H. Phillips, "Training the Child Voice," *Music Educators Journal* (December 1985), 57.

[12] The collection of fifty musical fingerplays, *Eye Winker, Little Tom Tinker, Chin Chopper* by Tom Glazer (New York: Doubleday and Company, Inc., 1973), has directions for "Eensie Weensie Spider," "The Bear Went Over the Mountain," "Charlie Over the Water," "Jack and Jill," "The Mulberry Bush," and many other enjoyable songs for young children.

[13] Merilyn Jones, "A Study of Vocal Pitch-Matching Skills Among Undergraduate Education Majors Using Classroom Instruments," *Update, The Applications of Research in Music Education,"* 7, no. 2 (Spring 1989), 39–41.

[14] National Endowment for the Arts, *Toward Civilization, A Report on Arts Education* (Washington, D.C.: National Endowment for the Arts, 1988), 80.

[15] Jeffrey Kimpton, "The Learning Tree," *General Music* 2, no. 2 (Winter 1988), 13–14.

[16] Marilyn P. Zimmerman, "State of the Art in Early Childhood Music and Research," *The Young Child and Music* (Reston, Va.: Music Educators National Conference, 1985), 67.

[17] Sylvesta Wassum, "Elementary School Children's Vocal Range," *Journal of Research in Music Education,* 27, no. 4 (Winter 1979), 214–26.

[18] Kurt Adler, *The Art of Accompanying and Coaching* (Minneapolis: University of Minnesota Press, 1965; Da Capo Press, paperback edition, 1976), 38–41.

[19] *See* Linda Swears, *Teaching the Elementary School Chorus* (West Nyack, N.Y.: Parker Publishing Co., Inc., 1985), 62–66.

[20] Dorothy Grant Hennings, *Words, Sounds and Thoughts* (New York: Citation Press, 1977), is a compendium of ideas for enriching communication skills.

[21] Paul F. Roe, *Choral Music Education,* 2d ed. (Englewood Cliffs, N.J.: Prentice-Hall, Inc., 1983), 96–98.

[22] Wilhelm Ehmann and Frauke Haasemann, *Voice Building for Choirs,* English trans. by Brenda Smith (Chapel Hill, N.C.: Hinshaw Music, Inc., 1982).

[23] *See* Graham F. Welch, "Poor Pitch Singing: A Review of the Literature," *Psychology of Music,* 7, no. 1 (1979), 50–58.

[24] The final verdict on the effects of accompanied singing remains to be heard, according to a review of research on this topic by Betty W. Atterbury. See *Bulletin of the Council for Research in Music Education* (Summer 1987), 69–78.

[25] From *Experiences in Music,* 2d ed, by R. Phyllis Gelineau (New York: McGraw-Hill, 1976), 21.

[26] Silver Burdett and Ginn's *World of Music,* Grade 8, includes a canon by Antonio Salieri with words that remind us throughout that a canon is not a cannon.

MUSIC READING AND WRITING 9

We use music reading skills whenever the eye helps the ear in learning music. Children apply music reading skills when learning a new song, when playing an instrument, when using notation to guide music listening, or when writing out the notes of an original arrangement or composition.

Progress in music reading is related to the child's chronological age, previous musical experience, and level of motivation. "One cannot expect a child who has had almost no contacts with music, who has never found out that music is something to be enjoyed and sought after, and who is perfectly indifferent to it, to be in any genuine sense ready to begin learning to read it."[1]

Like the written word, music notation is complex and abstract. At first, children represent their understanding of basic musical concepts through the *enactive* mode. They sing, play, and use movement to express what they know about loud/soft, long/short, slow/fast, high/low, same/different, and other concepts. *Ikons*—pictures or diagrams that look like what they represent—help children visualize rhythm patterns and pitch patterns. A diagram of stairsteps, for example, resembles the ascending or descending scale. Long and short lines picture long and short sounds. Rote songs, listening to music, and many other aural experiences prepare the way for music reading instruction.

TEACHING MUSIC READING

Building awareness of beat, tone color, dynamics, duration, tempo, and pitch precedes instruction in music reading. Young children can learn to distinguish between musical sounds that are relatively loud or soft, long or short, fast or slow, high or low, but they find verbal labeling more difficult than using speech, song, and movement to represent their musical understanding.[2]

TEACHING HIGH AND LOW

Children's invented notation for melody progresses from pictures and shapes to combinations of language and symbols. Staff notation with notes and other symbols comes later, because it is more abstract.[3] Primary grade children enjoy matching sounds with pictures and creating sounds to represent the high/low, loud/soft, long/short, fast/slow associations the pictures call to mind.

CHANTS

Singing and hearing chant-like melodies with two or three notes (such as "Rain, Rain, Go Away") develop aural and vocal skills used in the early stages of in-tune singing and music reading. Teachers often create chants to greet the children when they enter the room, carrying on musical conversations made from the *la-so-mi* pitches of "Rain, Rain, Go Away." Chants based on rhymes and other speech patterns offer many other possibilities.

See-Saw

See - saw, up and down, in the sky and on the ground.

Jack Be Nimble

Jack be nim - ble, Jack be quick, Jack jump ov - er the can - dle stick.

Bee, Bee, Bumble bee

Bee, bee, bum - ble bee, stung a man up - on the knee,

stung a pig up - on the snout, I de - clare that you are out.

MOVEMENT

Show pitch relationships with movement in space. "Listen to the (piano, bells, xylophone, etc.). Stretch up high or crouch down low to match the sounds you hear." After singing and listening to "Bounce High, Bounce Low," repeat the song and direct children to show higher or lower pitch by moving their hands higher and lower with the melody.

TEACHING MELODIC CONTOUR

Studies indicate that children learn the words, rhythm, and contour of a melody in that order.[4] Use lengths of yarn to show melodic *contours* on the felt board. Invite children to arrrange patterns on the board to represent contours of phrases from a known song and have them match contours with phrases by listening. Ask them which phrase occurs first, second, third, and so forth. Emphasize repetition and contrast by using matching or contrasting colors of yarn. Sing *higher* and *lower* sounds to match contour designs on posters.

HIGH AND LOW

Low to high moves from left to right on the horizontal piano keyboard. To clarify pitch direction, place small xylophones or bell sets in a vertical position. The slide whistle is another good instrument for demonstrating pitch movement between low and high. (Learning to play a tune on a slide whistle also gives the student opportunities for careful listening and ear training.) Commercial "step bells," available from music stores, show high and low as steps on a staircase. You can make an inexpensive staircase from styrofoam to support resonator bells. Place a 20 inch by 8 inch strip of two-inch thick styrofoam on the bottom. Make each higher step two inches shorter than the one beneath. Use one-inch thick sheets to show the half steps between *mi-fa* and *ti-do*.[5]

KEYBOARD CHARTS

Keyboard charts clarify pitch relationships. Half steps and whole steps look equidistant in staff notation, but can be visualized accurately with the keyboard. A large chart of the piano keyboard can be held in a vertical position to show high/low, and then moved to its normal horizontal position.

Hold the chart against your chest and point to the keys that correspond to the notes of a simple melody. (Use a bright colored pencil as a pointer to increase visibility.)

Have the children echo what you sing, then ask them to sing (using numbers, note names, or syllables) as you point.[6]

TEACHING STEPS, SKIPS, SCALES

Draw the rectangular shapes of resonator bells on oaktag with a felt marker. Diatonic "bell mats" help children visualize "steps and skips" or the idea that pentatonic scales can be formed by omitting steps four and seven from the major scale. Teach students to align the bells in order by placing them on the bell mat. Chromatic bell mats show the half step progression of the chromatic scale.

(*a*) Bells: C major scale;
(*b*) Bells: C pentatonic scale.

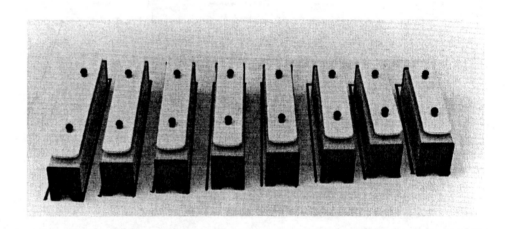

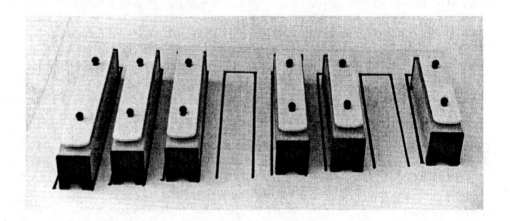

(The catalogs of music merchandise retailers include "Bellboards," which are durable, brightly colored outlines of instrument tone bars. Bellboards are available in sets of 25 desktop and one 17½ × 22½ chart size bellboard in diatonic or chromatic designs.)

LINE NOTATION

Draw higher and lower lines to show the melody's movement. Show long and short sounds with longer and shorter lines. Sing the song and point to the higher and lower lines. Ask the children to do the same on their "picture" of the melody.

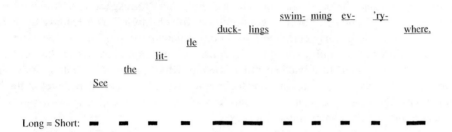

NUMBER NOTATION

The following example combines numbers with simplified rhythmic notation to show the melody of "Are You Sleeping?" ("*Frère Jacques*").[7]

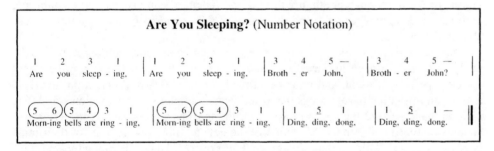

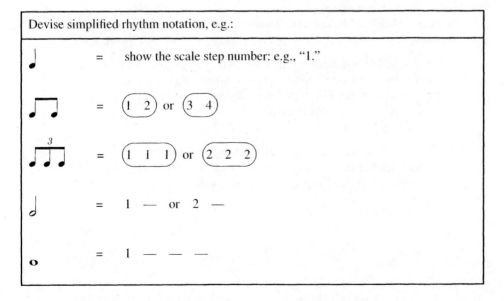

THE KODÁLY APPROACH

Many American music educators have been inspired by the ideals of the late Zoltán Kodály (1882–1967), who established a system of music education in Hungary that has gained international renown. Honored throughout the world for his achievements as a composer, musicologist, and music educator, Kodály insisted that music was for everyone, not just the most talented. He urged teachers to respect their students' musical potential: "Only the best is good enough for children." The Kodály approach emphasizes music in early childhood, unaccompanied singing, the use of selected folk songs and art music, and a carefully organized sequence of instruction that extends from early childhood to advanced musicianship. Rhythm syllables, hand signs, and movable *do* syllables are among the techniques Kodály selected in developing his approach. The main goals of the Kodály approach are to instill a love of music in children and to teach basic music literacy.

The classroom teacher can make use of basic principles and techniques derived from the Kodály approach, though Kodály pedagogy requires a level of musicianship and training far beyond the scope of a music fundamentals book. (Teachers seeking in-depth information should explore books on the Kodály approach and consider attending workshops or programs at universities offering Kodály training.)[8]

SYLLABLES

Kodály pedagogy includes singing games, visual aids, and instructional techniques that make music classes enjoyable as well as productive. ("A fundamental premise of Kodály's philosophy was that music and singing should be taught to provide pleasurable experiences rather than drudgery.")[9] Pitch notation is introduced through many gradual increments, each presented in a developmentally appropriate, child-centered learning sequence. High-low pitches in songs or chants lead to the use of syllables. Rote songs prepare children for *la so* and *mi.* New syllables are presented in a sequence moving from *la so* and *mi* to additional tones of the pentatonic scale (*do re mi so* and *la*). During the child's first-grade year, for instance, only *la so mi* and *do* are "made conscious," even though children will sing and listen to many songs that contain the entire scale. Syllables for pitch and rhythm help children identify and remember tonal and rhythm patterns.

Kodály teaching derives learnings from selected songs that children have previously sung and enjoyed in varied classroom activities.[10] Teachers use a three-stage pattern—prepare, present, and practice—to help children learn. Preparation involves singing and listening to rote songs that offer clear examples of the new element. After children have learned the songs thoroughly, the teacher uses questions to derive responses that lead children to conceptualize the new learning on the basis of their musical experiences. Children then strengthen their grasp of the new learning by applying it in new songs and contexts.[11]

Each new syllable adds new tonal possibilities as children continue to practice the tonal patterns already learned. Syllables are presented in the following sequence:

> **So, mi,** and **la** and the tonal patterns that contain these syllables.
> **Do** and tonal patterns containing *la so mi* and *do.*
> **Re** and tonal patterns containing pentatonic scale tones.
> Low **la** and **so** and other pentatonic tonal patterns.
> High **do** and other pentatonic tonal patterns.

> Each new syllable is prepared by learning numerous songs that contain the new tonal patterns. Examples of songs that might be chosen in learning a new tonal combination are shown here.

Rain, Rain Go Away

Rain, rain, go a - way. Come a - gain some oth - er day.

Bounce High

Children's Song

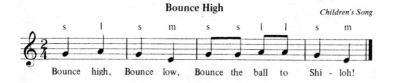

Bounce high, Bounce low, Bounce the ball to Shi - loh!

Ring Aroung the Rosy

Singing Game

Ring a - round the ro - sy, a poc - ket full of po - sies,

Ash - es, ash - es, we all fall down.

The Closet Key

Singing Game

1. I have lost the clo - set key, in my la - dy's gar - den,
2. Help me find the clo - set key, in my la - dy's gar - den,

I have lost the clo - set key, in my la - dy's gar - den.
Help me find the clo - set key, in my la - dy's gar - den.

(Solo)

3. I have found the closet key, in my lady's garden,
   I have found the closet key in my lady's garden.

From On the Trail of Negro Folk Songs *by Dorothy Scarborough,* © *1925 Harvard University Press; renewed 1953 by Mary McDaniel Parker. Reprinted by permission of the publishers.*

Who's That Tapping at the Window?

Singing Game

Who's that tap-ping at the win - dow? Who's that knock-ing at the door?
I am tap-ping at the win - dow. I am knock-ing at the door.

From On the Trail of Negro Folk Songs *by Dorothy Scarborough,* © *1925 Harvard University Press; renewed 1953 by Mary McDaniel Parker. Reprinted by permission of the publishers.*

From 150 American Folk Songs, *selected and edited by Peter Erdei and Katalin Komlos. Copyright © 1974. Boosey and Hawkes. Used by permission.*

Bluebird

The syllables *fa* and *ti* are presented after children have internalized pentatonic pitch sets. Notice that syllables are identified by their initial letter.

Syllable initials: A minor/C major

HAND SIGNS

Hand signs show the rise and fall of pitch through movement. Each syllable has its own hand sign, which is introduced in the same sequence as its syllable name. Sight, sound, and touch combine kinesthetic, aural, and visual learning modes for maximum impact. (Kinesthetic learning involves a linking of the physical response to the brain's information processing and memory centers.)[12] The child shows the hand signs with one hand: low *do* is at waist level and high *do* is above the head. By using both hands the child or teacher can show simultaneous pitches in order to practice intervals and intonation.[13]

Hand Signal Chart

Sight and Sound—Revised Curwen Signals

From Sight and Sound *by Arpad Darazs and Stephen Jay. Boosey and Hawkes, Inc.* © 1965. *Used by permission.*

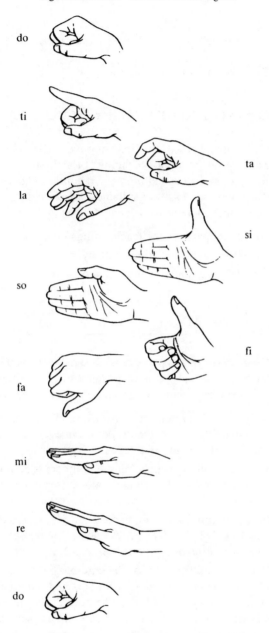

do

ti

ta

la

si

so

fi

fa

mi

re

do

SOL-FA NOTATION

Write syllable letters beneath rhythm stem notation to show melody in "sol-fa" notation. Sol-fa notation does not require knowledge of lines, spaces, clefs, and key signatures.

Love Somebody (solfa notation)

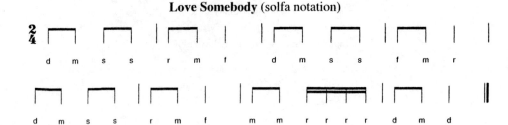

LEARNING TO SING AND IDENTIFY TONAL PATTERNS BY SOUND

Students' skill in recognizing tonal patterns improves with regular practice. Small amounts of daily practice in imitating ("echoing") tonal patterns from known songs develops "tonal thinking" skills needed in music reading. Echo tonal patterns first on a neutral syllable, then with the *do-re-mi* syllables. As skills increase, ask children to respond with *syllable* names to patterns presented on "loo."

■ Repeat ("echo") tonal patterns the teacher sings on "*loo*".

■ Repeat tonal patterns the teacher sings with syllables.

■ Respond with syllables to patterns presented on "loo."

lsm	msl	slm	lms	mls	mrd	drm	smd

Singing with Syllables Compared to Numbers and Letter Names

Numbers, letters, or syllables may be used to label pitch in singing.[14] Movable *do* syllables have certain advantages compared to numbers or letter names.

■ Movable-*do* syllables label pitch *relationships* in all keys and modes. Major scales begin on *do* and have the same syllables in every key. Minor scales begin on *la* and have the same syllables in every key.[15]

■ Numbers also indicate relationships, but the numbers used for major scales are the same as for minor scales, though the scales differ in construction and sound.

■ Numbers require counting backward, and skipping numbers for descending interval patterns (8-6-4-2, 8-5-3-1, 4-2-7-5, etc.) The numbers above or below the basic octave are confusing: "8-9-10" or " 8-2-3" or "high 1-2-3?"

■ There are syllables for all the notes of the chromatic scale and movable-*do* syllables match one sound to one note. Numbers and letter names may require words of more than one syllable for a single note ("sev-en," "E-flat"). Numbers and letter names are awkward when there are accidentals. (For example, in harmonic minor, "sharp seven" is harder to sing than changing the syllable from *so* to *si*.)

■ Pitch numbers are easy to confuse with fingering numbers on instruments. ("Hot Cross Buns" in G major uses scale numbers 3-2-1 but recorder fingers 1-2-3. Different sets of finger numbers are used for right or left hand at the keyboard.)

Chromatic syllables: do   di   re   ri   mi   fa   fi   so   si   la   li   ti   do

Descending chromatic syllables are changed to a spelling ending in "e": *do, ti, te* (tay), *la le* (lay), etc. The exception is *re,* which must be changed to *ra* (rah).

do   ti   te   la   le   so   se   fa   mi   me   re   ra   do

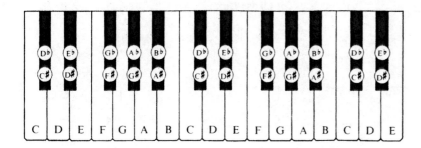

SING MELODIES FROM SOL-FA NOTATION

Melodies written in sol-fa notation help develop aural skills and familiarity with tonal and rhythm patterns. Review the following songs. Include one or more of the following activities:

1. Sing each song with words and syllables.
2. Clap and chant its rhythm syllables.
3. Show the hand signs.
4. Write the song in staff notation in the keys of C, F, G (if minor, in A, D, or E minor).
5. Sing it with letter names in each key.
6. Learn to sing the song with pitch syllables by memory.
7. Combine singing with conducting, hand signs or clapping a rhythmic ostinato.

Learn each song thoroughly before moving to the next one.

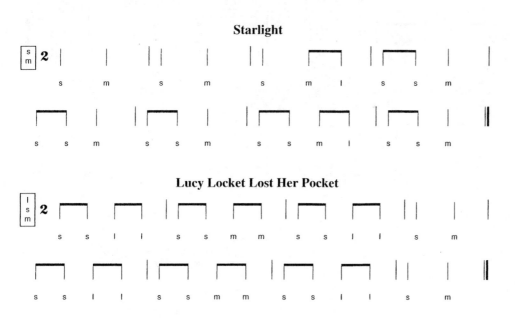

Starlight

Lucy Locket Lost Her Pocket

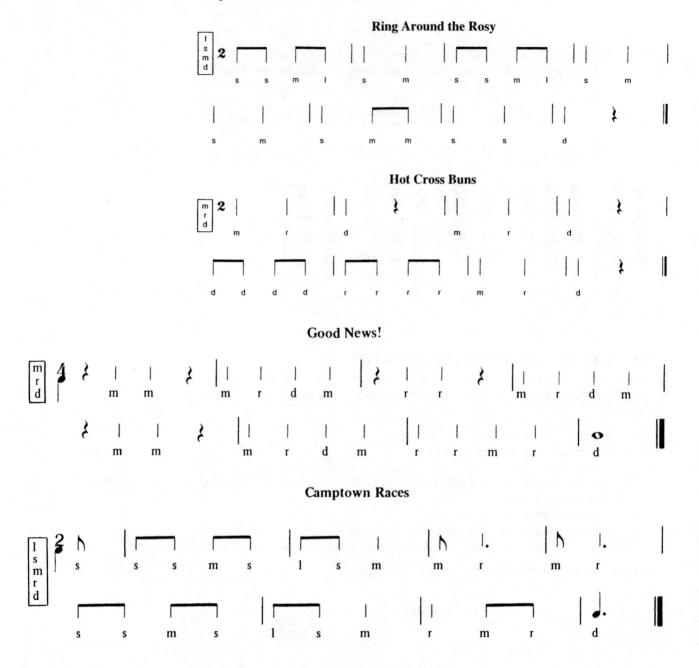

Old MacDonald Had a Farm

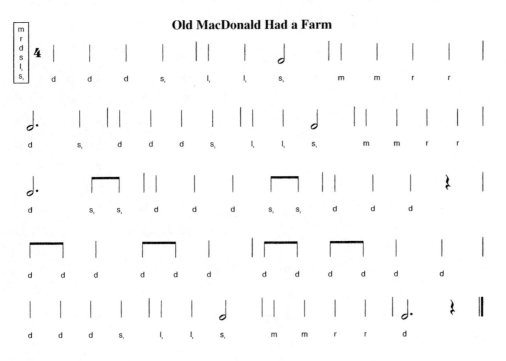

Scotland's Burning

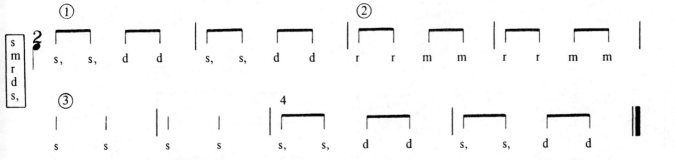

Hop Up, My Ladies

Twinkle, Twinkle Little Star

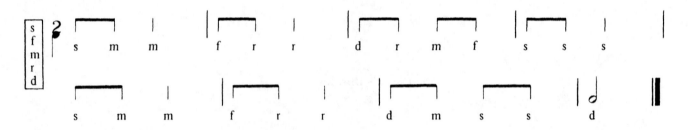

Lightly Row

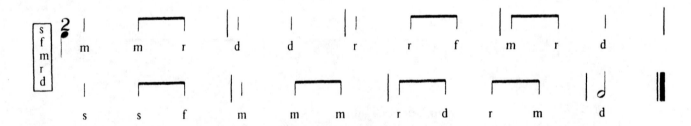

Go Tell Aunt Rhody

London Bridge

America

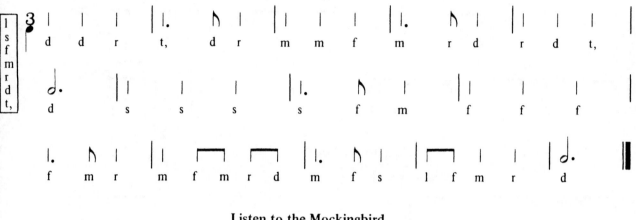

Listen to the Mockingbird

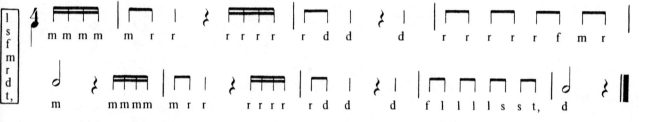

Jingle Bells

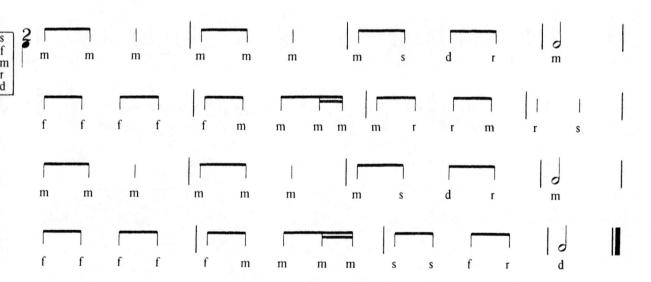

This Old Man

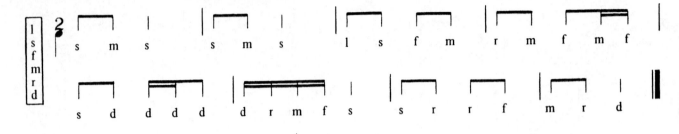

Skip to My Lou

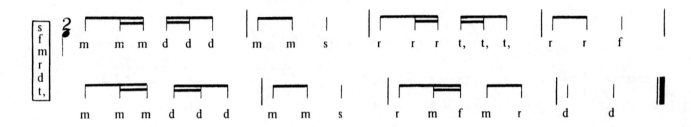

When The Saints Go Marching In

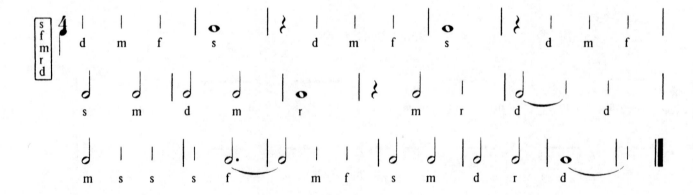

Taffy

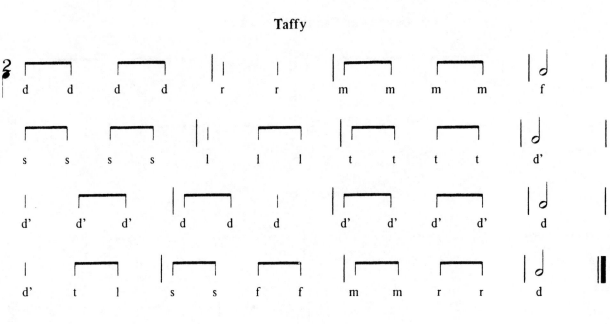

Sweet Betsy from Pike

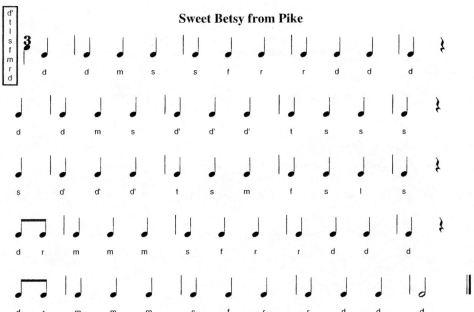

The Mulberry Bush

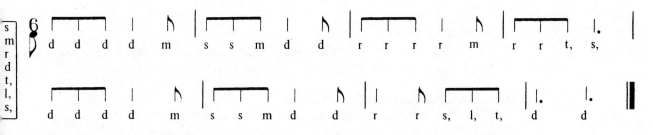

Oh, Dear! What Can the Matter Be?

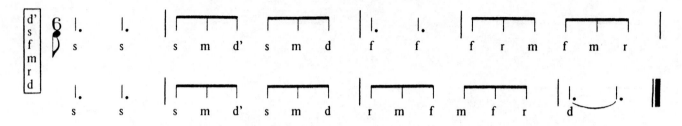

The Birch Tree

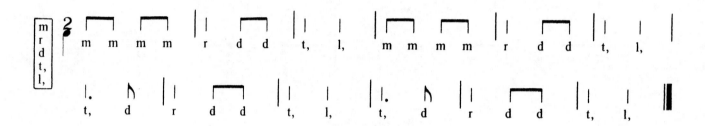

Old Abram Brown

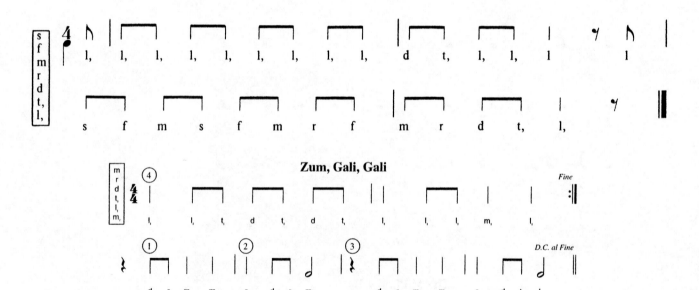

Zum, Gali, Gali

STAFF NOTATION

A *one-line* staff shows "on the line, above the line, or below the line." Some music reading materials add staff lines one at a time before introducing the five-line staff.

Instruments and Staff Notation

To show relationships between sounds and symbols, draw the music staff on the chalkboard or flannel board, using lines spaced to match the dimensions of tone bars from a set of melody bells (see page 187).[16]

Tuning Fork

After drawing a five-line staff on the chalkboard or on a poster, place a resonator bell or a tuning fork in the second space to show the position of A-440 (A above middle C) and strengthen the child's association of sight and sound.

Tuning fork

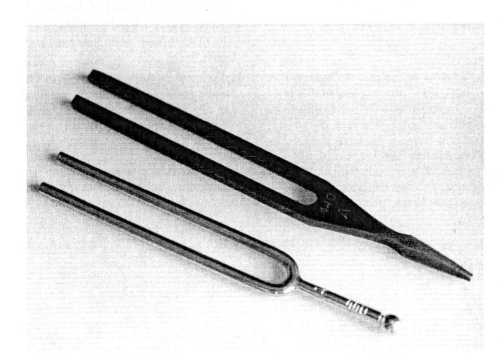

Felt Staves and Notes

Use a felt staff to help children learn that there are five lines and four spaces, that lines and spaces are counted from low to high, that notes can be in a space or on a line, and that familiar tonal patterns can be shown with notes on the staff.

> Making a felt staff. Draw music staff lines on felt with a marker. Cut out note heads from a contrasting colored piece of felt. Make each note oval shaped. It should fill the space between the lines without touching the line above or below. Prepare smaller felt staves for children's desktops. Attach a pocket beneath the lines in order to store the notes when they are not in use.

Magnetic Staff Board

You can make a magnetic staff board by drawing staff lines on a metal baking sheet. Sets of colored round magnets, available from office supply stores, make good notes.

Laminated Notes and Staves

Prepare sets of laminated note heads and music staves that children can use in developing understanding of pitch relationships.[17]

Floor Staff

A floor staff, made with masking tape lines on the floor, is all that is needed for activities such as the following. (A portable floor staff, printed on vinyl can be purchased or constructed, using black marker and a white, unpatterned, vinyl table cloth.)

Movement only

1. Hop from line to line or from space to space.
2. Hop from line one to line three, etc.

3. Hop from G to A, etc.

4. Three or four students "spell a musical word" by standing on the lines or spaces required by the word (e.g., BEE).[18]

Movement to sounds

1. Step on lines to show *so-mi* or *mi-so*. Step in spaces to show *so-mi* or *mi-so*.
2. Line two is *so*. Move the way the music moves. (Play *sls, sms, lsm,* etc.)
3. Three "notes" stand on BAG, FAC, or EDC. "Bend when you hear your note."
4. Three or four students "spell a musical word" by standing on the lines or spaces that match the tonal pattern the teacher plays (e.g., EGG).

Note-Name Stickers

Commercial electronic keyboard instruction books provide note-name stickers for piano keys so that beginners can match them to music notation that shows letter names inside note heads.

This Old Man

This old man,   he played one,   He played knick, knack,

Do *Clef*

The *do* clef (which resembles the prongs of an old-fashioned key) can be used to designate any line or space as *do,* thus offering great flexibility in showing tonal patterns. In the keys of C, F, or G, pentatonic songs have no sharps or flats in their key signatures. By introducing the basic elements of staff notation with pentatonic songs in these keys, the teacher can postpone explanations of accidentals and key signatures until a later stage of learning.

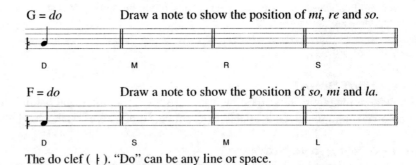

The do clef (⊦). "Do" can be any line or space.

Using Music Books

Music reading implies the ability to link sound and symbol—to "hear what you see and see what you hear." Long before functional music reading skills develop, however, children use visual cues from pictures, charts, and songbooks in learning new songs. Music reading is present to some extent whenever the notation of words and music facilitates learning. The intermediate stage between rote learning and music reading is sometimes called "rote-note" learning.

Pictures and diagrams supplement notation in music books, and children in the primary grades can use their reading skills to follow the words of the song, locate page numbers, and observe other details on the printed page. (As one music teacher describes it, the students "read the words, ignore the notes and pick up the melody by ear.")[19] Establish a routine for distributing and collecting music books and guide children in using them. Point out details such as the following:

> The song's words are written beneath the staff.
> Longer words are divided into syllables to fit the music.
> The words of the second verse are written beneath the words of the first verse.
> The words are read from left to right on the page, just as in language.
> The notes of the music may go up, down, or straight across.
> Repeat signs are used to save space.
> Each page has its own number.

INTERVALS

An interval is the distance between two pitches. Pitches played simultaneously are called *harmonic* intervals; pitches played one after the other are called *melodic* intervals.

To measure the size of an interval, call its lower note one and count up to the higher note. (Example: C D E F G; C up to G is a 5th.) The number of letter names or scale steps is the same as the size of any interval.

When one note is on a line and the other is in a space, the intervals are 2nds, 4ths, 6ths, and 8ths (octaves).When both notes are on lines or in spaces, the intervals are 3rds, 5ths, 7ths, and 9ths.

Intervals

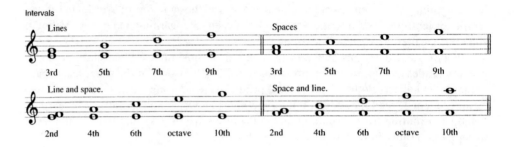

Intervals wider than an octave—9ths, 10ths, etc.—are known as *compound* intervals.

INTERVAL QUALITIES

From C to D♭ is a half step—a *minor* second; from C to D is a whole step—a *major* (large) second. From C to D♯ is a step and a half—an *augmented* second. The terms *major, minor, perfect, augmented,* and *diminished* indicate the precise size of each numerical interval.

Perfect intervals are the unison, 4th, 5th, and octave. In perfect intervals each note is in the major scale of the other. From C to G is a perfect fifth—C is in the G scale and G is in the C scale.

Major and minor intervals are the 2nd, 3rd, 6th, and 7th. Major intervals are always a half step wider than the corresponding minor intervals. From C to E is a *major* third; from C to E♭ is a *minor* third. An interval's exact size depends on the number of half steps it contains. Major intervals are always a half step wider than minor intervals.

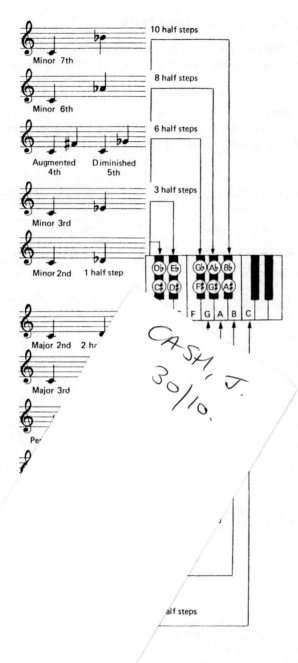

10 half steps
Minor 7th

8 half steps
Minor 6th

6 half steps
Augmented   Diminished
4th   5th

3 half steps
Minor 3rd

Minor 2nd   1 half step

Major 2nd   2 h

Major 3rd

Pe

Db Eb   Gb Ab Bb
C# D#   F# G# A#

F G A B C

CASH, J.
30/10.

alf steps

MUSIC NOTATION ACTIVITIES

Write music in staff notation after experiences in deriving and practicing tonal patterns and syllables from songs that were learned by rote. Practice the following notation skills.

Notes and Stems

Copy the indicated notes. Make note heads oval, not round. The whole note is horizontal to the staff. Other note heads slant upward.

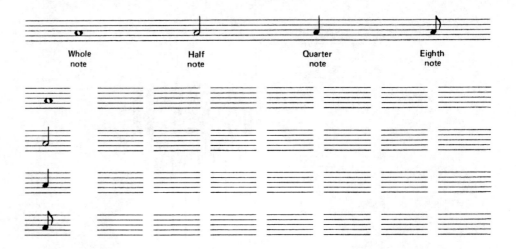

Draw stems about an octave in length. Use downward stems for notes above the third line and upward stems for notes below the third line. Notes on the third line may have upward or downward stems. Flags are always attached to the right of the stem.

Beams

Beams are used to group eighth notes and sixteenth notes and to group notes into beats. Avoid drawing beams in such a way that they can be confused with staff lines.

Some stems must be lengthened when using beams with notes of different pitch. The shortest stem should be approximately an octave in length. Slanted beams should not cross more than one staff line.

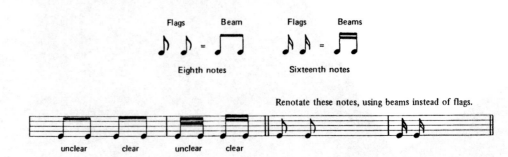

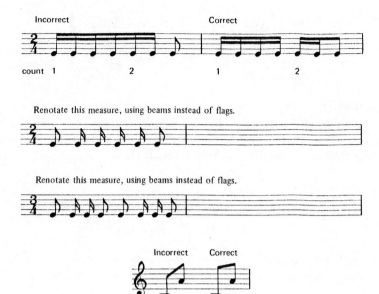

Renotate this measure, using beams instead of flags.

Renotate this measure, using beams instead of flags.

Rests

The *quarter rest* extends from the fourth space down to the second line of the staff. The shape of the engraved quarter rest is difficult to draw. A simpler shape, resembling a reversed letter "Z" is often used.

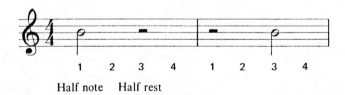

The *half rest* sits on the third line.

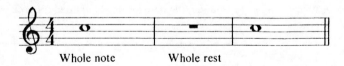

The *whole rest* is placed in the center of the measure and hangs beneath the fourth line.

A complete measure of rest is always shown with a whole rest, regardless of the time signature.

Dots and Ties

Place the tie on the side of the note that is opposite from the stem, except when there are other tied notes that are sung or played at the same time. Draw the tie above or below the note heads on the side opposite from the stems.

For whole notes, write the tie above notes higher than the third line of the staff and below notes lower than the third line (the same as if they had stems).

Place the dot to the right of a note. If the note is on a line, place the dot in the space above the line.

Bar Lines

Draw *bar lines* to divide each rhythm into measures corresponding with the time signature. Circle the accented note(s) in each measure.

> **Stem notation**
>
> When the staff is not used to indicate pitch, rhythm notation can be shown in shorthand *stem notation*. When using stem notation, the note heads are omitted for note values shorter than half notes.

Clefs

The treble clef shows the location of G.

    a. To draw the clef, begin with a slanted line on the staff.
    b. Add a loop that crosses at the fourth line of the staff.
    c. Continue, curving around the second line (G).
    d. Notice that the curve touches the bottom line and the third line.
    e. Draw treble clefs.

Treble Clef

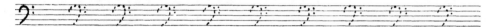

The bass clef has dots on either side of the fourth line (F).

Bass Clef

Accidentals

The accidentals used in notation, listed from low to high, are double flats, flats, naturals, sharps, and double sharps. When written before a note, the symbols should be in the same space or on the same line as the note.

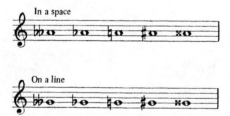

The natural sign has two vertical lines and two slanted lines that make an enclosed section.

Natural

Sharps have two parallel vertical lines and two thicker, slanted lines that cross the vertical lines. On the staff, place the sharp before (to the left of) the note. Write the sharp in the same space or on the same line as the note it affects.

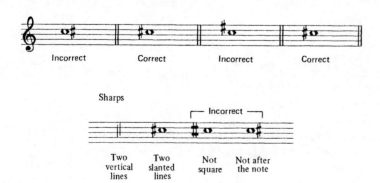

Flats have a vertical line, about two and one half spaces in height. The loop portion, about one space high, should be centered in front of the note head, in the same space, or on the same line as the note.

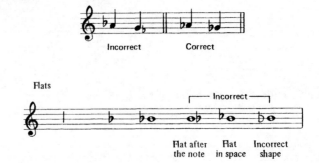

Place any required sharp(s) or flat(s) to the left of notes so as to form major scales.

Key Signatures

Write the indicated key signatures. The order of the flats (B E A D G C F) is the reverse of the order of the sharps (F C G D A E B). Copy the indicated key signatures on the staff below.

G major   E minor   E major   C-sharp minor

D minor   D major   F major   F minor

Finding the Keynote

The major keynote *do* is written on the staff. Write the name of the minor keynote (*la*) beneath the staff in problems 1, 2, 3.

The minor keynote (*la*) is written on the staff. Write the name of the major keynote (*do*) beneath the staff in problems 1, 2, 3.

Repeat Signs

Show how the following example could be notated more concisely with repeat signs.

Rewrite the following example, showing it as it would be written if first and second endings were *not* used.

SUGGESTED ACTIVITIES

1. Practice playing major and minor scales on bells, piano, recorder, or any other instrument.
2. Sing scales with the *do-re-mi* syllables, with letter names or numbers.
3. Review the rhythm syllables for all note values from whole notes to sixteenth notes.
4. Chant the rhythms of the songs in this chapter, using duration syllables as you pat the steady beat.

NOTES

[1] From *Music in American Schools* by James Mursell. (Silver Burdett Publishers, 1943).

[2] Patricia J. Flowers, "How to Communicate with Children About Music," *Music Educators Journal* (April 1985), 45–76.

[3] *See* Jerome Bruner, *Toward a Theory of Instruction* (Cambridge, Mass: Harvard University Press, 1966), 10–21, 27–31, 44–50, 155–57.

[4] Lyle Davidson, Patricia McKernon, and Howard E. Gardner, "The Acquistion of Song: A Developmental Approach," in *Documentary Report of the Ann Arbor Symposium: Applications of Psychology to the Teaching and Learning of Music* (Reston, Va.: Music Educators National Conference, 1981), 301–315.

[5] Directions for constructing bell stairsteps and many other useful music teaching materials are presented in the *Holt Music Activity Books* that accompany the *Holt Music* basic music series.

[6] *See* Sten G. Halfvarson, "Melodic Vocal Sight Reading," *The Illinois Music Educator* (Fall 1981), 19–20.

[7] Lloyd H. Slind and D. Evan Davis, *Bringing Music to Children* (New York: Harper and Row, 1964).

[8] Guides to lessons using Kodály techniques are provided in current music series. Teacher training in the Kodály approach is offered at a number of colleges and universities in the United States and Canada. Information about current programs is reported in the *Kodály Envoy,* the national publication of the Organization of American Kodály Educators. Contact Richard C. Merrell, Executive Director, the Organization of American Kodály Educators, 823 Old Westtown Rd., West Chester, PA 19382–5276 for additional information.

[9] Sr. Lorna Zemke, *The Kodály Concept—Its History, Philosophy and Development* (Champaign, Ill.: Mark Foster Music Company, 1974), p. 23.

[10] Accounts of nineteenth-century American music reading classes indicate that, although children learned many musical exercises and drills, they had difficulty relating their skills to actual songs. See Edward Bailey Birge, *History of Public School Music in the United States.*

[11] *See* Choksy, et al, *Teaching Music in the Twentieth Century* (Englewood Cliffs, N.J.: Prentice-Hall, 1986), 133.

[12] Kinesthetic feedback is also called proprioceptive feedback. Both terms refer to the belief that the higher mental processes are related to sensory feedback from movement. "Muscle memory is musical memory," writes neurologist Dr. Frank R. Wilson. See Rudolf Radocy and J. David Boyle, *Psychological Foundations of Musical Behavior,* 2d ed. (Springfield, Ill.: Charles C. Thomas, Publisher, 1988), 90–93.

[13] Kodály's *Let Us Sing Correctly* (New York: Boosey & Hawkes, 1952), provides a model for this training.

[14] *See* A. Malcolm Brown, "Letters, Syllables, Numbers, Intervals," *Music Educators Journal* (November 1974), 52–55, 101–3.

[15] A concise summary of the history of syllables is found under "Solmization" in the *New Harvard Dictionary of Music,* Don Michael Randel, ed. (Cambridge, Mass.: Harvard University Press, 1986).

[16] Directions for making a flannel board glockenspiel visual aid are presented in Bessie R. Swanson's *Music in the Education of Children,* 4th ed. (Belmont, Calif.: Wadsworth Publishing Co., 1981), 159–60.

[17] *See Holt Music* (1988) Activity Booklets from the Teacher's Resource Binder.

[18] Margaret Athey and Gwen Hotchkiss have written *A Galaxy of Games for the Music Class* (West Nyack, N.Y.: Parker Publishing Company, Inc., 1975), which contains many notation games.

[19] William Salaman, *Living School Music* (Cambridge, England: Cambridge University Press, 1983), 29.

PLANNING AND EVALUATION 10

The object of planning is to improve instruction and learning. As one teacher expresses it, "You can't just go into a classroom and try to pull things out of the sky. You do have to have an idea of what you're going to teach and its significance to the child."[1]

The topic of planning consumes sizable amounts of time in most education courses, and with good reason. The classroom teacher, teaching six or more subjects, can expect to prepare a great many lessons—more than one thousand each year in most schools.

MUSICAL EXPERIENCES

The music curriculum is built around the child's experiences with music. "Mere activity does not constitute experience," according to John Dewey, who emphasizes that experience leads to cumulative growth through finding relationships between activities and their outcomes: connecting cause and effect.[2]

What do we learn and how do we learn it? Children discover relationships among rhythm, melody, and the other elements of music through experiences in *performing, describing,* and *creating* music. To develop skills, knowledge, and understanding, however, the learning experience must focus on significant details in relation to a musical whole that is expressive and has musical meaning. Experiences are meaningful activities that involve perception and conceptualization.

Research suggests a guide to the sequence of learning: children need little training to discriminate between loud and soft, but the development of *pitch* and *rhythm* discrimination improves with practice and as the child's attention span increases with age. The perception of *harmony* (simultaneous sounds) develops last, perhaps at the age of eight.[3]

RESOURCES FOR PLANNING

For help in planning, teachers turn to various sources: national, state, or local curriculum guides, textbooks, consultants, personal experience, and educational research.

BASIC MUSIC SERIES AND RECORDINGS

The teacher's editions of the K–8 classroom music series are an important resource for planning and teaching. Written by experienced music educators, the books for each grade level contain songs, accompaniments, step-by-step lessons, information on teaching and evaluation, and suggestions for mainstreaming. Supplementary resource books for the teacher present information on numerous important topics, including the child voice, specific methods of teaching, classroom management, curriculum correlations, movement, multicultural music, music for special learners, signing, music reading, and music for the talented and gifted. Supplements include activity pages, evaluations, listening guides, progress reports, and reproducible black-line masters to facilitate the preparation of visual aids. Instructional technology includes computer software to reinforce the teaching of music fundamentals and music videotapes that present the instruments of the orchestra and many other vocal and instrumental sources of sounds.

Basic Music Series Publications[4]

1. **Holt Music** (1988) Holt, Rinehart and Winston, Inc., 1627 Woodland Avenue, Austin, Texas 78741. **Authors:** Eunice Boardman, Barbara Andress, Mary P. Pautz, and Fred Willman. **Components:** Pupil Book (1–8), Jumbo Book (K–1), Teacher's Edition (K–8), Recordings (K–8), Teacher's Resource Binder (K–8), Holiday Song Book (K–8), Computer Software (K–8), and Performance Cassettes (K–8). The Teacher's Resource Binders include Activity Sheets, Biographies, Curriculum Correlations, Enrichment, Evaluations, Mainstreaming, Kodály, and Orff.

2. **Music and You** (1991) Macmillan Publishing Company, 866 Third Avenue, New York, New York 10022. **Authors:** Barbara Staton, Merrill Staton, Marilyn Copeland Davidson, and Phyllis Kaplan. **Components (K–8):** Pupil Editions (1–6), Teacher Editions (K–6), Big Books (K–3), Piano Accompaniment Books (K–6), Teacher's Resource Package (K–6), Music Reading Charts (1–2), Recordings (records or compact discs, K–6). Macmillan/McGraw-Hill's 1994 series, *Share the Music,* was not available in time to be reviewed in the fourth edition of *Teaching Children Music.* For information about *Share the Music* call the Macmillan/McGraw-Hill Music Marketing Department at 212–353–5724.

3. **World of Music** (1991) Silver Burdett & Ginn, 250 James Street, Morristown, New Jersey 07960–1918. **Authors:** Jane Beethoven, Darrell Bledsoe, Carmen E. Culp, Jennifer Davidson, Lawrence Eisman, Mary E. Hoffman, Catherine Nadon–Gabrion, Mary Palmer, Carmino Ravosa, Mary Louise Reilly, Jean Sinor, Carol Rogel Scott, Jill Trinka, and Phyllis Weikart. **Components:** Pupil Books (1–8), Teacher Editions (K–8), Recorded Listening Library (records or compact discs, K–8), Listening Transparencies (1–8), Reading Music Charts (1–2) and Transparencies (3–6), Chart-Size Big Books (K–1), Orff Records (K–8), Theme Musical Cassettes (K–8), Music Magic Videos (4–8), and Teacher Resource Books (K–8). Silver Burdett Ginn's 1994 series, *The Music Connection* was not available in time to be reviewed for the fourth edition of *Teaching Children Music.* For information, call toll-free 1–800–848–9500 and ask to speak with the music specialist.

Music books for the primary grades reinforce reading skills development, and introduce the fundamentals of rhythm and melody notation. Attractive artwork and visual appeal combined with relevant information helps the teacher integrate music with other subjects. Teacher's editions include lessons, extensive information on music and pedagogy, and detailed guides to assist in planning and sequencing instruction at each grade level.

Recorded songs and listening selections are a vital component of the K–8 music series. Song recordings feature children's voices and may be used to introduce new songs and accompany classroom singing. Recorded listening lessons, integrated with lessons in the books, illustrate the sounds of conventional as well as unusual instruments and include many different types and styles of music.

This textbook assists you in preparing to use materials from the basic music series. No single textbook, however, includes the quantity of songs and activities, or the detailed sequence of lessons, recordings, and information available in the basic music series. Examine the teacher's edition for one or more grade levels carefully and you will gain a valuable overview of goals, activities, materials, and planning resources for music in the elementary school classroom.

CURRICULUM GUIDES

Curriculum guides are available in schools and from local, state, or national sources.[5] The Music Educators National Conference has published *The School Music Program: Description and Standards* 2nd ed. (1986), a book containing recommended achievements for each grade level and standards for implementing music programs, and *Teaching General Music, A Course of Study* (1991). The 1994 edition of *The School Music Program* was published after the manuscript for *Teaching Children Music* was completed. Readers should refer to this publication and it's companion volume, *Opportunity-to-Learn Standards for Music Instruction* to obtain information on the new national standards for K–12 music education.[6]

VARIABLES IN PLANNING

The availability of music books and curriculum guides may suggest that further efforts to plan music instruction are unneccesary. Why not simply follow the lessons in the music books or in the local curriculum plan? You can guess the reason: communities, schools, teachers, and students have different goals, needs, and resources.

Among the considerations that enter into the teacher's planning are (1) the students to be taught; (2) the materials and resources available; (3) scheduling and the time available for instruction; and (4) the situation in the school and the community.

THE STUDENTS

What can be effectively taught and learned is, of course, related to the child's level of intellectual, emotional, and physical development. While there may be no ideal sequence for a group of children, it is possible to establish "many tracks leading to the same general goal."[7] Like all teachers, music educators have shown great interest in contemporary research pertaining to developmental stages and to classifications of objectives in the cognitive, affective, and psychomotor domains.

Cognitive Development

A "spiral curriculum," in which essential concepts are studied repeatedly at an even higher level, is applicable to music as well as to other subjects.[8] Return to fundamental concepts to help learners discover new relationships and acquire greater understanding. Adapt your teaching to the ways children represent reality at each stage of their development.

In *Toward a Theory of Instruction,* Jerome Bruner describes three modes of representing experiences at any age level: enactive, iconic, and symbolic representation.[9]

Children in the enactive stage move, manipulate objects, or use other nonverbal behaviors to show how sounds move: faster or slower, higher or lower, and so forth. Iconic representation includes images, pictures, diagrams, graphs, and descriptive word pictures that describe melodic contour, meter, even or uneven rhythms, phrase length, and other musical characteristics. Enactive and iconic representation prepare the way for the use of more abstract verbal or musical symbols such as those found in conventional musical notation.

Physical Growth

The child's vocal development is one example of the influence of physical maturation on learning. Vocal range is relatively limited during the early years of school, and the ability to sing in tune may not be fully developed before the end of first or second grade. In the upper grades, boys whose voices are beginning the change to the adult male voice register encounter new challenges in singing and in their attitudes toward singing.

Very young children can play some types of instruments, including certain classroom percussion instruments, and some children begin lessons on the violin or the piano at an early age. With many instruments, better results are obtained by waiting for maturation to provide increased control and coordination. Recorder instruction usually begins in grade three or four and band lessons begin in grades four, five, or six.

Emotional Growth

Use age-appropriate music. The child who finds the words and actions of "Eency-Weency Spider" delightful during early childhood soon develops quite different song preferences as peer group opinions grow in importance and replace the self-centered perspective of early childhood.

The short attention span of the young child makes frequent changes in music activities advisable. Incorporate different learning modes—aural, visual, tactile. Include familiar and unfamiliar songs and keep the lesson moving with a variety of activities. Occasional lessons devoted to in-depth learning of a song or limited to a single activity may be feasible, but a change of focus usually improves attentiveness.

The classroom teacher often enhances learning by correlating music with other subject areas. For example, use a counting song as part of a math lesson or integrate a folk song or a patriotic song into a social studies lesson.[10] Seasonal music, multicultural music, experiments with homemade instruments, creative work with music and language, movement activities, or integrated studies relating music and the visual arts are among the numerous possibilities for correlating music with other studies.

MATERIALS, RESOURCES, AND FACILITIES

Instructional materials include music books and recordings. The 1994 MENC standards call for a complete set of music textbooks and accompanying sound recordings, not more than 6 years old, . . . for each grade level. (Teacher's editions of music textbooks should be available for music specialists and classroom teachers.)[11]

Rooms where music is taught should have a piano that is tuned at least three times a year and an assortment of pitched and non-pitched classroom instruments, including recorders, bells, fretted instruments, barred instruments, chorded zithers (e.g., Autoharps), and instruments from diverse cultures.

Teachers should have access to high quality sound reproduction equipment and additional electronic equipment, including earphones, tape recorders, synthesizers, microcomputers and notation sequencing software. In addition, classroom instruction makes use of compact discs, films, filmstrips, and videotapes. The instructional potential of any of these resources is, of course, affected by their availability at the right time and in the right place.

Even routine instruction depends upon planning. Forgetting to replace a burned-out projector lamp, find an extension cord, or reserve audiovisual materials ahead of time will upset what might have been a successful learning experience. Plans also must allow for time to present the lesson and bring it to a successful conclusion.

Permanent music rooms offer greater flexibility than makeshift space in storage rooms, lunchrooms, or noisy multi-purpose rooms. Rooms should have adequate size, lighting, ventilation, and instrument storage space, as well as a location that allows students to hear and make music without disturbing other classes. If the teacher travels from room to room, only a limited amount of equipment can be transported, and a well-designed equipment cart becomes imperative.

TIME AND SCHEDULE

The 1994 edition of *The School Music Program* recommends that each child in grades K–6 should receive general music instruction from a music specialist for a minimum of ninety minutes each week (not including time in elective band or choral ensembles). The work of the music specialist should be complemented by the classroom teacher in order to make music a part of each child's daily life.

The curriculum should provide a balanced and sequential program that includes singing, playing instruments, listening to music, moving to music, music reading, improvising music, composing music and instruction to help children understand music in relation to history, to other cultures and to other disciplines. Students should learn to use music terminology as they analyze and describe music and should develop criteria to allow them to make informed evaluations of music.[12]

The classroom teacher and music specialist can coordinate their roles in providing rich musical experiences for students. For example, the classroom teacher may provide opportunities for guided practice, reinforcement, and skill development using new material introduced by the music specialist. The classroom teacher is an important model in fostering enthusiasm for and positive attitudes toward music. Time and schedule constraints limit the specialist's opportunities to integrate music into the school environment, but the classroom teacher—who is with the same students for most of the school day—can offer music throughout the day and relate it directly to relevant learnings in other areas.

When integrating music with other subjects in the curriculum, it is essential to maintain the integrity of each discipline by careful attention to objectives and sequencing. For example, a counting song used to enhance kindergarten math should also be musically appropriate for kindergarten. A folk song that correlates with a fourth-grade social studies unit should be compatible with the musical objectives for that grade level.

OTHER CONSIDERATIONS

Issues such as religion, cultural diversity, and special education must also be considered. For example, school performances of Christmas songs may be controversial because of laws requiring separation of church and state.[13] Achieving a balance of music representing the ethnic and cultural diversity of the American people is also an important consideration. Similarly, teachers must plan instruction that takes into account the diversity of students, including the talented and gifted and those with learning disabilities.

Attitudes toward music also affect planning. Music is usually rated near the top of the list of subjects by children in the early grades, but it ranks lower in the upper grades, especially among those least or most advanced musically. Those who take private music lessons find the pace too slow; those with undeveloped skills can be frustrated by a pace that is beyond their ability.[14]

Inadequate music instruction in the early years may have a long-lasting influence. Researchers have reported that a child's musical potential must be developed by the age of nine if it is to be fully realized.[15] A similar conclusion has been reached in the area of languages, where studies have shown that it is difficult to achieve a correct, natural accent in a foreign language learned after the age of twelve.[16]

WHAT SHALL I TEACH?

The concepts and skills you have studied in the preceding chapters are similar to the concepts and skills you should teach children. Lessons on rhythm, for instance, might focus on beat, accent, duration, meter, rhythm patterns, syncopation, or related topics involving rhythm notation.

Use varied music of many types in a related sequence of lessons to assist children in reaching the long-term goals you have planned for the year. Build lessons around actual musical experiences, not just drills, musical crossword puzzles, or teacher-talk *about* music. Most lessons will include several songs and activities. The outcomes of lessons should include growth in conceptual understanding and in musical skills, along with increased knowledge of music from different times and places.

MUSICAL CONCEPTS

Concepts about the ingredients of music—sounds organized into rhythm, melody, harmony—help us to understand every kind of music. Here is a psychologist's definition of a concept:

When a symbol stands for a class of objects or events with common properties, we say that it refers to a concept.[17]

Music is the art of sound and its concepts are about musical sounds.

A musical concept is a musical meaning developed in the mind of a person as a result of his experiences with the sound of music. . . . The ability to think tones—to hear them in the mind when no sound is being produced—is prerequisite to the further development of musical concepts.[18]

Perceptions lead to concepts, which in turn serve to organize our musical experiences. According to research, children's musical concepts develop in the following order: volume, timbre, tempo, duration, pitch, and harmony.[19] Concepts help children learn to learn. We acquire concepts gradually through meaningful musical experiences, and so do children, who must perceive and differentiate patterns of sound for themselves in order to develop concepts about music.

We can help children learn to classify and organize aural, visual, and tactile inputs. Which sound is louder (or higher or longer)? Which instrument makes louder (or higher or longer sounds)? How can you show louder (or higher or longer) sounds?

Concepts stem from direct experience with actual music. The young child, however, knows more than he or she can put into words. Nonverbal responses—movement, performance, and the like—may be a better guide to the child's conceptual growth than the ability to describe music with words, which is difficult for anyone. Nevertheless, children need to develop a musical vocabulary because words/concepts make it possible for us to subsume the bits and pieces of our knowledge into categories. Learning the musical labels and categories enables children to describe and think about music in musical rather than extramusical ways.

SKILLS

Musical skills are not limited to the area of performance, but include listening, music reading, and movement to music. Singing offers children an approach to achieving expressive performance; instrumental experience is valuable in teaching music reading and musicianship. Skills, concepts, and musical subject matter are interdependent, like the cognitive, affective, and psychomotor domains.

HOW SHALL I PLAN?

Basic questions—such as who, what, where, when, and how to teach—affect all planning, but actual plans are usually designed on the basis of goals and objectives that have been selected in response to these basic questions.

OBJECTIVES

Teachers use fairly general statements of objectives to make long-term plans and more specific types of objectives for day-to-day plans. Daily lesson plans use instructional objectives to specify what students do when they learn.

Instructional objectives tell what the students are to do, describe the conditions under which the learning is to occur, and identify the level of achievement that is required.

Rather than saying, "To introduce the pentatonic scale," the teacher states the objective in terms of student responses. "Given the resonator bells for the C major scale, the student will select the bells required for a pentatonic scale." With some objectives, the level of success is *implied;* with others it is *stated.* In a recorder class, the teacher might state this objective: "The student will play a one-octave C major scale at a tempo of at least two notes per second with no mistakes."

State objectives with action verbs such as the following: arrange, chant, choose, clap, classify, compose, conduct, define, demonstrate, describe, echo, explain, hum, identify, imitate, improvise, label, memorize, notate, organize, play, rearrange, recite, select, show, spell, strum, sing, show, substitute, tap, tell, write.[20]

LESSON PLANS

Daily lesson plans usually contain the following elements:

1. A statement of the desired concepts and skills to be emphasized.
2. A statement of the instructional objective(s).
3. A list of needed materials.
4. A projection of the step-by-step procedures.
5. An indication of how the learning will be assessed.

The exact format of the lesson plan may vary. Lessons in *Holt Music* (Holt, Rinehart and Winston, 1988), for example, have the following headings: Lesson Focus, Materials, Introducing the Lesson, Developing the Lesson, and Closing the Lesson.

SAMPLE LESSON PLAN: GRADE 3

Concepts
Sounds may be longer than, shorter than, or the same as the length of one beat.
Beats may move in sets of two or three.
Melodies may be based on tones of major or minor scales.

Instructional Objectives
1. Students will identify sounds as longer than, shorter than, or the same as the length of one beat by performing with vocal sounds and duration syllables.
2. Students will identify meters in two or three by movement and by playing instruments.
3. Students will demonstrate familiarity with major and minor through singing, listening, and playing instruments.

Materials
Songs: "Don Gato," *World of Music*, Grade 4, or *Holt Music*, Grade 3.
   "El Coqui," *Teaching Children Music*, p. 117.
Instruments: resonator bells, Autoharp, hand drum, rhythm sticks, tambourine.
Recordings: "Don Gato" and "El Coqui" from music series.

Procedures
Review: Sing "Don Gato" and "El Coqui."
1. Echoing. Perform basic four-beat rhythm patterns using a hissing sound ("sss") to produce each duration. Have students echo each pattern. Switch to rhythm syllables and have students echo. Compare the sounds of *ta* (one sound to a beat) and *ti ti* (two sounds to a beat). Have students perform the rhythm of "Don Gato" and "El Coqui" using the "sss" in place of the melody as they tap the steady beat. Ask them to identify places where they heard one sound to a beat, two sounds to a beat, or sounds longer than one beat.
2. Play chord patterns in twos (duple meter). Students form one or more circles and step to the beat as they clap on the accented beat. Switch to chords in threes (triple meter). Ask what is different. Have the students step the beats and clap on the accented beat as you play the chords. Have students find a partner and devise a clapping pattern to show meter in twos and threes. Select a few percussion instruments and transfer the patterns of "twos" or "threes" to the instruments. Play the two melodies on an instrument, or from a recording, and have the students respond to the duple or triple meter of the song.
3. Distribute two sets of resonator bells: D F A and D F-sharp A. Identify the D F A sound (heard in "Don Gato") as minor and the D F-sharp A bells as major. Play the first measure of each song and ask students to play the set of bells that sounds the same. Play the Autoharp chord patterns indicated: Dm–A7–Dm (key of D minor); D–G–A7–D (key of D major). Have the students devise a gesture or movement to represent "Don Gato" (D minor) or "El Coqui" (D major). Conclude by singing "Don Gato" or "El Coqui" again, this time with students showing the conducting pattern for duple or triple meter.

Don Gato

English by Margaret Marks   *Mexican Folk Song*

1. Oh, Se - ñor   Don   Ga - to   was   a   cat, ____
2. "I   a - dore   you!" wrote   the   la - dy   cat, ____

On   a   high   red   roof   Don   Ga - to   sat, ____
Who   was   fluff - y   white   and   nice   and   fat, ____

He   went   there   to   read   a   let - ter, Meow, Meow, Meow,
There   was   not   a   sweet - er   kit - ty   Meow, Meow, Meow,

Where   the   read - ing light was   bet - ter, Meow, Meow, Meow,
In   the   coun - try   or   the   cit - y,   Meow, Meow, Meow,

'Twas   a   love   note   for   Don   Ga - to. ____
And   she   said   she'd   wed   Don   Ga - to. ____

SAMPLE INTERDISCIPLINARY LESSON PLAN: GRADE 2

Concepts and objectives in more than one discipline can be merged into a single lesson. The following lesson is part of a unit designed to build awareness and appreciation of several Native American cultures by comparing farming and harvesting practices and traditions with Euro-American practices and traditions. Concepts and objectives are defined in terms of social studies, emphasizing multicultural infusion, as well as music. The songs and some components of the lesson plan are adapted from Silver Burdett and Ginn *World of Music,* Grade 2.

Concepts

Musical Concepts
Steady beat
Accented and unaccented beats
Choosing appropriate dynamic level

Social Studies Concepts
The sun provides warmth and light and helps make crops grow.
People all over the world give thanks for the sun.
We can learn about different groups of people by studying their music, art, and literature.

Objectives

Musical Objectives
Students will indicate the steady beat through gestures or playing an instrument.
Students will discriminate between accented and unaccented beats.
Students will select an appropriate dynamic level for each song.

Social Studies Objectives
Students will read the text of each song and discuss the cultural implications of the text.

Materials

Song: "Thanksgiving" (Finnish folk tune, translated into English), *World of Music,* Grade 2, pp. 202–203.

Song: "Sunset," *World of Music, Grade 2,* pp. 156–157. Record (or CD), Grade 2, 7B, Band 3

Instruments: Finger cymbals, drums

Book: *The Way to Start a Day* by Byrd Baylor (New York: Charles Scribner's Sons, 1986).

Thanksgiving

English Words by Rosemary Jacques

Folk Tune from Finland

From World of Music, *Grade Two. Copyright © 1988, Silver Burdett and Ginn, Inc. Used by permission.*

2. For the corn and golden wheat,
   We are truly thankful.
   For the pears and apples sweet . . .
   For the good food that we eat . . .

3. For the joys of each new day . . .
   For each hour of work and play . . .
   For God's blessings, let us say,
   "We are truly thankful."

Sunset

Native American Song

From Music for Young Americans *© 1959 American Book Company. Reprinted by permission of D. C. Heath and Company.*

Procedures

1. Read *The Way to Start a Day* aloud to the class. (This poem, illustrated by Peter Parnall, describes how different cultural groups throughout the world give thanks for the sun by greeting it and offering gifts to it.)

2. Discussion: Ask the children to share their feelings about the sun. What do they like about it? Is there anything they do not like about it? Why do we need it?

3. Listen to a recording of "Thanksgiving." Focus: What are some of the things the song says people are thankful for? List them (sun, moon, stars, corn, wheat, pears, apples, good food, joys of each day, work and play, God's blessings).

SAMPLE INTERDISCIPLINARY LESSON PLAN: GRADE 2 CONT.

4. Listen, follow the score, and sing on the recurring phrase, "We are truly thankful."
5. Sing the first verse together while clapping the strong beat and patting the weak beat.
6. Add finger cymbals. Play on the strong beat only. Add verses 2 and 3.
7. Decide on an appropriate dynamic level for the song.
8. Divide the class in half. One half sings the phrases that list what we are thankful for. The other half sings "We are truly thankful" using an appropriate dynamic level. Switch parts and repeat.
9. Listen to "Sunset" (North American Indian song). Focus on dynamics. What is the dynamic level of the song? (soft) Why is this an appropriate dynamic level?
10. Discuss the text of "Sunset." Why do you think the Indians call the sun Father Sun? (Discuss our dependence on the sun and the oneness with nature that is a part of the spiritual life of many Native Americans.)
11. Sing the song while patting the steady beat.
12. Sing the song while playing the steady beat on drums.

Evaluation

Observe the children to determine if they are playing the steady beat.

Observe the children to determine if they can discriminate between the accented and unaccented beats.

Assess through class discussion the students' understanding of the text of each song and how the songs relate to dependence upon the sun for crops, harvest, and giving thanks.

Cross-Curricula Correlations

Art

Create water color washes of the sun and sky.

Draw Indian symbols that tell the story of the song. (See *World of Music, Grade 2,* p. 157.)

Language Arts

Creative Writing: Write a short paragraph that begins, "The way to start a day is this" and another paragraph that begins, "The way to end a day is this." Have the children share their paragraphs with a partner.

Science and Math

Conduct an experiment with plants in the classroom. Plant seeds in two different containers. Observe the plants for height (measure and chart). After a time put the container which has received less sun in the sunnier environment. Observe what effect more sun has on these plants.

LONG-RANGE PLANNING

Good daily plans are part of the task of planning, but without long-range plans and goals, daily lessons may lack sequence and coherence. Along with the ever-popular "winging it" approach, attempts to find a basis for long-range planning include emphasis on a sequence of *skills* or on *facts* about music.

Although plans based primarily on developing skills or memorizing musical facts may seem very logical, they risk omitting the kind of musical experiences that lead most directly to genuine musical growth. Such plans may also ignore the vast differences among children in each classroom and their divergent patterns of musical growth. Plans stressing intellectual responses to music, taught apart from direct involvement in musical experiences, misconstrue the nature of musical learning.

Long-range planning includes the selection of learning activities and musical subject matter. Learning activities should move from concrete to abstract; musical materials should progress from obvious to subtle. Methods should offer students exposure to a wide range of music and activities, all leading to increased growth in musicianship and the ability to solve musical problems independently.[21] The following plan illustrates the relationship between long-range, mid-range, and daily lesson plans.

LONG-RANGE PLANS

The following long-range planning sketch specifies the general goals for a semester teaching period as well as the areas to be emphasized each month:

LONG-RANGE PLANNING SKETCH

Planning Outline   **September-December, 19—**   **Grade 4**

General goals: By the end of this term, students will have improved in the following:

1. Playing the Autoharp
2. Playing simple tunes on the recorder
3. Singing with expression and good tone
4. Performing a song repertoire
5. Identifying orchestral instruments
6. Identifying voice categories
7. Using experiments with sounds to compose
8. Reading and writing music
9. Performing common rhythm and tonal patterns

General concepts: rhythm, melody, harmony, tone color, form

Areas to Emphasize:

September
Singing participation, posture, tone quality, enunciation
Playing Autoharp: beat, meter
Listening vocal timbre: adult, child
Experimenting Autoharp: strums, styles
Notation note values

October
Singing continue previous, learn seasonal songs
Playing Autoharp: I, IV, V7; bells, recorders, and percussion
Listening "Sound in Music" unit; *The Banshee, In The Hall of the Mountain King*
Experimenting create: vocal sounds, body sounds, piano, and Autoharp sounds
Notation original notation, minor mode, Halloween pieces

November
Singing continue previous, dynamics, add selected songs for the seasons
Playing continue previous
Listening woodwinds, live demonstrations
Experimenting interpretations of songs
Notation rhythm and tonal patterns from song literature

December
Singing continue previous, phrasing, dynamics, precision, blend
Playing music accompaniments: recorders, Autoharp, etc.
Listening seasonal music, choral and orchestral; tape recordings of class and student soloists
Experimenting interpretation: tempo, dynamics, tone color
Notation continue previous rhythm and tonal patterns

MID-RANGE PLANS

Mid-range planning sketches focus on one area of the long-range plan and present more detailed information. The following mid-range plan is based on daily music classes, with one day a week reserved for student-initiated activities, such as presenting piano pieces, individual projects, creative work, and instrumental solos.

MID-RANGE PLANNING SKETCH

Date	Review	Introduce
Oct. 2–3	"Old Abram Brown" Review natural minor scale pattern. "Dry Bones," Review half steps.	Autoharp—primary chords. "Who's That Tapping at the Window?" Practice chord changes in minor.
Oct. 5–6	"Who's That Tapping at the Window?" in minor. Learn bell part. Review minor scale. Work on Autoharp chords.	"The Old Black Cat" (See "The Old Grey Cat," page 243.) Rehearse in major. Change to parallel minor. Play on bells.
Oct. 9–10	"The Old Black Cat." Create sound effects for other verses. Review rhythm patterns in 6/8.	"Skin and Bones," page 245 Stress expressive singing and vocal tone. Recorder: B, A, G, E pattern
Oct. 12–13	"Monster Frankenstein." Review major and minor mode. "Skin and Bones," Recorders: B, A, G, E pattern.	Experiment with speech sounds. Experiment with instrument sounds. Play minor chords on Autoharp.
Oct. 16–17	"Old Abram Brown" "Who's That Tapping at the Window?" "The Old Black Cat" "Monster Frankenstein" Stress tone, posture, enunciation.	"The Pumpkin Man" Listening: *In the Hall of the Mountain King*, by Grieg. Record 2, Side B, Band 4. Develop movements to the music. Concepts of tempo and accelerando.
Oct. 19–20	Speech sounds for Halloween pieces. "Monster Frankenstein" "The Pumpkin Man"	Make tape recording of sounds. Begin original notation. Assign Halloween projects.
Oct. 23–24	Minor chords on Autoharp. Compare major and minor versions of "Frère Jaques."	"Skin and Bones" B-A-G-E Work on notation and projects. Listen: Mahler: Sym. 3rd Mvmt.
Oct. 26–27	"The Pumpkin Man" "Skin and Bones," Memorize words. "Monster Frankenstein," Diction, expression.	Listening. *The Banshee* by Henry Cowell. (Eerie sounds made by scraping against piano strings). Recording: CD 5–10.
Oct. 30–31	Have students rehearse their sound compositions and make tape recording to play for the haunted house at tomorrow's Halloween party.	

From On the Trail of Negro Folk Songs *by Dorothy Scarborough,* © *1925 Harvard University Press; renewed 1953 by Mary McDaniel Parker. Reprinted by permission of the publishers.*

Who's That Tapping at the Window?

Virginia Folk Song

Who's that tap-ping at the win - dow? Who's that knock-ing at the door?

The Old Black Cat

1. The old black cat is sleep-ing, sleep-ing, sleep-ing.
The old black cat is sleep-ing in the house. _____

2. The little mice are creeping . . .
3. The little mice are nibbling . . .
4. The old black cat is waking . . .
5. The little mice are running . . .

The Pumpkin Man

1. Oh, do you know the pump-kin man, the pump-kin man, the
2. Oh, yes I know the pump-kin man, the pump-kin man, the

pump-kin man. Oh, do you know the pump-kin man that lives in sca-ry lane?
pump-kin man. Oh, yes I know the pump-kin man that lives in sca-ry lane.

Monster Frankenstein

Words by Mary Lou Frierdich

Tune: Darling Clementine

1. In a cast-le in a moun-tain, near the dark and mur-ky Rhine,
2. In a grave-yard near the cast-le, when the moon re-fused to shine

Dwelt a doc-tor, the con-coc-tor, of the mon-ster Fran-ken-stein.
He dug for nos-es and for "toe-ses" for his mon-ster Fran-ken-stein.

Chorus

Oh my mon-ster, oh my mon-ster, oh my mon-ster, Frank-en-stein

You were built to last for-ev-er, Dread-ful sca-ry Frank-en-stein.

From Keeping Up with Orff Schulwerk in the Classroom. © 1976, *Keeping Up with Music Education, Muncie, Ind. Used by permission.*

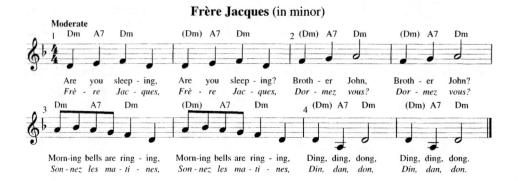

Frère Jacques (in minor)

Are you sleep - ing, Are you sleep - ing? Broth - er John, Broth - er John?
Frè - re   Jac - ques,   Frè - re   Jac - ques,   Dor - mez   vous?   Dor - mez   vous?

Morn-ing bells are ring - ing, Morn-ing bells are ring - ing, Ding, ding, dong, Ding, ding, dong.
Son - nez   les   ma - ti - nes,   Son - nez   les   ma - ti - nes,   Din,   dan,   don,   Din,   dan,   don.

Related Listening: Gustav Mahler: *Symphony No. 1* 3rd Movement. Bowmar Orchestral Library No. 62 or EM1 Classics CDD-64287.

DAILY PLANS

A daily lesson plan can be derived from the mid-range plan for the month. Notice that the plan shown stresses *music,* but also acknowledges a *seasonal* event, in this case, Halloween. Music classes should emphasize music rather than some other subject, but that does not mean that the music lesson should be taught in isolation from the child's world or the aims of the school.

DAILY LESSON PLAN

Date: October 27

A. Musical Learnings (The Banshee)
1. Unexpected musical events (e.g., sudden changes in volume) may produce suspense or tension in music.
2. Unusual tone colors may increase tension in music.
3. Unusual performance techniques may increase tension in music.

B. Students Will:
1. Accompany "Skin and Bones" in E minor on the Autoharp.
2. Explain the source of the sounds in a recording of *The Banshee* by Henry Cowell.
3. Imitate these sounds, after experimenting, on the Autoharp.

C. Materials
1. Autoharps
2. Music books
3. Recording: *The Banshee,* CD 5–10.
4. CD player

D. Procedures
Review

1. Sing "Skin and Bones" page 249.
2. Ask how many different chords are needed.
3. Ask whether to strum on every beat or just on chord symbols.
4. Invite children to accompany each verse on the Autoharp.
5. Repeat the song and let different children play. Ask the class to sing the verses with dynamic contrasts to match the story.

New

6. Ask children "What is the name for an Irish spirit?" (banshee).
7. Before playing the recording of "The Banshee," ask the children to listen and try to identify the instrument they will hear.
8. Play the recording.
9. Discuss answers. Play recording again if necessary.
10. Demonstrate. Strum, scrape, and pluck the strings inside the piano as one child holds down the right pedal. If no piano is available, illustrate similar effects on the Autoharp or let children experiment to discover them.
11. Remind children to bring their Halloween pieces for tomorrow's class.

MENC MUSICAL EXPERIENCES CHARTS

The following guide to the selection of musical experiences appropriate for children at different ages is suggested in the 1986 edition of *The School Music Program: Description And Standards*, published by the Music Educators National Conference. These statements offer teachers a concise summary of long-range goals that may be adapted to fit the particular situation in a school district or an individual classroom.

MENC MUSICAL EXPERIENCES CHART

Music Experiences for Infants

Infants and very young children experience music by hearing and feeling it. Children should experience music daily while receiving caring physical contact. Adults can encourage the musical development of infants by:

—singing and chanting to them;

—imitating the sounds infants make;

—exposing them to a wide variety of vocal, body, instrumental, and environmental sounds;

—providing exposure to selected recorded music;

—rocking, patting, touching, and moving with the children to the beat, rhythm patterns, and melodic direction of music heard; and

—providing safe toys that make musical sounds that the children can control.

Music Experiences for Two- and Three-Year-Old Children

Two- and three-year-old children need an environment that includes a variety of sound sources, selected recorded music, and opportunities for free improvised singing and the building of a repertoire of songs. An exploratory approach, using a wide range of appropriate materials, provides a rich base from which conceptual understanding may evolve in later years. A variety of individual musical experiences is important for children of this age, with little emphasis on musical activities that require children to perform together as a unit.

Ages 2–3. By four years of age, children are able to:

Performing/Reading

Sing in a freely improvised style as they play

Sing folk and composed songs, although not always on pitch or in time with others

Play simple rhythm instruments freely and explore sounds of rhythm instruments and environmental sources

Walk, run, jump, gallop, clap, and "freeze" while an adult responds to the child's movements with sound on a percussion instrument

Recognize printed music and label it as music

Creating

Explore the expressive possibilities of their own voices

Improvise songs as they play

Create sounds on instruments and from other sound sources in their environment

Listening/Describing

Listen attentively to a selected repertoire of music

Move spontaneously to music of many types

Recognize the difference between singing and speaking

Demonstrate awareness of sound and silence through movement and "freezing"

Improvise movements that indicate awareness of beat, tempo, and pitch

Valuing

By four years of age, children:

Enjoy listening to music and other sounds in their environment

Like being sung to

Enjoy singing as they play

Enjoy making sounds with environmental, body, and instrumental sound sources

Music Experiences for Four- and Five-Year-Old Children

Four- and five-year-old children are becoming socially conscious. Appropriate music-making experiences include group activities such as singing and playing song games and playing classroom instruments. Many opportunities for individual exploration of voice, body, nature, and instrument sounds should also be included. Movement is the most effective means for children of this age to describe their musical experiences. They enjoy playing with ideas, movements, language, and sounds. Music activities that allow opportunities for free exploration provide the most positive foundation for creative musical growth later.

**MENC MUSICAL EXPERIENCES CHART
CONT.**

Ages 4–5. By the completion of kindergarten children are able to:

Performing/Reading

Utilize the singing voice, as distinct from the speaking voice

Match pitches and sing in tune within their own ranges most of the time

Show an awareness of beat, tempo (e.g., fast-slow), dynamics (e.g., loud-soft), pitch (e.g., high-low), and similar and different phrases through movement and through playing classroom instruments

Enjoy singing nonsense songs, folk songs, and song games

Utilize pictures, geometric shapes, and other symbols to represent pitch, durational patterns, and simple forms

Creating

Explore sound patterns on classroom instruments

Improvise songs spontaneously during many classroom and playtime activities

Complete "answers" to unfinished melodic phrases by singing or playing instruments

Express ideas or moods using instruments and environmental or body sounds

Listening/Describing

Give attention to short musical selections

Listen attentively to an expanded repertoire of music

Respond to musical elements (e.g., pitch, duration, loudness) and musical styles (e.g., march, lullaby) through movement or through playing classroom instruments

Describe with movement or language similarities and differences in music such as loud-soft, fast-slow, up-down-same, smooth-jumpy, short-long, and similar-contrasting

Classify classroom instruments and some traditional instruments by shape, size, pitch, and tone quality

Use a simple vocabulary of music terms to describe sounds

Valuing

By the completion of kindergarten, children:

Demonstrate an awareness of music as a part of everyday life

Enjoy singing, moving to music, and playing instruments alone and with others

Respect music and musicians

Subject Matter Achievements for Grades 1–3

The primary school years are a time of growth, wonder, excitement, exploration, and discovery. These years are crucial as the child develops a concept of music, gains fundamental skills, and acquires a sensitivity to musical sounds and their beauty. All children need to have regular and continuing musical experiences that lead to satisfaction through success in producing musical sounds, using them enjoyably, and responding to them with pleasure.

Grades 1–3. By the completion of the third grade, students are able to:

Performing/Reading

Sing in tune alone or with a group using a clear, free tone

Sing from memory a repertoire of folk and composed songs

Sing with appropriate musical expression

Respond to the beat in music by clapping, walking, running, or skipping

Play simple pitch patterns on melodic instruments such as bells or xylophones

Play simple rhythmic patterns on classroom percussion instruments to accompany songs and rhythm activities

Sing a simple ostinato with a familiar song

Sing a part in a round while maintaining a steady tempo

Creating

Create "answers" to unfinished melodic phrases by singing or playing on classroom instruments

Create short melodic patterns on classroom instruments or by singing

Improvise songs and accompaniments to physical movement using classroom instruments

Create short pieces consisting of nontraditional sounds available in the classroom or with the body (e.g., snapping fingers, rubbing fingers on a table top)

Create, in class, new stanzas to familiar melodies

Dramatize songs and stories

Performing/Reading

Interpret the basic notational symbols for rhythm patterns, including quarter, eighth, and half notes and rests, by engaging in appropriate movement, such as clapping or walking, playing on classroom instruments, or chanting

Recognize the basic features (e.g., form, melodic contour, expressive qualities) of unfamiliar songs by studying their notation

Use correct notational symbols for pitch and expression

Use a system (e.g., syllables, numbers, letters) for reading notation

Listening/Describing

Recognize aurally the difference between long and short sounds, repeated and contrasting phrases, slow and fast tempos, duple and triple meters, major and minor modes, and other contrasting sound patterns

Indicate aural recognition of high and low pitches by making directional hand movements that follow the pitch of a melodic line

Recognize aurally the timbre of basic wind, string, and percussion instruments

Describe in simple terms the stylistic characteristics of some of the music they sing or listen to

Use musical terms and concepts to express thoughts about music (e.g., loud, short, high, melody, rhythm)

Use hand motions and other body movements or graphic designs to indicate how portions of a musical work sound

Identify the patterns of simple forms (e.g., AB, ABA)

Valuing

By the completion of the third grade, students:

Realize that music is an important part of everyday life

Feel a sense of respect for music and its performance and creation

Display a sense of enjoyment when participating in music

Use music as a means of personal expression

Subject Matter Achievements for Grades 4–6

Students in grades 4–6 continue to develop many of the skills, understandings, and values that were introduced in the earlier grades while adding many more. It may appear that there are similarities between the objectives of music instruction in grades 1–3 and grades 4–6. There are, however, sizeable differences in the nature and quality of the learning. The main difference lies in the greater accuracy, facility, clarity, and ease of learning that should be evident in grades 4–6.

Grades 4–6. By the completion of the sixth grade, students are able to:

Performing/Reading

Sing songs accurately and independently, reflecting an understanding of tonal and rhythmic elements

Control their voices in order to produce the desired musical quality to communicate expressive intent

Perform basic tonal patterns, rhythm patterns, and simple songs on recorder, keyboard, electronic synthesizer, and other classroom instruments

Provide chordal accompaniments with instruments such as guitar and Autoharp-type instruments

Creating

Make thoughtful alterations and variations in existing songs

Improvise simple ostinato-like accompaniments on pitched instruments

Improvise rhythmic accompaniments for songs

Create simple descants, introductions, and codas

Experiment with variations in tempo, timbre, dynamics, and phrasing for expressive purposes

Utilize diverse sound sources, including electronic, when improvising or composing

MENC MUSICAL EXPERIENCES CHART
CONT.

Conduct songs in 2–, 3–, and 4–beat meter
Sing one part alone or in a small group while
    others sing contrasting parts
Sing harmonizing parts in thirds and sixths
Perform simple accompaniments by ear
Recognize tonal and rhythm patterns and
    musical forms from examining the notation
Continue the use of a systematic approach to
    music reading
Demonstrate growth in the ability to sing or play
    music from notation

Listening/Describing	Valuing
Listen to and demonstrate an understanding of rhythm by responding physically or with the use of rhythm instruments	By the completion of the sixth grade students:
	Demonstrate an increased awareness of music as an important part of everyday life
Notate correctly simple pitch and rhythm patterns presented aurally	Participate in music through singing and playing instruments
Identify by listening a basic repertoire of standard orchestral and vocal compositions	Enjoy listening to most types of music
	Discuss personal responses to works of art
Use correct terminology to discuss the characteristics of a work, including melody, rhythm, meter, key, form, expressive qualities, and style	Describe the musical phenomena on which their observations are based
Discuss in their own words the qualities of a work of music	
Identify by listening: most orchestral instruments and classifications of voices; formal patterns such as AB, ABA, rondo, and theme and variations; salient musical features such as tempo, dynamic level, major and minor modes, meter, counterpoint; and types of music (e.g., electronic, folk, orchestral, jazz, choral)	

From *The School Music Program: Description and Standards,* 2d ed. Copyright © 1986. Music
    Educators National Conference. Used by permission.

EVALUATION OF MUSICAL LEARNING

Evaluation is used to assess progress toward goals and to guide future learning. It may
also serve to stimulate effort and produce information helpful in guidance and curriculum revision.

FORMAL AND INFORMAL EVALUATION

Informal evaluation is a natural part of daily instruction, while formal evaluation suggests the use of tests to measure musical aptitude or achievement. In music, the teacher listens to children sing or play, assists them by correcting errors, encourages them by reinforcing things done well, and estimates the need for review, clarification, or additional practice when planning subsequent instruction.

The outcomes of musical learning include knowledge, understanding, skills, attitudes, habits, and appreciation.[22] Evaluation, therefore, should not be limited to tests of factual knowledge. Narrow concepts of evaluation may cause us to "teach for the test," ignoring attitude or other considerations, such as the fact that music allows every student to succeed at some level, provided that the teacher provides a degree of individualized instruction.

Because success can be measured in many ways, achievement scores vary in different situations, as is apparent in the report of the First National Assessment of Musical Performance:

> *Very few individuals were able to accurately sight-read a line of music, either vocally or instrumentally. And although about a quarter of the population claimed to play an instrument, very few were able to give acceptable performances. . . .Although 70 percent of the adults gave an acceptable [singing] performance of "America," only about 45 percent were able to give an acceptable performance of the round ["Frère Jacques"].*[23]

Information from standardized music tests can help teachers match instructional goals to realistic expectations. For example, the *Primary Measures of Music Audiation* test the tonal and rhythmic aptitude and musical potential of children in grades K–3. (An intermediate level for grades 1–4 is also available.)[24] The music series *Jump Right In* (G.I.A. Publications, Inc., 1986), employs these aptitude tests to classify students as high, medium, or low in order to focus "learning sequence activities" on individual needs. By selecting and teaching the appropriate *tonal and rhythm pattern cards,* instructors correlate student aptitude with item difficulty. *Classroom activity cards* correspond to the level of difficulty in the "learning sequence activities."[25]

Achievement tests and evaluation projects are available as components of current music series. Teacher-made tests should also be considered for evaluating daily instruction, although much of the daily evaluation will be informal and based on observation. A few notes jotted on each lesson plan will help teachers maintain records of individual student's progress or difficulties and will also be advantageous in revising lessons for future use. Information gathered from evaluation is useful in preparing progress reports for use in parent-teacher conferences, and as a means of informing administrators and the community about the work of the school.

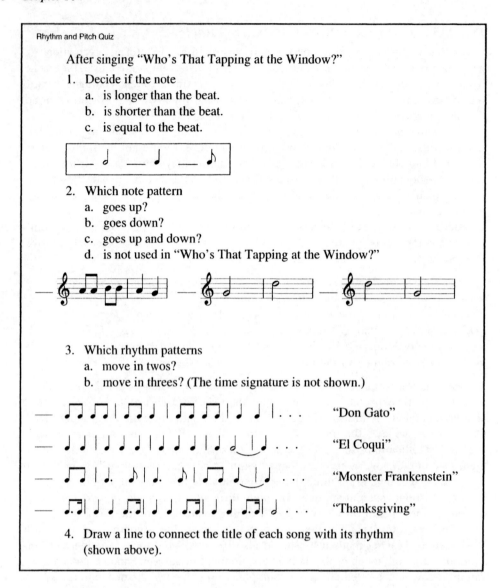

After singing "Who's That Tapping at the Window?"

1. Decide if the note
   a. is longer than the beat.
   b. is shorter than the beat.
   c. is equal to the beat.

2. Which note pattern
   a. goes up?
   b. goes down?
   c. goes up and down?
   d. is not used in "Who's That Tapping at the Window?"

3. Which rhythm patterns
   a. move in twos?
   b. move in threes? (The time signature is not shown.)

   ——   "Don Gato"

   ——   "El Coqui"

   ——   "Monster Frankenstein"

   ——   "Thanksgiving"

4. Draw a line to connect the title of each song with its rhythm (shown above).

Still another aspect of informal evaluation is the use of audio or video tape recordings to review work in the class, or even to review your own presentation. A recording, which can be studied apart from the normal activity of the classroom, may be very helpful to you in identifying the strengths and weaknesses of individual students, of lessons, or of your own preparation.

Major or Minor Quiz

Listen to the following tonal patterns as they are played on the (piano, bells, recorder, xylophone, etc.). Decide if the pattern sounds like

    a. Major.

    b. Minor.

    (Student or teacher plays the following pitches:)

_____	C	E	G
_____	C	E♭	G
_____	A	B	C
_____	A	B	C♯
_____	G	E♭	C
_____	G	E	C

Play the following chords on the autoharp. Have your partner listen and tell whether the chord was major or minor.

_____	C
_____	Am
_____	F
_____	Gm
_____	G

Have your partner choose five major or minor chords. Listen and decide whether each chord was major or minor.

_____ ◯ (chord)

_____ ◯ (chord)

_____ ◯ (chord)

_____ ◯ (chord)

_____ ◯ (chord)

Listen to these songs. Which ones are in major? In minor?*

_____ "Skin and Bones"

_____ "The Muffin Man"

_____ "Monster Frankenstein"

_____ "The Pumpkin Man"

_____ "My Darling Clementine"

    *Play or hum the melody *without* the words.

SUGGESTED ACTIVITIES

1. Plan a learning experience emphasizing a musical concept or skill, and present it to a classmate through a musical activity.
2. Analyze several lessons in one of the current music series: list the musical learnings, concepts, and content of the lessons in a lesson plan format.
3. Prepare a concise list of basic musical concepts about rhythm, melody, harmony, form, and timbre.[26] (Examine the concepts listed in current music series, and those included in the preceding chapters of this book.)

NOTES

[1] Quoted in *The Real Teachers,* ed. Philip Sterling (New York: Vintage Books, 1972), p.304.

[2] John Dewey, *Democracy and Education* (New York: Macmillan, 1916, 1944), p.39.

[3] Marilyn P. Zimmerman, *Musical Characteristics of Children* (Reston, Va.: Music Educators National Conference, 1971).

[4] Materials designed for specific teaching approaches include the following:

Jump Right In (1986) by Edwin E. Gordon and David G. Woods. G.I.A. Publications, Inc., 7404 South Mason, Chicago, IL 60638. Components: Guide for Teachers, Reference Handbook, *Jump Right In!* card boxes (tonal and rhythm pattern cards and activity cards), two-volume song collection, activity books for grades one through eight, register books, tonal and rhythm learning sequence pattern transparencies, and indexes.

Music in Education™ Yamaha Corporation of America, Band and Orchestral Division, 3445 East Paris Avenue, S.E., P.O. Box 899, Grand Rapids, MI 49512–0899. A technology assisted music program using the Macintosh computer, keyboards, compact disc players, overhead transparencies, individual student song sheets, listening materials, charts, and worksheets for teaching music concepts and understanding keyboard skills. A non-graded curriculum organized into 145 modules emphasizes experiences in listening, discussing and describing, making, and creating music. All students begin with the first module and progress at a rate based on their varying levels of ability.

[5] *See A Guide to Curriculum Planning in Music Education* (Madison, Wis.: Department of Public Instruction, 1986).

[6] Music Educators National Conference, 2d ed. Music Educators National Conference, 1806 Robert Fulton Drive, Reston, VA 22091–4348. (Reston, Va., 1986).

[7] Jerome Bruner, *Toward a Theory of Instruction* (Cambridge, Mass.: Harvard University Press, 1967), p.71.

[8] *See* Jerome Bruner, *The Process of Education* (Cambridge, Mass.: Harvard University Press, 1963).

[9] Bruner, pp.10–14, 44–50, 155–157.

[10] See, for example, "She Wrote America's Favorite Song," *Reader's Digest,* July 1993, pp.90–92 ("America the Beautiful") or find out about the history of "Yankee Doodle." Robertson Davies tells us how it was viewed by the British soldiers in his novel, *Murther and Walking Spirits* (Viking-Penguin, 1991), pp.48–52.

[11] MENC, Opportunity-to-Learn Standards, p.6.

[12] Ibid., pp.1–5.

[13] "Can We Still Sing Christmas Carols in the Public Schools?," *Music Educators Journal* (November 1976), pp.71–73.

[14] Oliver Broquist, "A Survey of the Attitudes of 2594 Wisconsin Elementary School Pupils Toward Their Learning in Music." Unpublished doctoral dissertation (University of Wisconsin, 1961). Reviewed in the *Bulletin of the Council for Research in Music Education,* 2, p.36.

[15] Edwin E. Gordon, "A Factor Analysis of the Music Aptitude Profile, The Primary Measures of Music Audiation, and the Intermediate Measures of Music Audiation," *Bulletin of the Council for Research in Music Education,* 87, p.19.

[16] Frank B. McMahon, *Psychology, the Hybrid Science,* 2d ed. (Englewood Cliffs, N.J.: Prentice-Hall, 1972), p.55.

[17] Ernest Hilgard, *Introduction to Psychology* (New York: Harcourt, Brace, and World, 1962).

[18]Frederick Beckman, et al., *The Magic of Music,* Book 6 (Boston: Ginn and Co., 1968), pp.1–10.

[19]Marilyn P. Zimmerman, "Developmental Processes in Music Learning," *Symposium in Music Education,* ed. by Richard Colwell (Urbana-Champaign, Ill.: University of Illinois, 1982), 38.

[20]*See* Norman E. Gronlund's *How to Construct Achievement Tests,* 4th ed. (Boston: Allyn and Bacon, 1991) for more extensive information.

[21]From *Foundations and Principles of Music Education* by Charles Leonhard and Robert W. House. Copyright © 1972. McGraw-Hill Book Co.

[22]From *Foundations and Principles of Music Education* by Charles Leonhard and Robert W. House. Copyright © 1972. McGraw-Hill Book Co.

[23]*The First National Assessment of Musical Performance,* Report 03–MU–01 (Ann Arbor, Mich.: National Assessment of Educational Progress, 1974).

[24]Edwin E. Gordon, *Primary and Intermediate Measures of Music Audiation* (Chicago: G.I.A. Publications, Inc., 1979, 1982).

[25]Edwin E. Gordon and David G. Woods, *Jump Right In, The Music Curriculum* (Chicago: G.I.A. Publications, Inc., 1986).

[26]*See The Study of Music in the Elementary School—A Conceptual Approach,* ed. Charles L. Gary (Reston, Va.: Music Educators National Conference, 1967).

Song Supplement

All the Pretty Little Horses

Quietly

Folk Song from Southern United States

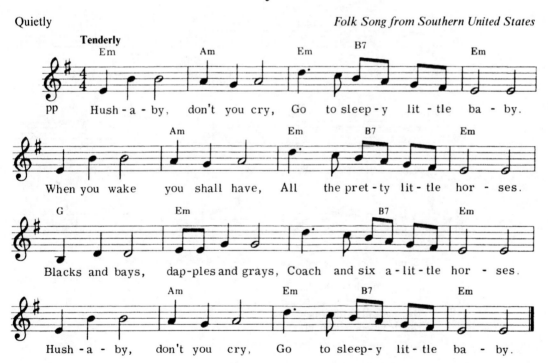

Related Listening: Aaron Copland: "Old American Songs," *Copland Conducts Copland*, William
Warfield, Baritone, CD: CBS MK 42430

All Through the Night

British Isles

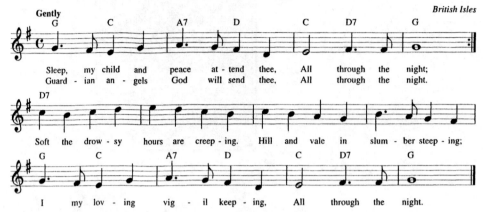

Sleep, my child and peace at - tend thee, All through the night;
Guard - ian an - gels God will send thee, All through the night.

Soft the drow - sy hours are creep - ing. Hill and vale in slum - ber steep - ing;

I my lov - ing vig - il keep - ing, All through the night.

At the Gate of Heaven

TR. A. D. Zanzig

Spain

1. At the gate of heav'n lit - tle shoes they are sell - ing

For the lit - tle bare - foot - ed an - gels there dwell - ing.

Chorus

Slum - ber, my ba - by, slum - ber my ba - by,

Slum - ber, my ba - by, a - rru, a - rru.

A la puerto del cielo Venden zapatos,
Para los angelitos que endan descalzos
Duermete niño, duermete, niño,
Duermete, niño, arru, arru.

Au Clair de la Lune

Moderato

French Folk Song

Au clair de la lu - ne! Mon a - mi, Pier - rot, Prê - te moi ta
plu - me pour é crire un mot; Ma chan - delle est mor - te,
Je n'ai plus de feu. Ou - vre moi ta por - te, Pour l'a - mour de Dieu.

In the evening moonlight, My good friend, Pierrot,
Lend me please your quill pen, I would write a note.
My candle is burned out, And my fire's out too;
Please unlock your door now, Please, I beg of you.

Aura Lee

Words by
W. W. Fosdick

Music by
George R. Poulton

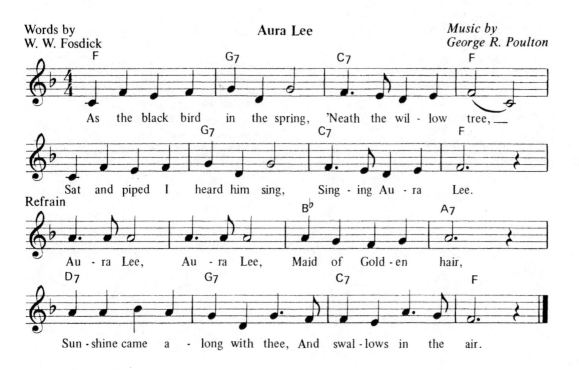

As the black bird in the spring, 'Neath the wil - low tree, —
Sat and piped I heard him sing, Sing - ing Au - ra Lee.

Refrain

Au - ra Lee, Au - ra Lee, Maid of Gold - en hair,
Sun - shine came a - long with thee, And swal - lows in the air.

Barbara Allen

English Folk Song

Sadly

1. In Scar-let town where I was born, there was a fair maid dwell-in', Made
ev'-ry youth __ cry, __ "Well - a - day." Her name was Bar - bara Al - len.

2. All in the merry month of May
   When green buds they were swellin',
   Young Jimmy Grove on his deathbed lay
   For love of Barbara Allen.

3. He sent his man unto her then,
   To the place where she was dwellin',
   To bring her to poor Jimmy Grove,
   The lovely Barbara Allen.

4. And death was printed on his face,
   And o'er his heart was stealin',
   Before she came to comfort him,
   The willful Barbara Allen.

5. So slowly, slowly she came up,
   And slowly she came nigh him,
   And all she said, when there she came,
   "Young man, I think you're dying."

6. He said, "I am a dying man,
   One kiss from you will cure me."
   "One kiss from me you will never get,"
   Said cruel Barbara Allen.

7. As she was walking o'er the fields,
   She heard the death bells knellin'
   And every peal did again reveal
   How cruel Barbara Allen.

8. When he was dead and in his grave,
   Her heart was struck with sorrow,
   "Oh, mother, mother make my bed,
   For I shall die tomorrow."

9. And on her deathbed as she lay,
   She begged a place beside him,
   And sore repented of that day
   That she did e'er deny him.

10. "Farewell," she said, "ye virgins all,
    And shun the fault I fell in,
    Henceforth take warning by the fall
    of heartless Barbara Allen."

11. Then she was buried on the moor,
    And he was laid beside her,
    Above his grave red roses grew,
    Above hers, a green briar.

The Boatmen

American Minstrel Song

From *Making Music Your Own,* Grade Six. Copyright © 1968, Silver Burdett. Used by permission of Silver Burdett and Ginn, Inc.

Hi - ho, the boat - men row, Float - in' down the riv - er, the O - hi - o.

Hi - ho, the boat - men row, Float - in' down the riv - er, the O - hi - o. *Fine*

Verse

1. The boat - men dance, The boat - men sing, The boat - men up to ev - 'ry - thing.
2. The oys - ter boat should keep to the shore, The fish - ing smack should ven - ture more,
3. When you go to the boat - men's ball, Dance with your wife or not at all;

And when the boat - man gets on shore, He spends his cash and works for more.
The schoon - er sails be - fore the wind, The steam - boat leaves a streak be - hind.
Sky - blue jacket and tarpau - lin hat, Look out, my boys, for the nine - tail cat.

Refrain

Then dance, the boat - men, dance! Oh, dance, the boat - men, dance!

Oh, dance all night till the broad day - light, And go

D.C. al Fine

home with your pals in the morn - ing.

Related Listening: Aaron Copland: "Old American Songs," *Copland Conducts Copland,* William Warfield, Baritone, CD: CBS MK 42430

The Bridge of Avignon
(Sur le Pont d'Avignon)

French Folk Song

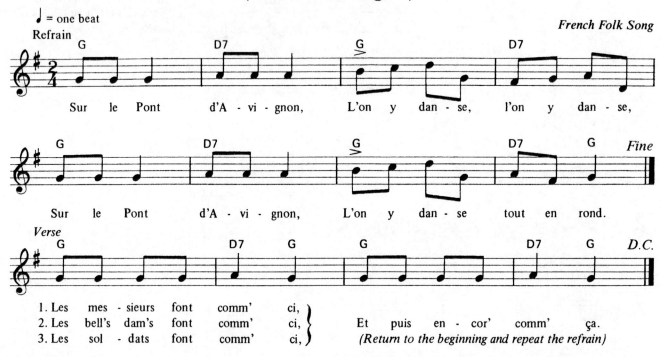

♩ = one beat

Refrain

Sur le Pont d'A - vi - gnon, L'on y dan - se, l'on y dan - se,

Sur le Pont d'A - vi - gnon, L'on y dan - se tout en rond.

Verse

1. Les mes - sieurs font comm' ci,
2. Les bell's dam's font comm' ci,
3. Les sol - dats font comm' ci,

Et puis en - cor' comm' ça.

(Return to the beginning and repeat the refrain)

On the bridge (of) Avignon,
There is dancing, there is dancing,
On the bridge (of) Avignon,
There is dancing all around.

1. Gentlemen do like this, then again do like that.
2. Ladies, too, do like this, then again do like that.
3. Soldiers, too, do like this, then again do like that.

Bye'm Bye

Texas Folk Song

Bye'm bye, bye'm bye, Stars shin - ing, count - ing, num - ber one,

num - ber two, num - ber three, num - ber four, num - ber five,

Oh my! Bye'm bye, bye'm bye, Oh my! Bye'm bye.

Camptown Races

With Spirit

Stephen Foster

The Camp-town la - dies sing this song, Doo - dah! Doo - dah! The
Oh see those hor - ses round the bend,

Camp-town race - track five miles long, Oh, Doo - dah day!
Guess that race will nev - er end,

Chorus
Goin' to run all night! Goin' to run all day! I'll ___

bet my mon - ey on a bob - tail nag, Some - bod - y bet on the bay.

Related Listening: Aaron Copland: *A Lincoln Portrait.* Bowmar Orchestral Library No. 75 (cassette), or CD: RCA 09026–60983.

Chichipapa

Japanese Folk Song

(Teacher) Chi - chi - pa - pa chi - pa - pa. I am the teach-er of a spar - rows' school.
(Children) Chi - chi - pa - pa chi - pa - pa. She/He is the teach-er of a spar - row's school.

We learn to sing a song by lis - ten - ing. We learn to step and flut - ter just like this.
We learn to sing a song by lis - ten - ing. We learn to step and flut - ter just like this.

Sing a lit - tle song and sing it ver - y well. We can sing it bet - ter, spar-rows, try a - gain.
Sing a lit - tle song and sing it ver - y well. We can sing it bet - ter, spar-rows, try a - gain.

Chi - chi - pa - pa chi - pa - pa.
Chi - chi - pa - pa chi - pa - pa.

From *Holt Music,* Teacher's Edition, Kindergarten Book. © 1988 Holt, Rinehart and Winston, Inc. Used by permission.

Come, Follow Me

John Hilton (1599–1657)

With spirit

1. Come, fol - low, fol - low, fol - low, fol - low, fol - low, fol - low me!

2. Whith-er shall I fol - low, fol - low, fol - low, whith-er shall I fol - low, fol - low thee?

3. To the green-wood, to the green-wood, to the green-wood, green - wood tree.

Dipidu

Uganda

Verse
Solo   Class   Solo   Class

Good morn - ing! The same to you! Good morn - ing! A - dip - i - du.

Refrain

Dip, dip, dip - i - du, dip - i - du, a dip - i - du.

Dip, dip, dip, dip, dip - i - du, dip - i - du, a dip - i - du.

Down in the Meadow

Southern Folk Song

Gaily

1. Down in the mead - ow, hop a doo - dle, hop a doo - dle,
2. Down in the barn - yard, hop a doo - dle, hop a doo - dle,

Down in the mead - ow, hop a doo - dle doo!
Down in the barn - yard, hop a doo - dle doo!

Down in the mead - ow, the colt be - gan to prance, The
Down in the barn - yard, the goose be - gan to sing, The

cow be - gan to whis - tle, and the pig be - gan to dance.
hen be - gan to cack - le, as the roost - er flapped a wing.

The Drunken Sailor

With Spirit

Capstan Chantey

1. What shall we do with a drunk - en sail - or? What shall we do with a
2. Hoist him ___ up with a run - ning bow - line, Hoist him ___ up with a
3. Put him in the long boat un - til he's so - ber, Put him in the long boat un -

drunk - en sail - or? What shall we do with a drunk - en sail - or
run - ning bow - line, Hoist him ___ up with a run - ning bow - line,
til he's so - ber, Put him in the long - boat un - til he's so - ber,

Ear - lye in the morn - ing? Way, hey, and up she ris - es, Way, hey, and

up she ris - es, Way, hey, and up she ris - es Ear - lye in the morn - ing.

4. Pull out the plug and wet him all over, . . .
5. Tie him to the mast until he's sober, . . .
6. That's what we do with a drunken sailor, . . .

The Farmer in the Dell

England

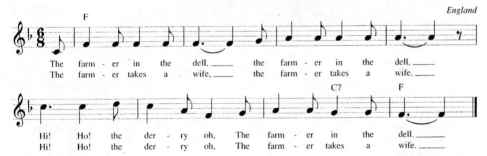

The farm - er in the dell, ___ the farm - er in the dell, ___
The farm - er takes a wife, ___ the farm - er takes a wife, ___

Hi! Ho! the der - ry oh, The farm - er in the dell. ___
Hi! Ho! the der - ry oh, The farm - er takes a wife. ___

3. The wife takes a child,
   The wife takes a child,
   Hi-ho, the derrio,
   The wife takes a child.

4. The child takes a nurse, *etc.*

5. The nurse takes a dog, *etc.*

6. The dog takes a cat, *etc.*

7. The cat takes a rat, *etc.*

8. The rat takes the cheese, *etc.*

9. The farmer runs away, *etc.*

10. The wife runs away, *etc.*

11. The child runs away, *etc.*

12. The nurse runs away, *etc.*

13. The dog runs away, *etc.*

14. The cat runs away, *etc.*

15. The rat runs away, *etc.*

16. The cheese stands alone,
    The cheese stands alone,
    Hi-ho, the derrio,
    The cheese stands alone.

For Health and Strength

American Round

For health and strength and dai - ly food we bless Thy name, O Lord.

The Frogs

Round

Hear the live - ly song of the frogs in yon - der pond.

Crick, crick, crick - e - ty crick,

Brr - ump.

The Goat

Traditional

There was a man, _____ Now please take note, _____ There was a
(There was a man)   (now please take note)

man, _____ who had a goat, _____ He loved that goat, _____ in-deed he
(There was a man,)   (who had a goat,)   (He loved that goat.)

did, _____ He loved that goat, _____ Just like a kid. _____
(in - deed he did,)   (He loved that goat,)   (Just like a kid.)

2. One day that goat (echo each phrase)
   Felt frisk and fine . . .
   Ate three red shirts . . .
   Right off the line . . .
   The man, he grabbed . . .
   Him by the back . . .
   And tied him to . . .
   A railroad track . . .

3. Now, when that train . . .
   Hove into sight . . .
   That goat grew pale . . .
   And green with fright . . .
   He heaved a sigh . . .
   As if in pain . . .
   Coughed up those shirts . . .
   And flagged the train . . .

Good Night, Ladies

Traditional

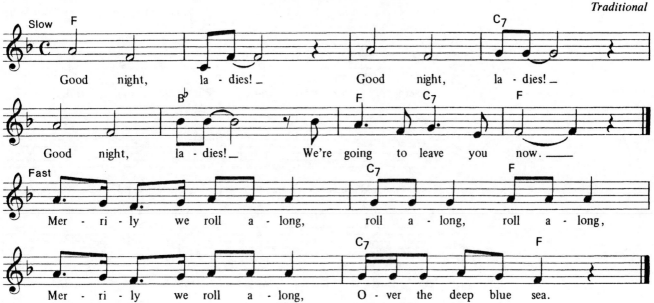

Good night, la - dies! _ Good night, la - dies! _

Good night, la - dies! _ We're going to leave you now. ____

Mer - ri - ly we roll a - long, roll a - long, roll a - long,

Mer - ri - ly we roll a - long, O - ver the deep blue sea.

Related Listening: Meredith Willson: "Pick-A-Little, Talk-A-Little," from *The Music Man,* CD: Warner Brothers 1459–2, or Telarc CD-80276. and Charles Ives: "Washington's Birthday," *Holidays Symphony,* CRI (C-163 (cassette) or CD: Vox Box-2-CDX 5035.

Hey, Betty Martin

American Folk Song

Hey, Bet - ty Mar - tin, tip - toe, tip - toe, Hey, Bet - ty

Mar - tin, tip - toe fine, Hey, Bet - ty Mar - tin,

tip - toe, tip - toe, Hey Bet - ty Mar - tin, Please be mine.

Hickory, Dickory, Dock

Mother Goose Rhyme

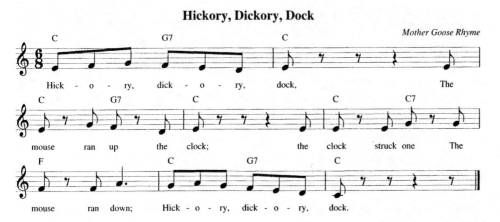

Hick - o - ry, dick - o - ry, dock, The

mouse ran up the clock; the clock struck one The

mouse ran down; Hick - o - ry, dick - o - ry, dock.

Johnny Has Gone for a Soldier

American Revolutionary War Song

There   I   sat   on   But - ter - milk   Hill.

Who   could   blame   me,   cry   my   fill?   And

ev 'ry   tear   would __   turn   a   mill;

John - ny   has   gone   for   a   sol - dier.

Lavender's Blue

English Singing Game

Lav - en - der's   blue,   dil - ly,   dil - ly,   Lav - en - der's   green;

When   I   am   king,   dil - ly,   dil - ly,   You   shall   be   queen.

Lazy Mary

Traditional

1. La - zy Ma - ry, will   you   get up? Will   you   get up? Will   you   get up?
2. Yes,   dear Moth - er,   I   will   get up,   I   will   get up,   I   will   get up!

La - zy Ma - ry, will   you   get up? Will   you   get up   this   morn - ing?
Yes,   dear Moth - er,   I   will   get up,   I   will   get up   to - day!

Related Listening: Edwin Franko Goldman: *Children's March*. CD: Mercury Living Presence 432–019–2MM.

Li'l 'Liza Jane

American Folk Song

3. I got a house in Baltimore, Li'l 'Liza Jane
   Silver doorplate on the door, Li'l 'Liza Jane.

4. I got a house in Baltimore, Li'l 'Liza Jane
   Brussel's carpet on the floor, Li'l 'Liza Jane.

London Bridge

Traditional

2. Build it up with iron bars
3. Iron bars will rust and break
4. Build it up with sticks and stones
5. Sticks and stones will tumble down
6. Here's a prisoner I have found
7. Off to prison he (she) must go
8. Have the jailer lock him (her) up

Related Listening: Edwin Franko Goldman: *Children's March*. CD: Mercury Living Presence 432–019–2MM.

Mary Ann

West Indian Calypso Song

All day, _ all night, _ Miss Ma - ry Ann, ___ Down by _ the

sea - side, _ sift - ing sand; ___ All the lit - tle chil - dren _ love

Ma - ry Ann, ___ Down by _ the sea - side _ sift - ing sand. ___

Mary Had a Little Lamb

SARA J. HALE

1. Mar - y had a lit - tle lamb, lit - tle lamb, lit - tle lamb,

Mar - y had a lit - tle lamb, Its fleece was white as snow.

2. Everywhere that Mary went the lamb was sure to go.
3. It followed her to school one day which was against the rule.
4. It made the children shout and play to see the lamb in school.
5. And so the teacher turned it out but home it would not go.
6. It waited there till school was out for it loved Mary so.

Also-
Mary had a little lamb,
You've heard this tale before.
But did you know she passed her plate
And had a little more?

Related Listening: Edwin Franko Goldman: *Children's March*. CD: Mercury Living Presence 432–019–2MM.

Mary's a Grand Old Name

George M. Cohan

For it is Ma - ry, Ma - ry, plain as an - y name can be;_____

But with pro - pri - e - ty, so - ci - e - ty will say Ma - rie._____

But it was Ma - ry, Ma - ry, long be-fore the fash - ions came;_____

And there is some - thing there that sounds so fair, it's a grand old name. _____

Related Listening: "Star Spangled Spectacular," George M. Cohen, arr. by John Cacaves. *American Jubilee,* Erich Kunzel and the Cincinnati Pops Orchestra. C. D.: Telarc 80144

Michael, Row the Boat Ashore

Spiritual/Georgia Islands

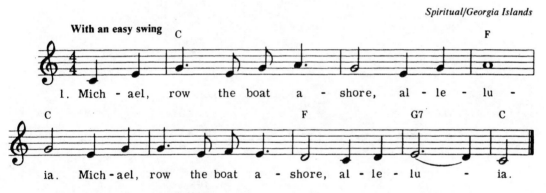

1. Mich - ael, row the boat a - shore, al - le - lu - ia. Mich - ael, row the boat a - shore, al - le - lu - ia.

2. Sister, help to trim the sail, alleluia, (twice)

   (repeat verse 1 after each verse)

3. River Jordan's deep and wide, alleluia, (twice)

4. River Jordan's chilly and cold, alleluia, (twice)

Mistress Moore

American Folk Song

Mis - tress Moore lives on the shore; she has daugh - ters by the score.

Eld - est one is twen - ty four; mar - ried to a sail - or.

Partner Songs: "Bow Belinda," "Mistress Moore," "Mulberry Bush," "Paw Paw Patch," "Sandy Land," "Skip to My Lou," "This Old Man."

No Bears Out Tonight

1. No bears out to - night, no bears out to - night,
2. One bear out to - night, no one bear out to - night,

No bears out to - night, they're all in their cave.
One bear out to - night, the rest are in their cave.

3. Two bears . . .
4. Three bears . . .
   etc.

Old Brass Wagon

American Singing Game

Lively
G   D7   G

1. Cir - cle to the left, old brass wag - on cir - cle to the left, old brass wag - on

C   D7   G

cir - cle to the left, old brass wag - on You're the one, my dar - ling.

2. Circle to the right, old brass wagon . . .

3. Swing, oh swing, old brass wagon . . .

4. Promenade around, old brass wagon . . .

Game
Circle formation of partners, girls on boys' right.
Verse 1. All circle left, hands joined.
Verse 2. All circle right, hands joined.
Verse 3. Partners face, swing around once.
Verse 4. Promenade–partners with hands in skating position.

Words by
Dan Emmett
With humor

Old Dan Tucker

Music by
Dan Emmett (1843)

1. I came to town the oth-er night, I heard the noise and saw the fight. The
watch-man, he was run-ning 'round, said, "Old Dan Tuck-er's come to town."

Chorus
Get out the way, old Dan Tuck-er, Get out the way, old Dan Tuck-er,
Get out the way, old Dan Tuck-er, You're too late to come to sup-per.

2. Old Dan Tucker was a fine old man, he
   washed his face in a frying pan,
   Combed his hair with a wagon wheel
   and died with a toothache in his
   heel.
   (*Chorus*)

3. Now Old Dan Tucker he came to town
   to swing the ladies all around,
   Swing them right and swing them left,
   then to the one he liked the best.
   (*Chorus*)

Old Joe Clark

American Folk Song

Fare you well, old Joe Clark, Fare you well, I say,
Fare you well, old Joe Clark, I ain't got long to stay.

Stanza
Joe Clark had a vi-o-lin, he fid-dled all the day,
Ev-'ry bo-dy had to dance when-ev-er Joe did play.

2. Old Joe Clark had a house twenty stories high,
   And every story in that house was filled with chicken pie.
3. I used to live on the mountain top, Now I live in town,
   I'm staying at the big hotel, courting Betsy Brown.

On Top of Old Smoky

American Folk Song

On top of Old Smok - y, ____ All cov ered with snow, ____

____ I lost my true lov - er, ____ By court -ing too slow. ____

On Springfield Mountain

American Folk Song

On Spring - field Moun - tain there did dwell, A love - ly

youth, I knew him well. Too roo - de - nay too roo - de -

noo, Too roo - de - nay too roo - de - noo.

Related Listening: Aaron Copland: *A Lincoln Portrait*. Bowmar Orchestral Library No. 75 (cassette), or CD: RCA 09026–60983.

Over the River and through the Wood

LYDIA MARIA CHILDS

U.S.

Oh Where, Oh Where Has My Little Dog Gone?

From *On the Trail of Negro Folk Songs* by Dorothy Scarborough, © 1925 Harvard University Press; renewed 1953 by Mary McDaniel Parker. Reprinted by permission of the publishers.

Riding in the Buggy

Americn Folk Song

Rid-ing in the bug-gy, Miss Mar-y Jane, Miss Mar-y Jane, Miss Mar-y Jane,

Rid-ing in the bug-gy, Miss Mar-y Jane, I'm a long way from home.

Refrain

Who waits for me? Who waits for me?

Who waits for me, my dar-ling? Who waits for me?

Row, Row, Row Your Boat

Round

Row, row, row your boat, gent-ly down the stream,

mer-ri-ly, mer-ri-ly, mer-ri-ly, mer-ri-ly, life is but a dream.

Sandy Land

Partner Songs: "Bow Belinda," "Mistress Moore," "Mulberry Bush," "Paw Paw Patch," "Sandy Land," "Skip to My Lou," "This Old Man."

Briskly

Oklahoma

1. Make my liv-ing in sand-y land, Make my liv-ing in sand-y land,

Make my liv-ing in sand-y land, La-dies, fare-you well.

2. Raise potatoes in sandy land, etc.
3. Dig potatoes in sandy land, etc.
4. I'm through digging in sandy land, etc.
5. Gave up working in sandy land, etc.
6. I'm all through with sandy land, etc.

See the Little Mouse

Leon Burton

See the lit - tle mouse,____ crawl - ing up to me.____

See him get - ting clos - er. Now he's on my knee!

*Continue crescendo throughout song.

Shoo, Fly, Don't Bother Me

BILLY REEVES

FRANK CAMPBELL

Enthusiastically

Shoo, fly, don't both - er me, Shoo, fly, don't both - er me,

Shoo, fly, don't both - er me, For I be - long to some - bod - y.

Verse

1. I feel, I feel, I feel, I feel like a morn - ing star, I

feel, I feel, I feel, I feel like a morn - ing star.

2. I feel, I feel, I feel, I feel, like my mother said,
   Like angels pouring 'lasses down on my little head.

Simple Gifts

Related Listening: Aaron Copland: *Appalachian Spring*. CD: CBS MK 42430 and Aaron Copland: "Old American Songs (Set I, No. 4)," *Copland Conducts Copland,* William Warfield, Baritone, CD: CBS MK 42430

American Shaker Melody

'Tis the gift to be sim-ple, 'Tis the gift to be free, 'Tis the gift to come down where we ought to be, And when we find our-selves in the place just right, 'twill be in the val-ley of love and de-light.

When true sim-plic-i-ty is gained, to bow and to bend we shan't be a-sham'd, to turn, turn will be our de-light 'till by turn-ing, turn-ing we come round right.

Sing a Song of Sixpence

J. W. Elliott
Mother Goose Rhyme

Lively

1. Sing a song of six-pence, a pock-et full of rye;
Four and twen-ty black-birds baked in a pie;
When the pie was o-pened, the birds be-gan to sing;
Was-n't that a dain-ty dish to set be-fore a king?

2. The king was in the counting house counting out his money;
The queen was in the parlor eating bread and honey;
The maid was in the garden hanging out the clothes;
Along came a blackbird and nipped off her nose.

Solmisation

English Words by Alice Firgau

Luigi Cherubini (1760–1842)

From *Making Music Your Own,*
Grade 5, Copyright © 1968,
Silver Burdett and Ginn. Used
by permission.

Do do so la mi fa so! Oh, sing a

song, You can sing it loud and long, And you ne - ver will be

wrong If you sing la ti ti do. The gam - ut you can

run. And then your song is done. Ti do so mi so do!

Starlight

Star - light, star bright, First star I see to - night

wish I may, wish I might, Have the wish I wish to - night.

Related Listening: Roy Harris: *American Ballads for Piano*. CD: Etcetera KTC 1036.

The Streets of Laredo

American Folk Song

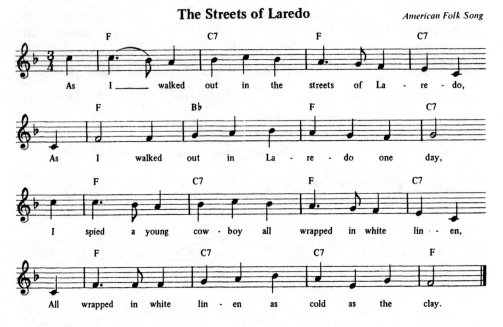

2. "I see by your outfit that you are a cowboy."
   These words he did say as I boldly stepped by;
   "Come, sit down beside me and hear my sad story,
   I'm shot in the breast and I'm going to die."

3. "Now once in the saddle I used to go dashing,
   Yes, once in the saddle I used to be gay.
   I'd dress myself up and go down to the card-house,
   I got myself shot and I'm dying today."

4. "Get six husky cowboys to carry my coffin,
   Get ten lovely maidens to sing me a song,
   And beat the drum slowly and play the fife lowly,
   For I'm a young cowboy who knows he was wrong."

5. "Oh, please go and bring me a cup of cold water
   To cool my parched lips, they are burning," he said.
   Before I could get it, his soul had departed
   And gone to its Maker, the cowboy was dead.

6. We beat the drum slowly and played the fife lowly
   And wept in our grief as we bore him along.
   For we loved the cowboy, so brave and so handsome,
   We loved that young cowboy although he'd done wrong.

Take Me Out to the Ball Game

Words by Jack Norworth

Music by Albert von Tilzer

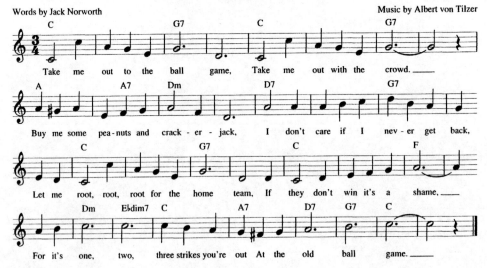

Tallis's Canon

Thomas Ken

Thomas Tallis (c. 1505–1585)

All praise to Thee, my God, this night,

For all the bless - ings of the light,

Keep me, oh keep me, King of kings

Be - neath Thine own Al - might - y wings.

Wade in the Water

REFRAIN

Chorus:

Spiritual

Wade in the wa - ter,__ wade in the wa - ter, child - ren,

Fine

Wade in the wa - ter,__ God's gon - na trou - ble the wa - ter.__

VERSE

Leader:

Chorus:

'Mem - ber one thing an' it's cer - tain - ly sho',__ Wade in the wa - ter,__

Leader:

Chorus:

D.C. al Fine

Judge - ment's com - in' an' I don't __ know,__ Wade in the wa - ter.__

We Wish You a Merry Christmas

Traditional

We wish you a Mer-ry Christ-mas, We wish you a Mer-ry
Christ-mas, We wish you a Mer-ry Christ-mas, And a
Hap-py New Year! Good ti-dings to you, And all of your
kin, Good ti-dings for Christ-mas and a hap-py New Year.

Yankee Doodle

American Revolutionary War Song

1. O fath'r and I went down to camp, a - long with Cap-tain Good' - in, And there we saw the men and boys as thick as hast - y pud - din'.'

Chorus

Yan - kee Doo-dle keep it up, Yan - kee Doo - dle Dan - dy,
Mind the mu - sic and the step, And with the girls be hand - y.

2. And there was Captain Washington upon a slapping stallion,
   A-giving orders to his men; I guess there were a million.

3. And there I saw a swamping gun, large as a log of maple,
   Upon a mighty little cart; a load for father's cattle.

4. Ev'ry time they shot it off it took a horn of powder,
   And made a noise like father's gun only a nation louder.

5. There I saw a wooden keg with heads made out of leather,
   They knocked upon it with some sticks to call the folks together.

6. Then they'd fife away like fun and play on cornstalk fiddles,
   And some had ribbons red as blood all bound around their middles.

7. Troopers too would gallop up and shoot right in our faces,
   It scared me almost half to death to see them run such races.

8. I can't tell you all I saw they kept up such a smother,
   I took my hat off, made a bow and scampered home to mother.

A PPENDIX 1

MUSIC FOR SPECIAL LEARNERS

The 1975 passage of Public Law 94–142 guaranteed the right of children with special needs to have educational opportunities in the "least restrictive environment commensurate with their needs." In compliance with the law, teachers have developed techniques and materials to meet the challenge of integrating children with disabilities and children without disabilities in regular general music classes.

When a child requires specialized instruction in order to study music in the classroom, a multidisciplinary team prepares a written Individualized Education Program (IEP) for the child. The planning should include all the teachers who will work with the child, including the music educator.

Classroom teachers in many schools are required to provide some music instruction, or to teach the complete music program if there is no full-time music specialist. Accordingly, concern for music in special education is shared by classroom teachers along with music specialists.

Experienced music educators suggest that not more than three students with disabilities should be assigned to a single music class, and that children with different types of disabilities should not be placed in the same classroom.[1] Although the specific needs of students with disabilities often involve nonmusical activities and goals, the general purpose of music education remains the same for all: to develop each student's aesthetic potential.

Music instruction can be adjusted to encourage success by placing greater or less emphasis on the learning mode (visual, auditory, or tactile) and the activity (singing, listening, moving, or playing instruments).[2] Accommodating many learning modes and various special needs calls for planning as well as preparation of other students involved in a mainstreamed classroom so as to provide an environment of acceptance and rapport within the group.

MENTAL DISABILITIES

Students with mental disabilities in mainstreamed classes include the borderline intellectually disabled, with IQ scores between 70 and 85, and the mildly disabled, with IQ scores between 55 and 70. Children with scores between 35 and 55 are considered to be moderately disabled, and usually receive instruction in a self-contained classroom setting.

Music can be a source of joy and a way to build self-confidence for students with mental disabilities. Rhymes, poems, and rhythmic speech patterns develop vocabulary, and musical activities encourage group experiences that are especially important for these students.

Even though some mainstreamed students with disabilities learn at only about one-half to three-fourths the rate of other learners,[3] writers on music for people with mental disabilities caution teachers not to underestimate what a student might achieve. The use of smaller increments of instruction together with a slower rate of presentation and a greater amount of repetition are helpful. Instruction similar to that for younger children can be adapted to meet the needs of children with mental disabilities—provided that the materials fit the social level of the children. Most children with disabilities respond to music and benefit from experiences in singing, playing instruments, and moving to music.

General Guidelines

1. Help children improve their feeling of self-esteem and personal worth. ("Peer acceptance is the most serious obstacle facing the mainstreamed exceptional child.")[4]

   a. Let students assume leadership tasks such as conducting changes in dynamics (louder/softer) or changes in tempo (faster/slower) as the class sings a familiar song.

   b. Special days, special events, and the child's name offer opportunities to build self-esteem. Many songs can be adapted to include names of children in the classroom. Hap Palmer's "What Is Your Name?" (Recording: *Learning Basic Skills Through Music,* vol. 1) is one example. Songs such as "If You're Happy And You Know It" offer possibilities for names and creative responses: "If your name is _____ , clap your hands (blink your eyes), etc.

   c. Individual name tags can be used to extend learning activities. Add pictures or musical symbols to the name tags and have children find a tag that matches their own, or ask them to stand when you hold up a card with a matching symbol.[5] Two excellent sources for ideas are *Music and Perceptual-Motor Development* by Katherine Crews (New York: The Center for Applied Research in Education, Inc., 1975) and *Alike and Different, the Clinical and Educational Use of Orff-Schulwerk* by Carol Hampton Bitcon (Santa Ana, Calif.: Rasha Press, 1976).

   d. When possible, involve all of the students in an activity, not just the students with disabilities. Music instruction can combine simpler and more difficult tasks, and the use of repetition, graphic notation, or nonverbal responses through movement can be worthwhile for regular and special learners.

   e. Praise good work, but do not use praise indiscriminately.

2. Simplify tasks when necessary.

   a. Practice songs in a slower tempo, especially those that are recorded at a tempo too fast for the children to use when learning a new song.

   b. If a child has difficulty doing two things at once (e.g., clapping while singing), have the child do only one of the two activities until he or she is able to do more.

3. Present less material with more repetition.

   a. Build tasks in layers, one thing at a time (e.g., practice the steady beat by tapping different parts of the body; transfer a rhythm from speech to the body and then to an instrument).

   b. Help children focus on the task. Observing a chart or the chalkboard may be simpler than finding a detail in a music book. When using activity sheets or books, a marker cut from oaktag can be moved beneath each line of words or pictures as the child follows the lesson.

4. Use graphics, objects, manipulative materials, and color coding to clarify explanations.
   a. Pictures of colored and numbered resonator bells can substitute for staff notation when presenting simple melodies (e.g., "Hot Cross Buns"). The child could also use hand levels (higher/lower/same) to practice the melody before trying it on the bells.
   b. Write words, letters, or chord symbols in colored chalk to match colored tape on bells, piano keys, or Autoharp chord bars.
   c. Prepare colored construction paper shapes (circles, triangles, rectangles, etc.) to clarify and reinforce concepts of similar/different phrases in songs.
   d. Colored outlines of hands or feet (e.g., green for left, blue for right) help children learn right/left differentiation. Have children tap or step to the beat as they alternate left to right. Colored yarn or ribbon can be tied to wrists or ankles as an aid. Reminder: Children in the regular classroom usually are not expected to respond to "right" or "left" until second grade.[6]
5. Make learning concrete rather than abstract.
   a. Use step bells to show high and low and the scale.
   b. Use movement (e.g., hand levels, hand signs) to show higher/lower, step/skip, and the like.
   c. Prepare large, melody contour charts. Let students trace the contour shapes on the charts with their hands and arms and then make similar vocal contours. The music series *Jump Right In* suggests a balloon activity: Blow up a balloon and release it, letting the air propel it around the room. Have children show the contour of the balloon's path with their hands.[7]

PHYSICAL DISABILITIES

Students with physical disabilities often need unobstructed access to the music room, and may require some rearrangement of furniture within the room. Because of the large variety of specific disabilities, there are few general solutions. Participation in movement activities may be affected by a particular disability, but whatever participation is feasible should be encouraged. The teacher should consult with the school physical therapist, other teachers, and parents to learn more about each student's limitations and possibilities.

Possible adaptations of movement activities for students restricted to wheelchairs include the use of a partner to move the wheelchair, electric wheelchairs that the student can operate, and movements while remaining in the chair.

■ With the consent of the child with the physical disability, a responsible partner can push the chair in dances or games. The student in the wheelchair might be the engineer of a train, the driver of the bus, etc.

■ Students can use alternative responses for dance movements: patschen on knees, "walking" with the fingers, slightly rocking the chair, rolling it back and forth while the dancers move, playing percussion instruments, clapping rhythms, or devising original responses.

Classroom Instruments

Classroom instruments or playing techniques can be modified to allow students with physical disabilities to participate.

■ Place tape over holes of the recorder to enable players who do not have the use of both hands to participate in a particular song or ostinato (e.g., taping the left hand holes will allow a student with a disability to play the lower tones with his or her right hand).

■ Hang small drums, cymbals, cowbells, etc., to a string attached to a frame (a rack or stand such as a chart holder) at a height suitable for a student in a wheelchair. Fasten a tray or shelf to a wheelchair to hold small instruments or other materials.

■ Use open string tunings with the ukulele or guitar to simplify playing techniques.

■ Tape a holder to a desk to support a tone block, triangle, or other small percussion instrument. Small instruments that might accidentally be dropped can be fastened to the player's clothing.

■ Insert the mallet stick in the center of a small rubber ball to assist children who cannot grasp a narrow object. Students who have difficulty gripping an Autoharp pick may be able to strum with a plastic spatula, a rubber doorstop, or some other substitute. (More detailed information can be found in *Clinically Adapted Instruments for the Multiply Handicapped* by Donna M. Chadwick and Cynthia A. Clark [St. Louis: Magnamusic-Baton, 1979]).

■ Students with perceptual-motor development problems may benefit from simplified performance techniques. If a student cannot strum and press the Autoharp chord bars at the same time, divide the task between partners. If a student has difficulty crossing the midline (playing from right to left on bells, for example), devise a less complicated pattern.

VISUAL IMPAIRMENTS

Students who are visually impaired or partially sighted may have highly developed listening skills, but musical activities involving notation or visual aids and activities requiring locomotor movement must be adapted to accommodate their needs. The following suggestions are examples of ways to adjust instruction.

1. Describe what is on a page in the music book or on a chart or transparency being shown to the class.

2. Prepare tactile materials.
   a. Make shapes from textured materials (felt, cotton, carpet, paper, tagboard, sandpaper, etc.) to represent *same/different* discriminations.
   b. Represent *long/short sounds* with long and short lengths of sandpaper or felt. Prepare cards to indicate duple or triple meter: glue sandpaper rectangles to the cards in groups of two's or three's. Use Cuisenaire rods to show relationships between note lengths. (Cuisenaire rods are graduated by length from one to ten, with each length in a different color. Their great advantage is that a child can learn number relationships through a concrete rather than a verbal operation.)
   c. Make raised lines by gluing yarn, pipe cleaners, shoe laces, and similar materials to charts that diagram melodic direction, musical stairsteps, musical forms, etc.[8]
   d. Use small loops of masking tape to attach textured circles to piano keys to designate the keys used in chords. Use sandpaper circles to make a recorder fingering chart.

3. Assist students in finding successful instrument playing techniques. Play claves, finger cymbals, or woodblocks by holding one hand stationary and moving the other. Hold the triangle striker *inside* the triangle. Students who are visually impaired can be aided when playing the Autoharp or a keyboard instrument if you provide cues such as raised labels, Braille symbols, or large, wide-line staff notation.[9] Audiotaped instructions can guide individuals during independent practice.

4. Let students touch various orchestral instruments that are brought to the classroom; describe those instruments that are not available (e.g., the string bass) to help children discover how instruments differ in size and shape. Compare resonator bells to learn that larger bells (and instruments) make lower sounds. Place bells on miniature stairsteps to teach melodic direction and intervals. (To make interval learning concrete, students can count the steps between bell pitches.)

5. To guide movement activities, a length of cotton rope may be inserted through a large plastic ring. The student who is visually impaired holds the ring in one hand and slides it along the rope, which is suspended at waist height, or held by two other students.

6. Materials to construct a Braille keyboard from oaktag are provided in *Holt Music*, Grade 3, "Mainstreaming Activities." The child can use this aid to establish the sequence of pitches to be played, before going to the piano. The authors also suggest attaching Braille letters to the piano keyboard.

New technology makes music learning opportunities greater for students who are visually impaired. As a result of developments such as the computer, Autobraille, the Electric Baton, and the Optacon, "For many visually impaired persons, bulky braille scores are a thing of the past. Using Autobraille, music on file in the Library of Congress can be transmitted anywhere in the country—via telephone modem—and recorded on a cassette player with a braille display (which can store over two hundred pages of musical braille)."[10]

HEARING IMPAIRMENTS

Hearing is affected by any loss in perception of loudness (measured in decibels) or pitch frequency (measured in Hertz [Hz.]). Students with a mild to a moderate hearing loss are found in the regular classroom, while those with a more severe loss may require special learning environments.[11]

Because hearing loss interferes with speech development and language reception, a hearing impairment may affect both academic achievement and social development. The teacher should consult the audiologist and the speech therapist in planning appropriate musical activities for the student who is hearing impaired. A few general suggestions are presented here.

1. Speak clearly, but do not shout. (Despite advances in the design of hearing aids, "the user may be annoyed by people who believe they must shout to make themselves heard.")[12]

2. Speech reading (lip reading) is difficult at best. Remember to face the child, not the chalkboard, when you speak.

3. Approach the child within the field of vision to avoid startling him or her.

4. Be patient. Children who cannot hear their own speech may be hard to understand.

5. Teachers of students who are hearing impaired may need to gather information from speech therapists as well as information about hearing aids. Electronic hearing aids continue to improve, but their sound quality has been compared to that of a cheap pocket radio. There are other problems as well, including weak batteries. One study reported that more than half of the hearing aids used in schools operate poorly or not at all.[13] Hearing aids may produce an irritating and tiring amount of background noise, and they are subject to acoustic feedback (often a result of the earmold being dislodged during the child's play).

Speech reading is another concern. "Fifty percent of the words in the English language are estimated to have some other word or words homophonous to them, thus indicating the difficulty of speech reading."[14] To the speech reader, words such as *mommy* and *Bobby* look almost exactly the same. Words and sounds, such as *hang, kick*, k, g, h, are nearly impossible to recognize visually.[15]

Tactile responses to vibrations are important in work with students who are hearing impaired. According to Robert H. Brey, sensors in the skin allow perception of vibro-tactile stimulation in frequencies from 125–1300 Hz.[16]

The following suggestions indicate ways to assist students who are hearing impaired in the study of music.

1. Let children who are hearing impaired feel the vibrations of the piano, Autoharp, drums, hi-fi speakers, or other instruments. Placing the Autoharp on a wooden desk or some other resonator will help to increase its volume. Have the child place both hands against the sides of a bass xylophone as it is played. Contrabass resonator bars, used with other Orff instruments, are considered especially effective in improving the rhythmic and melodic speech of the deaf and hard of hearing.

2. Use many visual aids related to classroom songs and music. Picture cards that illustrate verses to cumulative songs (such as "The Twelve Days of Christmas") are helpful.[17]

3. Techniques for finding the singing voice and learning to make high and low vocal sounds (see chapter 8) have value to the hearing impaired as an aid to improving their ability to speak with improved vocal inflections. Basic rhythmic learning is also essential in the development of speech.[18]

4. Instruments that produce relatively low volume, such as maracas, sand blocks, or rhythm sticks, may be less promising for some students who are hearing impaired than instruments such as a drum, an electric organ, or an amplified guitar.

5. Students with normal hearing can hear frequencies from about sixteen to twenty thousand Hertz, but some children who are hearing impaired perceive only the lower frequencies. The high pitch of triangles, finger cymbals, bells, or recorders makes these instruments less suitable for many students with a hearing loss.

6. Instruments such as the piano and drums, which do not require fine pitch discrimination, are usually more rewarding for students who are hearing impaired than instruments requiring a keen sense of pitch, such as the violin.

7. Sign language is shown in current music series with drawings or photographs of signs to words of songs. Some music teachers have found that all students develop greater awareness of what it means to be disabled when they learn and use sign language along with the students who are hearing impaired.[19]

LEARNING DISABILITIES

There are many causes for academic achievement or underachievement, including the quality of instruction, home conditions, opportunity to learn, and attendance at school. Some children who perform below grade level have a learning disability and require special education. The term *learning disability* applies to more than fifty physiological impairments that afflict children with normal or above normal intelligence, but it excludes mental disabilities, emotional disturbance, or sensory impairment, although students with these disabilities may also have a learning disability.[20]

The screening and classification of children who display symptoms of a perceptual disability are usually done by a multidisciplinary team. Learning disabilities are related to a wide range of problems, including motor development, perception, memory, communications, mathematics calculation, and reasoning. Students with learning disabilities are likely to have one or more problems, such as inconsistent performance, lack of understanding of abstract concepts, memory lapses, confusion in reading, difficulty with space relationships (left-right, up-down), lack of motor coordination, social immaturity, hyperactivity, or hypoactivity (too little activity). Not surprisingly, ". . . *learning disabilities* has become a wastebasket term for labeling children whom teachers fail to reach in any academic area."[21]

Problems encountered by students with learning disabilities in music classes may involve music notation, doing two things at once (e.g., singing and clapping), or executing a series of movements in a dance or singing game. To a child who thinks in concrete terms, a "sharp" may signify something with a cutting edge. Music can be confusing: a horizontal keyboard has notes that go "up and down"; white keys look flat, but raised black keys are called "flats"; whole rests look like half rests; quarter notes are called black notes but they look white when they are written on the chalkboard, etc. Failing to perform a movement activity (e.g., stepping the beat while singing a song) is dismaying. A series of frustrations may cause emotional reactions, or behavior that is less mature than the child's age level.

Instructional adaptations for children with learning disabilities must be based on each child's particular needs. The teacher should try to provide opportunities for the student to do those things he or she can do easily and remember not to bypass strengths in order to correct weaknesses.

- Use teaching methods that call upon all of the student's senses.
- Find out if a child understands a concept by asking the child to repeat it in his or her own words.
- Sequence the lesson in tiny steps.[22]
- Establish space boundaries with stickers, masking tape, carpet squares or a hula hoop when "staying put" becomes a problem during classroom activities.[23]
- Use color coding to highlight same/different concepts.
- Prepare a chart of Autoharp chords rather than playing from the cluttered page of music notation.
- Emphasize large muscle motor activities.
- Simplify problems so that only one thing at a time is called for, then build from there.
- Encourage participation (for instance, invite the reluctant singer to do only the motions of an activity song).
- Use a visual, auditory, or tactile learning mode to reinforce learning: for example, assist left-right discrimination with colors and pictures of hands or feet.
- Clarify language for directions and movement (say, "say and do, whisper and do, think and do"). Make word and picture bridges between the student's experiences and the specific meanings of music language and symbols. Communicate in terms to which the student can relate easily.

BEHAVIOR DISORDERS

Structure and awareness of boundaries help reduce conflicts and bring order to the situation involving children with emotional needs. Often-heard suggestions include the following: assign special tasks as positive reinforcement; use a few, consistently enforced rules; establish classroom routines (e.g., a procedure for distributing instruments); emphasize movement activities (remembering to enforce rules against bumping others); employ effective "time-out" techniques to allow children to regain control of their emotions; provide opportunities for creative response; emphasize active involvement; maintain a high level of awareness.

Careful planning, reducing distractions, narrowing the number of choices, varying the lesson to cope with short attention spans, interacting one-on-one with the student, and ongoing study of relevant information from resource teachers and publications are among the options that teachers should explore in seeking solutions to the complex and difficult problems related to instruction of students with emotional disabilities.

ISSUES IN MAINSTREAMING

Reports on problems of mainstreaming indicate that elementary school music educators have found inconsistencies between recommendations and actual practices in schools. Administrators, for example, have tended to assign children with disabilities to music classes for social rather than musical objectives, with the result that some mainstreamed children have not had successful musical learning experiences. A 1984 study reports that some music teachers feel less confident that they can cope with the demands of mainstreaming than they did five years earlier. Inadequate preparation for teaching music to students with disabilities and a lack of administrative support (e.g., providing sufficient planning time to allow for individualization) are problems that have not been overcome, according to recent studies.[24, 25]

Further information on mainstreaming in music classes is found in the following references. In addition, the reader should examine current music series and consider supplementary workshops and course work.

REFERENCES

Books

Alvin, Juliette. *Music for the Handicapped Child.* London: Oxford University Press, 1965.

Atterbury, Betty W. *Mainstreaming Exceptional Learners in Music.* Englewood Cliffs, NJ: Prentice-Hall, 1990.

Birkenshaw-Fleming, Lois. *Music for Fun, Music for Learning,* 3d ed. St. Louis: MMB Music, Inc., 1982.

——— *Come On Everybody, Let's Sing.* Toronto: Gordon V. Thompson Music, 1989.

——— *Music For All: Teaching Music to People With Special Needs.* Toronto: Gordon V. Thompson Music, 1993.

Bitcon, Carol Hampton. *Alike And Different, The Clinical And Educational Use of Orff Schulwerk.* Santa Ana, CA: Rosha Press, 1976.

Crews, Katherine. *Music And Perceptual Motor Development.* New York: The Center for Applied Research in Education, Inc., 1975.

Graham, Richard M. *Music for the Exceptional Child.* Reston, VA: Music Educators National Conference, 1975.

Graham, Richard M., and Alice S. Beer. *Teaching Music to the Exceptional Child.* Englewood Cliffs, NJ: Prentice-Hall, 1980.

Nocera, Sona D. *Reaching the Special Learner Through Music.* Morristown, NJ: Silver Burdett Co., 1979.

Pratt, Rosalie Rebollo, ed. *Second International Symposium of Music Education for the Handicapped.* Bloomington, IN: Frangipani Press, 1983.

Ward, David. *Sing a Rainbow.* London: Oxford University Press, 1979.

Articles

Atterbury, Betty W. "Success Strategies for Learning-Disabled Students." *Music Educators Journal* (April 1983), pp. 29–31.

——— "Success in the Mainstream of General Music." *Music Educators Journal* (March 1986), pp. 34–36.

Chadwick, Donna M., and Cynthia A. Clark. "Adapting Music Instruments for the Physically Handicapped." *Music Educators Journal* (November 1980), pp. 56–59.

Darrow, Alice-Ann. "Music for the Deaf." *Music Educators Journal* (February 1985), pp. 33–35.

Gilbert, Janet Perkins. "Mainstreaming in Your Classroom: What to Expect." *Music Educators Journal* (February 1977), pp. 64–68.

Kersten, Fred. "Music as Therapy for the Visually Impaired." *Music Educators Journal* (March 1981), pp. 62–65.

Levinson, Sandra, and Kenneth Bruscia. "Putting Blind Students in Touch with Music." *Music Educators Journal* (October 1985), p. 49.

Catalog

A list of publications on therapy in music, dance, art, and drama is available from MMB Music, Inc., 10370 Page Industrial Boulevard, St. Louis, MO 63132.

NOTES

[1] Eunice Boardman Meske, Barbara Andress, Mary P. Pautz, and Fred Willman, *Mainstreaming Activities, Holt Music* (New York: Holt, Rinehart and Winston, 1988).

[2] Wilma F. Sheridan, "The Oregon Plan for Mainstreaming in Music," *Second International Symposium of Music Education for the Handicapped* (Bloomington, IN: Frangipani Press, 1983), p. 87.

[3] Kate Gfeller, "Adapting Orff Activities for the Handicapped Student: Part III-Cognition," *Iowa Music Educator* (December 1986), p. 41.

[4] Lloyd M. Dunn, quoted by Janet Perkins Gilbert in "Mainstreaming in Your Classroom, What to Expect," *Music Educators Journal* (February 1977), p. 65.

[5] *See* "Name Games" by Linda Damer White, *Music Educators Journal* (March 1981), for more ideas on using names in the music class.

[6] Phyllis Weikart, *Round the Circle,* (Ypsilanti, MI: High/Scope Press, 1987), p. 19.

[7] Edwin E. Gordon and David G. Woods, *Jump Right In* (Chicago: G.I.A. Publications, Inc., 1986).

[8] *See* "Integrating Blind and Sighted Through Music," by Rita C. Lam and Cecilia Wang, *Music Educators Journal* (April 1982), pp. 44–45.

[9] Sources of materials for the visually impaired are listed in the March 1981 *Music Educators Journal.* These include the Music Section of the National Library Service for the Blind and Physically Handicapped (Library of Congress, Washington, D.C. 20542).

[10] Fred Kersten, "Musical Communications for the Visually Impaired Through Audio-Visual Technology," *College Music Society Proceedings,* ed. Paul Hawkshaw (Boulder, CO: The College Music Society, 1987), p. 25.

[11] Samuel A. Kirk and James J. Gallagher, *Educating Exceptional Children,* 4th ed. (Boston: Houghton Mifflin Co., 1983), pp. 232–34. According to Kirk and Gallagher, approximately one in a thousand children is hearing impaired, and from three to five children per 1,000 are hard of hearing. Those described as "hard of hearing" have a hearing loss of from 35–69 decibels (dB). Students with a moderate hearing loss of 41–55 dB can understand conversational speech, but may require speech therapy and hearing aids. Most children with a mild hearing loss (27–40 dB) are found in regular public schools, but the majority of deaf students are taught in special learning environments.

[12] Oliver Bloodstein, *Speech Pathology, An Introduction,* 2d ed. (Boston: Houghton Mifflin Company, 1984), p. 251.

[13] Kirk and Gallagher, p. 252.

[14] Ibid., p. 260.

[15] Bloodstein, p. 261.

[16] Robert H. Brey, "Hearing Tutorial for Music Educators of the Hearing Impaired," *Second International Symposium of Music Education for the Handicapped* (Bloomington, IN: Frangipani Press, 1983), p. 17.

[17] Gail Schaberg. "Tips, Teaching Music to Special Learners" (Reston, VA: Music Educators National Conference, 1988), p. 15.

[18] *See* "Bypassing the Ear: The Perception of Music by Feeling and Touch" by Joan Dahms Fahey and Lois Birkenshaw, *Music Educators Journal* (April 1972), pp. 44–49, 127–128.

[19] "The Conquest of Silence with Sign and Song," *MENC Soundpost* (Summer 1987), vol. 3, no. 4.

[20] Milton Brutten, Sylvia O. Richardson, and Charles Mangel, *Something's Wrong With My Child, A Parent's Book About Children With Learning Disabilities* (New York: Harcourt Brace Jovanovich Publishers, 1979).

[21] Sona D. Nocera, *Reaching the Special Learner Through Music* (Morristown, NJ: Silver Burdett, 1979), p. 237.

[22] Adapted from "What to Do with the Learning Disabled" by Dorothy Gilles and Valerie Kovitz, *Clavier* (September 1973), pp. 14–17.

[23] Schaberg, p. 13.

[24] Kate Gfeller and Alice-Ann Darrow, "Ten Years of Mainstreaming: Where Are We Now?" *Music Educators Journal* (October 1987), pp. 27–30.

[25] Betty W. Atterbury, "The Perplexing Issues of Mainstreaming," *Bulletin of the Council for Research in Music Education* (Fall 1987), pp. 17–27.

APPENDIX 2

JAQUES-DALCROZE, KODÁLY, AND ORFF

The teaching approaches developed by Émile Jaques-Dalcroze (1865–1950), Zoltán Kodály (1882–1967), and Carl Orff (1895–1982) have influenced music teachers throughout the world. Although each approach requires specialized training, many of the principles and teaching techniques associated with these approaches have wide applications for all classroom music instruction.

THE DALCROZE APPROACH

Emilé Jaques-Dalcroze was born to Swiss parents in Vienna on July 6, 1865. He began composing music at the age of seven and later studied with the composers Léo Delibes, Gabriel Fauré, and Anton Bruckner. He was appointed to the staff of the Conservatory of Geneva in 1892 and by 1911 had established his own school in Hellerau, Germany. (Among the important musicians, actors, dancers, writers, and teachers who visited the school were Sergei Rachmaninov, Ernest Block, Serge Diaghilev, Vaslav Nijinsky, Marie Montessori, George Bernard Shaw, and Carl Orff.) With the outbreak of World War I, Jaques-Dalcroze returned to Geneva, where he established the Institut Jaques-Dalcroze. Other schools based on his method were soon established in Paris, London, and New York. By the time of his death in 1950, his method had become one of the most influential approaches in the history of music education.

The Dalcroze approach integrates three main areas of study: eurhythmics (rhythmic movement), solfége (ear training and singing with syllables), and improvisation based on creative responses to musical problem solving. The term "eurhythmics" means "good movement" in relation to the flow of music through time. The study of eurhythmics requires careful listening and consists of bodily responses to music improvised at the piano or on percussion instruments.

Direct experiences with music combine aural and kinesthetic learning modes, linking mind and body to develop musical understanding. Instinct precedes intellectual analysis. The ear perceives, the brain analyzes, and the body responds. Basic examples of learning experiences include the following: 1) Students respond to sound and silence by moving or stopping when the music sounds or ceases. 2) Students walk to the sound of quarter notes, run to eighth notes, step and bend to half notes. 3) Students show meter by conducting to match the rhythms improvised by the Dalcroze teacher. 4) Students wear cards showing various note values. They listen and move when they hear the pattern notated on their card. 5) Students show contrasting rhythms with different parts of the body, as in stepping to the beat and clapping a rhythm pattern. 6) Students show form by moving in a new direction for each new phrase. 7) Students participate in games such as bouncing and catching a ball in different tempi, or different meters.

8) Students move in canon to a musical rhythm, showing the pattern they have heard as they listen to the next pattern. 9) Students interpret musical concepts (such as crescendo or accelerando) by responding with movement to the music they hear. 10) Students improvise a melody and show its contour with arm movements. 11) Students listen to the piano and move higher or lower as the pitch ascends or descends. Pitch studies involve the use of *fixed-do* (C is always *do*, D is always *re*, etc.) with Roman numbers used to indicate the function of the pitch within the scale. The study of notation moves from a one-line staff and progresses to the regular five-line staff. Rhythms are shown at first with dots and dashes of various lengths, corresponding to the lengths of the sounds perceived. Studies may begin with very young children and progress to advanced levels.

Certification to teach Dalcroze Eurhythmics requires intensive and extensive musical preparation. There are three levels: certificate, license, and diploma (the latter available only at the Institut Jaques-Dalcroze in Geneva, Switzerland). Programs to obtain the certificate and the license are offered at several training centers in the United States.

Additional information may be obtained from the Dalcroze Society of America,
P.O. Box 6804, Pittsburgh, PA 15212, or the Dalcroze International School of Music,
161 East 73rd Street, New York, NY 10021.

THE KODÁLY APPROACH

The Hungarian composer Zoltán Kodály was also renowned as a musicologist, teacher, and linguist. His compositions include the *Concerto for Orchestra, Psalmus hungaricus, Dances of Galánta, Dances of Marosszék,* the *Peacock Variations,* the opera *Háry János,* and a large number of choral works and works for children's voices.

Kodály advocated music education for every child and insisted that only the best music was good enough. The Kodály approach includes singing (especially unaccompanied singing), movement, listening, aural skill development, and reading and writing music. The materials for study include children's chants, songs, singing games, and folk music. These are followed by folk music from other cultures and by music of master composers.

Kodály believed that effective music education begins in early childhood. The Kodály approach follows a child-developmental learning sequence that takes account of the young child's limited vocal range and associates rhythmic learning with movement. For example, quarter notes and eighth notes (walking and running) precede half notes and whole notes, in keeping with the young child's enjoyment of activity. Pentatonic music, without half steps, encourages in-tune singing and allows for early opportunities to sing in two parts with melodies and ostinati. Canons and rounds also develop singing and listening skills and the ability to carry an independent vocal line. Singing and basic musicianship training precede the study of instruments, which may include recorders and percussion instruments such as xylophones.

Singing games and children's songs help students build a vocabulary of tonal and rhythm patterns and prepare the way for the introduction of music reading activities. "A fundamental premise of Kodály's philosophy was that music and singing should be taught to provide pleasurable experiences rather than drudgery."[1] Each new learning is *prepared* with numerous songs, *presented* and identified (usually by guiding the children with questions to help them derive answers) and then *practiced* in various contexts to assure the learning is assimilated. New tonal or rhythm patterns are extracted from familiar songs the children have learned by rote. The sequence of learnings is carefully structured and moves gradually to more complex tasks. The emphasis is on live performance, though careful listening is developed through a variety of "inner hearing" techniques such as singing silently on signal, then resuming singing aloud at the next signal.

Suggested Listening: *Concerto for Orchestra* (CD: DG. 427408-s GDO); *Psalmus hungaricus* (CD: London 433080–2LM); and (on one CD) the *Dances of Galánta, Dances of Marosszék, Peacock Variations,* and the *Suite* from *Háry János* (CD: London 425034–2-LM).

Syllables based on movable *do* express tonal functions and are aids to learning and remembering tonal relationships. Hand signs are introduced with each new syllable and offer a kinesthetic response to pitch movement. The pitch sequence begins with tones of the pentatonic scale (*la-so-mi-re-do*). *Fa* and *ti* complete the major scale, which is followed by the study of major, modal, and chromatic scales. The grade-by-grade tonal-learning sequence is usually similar to the following: Grade 1 *so mi la do;* Grade 2, present *re;* Grade 3, present low *la* and *so* and high *do;* Grade 4, present *fa* and *ti.* Singing is not limited to music containing only the pitches *presented* in the music reading sequence, however, and children sing many diatonic songs by rote before the study of tonal patterns with *fa* and *ti.* Pitch may be notated with the initial letter of each syllable before introducing staff notation, clefs, sharps, flats, accidentals, and key signatures.

Rhythm syllables label note values (*ta* for the quarter note, *ti* for eighth notes) and serve as memory devices in voicing and learning rhythms, which are written in stem notation and then in conventional notation. A carefully designed learning sequence is followed in presenting each new rhythmic value. (See chapter 2.)

Training in the Kodály approach is offered at numerous colleges and universities, which are listed in the *Music Educators Journal* or in the *Kodály Envoy,* the national publication of the Organization of American Kodály Educators (OAKE).

Kodály Envoy, Alan D. Strong, ed., Department of Music, Sam Houston State University, Huntsville, TX 77341.
Dr. Richard C. Merrell, OAKE Executive Director, 823 Old Westtown Road, West Chester, PA 19382–5276.

THE ORFF APPROACH

Born in Munich, Carl Orff had a long, active career and is famous as the composer of *Carmina Burana* a work that has been frequently performed ever since its initial success in 1937. Other compositions include *Catulli Carmina* and the operas *Die Kluge* and *Der Mond.*

The combination of music and movement attracted Orff when he became familiar with the work of Jaques-Dalcroze and Rudolf von Laban and their pupil, Mary Wigman. Orff's involvement with music education dates back to 1924 in Munich, when he and the dancer Dorothee Günther opened the *Güntherschule* (bombed during World War II) to train future teachers of music, gymnastics, and dance. Following World War II, Orff and Gunild Keetman developed pedagogical ideas and materials that have influenced music education throughout the world.

During the years 1950–1954, Orff wrote five volumes of *Music for Children* as part of the *Schulwerk* (School Work). These compositions, intended as models for children's creative music-making, contain exercises in speech, rhythm, melody, and harmony. English language adaptations of these volumes were prepared by Doreen Hall and Arnold Walter (1952) and by Margaret Murray (1957–1966).

In America, the *Orff-Schulwerk Association* (AOSA), with over 4,000 members, plays an active role in promoting and developing the approach created by Carl Orff. The three-volume American edition of *Music for Children* (1977, 1980, 1982) offers classroom-tested examples of music-making based on work by leading American Orff teachers. More recently, Jane Frazee's *Discovering Orff* (1987) and Arvida Steen's *Exploring Orff* (1992) have supplied additional guidelines to lead teachers and children toward a realization of Orff's creative and educational goals.

The Orff approach is based on active participation using movement, speech, body rhythms, singing, and critical listening to develop skills and aesthetic judgment. Orff called it an elemental approach, referring in part to Ernst Haeckel's "Law of

Suggested Listening: *Carmina Burana* (CD: DG 415136–2GH); *Catulli Carmina* (New Port Classic NCD 60118); *Die Kluge* and *Der Mond* (both on 2 Angel Studio discs CDMB-63712).

Recapitulation," a theory based on the idea that the child's development retraces that of the human race ("ontogeny recapitulates phylogeny"), or as paraphrased "An animal climbs its family tree."[2]

Rhythm is the starting point. The child begins with the voice, which is the basic instrument, and creates speech rhythms: rhymes, chants, calls, proverbs, sayings, names, and so forth. The child uses the sounds of language to express duration, accent, and meter as well as dynamics, tempo, and tone color. Rhythms are joined with body movement and body rhythms (finger snapping, clapping, *patschen* [patting the thighs], and foot taps) along with other movements, including running, skipping, and dance.

The exploration of pitch begins with the pentatonic scale, which is found in music the world over. The absence of half steps in the pentatonic scale facilitates improvisation and creative activities, which are at the heart of the Orff approach. Pentatonic music is followed by diatonic music in major, then in minor and in various other modes. Melody is combined with harmony through singing rounds and canons, adding ostinati parts and by accompanying singing with instruments.

The teacher's musical models of simple chants and melodies and basic accompaniment patterns encourage the child to explore harmony and basic techniques for improvisation. Ostinati (repeated tonal or rhythmic patterns), drones ("borduns") formed by tones a fifth apart, rounds and canons, and chordal accompaniments are presented and learned in a gradual sequence of difficulty appropriate for the child's developmental level. Combinations of basic patterns result in layers of sound that often combine simple means with musically sophisticated results.

The child's understanding of form grows through the combination of speech, movement, and music-making activities. Patterns of repetition and contrast help learners discover phrases, binary and ternary forms, rondo patterns (such as ABACA), and theme and variations form.

High quality, specially designed Orff instruments are relatively easy to play, and are capable of producing a great variety of musical sounds and styles, often with tone colors like those of non-Western music. The instruments include pitched and unpitched percussion instruments, string instruments (guitar, cello), and wind instruments, especially the recorder. Today's Orff teachers include a wide variety of instruments from non-Western cultures as well: African kalimbas (thumb pianos), Latin American "rainsticks" (seeds strike against thorns inside a cactus shell), Caribbean steel drums, Chinese bells, and many others.

Instruments with removable tone bars—glockenspiels, metallophones, and xylophones—are supplied with extra F-sharp and B-flat tone bars that allow the instruments to produce the scales of C, F, and G major and their relative minors along with various modes and pentatonic scales. Sounds precede notation symbols, and children learn to play from memory rather than attempting simultaneous music reading and instrument performance. Notation is used to record individual or group creative work: arrangements, improvisations, or longer compositions.

Training in the Orff approach is available at colleges and universities all over America. Information about courses and schedules is available from the American Orff-Schulwerk Association, P.O. Box 391089, Cleveland, OH 44139–8089, and in *The Orff Echo*, the official publication of AOSA.

NOTES

[1] Sr. Lorna Zemke, *The Kodály Concept—Its History, Philosophy and Development* (Champaign, IL: Mark Foster Music Company, 1974), p. 23.

[2] P. B. Medawar and J. S. Medawar, *Aristotle to Zoos, A Philosophical Dictionary of Biology* (Cambridge, MA: Harvard University Press, 1983).

$\mathcal{A}$PPENDIX 3

GUITAR CHORDS

Guitar Chords

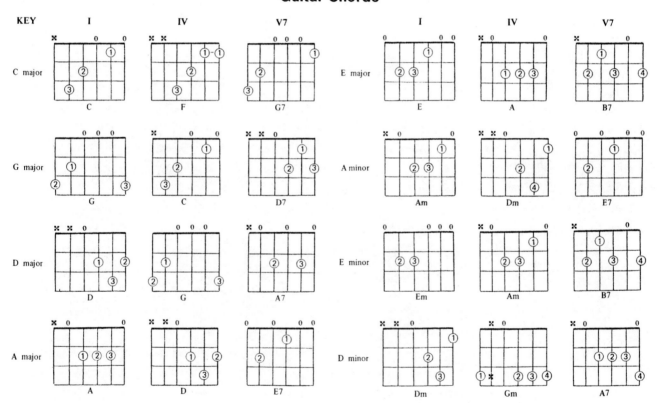

$\mathcal{A}$PPENDIX 4

SOPRANO RECORDER FINGERINGS
(BAROQUE SYSTEM)

Soprano Recorder Fingerings (Baroque System)

Fingerings are indicated visually and with numbers for the single or double holes on the front of the recorder.

*A*PPENDIX 5

MUSICAL TERMS AND SIGNS

Articulation

accents   tenuto
(sustained
full value)

tie   slur
(sustained for   (connected,
combined   smooth legato)
note values)

staccato   fermata
(detached,   (sustained
separated)   longer than
usual value)

Pitch

High

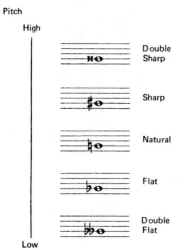

Double
Sharp

Sharp

Natural

Flat

Double
Flat

Low

Dynamics

pp	*pianissimo*	....	very soft
p	*piano*	....	soft
mp	*mezzo piano*	....	medium soft
mf	*mezzo forte*	....	medium loud
f	*forte*	....	loud
ff	*fortissimo*	....	very loud
$<$	*crescendo*	....	gradually louder
$>$	*diminuendo*	....	gradually softer

Repeat Signs

   Repeat the section between the repeat signs.

   Repeat the previous measure.

1.	2.	First and second endings.

Da capo al Fine (*D. C. al Fine*)   Return to the beginning and repeat to *Fine*.

Dal segno (D. S. 𝄋)   Return to the sign 𝄋 and repeat.

APPENDIX 6

INSTRUCTIONAL MATERIALS

SELECTED BOOKS ON MUSIC IN EARLY CHILDHOOD

Aaron, Tossi, ed. *Musicbook O: Songs, Games, Movement Activities for Teaching Music to Young Children.* St. Louis: Magnamusic/Edition Wilhelm Hansen, U.S.A., 1976.

Andress, Barbara. *Music Experiences in Early Childhood.* New York: Holt, Rinehart and Winston, 1980.

Aronoff, Frances Webber. *Music and Young Children.* Expanded edition. New York: Turning Wheel Press, 1979.

Batcheller, John. *Music in Early Childhood.* New York: The Center for Applied Research in Education, 1975.

Birkenshaw, Lois. *Music for Fun, Music for Learning.* 3d ed. St. Louis, MO: MMB Music, Inc., 1982.

Boswell, Jacquelyn, ed. *The Young Child and Music, Contemporary Principles in Child Development and Music Education.* Reston, VA: Music Educators National Conference, 1985.

Forrai, Katalin (Translated and adapted by Jean Sinor). *Music in Preschool.* Budapest: Franklin Printing House, 1990.

Greenberg, Marvin. *Your Children Need Music.* Englewood Cliffs, NJ: Prentice-Hall, 1979.

Haines, B., Joan E., and Linda Gerber. *Leading Young Children to Music.* 2d ed. Columbus, Ohio: Charles E. Merrill, 1984.

Hotchkiss, Gwen, and Margaret Athey. *Complete Handbook of Music Games and Activities for Early Childhood.* West Nyack, NY: Parker Publishing Co., Inc. 1982.

McDonald, Dorothy T., and Gene M. Simons. *Musical Growth and Development, Birth Through Six.* New York: Schirmer Books, 1989.

Moorehead, Gladys, and Donald Pond. *Music of Young Children.* 4 vols. Santa Barbara, CA: Pillsbury Foundation for Advancement of Music Education, 1978.

Nye, Vernice Trousdale. *Music for Young Children.* 3d ed. Dubuque, IA: Wm. C. Brown Publishers, 1983.

Simons, Gene M., ed. *Early Childhood Musical Development: A Bibliography of Research Abstracts, 1960–1975.* Reston, VA: Music Educators National Conference, 1978.

Weikart, Phyllis S. *Round the Circle, Key Experiences in Movement for Children Ages 3 to 5.* Ypsilanti, MI: High/Scope Press, 1987.

Wood, Donna. *Move, Sing, Listen, Play.* Toronto, Canada: Gordon V. Thompson, Ltd., 1982.

SELECTED BOOKS ON MUSIC IN THE ELEMENTARY SCHOOL

Abramson, Robert M. *Rhythm Games for Perception and Cognition.* Pittsburgh, PA: Volkwein Brothers, Inc., 1978.

Anderson, William M., and Patricia Shehan Campbell. *Multicultural Perspectives in Music Education.* Reston, VA: Music Educators National Conference, 1989.

Ardley, Neil. *Eyewitness Books: Music.* New York: Alfred A. Knopf, 1989.

Blackwood, Alan. *The Orchestra, A First Guide.* Brookfield, CT: The Millbrook Press, 1993.

Broekel, Ray. *Sound Experiments.* Chicago: Childrens Press, 1983.

Carder, Polly, ed. *The Eclectic Curriculum in American Music Education: Contributions of Dalcroze, Kodály and Orff,* Revised Edition. Reston, VA: Music Educators National Conference, 1990.

Choksy, Lois. *The Kodály Method.* 2d ed. Englewood Cliffs, NJ: Prentice-Hall, Inc., 1988.

Choksy, Lois, and David Brummitt. *120 Singing Games and Dances for Elementary Schools.* Englewood Cliffs, NJ: Prentice-Hall, Inc., 1987.

Choksy, Lois, et al. *Teaching Music in the Twentieth Century.* Englewood Cliffs, NJ: Prentice-Hall, Inc., 1986.

Cline, Dallas. *Homemade Instruments.* New York: Oak Publications, 1976.

Crews, Katherine. *Music and Perceptual-Motor Development.* New York: Center for Applied Research in Education, 1975.

Dennis, Brian. *Experimental Music in Schools.* London: Oxford University Press, 1970.

Drew, Helen. *My First Music Book (A Life-Size Guide to Making and Playing Simple Musical Instruments).* New York: Dorling Kindersley, Inc., 1993.

Findlay, Elsa. *Rhythm and Movement.* Evanston, IL: Summy-Birchard, 1971.

Frazee, Jane, with Kent Kreuter. *Discovering Orff, A Curriculum for Music Teachers.* New York: Schott Music Corporation, 1987.

Gary, Charles L., ed. *The Study of Music in the Elementary School—A Conceptual Approach.* Reston, VA: Music Educators National Conference, 1967.

Graham, Richard M., and Alice S. Beer. *Teaching Music to the Exceptional Child.* Englewood Cliffs, NJ: Prentice-Hall, Inc., 1980.

Gray, Vera, and Rachel Percival. *Music, Movement and Mime for Children.* London: Oxford University Press, 1962.

Hotchkiss, Gwen, and Margaret Athey. *A Galaxy of Games for the Music Class.* West Nyack, NY, 1975.

———— *Treasury of Individualized Activities for the Music Class.* West Nyack, N.Y.: Parker Publishing Co., 1977.

Jones, Bessie, and Bess Lomax Hawes. *Step It Down.* New York: Harper and Row, 1972.

Lavender, Cheryl. *Making Each Minute Count: Time-Savers, Tips, and Kid-Tested Strategies for the Music Class.* Milwaukee: Jenson Publications (Hal Leonard Publishing Corporation), 1991.

Mandell, Muriel, and Robert E. Wood. *Make Your Own Musical Instruments.* New York: Sterling Publishing Co., Inc., 1975.

Martin, Will. *The Guitar Owner's Manual: Buying, Repairing and Maintaining an Acoustic Guitar.* Sante Fe, NM: John Muir Publications, 1983.

Nash, Grace C. *Creative Approaches to Child Development with Music, Language and Movement.* New York: Alfred Publishing Co., 1974.

Nocera, Sona D. *Reaching the Special Learner Through Music.* Morristown, NJ: Silver Burdett Co., 1979.

Nye, Robert E., and Meg Peterson. *Teaching Music with the Autoharp.* Northbrook, IL: Music Education Group, 1982.

Orr, Hugh. *Basic Recorder Technique.* Toronto, Canada: Berandol Music, Ltd., 1961.

Peery, J., et al. *Music and Child Development.* New York: Springer-Verlag, 1987.

Phillips, Kenneth H. *Teaching Kids to Sing.* New York: Schirmer Books, 1992.

Regner, Hermann, coordinator. *Music for Children.* American Edition, vol. 1 (1982), vol. 2 (1977), vol. 3 (1980). New York: Schott Music Corporation.

Salaman, William. *Living School Music.* Cambridge, England: Cambridge University Press, 1983.

Schafer, R. Murray. *Creative Music Education.* New York: Schirmer Books, A Divison of Macmillan Publishing Co., Inc., 1976.

Simpson, Kenneth, ed. *Some Great Music Educators.* London: Novello and Co., 1976.

Steen, Arvida. *Exploring Orff, A Teacher's Guide.* New York: Schott Music Corporation, 1992.

Walther, Tom. *Make Mine Music!* Boston: Little, Brown and Company, 1981.

Warner, Brigitte. *Orff-Schulwerk. Applications for the Classroom.* Englewood Cliffs, NJ: Prentice-Hall, Inc., 1991.

Weikart, Phyllis S. *Teaching Movement and Dance, A Sequential Approach to Rhythmic Movement.* Ypsilanti, MI: The High/Scope Press, 1982.

Wollitz, Kenneth. *The Recorder Book.* New York: Alfred A. Knopf, 1982.

Zimmerman, Marilyn P. *Musical Characteristics of Children.* Reston, VA: Music Educators National Conference, 1971.

ACTION SONGS, FINGERPLAYS, FOLK SONGS, SINGING GAMES.

Axelrod, Alan, and Dan Fox. *Songs of the Wild West* (Metropolitan Museum of Art). New York: Simon and Schuster, 1991.

Bley, Edgar S. *The Best Singing Games for Children of All Ages.* New York: Sterling Publishing Co., Inc., 1957, 1985.

Bradford, Louise Larkins. *Sing It Yourself: 220 Pentatonic American Folk Songs.* Van Nuys, CA: Alfred Publishing Co., 1978.

Choksy, Lois, and David Brummit. *120 Singing Games and Dances for Elementary Schools.* Englewood Cliffs, NJ: Prentice-Hall, 1987.

Cohn, Amy L. *From Sea to Shining Sea, A Treasury of American Folklore and Folk Songs.* New York: Scholastic, Inc., 1993.

Erdei, Peter, and Katalin Komlos. *150 American Folk Songs to Sing, Read and Play.* New York: Boosey and Hawkes, 1974.

Fukuda, Hanako. *Favorite Songs of Japanese Children.* Van Nuys, CA: Alfred Publishing Co., 1990.

Gellineau, R. Phyllis. *Songs in Action.* New York: McGraw-Hill Book Company, 1974.

Kemp, Helen. *Where in the World: Folksong Warmups from Many Lands.* Minneapolis: Augsburg Fortress, 1989.

Krull, Kathleen. *Gonna Sing My Head Off! American Folk Songs for Children.* New York: Alfred A. Knopf, 1992.

Langstaff, John. *Climbing Jacob's Ladder: Heroes of the Bible in African-American Spirituals.* New York: Macmillan Publishing Company, 1991.

Locke, Eleanor G. *Sail Away. 155 American Folk Songs to Sing, Read, and Play.* New York: Boosey and Hawkes, 1981.

Marks, Claude, and Dan Fox. *Go In and Out the Window, An Illustrated Song Book for Young People* (The Metropolitan Museum of Art). New York: Henry Holt and Co., 1987.

Mattox, Cheryl Warren. *Shake It to the One That You Love the Best: Play Songs and Lullabies from Black Musical Traditions.* Nashville, TN: JTG of Nashville, 1024C 18th Ave So., Nashville TN 37212.

Nelson, Esther. *Singing and Dancing Games for the Very Young.* New York: Sterling Publishing Co., Inc., 1977, 1982.

Nocera, Sona D. *Reaching the Special Learner Through Movement.* Morristown, NJ: Silver Burdett Company, 1979.

Reeves, Harriet R. *Song and Dance Activities for Elementary Children.* West Nyack, NY: Parker Publishing Co., Inc., 1985.

Rohrbough, Lynn. Revised by Cecilia Riddell. *Handy Play Party Book.* Burnsville, NC: World Around Songs, 1940, 1982.

Seeger, Ruth Crawford. *American Folk Songs for Children.* New York: Doubleday and Co., 1948.

Sharon, Lois and Bram. *Elephant Jam.* Toronto, Canada: McGraw-Hill Ryerson, Ltd., 1980.

Stassevitch, Verna, Patricia Stemmler, Rita Shotwell, and Marian Wirth. *Musical Games, Fingerplays and Rhythmic Activities for Early Childhood.* West Nyack, NY: Parker Publishing Co., 1983.

Trinka, Jill. *Folksongs, Singing Games, and Play Parties, vols 1–4.* Austin, TX: Jill Trinka, 1716 Rustling Road, 1983–1994. (See West Music Company catalog.)

SOURCES OF MUSIC EDUCATION CATALOGS, EQUIPMENT, AND MATERIALS

Belwin Mills Publishing Corporation/Columbia Pictures Publications, 15800 NW 48th Avenue, Miami, FL 33104 *(Bowmar Orchestral Library*—recordings with teaching guides, theme charts, and transparencies—and *Andre Previn's Guide to Music*—a complete music appreciation package for schools).

Backyard Music Dulcimers, P.O. Box 9047, New Haven, CT 06532 (kits for instrument building).

Boosey & Hawkes, Inc., 52 Cooper Square, 10th Floor, New York, NY 10003–7102.

Canyon Press, Inc., Box 1235, Cincinnati, OH 45201 (*Juilliard Repertory Library,* selected music from differing eras and cultures for use in school music classes).

Choristers Guild, Inc., 2834 West Kingsley Road, Garland, TX 75041 (children's choir materials).

Clarus Music, Ltd., 340 Bellevue Avenue, Yonkers, NY 10703 (records, cassettes, books, musical plays, teaching aids).

Concordia Publishing House, 3558 South Jefferson Avenue, St. Louis, MO 63118–39687 (videocassettes of instruction by children's choral specialist Helen Kemp).

Educational Audio Visual Inc., Pleasantville, NY 10570 (books, cassettes, records, filmstrips [including *The Banshee*], *Threshold to Music* charts).

Electronic Courseware Systems, Inc., 1210 Lancaster Drive, Champaign, IL 61821 (music instruction software catalog).

European-American Music Distributors Corporation, P.O. Box 850, Valley Forge, PA 19482 (Schott Music Corporation publications, American Orff-Schulwerk volumes, etc.).

Gamble Music Co., 312 South Wabash Avenue, Chicago, IL 60604.

Hansen House, 1870 West Avenue, Miami Beach, FL 33139 (John Brimhall piano method books, guitar methods, easy arrangements of popular music).

Library of Congress, Archive of Folk Song, Music Division, Washington, DC 20540.

Lyons Music Products, P.O. Box 1003, Elkhart, IN 46515 (instruments, filmstrips, teaching aids/equipment, records).

MMB Music, Inc., 10370 Page Industrial Boulevard, St. Louis, MO 63132 (Studio 49 Orff instruments; books and music for music education and music therapy).

Music Educators National Conference, 1806 Robert Fulton Drive, Reston, VA 22091 (*Music Educators Journal, Journal of Research in Music Education,* catalog of music education publications).

Oscar Schmidt International and Music Education Group, Divisions of Washburn International, 230 Lexington Drive, Buffalo Grove, IL 60089 (Autoharps, classroom instruments, electronic tuners for guitars and Autoharps).

Pop Hits Publications, 3149 Southern Avenue, Memphis, TN 38111.

Rhythm Band Inc., P.O. Box 126, Fort Worth, TX 76101 (music, records, classroom instruments, electronic instruments, music instruction for computer).

Schwann *Opus* (classical CDs, cassettes, and laserdiscs) and Schwann *Spectrum* (Today's Music: CDs, tapes, LPs). Stereophile, Inc., 208 Delgado Street, Santa Fe, NM 87501.

Smithsonian/Folkways Mail Order, 416 Hungerford Drive, Suite 320, Rockville, MD 20850. (Folkways recordings of ethnic, blues, folk, jazz, classical, and children's music.)

Suzuki Musical Instrument Corporation, P.O. Box 261030, San Diego, CA 92126 (recorders, Orff instruments, Omnichords, tone chimes, electronic pianos).

Temporal Acuity Products, Inc., 300 120th Avenue NE, Building 1, Suite 200, Bellevue, WA 98005 (*TAP Master* and *Pitch Master* for teaching rhythmic and sightreading skills; music software for computer-assisted instruction).

University of Illinois Film Center, 1325 South Oak Street, Champaign, IL 61820 (*Performing Arts* catalog: films and video resources for rental and purchase).

West Music Company, P.O. Box 5521, 1212 5th Street, Coralville, IA 52241 (books, classroom instruments, music, records, electronic instruments, and software).

World Around Songs, Inc., 5790 Highway 80 South, Burnsville, NC 28714 (pocket songbooks with songs from all countries).

World Music Press, P.O. Box 2565, Danbury, CT 06813 (multicultural materials for educators).

Yamaha Music Corporation, USA, 6600 Orangethorpe Avenue, Buena Park, CA 90620 (electronic keyboards, computer-assisted equipment, digital synthesizers).

SONG INDEX

NAME INDEX

SUBJECT INDEX